Method Today

NAASR Working Papers

Series Editor: Brad Stoddard, McDaniel College in Westminster, Maryland.

NAASR Working Papers provides a venue for publishing the latest research carried out by scholars who understand religion to be an historical element of human cognition, practice, and organization. Whether monographs or multi-authored collections, the volumes published in this series all reflect timely, cutting edge work that takes seriously both the need for developing bold theories as well as rigorous testing and debate concerning the scope of our tools and the implications of our studies. NAASR Working Papers therefore assess the current state-of-the-art while charting new ways forward in the academic study of religion.

Published:
"Religion" in Theory and Practice: Demystifying the Field for Burgeoning Academics
Russell T. McCutcheon

Forthcoming:
Constructing "Data" in Religious Studies: Examining the Architecture of the Academy
Edited by Leslie Dorrough Smith

Method Today

Redescribing Approaches to the Study of Religion

Edited by
Brad Stoddard

SHEFFIELD UK   BRISTOL CT

Published by Equinox Publishing Ltd.

UK: Office 415, The Workstation, 15 Paternoster Row, Sheffield, South Yorkshire S1 2BX

USA: ISD, 70 Enterprise Drive, Bristol, CT 06010

www.equinoxpub.com

First published 2018

© Brad Stoddard and contributors 2018

All rights reserved. No part of this publication may be reproduced or transmitted in any form or by any means, electronic or mechanical, including photocopying, recording or any information storage or retrieval system, without prior permission in writing from the publishers.

British Library Cataloguing-in-Publication Data

A catalogue record for this book is available from the British Library.

ISBN-13 978 1 78179 567 5 (hardback)
         978 1 78179 568 2 (paperback)
         978 1 78179 704 4 (ePDF)

Library of Congress Cataloging-in-Publication Data

Names: Stoddard, Brad, editor.
Title: Method today : redescribing approaches to the study of religion / edited by Brad Stoddard.
Description: Sheffield, UK ; Bristol, CT : Equinox Publishing, Ltd, 2018. | Includes bibliographical references and index.
Identifiers: LCCN 2017061870 (print) | LCCN 2018023066 (ebook) | ISBN 9781781797044 (ePDF) | ISBN 9781781795675 (hardback) | ISBN 9781781795682 (paperback)
Subjects: LCSH: Religion--Methodology.
Classification: LCC BL41 (ebook) | LCC BL41 .M48 2018 (print) | DDC 200.71--dc23
LC record available at https://lccn.loc.gov/2017061870

Typeset by JS Typesetting Ltd, Porthcawl, Mid Glamorgan

Printed and bound in Great Britain by Lightning Source UK Ltd., Milton Keynes and in the USA by Lightning Source Inc., La Vergne, TN

Contents

Introduction   1
Brad Stoddard

Part I

1. Comparison   15
   Aaron W. Hughes
2. He Who Knows One Language Knows None: On the Inevitabilities of Comparison and Translation   36
   Lucas Carmichael
3. Comparison and the Production of Knowledge   47
   Thomas J. Carrico, Jr.
4. On Z-Factors and Empires   54
   Andrew Durdin
5. Complicating "Comparison": On Perspective, Rhetoric, and Recognition in the Study of Religion   64
   Stacie Swain
6. Response   70
   Aaron W. Hughes

Part II

7. Forget about Defining "It": Reflections on Thinking Differently in Religious Studies   79
   Naomi Goldenberg
8. Preaching to the Choir? Religious Studies and Religionization   96
   Ian Alexander Cuthbertson
9. Religion and Description   106
   Daniel O. McClellan
10. Perhaps Action Enough   114
    Emily D. Crews
11. In Pursuit of a Pushier Study of Those Words we Like to Put in Quotes   119
    Neil George
12. Response to the Responses   128
    Naomi Goldenberg

Part III

13	Explanation and the Study of Religion *Egil Asprem and Ann Taves*	133
14	"Constitutional God-Given Rights": Explaining Religion and Politics in the Malheur Occupation *Spencer Dew*	158
15	Ontological versus Axiological Approaches to Religion *Joel Harrison*	168
16	Is Explanation Existential? *Paul Kenny*	178
17	Causal Explanations in the Study of Religion *Erin Roberts*	186
18	To Our Critics *Egil Asprem and Ann Taves*	192

Part IV

19	Interpretation and the Study of Religion *Kevin Schilbrack*	205
20	Homo Interpretans *Jennifer Eyl*	222
21	Combining and Constituting *Mark Q. Gardiner and Steven Engler*	228
22	Subjectivity and Meaning *Joshua Lupo*	237
23	Interpretation *Matt Sheedy*	245
24	A Reply to My Critics *Kevin Schilbrack*	252

Afterword 259
Gregory D. Alles

Index 275

Introduction

Brad Stoddard

In 1959, Mircea Eliade and Joseph Kitagawa published *The History of Religions: Essays in Methodology*, an edited volume devoted to questions of method and methodology in what was then the growing "history of religions" (*Religionsgeschichteschule*) approach to the academic study of religion. The stakes were quite high, they surmised, as the legitimacy of their young and promising field required scholars to develop a unique approach to gathering and handling religious data. In the volume's Preface, Jerald Brauer summarized their concerns when he wrote,

> it will not be easy for the history of religions to establish itself as one of the leading scholarly activities in the modern university. In fact, the great danger is that it will be completely absorbed by certain other fields. The history of religions deals with materials handled also by philosophy of religion, psychology, sociology, anthropology, history and theology. Its problem is to demonstrate that it is not merely ancillary to these other studies but is a discipline in its own right, drawing upon, yet making unique additions to, these areas of knowledge. (Brauer 1959: ix)

He concluded, "Unless a satisfactory answer can be found concerning the content and method adopted by the history of religions, it will not be able to fill its potential role" (ibid.). As this suggests, the issue of "method" loomed large in his assessment. The field required a unique or distinct method, Brauer argued, to help prevent the history of religions from falling into the disciplinary orbits of other established disciplines.

Depending on one's perspective, Brauer had legitimate concerns. The academic study of religion began in earnest in the late 1800s, when European scholars first expressed academic interest in the non-devotional, non-confessional, and non-theological study of religion. In the process, they helped create many of the fields of study that, according to Brauer, threatened to appropriate the history of religions.

Consider, for example, the work of F. Max Müller, typically considered a pioneer in what would later become the academic study of religion. In 1873, he developed what he called the science of religion (*Religionswissenschaft*) as a method or methodology distinct from theology. Müller's work, which was primarily philological and comparative, helped create multiple fields of academic study, including philology. Other scholars of that era similarly interested in religion helped create or shape their budding disciplinary frameworks. To name but a few, these scholars include Edward Burnett Tylor and James Frazer, who influenced the field of anthropology; Émile Durkheim and Max Weber, who influenced the field of sociology; Sigmund Freud, who influenced the field of psychology; and Friedrich Nietzsche and Karl Marx, who influenced the field of philosophy. Despite their diverse methodological approaches to their subjects, these scholars shared an interest in studying religion as a human phenomenon and in identifying its relationship to other social, cultural, economic, or political projects. According to Paul Ricoeur, several of these scholars approached the study of religion with a "hermeneutic of suspicion" that motivated them to identify what Ricoeur referred to as "the lies and illusions of consciousness" (Ricoeur 1970: 32). Religion, of course, fell squarely within their gazes. From the beginning, then, the academic study of religion—at least as practiced by this admittedly diverse group of writers—was connected to the very disciplines that Brauer sought to distinguish it from.

To sustain itself as a distinct field of academic inquiry, Brauer argued that the history of religions had to develop a distinct "methodology appropriate to the discipline." This methodology, he argued, "seeks to penetrate one of the few cardinal facts of life—the phenomenon of man as a religious being. To properly investigate and explore this fundamental, one must begin with an attitude of respect and openness toward the religious reality itself as it is encountered in specific historical forms" (Brauer 1959: viii). This methodology assumes that our object of study is what some scholars have referred to as *homo religiosus* (the idea that humanity has a natural and deep desire to experience the sacred—see Kitagawa 1985), and thus, that the academic study of religion needs to respect the inherently religious worlds of the groups they study, and that scholars should therefore allow *homo religiosus* to be studied on its own terms. Later described as phenomenology (or epoché), this methodology was based on philosophically idealist assumptions about the nature of religion as *sui generis*, that is, distinct or unique from other quotidian aspects of life, and therefore incapable of being reduced to any mundane aspect of human life. This approach to the academic study of religion—built, as many would later argue, on questionable epistemological assumptions—conflicted with what had emerged as the academic study of religion in Europe, but it overlapped significantly and proved quite compatible with the theological interests of many "religious" people who similarly argued that their religions—or, for some perennialists, that all religions—are unique, are non-reducible, and should be treated with the upmost respect (if not empathy).

The convergence of phenomenology and theology was evident in the field's leading academic organization, the American Academy of Religion (AAR). The AAR grew out of the National Association of Biblical Instructors (NABI), originally created in 1933 to provide an organizational home primarily for ecumenical Protestants interested in biblical hermeneutics, "church history," exegesis, and pedagogy. The organization changed its name to the American Academy of Religion in 1963, within months of the U.S. Supreme Court's decision in *Abington School District v. Schempp*, where the Court ruled that school-sponsored devotional Bible reading violated the First Amendment's Establishment Clause which prohibited the government from engaging in sectarian endorsement of religion. The

Court's decision did not completely forbid the teaching of religion, however, provided the teaching of the Bible or of religion in general were, as the majority decision stated, "presented objectively as part of a secular program of education." In other words, the Court forbade the teaching of religion for strictly devotional purposes, opting instead to allow scholars and historians to teach what the Court called "comparative religion or the history of religion and its relationship to the advancement of civilization." Several months after this decision, NABI changed its name; however, theological undertones continued to exist in AAR-related scholarship. These undertones were evident in the AAR's new journal, the *Journal of the American Academy of Religion* (JAAR), first published in 1966. As history soon demonstrated, the *JAAR* provided an academic home for scholarship sympathetic to the emerging liberal, ecumenical pluralism that came to dominate the field. The editor of *JAAR* in 1979 acknowledged as much when he noted that the *JAAR* published few articles in the period 1970–1976 that he classified as the "academic study of religion" (Hart 1979: 513). The bulk of the journal instead focused on the histories of Christianity and Judaism, Biblical literature, and philosophy/theology of religion. Sixteen years after Hart's assessment, Hans Penner reflected not on the *JAAR*, but on the field itself when he suggested that it continued to have a theological focus. "When you review the theoretical status of the study of religion over the past decade," he wrote, "I believe you will agree with me that not much, if anything has happened. We speak and write metaphorically rather than theoretically, concerned with things like 'thick descriptions.' The academy, for the most part, continues to be interested in religious dialogue and experience rather than criticism" (Penner 1994: 977).

Together, the theological interests of the AAR and the perennialist assumptions of academic phenomenologists combined to create a field of religious studies in the U.S. that according to scholar Bruce Lincoln, "provide[d] a comfortable place in a hostile environment for those who had either religious commitments of their own or religious desires of their own that they felt were unwelcome in the American academy of the 1950s, 60s, [and] 70s."[1]

To understand this latter point, consider that religious studies departments (as they mostly came to be known in the U.S.) emerged concurrently with larger changes in the American academy. The development of religious studies departments were but one of these changes. Other changes included the development of identity studies (gender, feminist, race, and ethnicity, for example) Marxist studies, and postcolonial studies, among others. The scholars who developed these disciplines criticized as oppressive many of the traditional forms of religiosity previously celebrated by groups such as NABI and then the AAR. Yet the history of religions as practiced by Brauer, Eliade, and Kitagawa provided religious scholars with what they perceived as theoretically rigorous academic dispositions that helped defend themselves against their newfound critics. To their credit, they were modestly successful. Though they failed to influence the larger academy, they did create what Lincoln referred to as a "comfortable place in a hostile environment."

By the mid-1980s, then, what passed as the academic study of religion in America seemed to some critics to bear an unfortunate resemblance to the departments of theological studies that they replaced, as their methods and methodologies seemed quite compatible. Backed by these methods and methodologies, scholars such as Eliade, Kitagawa, and Brauer might have (rather ironically) "saved" the field from being consumed by ancillary academic disciplines, but in the process of saving the discipline from outside threats, they aligned the discipline with many of the (predominantly liberal) religious groups they studied. The compatibility of methods was the hinge that helped solidify this new alliance.

The North American Association for the Study of Religion

To develop a space in North America for more rigorous academic reflections on so-called "religious" data and to develop and encourage more academic methods and methodologies, in 1985, E. Thomas Lawson, Luther H. Martin, and Donald Wiebe founded the North American Association for the Study of Religion (NAASR). As they wrote in their invitation to prospective members:

> [It] become apparent to a number of scholars, especially those engaged in the history or [sic] religions, comparative religions, or the scientific study of religions, or simply those who [felt] the need for theoretical work in the field, that the American Academy of Religion [had] become such a complex and competing repository of interests that the academic study of religion was in danger of being lost in the process. (Martin and Wiebe 2014)

Building off the work of scholars such as Jonathan Z. Smith and the aforementioned Bruce Lincoln, NAASR's founders created NAASR "to encourage the historical, comparative and structural study of religion in the North American community of scholars, to promote publication of such scholarly research, and to represent North American scholars in the study of religion to, and connect them with, the international community of scholars engaged in the study of religion." Michael Stausberg discussed the significance of NAASR when he wrote, "It was only with the founding of the North American Association for the Study of Religion (NAASR) in 1985 that the firmly non-religious study of religion assumed an organizational framework in the United States" (Stausberg 2016: 791).

Four years after its founding, NAASR adopted *Method and Theory in the Study of Religion* (*MTSR*)—a journal created in 1989 by graduate students at the University of Toronto—as its official journal. *MTSR* (published by Brill of the Netherlands) continues to be NAASR's journal today, as it has grown into the eminent peer-reviewed journal concerned with method and theory in the academic study of religion. The association of NAASR and *MTSR* brought to NAASR more than a growing journal, it solidified the association of NAASR with the phrase "method and theory." The founders of NAASR therefore agreed with the likes of Brauer that questions about method and methodology were crucial to the academic study of religion.[2] They disagreed, however, on, well, most everything else—including which of those methods were best suited to an academic study of religion.

To understand the disagreements over a seemingly simple term—method—consider that the search for "proper method" long predates the academic study of religion. The modern concern with the investigator's relationship to the material she gathers dates at least back to the seventeenth century, when René Descartes wrote his classic *Discourse on Method*. Scholars looking to Descartes for influence or inspiration are often frustrated by his treatise, which lacks an extensive explanation of his method, focusing instead on applied method or method in practice. This ambiguity over "proper method" continues today, as is evident by competing understanding of the word itself.

For example, religious studies scholar Jon Stone attempted a definition of these terms when he wrote:

> By definition, method is the way one collects data, the means or process of selecting information for analysis. By contrast, methodology is properly defined as the assumptions and preconceptions that influence one's analysis and interpretation of data, that is, the theoretical and analytical framework, even personal feelings, one brings to the task of organizing and analyzing facts. (Stone 1998: 6)

Russell McCutcheon, however, conceived of "methodology as the systematic study of the methods (i.e., tools and assumptions) that scholars use to go about their work," just as psychology is the systematic study of the psyche, etc. (McCutcheon 2014: 30). These scholars agree that "method" relates to the gathering of data, but they disagree on the issues of "assumptions" and "methodology." According to Stone, all scholars have methodologies insofar as we have personal agendas and biases that influence or even dictate our work. McCutcheon, however, suggests that methodology is the study of those agendas and biases.

As evidenced by these brief examples, scholars disagree over the definition of these important terms; however, despite their disagreements, some degree of consensus emerges. First, "method" refers to the gathering of data. Müller, for example, used the comparative method. Sigmund Freud used a psychological method. Clifford Geertz used anthropological methods (i.e., ethnography). All scholars who gather so-called "religious" data must use some *method* to gather said data. As evidenced by the previous paragraph, some scholars also suggest that personal biases or structural conditions can impact both the gathering of data and the use of said data, ultimately influencing the construction of "religion" in the products of their research—indicating that there may be a place for reflecting on one's methods, their motives and implications. The latter point deserves additional consideration, as questions of method and methodology are often neglected topics, and rarely are they sufficiently interrogated as constructive agents that help create the purported object of study.

Building off this latter point, I would suggest, contra Brauer, that scholars of religion need not attempt to identify a unique method for handling so-called "religious" data. I agree completely with Robert Segal, who argued "religious studies does not require either a distinctive method or a distinctive explanation to be worthy of disciplinary status" (Segal 2009: xvii). Instead, the focus on "method" calls religious studies scholars to pay attention to the contested and subjective means they deploy in pursuit of questions that are germane to their interests; questions that do not lead us to *sui generis*, perennial, or irreducible "religion." This important shift refocuses the academic study of religion to (re)consider both the so-called "data" and the scholar herself as data. To borrow a line from Russell McCutcheon, the shift in focus helps to examine "the prior conditions that make seemingly commonsense knowledge about religion possible" (McCutcheon 2014: 5). In this particular instance, the "prior conditions" are the scholar's methods and methodologies. In short, the attention to "method," both as a reflexive move on the part of the individual scholar, and as a primary object of study itself, helps fulfill Jonathan Z. Smith's call that scholars make "rigorous self-consciousness" their "foremost object of study" (Smith 1982: xi). Building off this important insight, the noun "method" in "method and theory" is not "neutral filler," to borrow a phrase from Bruce Lincoln (Lincoln 1996); rather, it signifies a self-reflexive awareness on the part of the scholar. Going full circle, so to speak, it includes questions of method and methodology as important objects of study as consistent with NAASR's founders who wanted to solidify a place in North America for the academic study of religion.

Aaron Hughes (among others) recently noted in the companion volume to this book that "method and theory"—a term previously associated with critical analysis, discourse analysis, and reductionist scholarship—is now commonplace (Hughes 2017). As Hughes wrote, "the terms 'method and theory' are now regularly found in course titles, degree requirements, and as the subjects of comprehensive exams, regardless of subfield" (ibid.: 5). The proliferation of "method and theory" might suggest that NAASR, and that scholars sympathetic to NAASR's goals, have successfully influenced the larger field. As Willi Braun (once NAASR's President) recently argued, however, as the terms "method and theory" (and, I would add, its attendant move toward self-reflexivity) have become more mainstream and widespread, they lost their provincial meaning (Braun 2016). Today, scholars deploy the terms "method and theory" to justify any scholarship, including the more overtly theological scholarship.

Mainstreamed "Method"

Scholars' inability—or reluctance—to acknowledge the constructive role of method and methodology continues to influence religious studies scholarship. Consider, for example, a recent article in the *Journal of the American Academy of Religion*, where Mary Dunn invoked what she deemed a "Jamesian radical empiricism" used by such scholars as Michael Jackson and Robert Orsi (Dunn 2016: 881). "Jamesian," of course, refers to William James, a familiar name both inside and beyond the academic study of religion, who in the early 1900s called his audiences to acknowledge religious experience as the irreducible core of religion. The emphasis on experience is evident in his definition of religion, which he famously defined as "the feeling, act, and experiences of individual men in their solitude, so far as they apprehend themselves to stand in relation to whatever they may consider the divine" (James 2012: 22). This theory of religion, however, proved quite compatible (and attractive) to his Christian (and more specifically, Protestant) audiences who similarly believed that personal religious experience with god was the core of authentic religiosity. This approach to theorizing religion conflicted with the academic study of religion as it had emerged in European scholarship, but perhaps that was precisely the point, as James claimed to bring an academic disposition to the study of religion. Contra scholars like Tylor, Frazer, Nietzsche, or Marx, however, James's approach offered a more sympathetic approach to study and theorize about religion. Roughly 115 years later, Dunn invoked James to highlight the "something about religion that exceeds what can be observed in the material conditions of its existence" (Dunn 2016: 881).

No shortage of scholars have criticized James, and Dunn is aware of many of these critics, particularly Donald Wiebe, Bruce Lincoln, and Russell McCutcheon, whom she collectively refers to as scholars interested in the scientific study of religion (a label at least one of these scholars would not reject, whereas another would rigorously defend it). Dunn sidesteps their various criticisms—about both *sui generis* religion and the material interests that drive so-called "religious" thought and action—when she dismissively argued, "good work in religious studies must make room for the abundant reality of human experience and propos[e] a methodological approach to the study of religion by which even the historian might attend to and account for this 'unknowable more'" (Dunn 2016: 884). According to Dunn, method and methodology help legitimize her notion of *sui generis* religion.

To acknowledge this "unknowable more" that comprises the core of religiosity, Dunn suggests that we develop a new and more inclusive methodological pluralism that includes "the theological, the aesthetic, the embodied, *and* the natural scientific" (Dunn 2016: 887; italics original). The latter, she argues, reflects some of Wiebe's, Lincoln's, and McCutcheon's criticisms as it incorporates the best—in her estimation—part of the natural sciences while it ignores the more destructive or corrosive elements. This new methodological pluralism is no simple task, she acknowledges, as it requires the "scholar's self-conscious juxtaposition of a multiplicity of narratives—historical, sociological, psychoanalytic, theological, *and autobiographical*" to help "engineer an encounter between her own world and the world of her subject, practicing something like radical empiricism from that medial site between observer and observed" (ibid.: 885; italics original). In other words, the attention to self-consciousness and methodology justify the very conclusions that are at odds with traditional notions of "method and theory" at least as understood by and expressed in NAASR meetings and in *MTSR*.

Dunn's preferred method and methodology are on full display in Robert Orsi's most recent book. In *History and Presence*, Orsi, a Catholic scholar of American religious history (and former President of the AAR), used the notion of "presence" as typically understood in the Catholic Mass as a metaphor for the *real* presence of god (broadly conceived) in the lives of the religious subjects he studies (2016). He employs the methodological pluralism as articulated by Dunn—for Orsi this pluralism includes history, anthropology, psychology, and theory—to describe the presence of god or the gods (Orsi 2016: 7), which for Orsi, are legitimate and real forces that motivate human behavior and that provide comfort during difficult times. He concludes, "I am proposing that we let the gods out of their assigned places and that we approach history and religion through a matrix of presence" (ibid.: 251). He continues, "If the presence of the gods in the old Catholic sense is an absolute limit that contemporary scholars of religion and history refuse to cross, then they will miss the empirical reality of religion in contemporary affairs and they will fail to understand much of human life" (ibid.: 252). "Critical reflection" (ibid.: 8), he argues, sustains his conclusion. In other words, instead of belittling, demeaning, or "explaining away" religious belief and behavior, critical reflection validates religiosity and sustains the theological claims of his religious subjects.

Orsi broached one of the perils of his method and methodology only briefly when he discussed the Catholic sex abuse scandal. As Orsi described it, one particular priest "assured one of his victims that taking the priest's ejaculate into his mouth was 'another way of receiving Holy Communion'" (Orsi 2016: 219). In this example, it is important to understand that for Orsi, the priest *used* the rhetoric of presence as a coercive tool as he deployed the Catholic notion of presence to advance his own pedophilic desires. Unfortunately, this appears to be a larger trend, as evidenced by the Netflix show *The Keepers*, where a now adult woman recalled in graphic detail similar instances where priests allegedly told their victims that Christ was similarly present in their ejaculate. At least one priest used his ejaculate to form the cross on the young woman's stomach. Obviously, this is not the type of presence that Orsi seeks to valorize, as evidenced by his characterization of such priests as "evil" and "predator priests" (ibid.: 219). Behind these tragic and unfortunate events, however, lies the larger fact that the rhetoric of presence—Orsi's purported object of study—provided an authority figure with the power to coerce people to behave in a manner that was perhaps contrary to their own interests. In other words, the rhetoric of presence functioned as a control mechanism. Orsi faced two choices: he could continue to explore the function of the rhetoric of presence in other instances, or he could ignore an example that contradicted his overall goal and proceed as planned. Not surprisingly, he chose the latter.[3]

The work of Dunn and Orsi provide a prime example of the appropriation of terms traditionally associated with critical scholarship in service of traditional status quo theological apologetics. Their understanding of the terms method, methodology, theory, self-consciousness, and critical scholarship invert the academic dispositions as traditionally conceived by NAASR and in *MTSR*. The fact that Dunn and Orsi represent the field's majority is one example of what NAASR and *MTSR* have addressed in the last several years at their annual meetings.

The 2016 NAASR Program

In November 2015, NAASR members gathered at their annual meeting to discuss the issue of "theory." The proceedings from that meeting were published in an already mentioned book entitled *Theory in a Time of Excess*. A year later, NAASR members gathered in San Antonio, Texas to discuss and debate issues surrounding the often related term "method." As both meetings demonstrated, questions about method and theory always and necessarily involve one another. The format at the 2016 meeting consisted of four main panels, each organized around a main paper concerning a key method common to many in the field, authored (or in the case of Ann Taves and Egil Asprem, co-authored) by a senior scholar in the academic study of religion. NAASR pre-circulated these papers by posting them online for roughly a month before the meeting. The authors then summarized their papers at NAASR's annual meeting, followed by four respondents who were predominately either graduate students or early-career scholars. As the executive secretary and treasurer of NAASR and editor of this book, I chaired each panel and moderated the Q&A that followed.

Naomi Goldenberg began the meeting when she presented her paper on "Description," where she interrogated the utility of the category of "religion"—a topic undoubtedly familiar to NAASR members. In the second panel, Kevin Schilbrack summarized his paper on "Interpretation," where he argued that all academic inquires (critically informed or otherwise) inevitably contain some degree of phenomenological representation. Aaron Hughes provided the main paper for the panel on "Comparison," where he defended historical and local approaches to comparison. In the fourth and final paper, Ann Taves presented the paper that she co-authored with Egil Asprem on the topic of "Explanation," where they summarized their explanatory model of religion that combines natural and social sciences.

Method Today includes modified versions of the papers and responses that were presented at the annual meeting in San Antonio. This book also contains responses from the authors of the main papers, where they reflect on the respondents' essays, offering points of clarification, agreement, or refutation. These papers are by no means the final words on these topics, although we hope that they will inspire and influence future conversations both in print and at future meetings.

Finally, it was an honor and a pleasure to ask my friend and colleague at McDaniel College, Gregory Alles, to write the afterword. Anyone familiar with the history of NAASR will recognize that Greg was also a former president of NAASR (and current editor of the International Association for the History of Religions journal, *Numen*). Greg has taught at McDaniel College since 1987, where he experienced personally the aforementioned give and take between the academic study of religion and theology. Consider that when McDaniel College was founded in 1867 as Western Maryland College (it changed its name to McDaniel College in 2002), it had a formal affiliation with the Methodist Protestant Church. This affiliation continued until 1974, when the two groups officially severed ties. Despite its new independence, liberal pluralism continued to be the norm at Western Maryland College for decades to come.

Change in the Religious Studies Department at McDaniel College has taken decades, but the addition of Greg as faculty proved to be important not only for the future of the department, but for the relationship between NAASR and McDaniel College. As president of NAASR from 2002–2005, Greg helped sustain a link between McDaniel College and NAASR that began with Luther Martin, who graduated as an undergrad from Western Maryland College in 1959. Luther, as you recall, was one of the three NAASR cofounders. I then became the next link in 2016, when NAASR's executive committee elected me to succeed Craig Martin as NAASR's executive secretary and treasurer. I joined the faculty of McDaniel College in 2015, and with Greg's support and gentle nudging, I agreed to follow Craig. Later in 2017 I replaced Russell McCutcheon as NAASR President. Today, NAASR is twenty-seven years old and we have many affiliations and relationships both in North American and beyond. The McDaniel/NAASR link is just one example, but it gives me great pleasure to work on this project with Greg, and with all the contributors as well.

Brad Stoddard is an assistant professor of religious studies at McDaniel College in Westminster, Maryland, and is the president of the North American Association for the Study of Religion. His research explores religion and public policy, particularly as they relate to criminal justice policies in the era of faith-based initiatives.

Notes

1 Religious Studies Project, interview with Bruce Lincoln, "The Critical Study of Religion." See www.religiousstudiesproject.com/podcast/the-critical-study-of-religion.
2 By no means, do I mean to imply that all NAASR members agree universally on these issues.
3 For a more comprehensive critique of Orsi's selective use of his own method and methodology, see McCutcheon (2006).

References

Brauer, Jerald. 1959. "Preface," in Mircea Eliade and Joseph Kitagawa (eds), *The History of Religions: Essays in Methodology*, vii–x. Chicago, IL: University of Chicago Press.
Braun, Willi. 2016. "Colloquium on Method and Theory: Introduction," *Method & Theory in the Study of Religion* 28(1): 1–2.
Descartes, René. 1998 [1637]. *Discourse on Method*. Indianapolis, IN: Hackett Publishing Company.
Dunn, Mary. 2016. "What Really Happened: Radical Empiricism and the Historian of Religion," *Journal of the American Academy of Religion* 84(4): 881–902.
Eliade, Mircea and Joseph Kitagawa (eds). 1959. *The History of Religions: Essays in Methodology*. Chicago, IL: University of Chicago Press.
Hart, Ray L. 1979. "*JAAR* in the Seventies: Unconcluding Scientific Postface," *Journal of the American Academy of Religion* 47(4): 509–516.
Hughes, Aaron (ed.). 2017. *Theory in a Time of Excess*. Sheffield: Equinox Publishing.
James, William. 2012 [1902]. *The Varieties of Religious Experience*. Bedford: St. Martin's Press.
Kitagawa, Joseph M. (ed.). 1985. *The History of Religions: Retrospect and Prospect*. New York: Macmillan.
Lincoln, Bruce. 1996. "Theses on Method," *Method and Theory in the Study of Religion* 8: 225–227.
Martin, Luther H. and Donald Wiebe. 2014. "Establishing a Beachhead: NAASR, Twenty Years Later." Retrieved from https://naasrreligion.files.wordpress.com/2014/01/establishingabeachhead.pdf (accessed March 7, 2018).

McCutcheon, Russell. 2006. "'It's a Lie. There's No Truth in It! It's a Sin!': On the Limits of the Humanistic Study of Religion and the Costs of Saving Others from Themselves," *Journal of the American Academy of Religion* 74(3): 720–750.
McCutcheon, Russell. 2014. *A Modest Proposal on Method: Essaying the Study of Religion*. Boston, MA: Brill.
Orsi, Robert. 2016. *History and Presence*. Cambridge, MA: The Belknap Press of Harvard University Press.
Penner, Hans. 1994. "Holistic Analysis: Conjectures and Refutations," *Journal of the American Academy of Religion* 62(4): 977–996.
Ricoeur, Paul. 1970. *Freud and Philosophy: An Essay on Interpretation*. New Haven, CT: Yale University Press.
Segal, Robert A. 2009. "Introduction," in Robert A. Segal (ed.), *The Blackwell Companion to the Study of Religion*, xiii–xix. Chichester: Blackwell Publishing.
Smith, Jonathan Z. 1982. *Imagining Religion: From Babylon to Jonestown*. Chicago, IL: University of Chicago Press.
Stausberg, Michael. 2016. "History," in Michael Stausberg and Steven Engler (eds.), *The Oxford Handbook of the Study of Religion*, 775–803. Oxford: Oxford University Press.
Stone, Jon R. 1998. *The Craft of Religious Studies*. New York: Palgrave.

Part I

Chapter 1

Comparison

Aaron W. Hughes

Introduction

"To know one," F. Max Müller once famously quipped in the early part of the twentieth century, "is to know none." This phrase has functioned as the guiding inscription emblazoned upon the entranceway to the temple of religious studies ever since. Implicit in this locution is the idea that one cannot fully appreciate the breadth and depth of religion without putting at least two of them in counterpoint. It is their juxtaposition that is believed to show similarities, differences, and a host of other family resemblances. While I here put this assumption to the test, it is safe to assume that, by the end, comparison will be left standing. It will, I trust, be a somewhat different type of comparison than the kind that Müller had in mind over a century ago. If I could frame this essay in equally poetic terms, it would be along the lines of "she who knows one religion really well knows that she cannot fall under phenomenology's spell."

What is comparison? It is, first and foremost, a literary conceit. It is an activity that selects, juxtaposes, and manipulates two or more unrelated objects that an individual perceives to share one or more similar or overlapping characteristics. On a poetic register, these characteristics can be as obvious as comparing love to a rose or as arcane, as in the hands of Donne, of comparing love to the two legs of a drafting compass.[1] The goal of such comparisons is presumably to invoke a sense of wonder in the reader by showing the interconnectedness of the natural world and our place therein.

Yet, to show the resemblance of two contradictory or different objects, one must explicate the logic that comprises the comparison and try to illumine the gossamer threads that are perceived to hold them delicately together. Love is neither a rose nor is it a drafting compass. Yet, if one wants to talk about love, describe it, and analyze it one needs metaphors and a comparative grid on which to plot it. Since literary conceits portray one thing as something else, they make sense on the level of the imagination, but the intellect demands clarification. Although such clarificatory skill is thankfully not in the job description of the poet, it ought to be in that of the scholar. In this chapter, I wish to suggest that while there are good comparisons and bad comparisons, common to both is the sheer artificiality of the enterprise. This stems from the notion that if things are exactly alike, then they must necessarily be the same thing (see Neusner 1991:

175). Since no two things can be exactly alike—love is not nor ever can be a drafting compass; Islam is not Judaism; Hinduism is not Christianity—it is up to the juxtaposer or the comparativist to tell us why they resemble one another. And, just as importantly:

1 when they do;
2 for how long; and
3 for what purpose.

Too often, however, these latter aspects are muted and we return to a model in which specific religions are imagined to manifest timeless and disembodied truths.

The academic study of religion, to be sure, is certainly a more mundane and quotidian affair than poetry. There are no Donnes or Blakes who can help us imagine the world anew by drawing a set of comparisons between disparate social expressions signified as "religious" by their practitioners. Instead comparison in our chosen field has been used for a host of apologetical and often highly ideological ends. So much so that many doubt or at the very least question its utility (e.g., Smith 1982; Patton and Ray 2000: 1–4). Too many times we have read articles or monographs that purport to tell us how "x" in one religion resembles, is similar to, or is different from "y" in another. What, if anything, we have to ask ourselves, is gained by such an activity? Despite all the bad and faulty comparisons that litter our field, is it worth proceeding? If yes, we need to think about what a responsible comparison might look like. If not, we still have to acknowledge that, despite our best intentions, there is something comparative built into the way we know and describe things. Things can and do remind us of other things. Since we engage our world comparatively, comparison is a natural part of our cognitive framework. However, and this is the paradox, *while the comparative act might be natural, specific comparisons are not.*

Unfortunately, comparison habitually finds itself gravitating towards two ends of an ideological continuum: either (1) to show how two or more things are either entirely different or (2) to demonstrate how they are essentially the same. Despite their rather different ends, however, the hermeneutic that informs them both would seem to be based on a set of often extra-scholarly concerns.[2] If the former not infrequently wants to show how one's own religion is superior to others (e.g., the Christ-event is qualitatively of a different nature than those of, say, mystery cults of antiquity), the latter is informed by a set of irenic concerns premised on interfaith or interreligious dialogue (e.g., "Abrahamic religions" should be able to get along because they all share the same ethos). But we all know, or at least should know, the results of such endeavors. With few exceptions, such endeavors revolve around the assumption that comparison is or can be a valid method in the field. However, there is often very little to no theoretical reflection on the method, but simply an acknowledgement that it is as natural an activity as can be.

But to compare comparative schemes and to choose which one offers the best model is perhaps not the best way to proceed. I will suggest a few antecedents in the "History" section below, but allow me now to begin with my argument: *If comparison is to be an effective method it must be historical and not phenomenological, local and not global.* By this, I mean that while cross-cultural comparisons may appear eye-catching or useful ("x in Hinduism," for example, "is like y in Christianity"), such results are at best idiosyncratic, that is, contingent on the particular needs of the comparativist, and rarely if ever verifiable. A much more useful type of comparison is one that emerges from those places where contiguous or overlapping social groups speak the same literal language and think with the same metaphorical language. Since these localized interactions not infrequently occur on the margins, they tend to give definition to centers. Since they are marginal, however, they are often overlooked or written off as non-normative.

History provides one of the greatest antidotes to the type of essentialist reifications that have plagued and continue to plague religious studies. Such reifications (e.g., "Christianity says ...," "*the* Christian believes ...") have resulted in the most egregiously superficial frameworks of comparison.[3] The historical record, however, bequeaths us actual and verifiable material, textual, economic, political, intellectual, and social interactions between groups. Lest I appear as a historical positivist and claim that "the facts do not lie," it should go without saying that historians are often not the most theoretically sophisticated when it comes to comparative frameworks. This space between or intersectionality of historical data and theoretical sophistication is where comparison ought to be located. To do history like a historian (complete with linguistic and cultural expertise) and engage in social theory like a social theorist is, for me, the perhaps unattainable task of comparison.

As someone who works on the interface of, for lack of better terms, "Judaism" and "Islam," presumably I work on comparison. Though I have never called myself a "comparativist" or someone who engages in the task of "comparative religion," I guess I am and I do. I imagine that this is because I do not see myself as doing the type of essentialist comparative work that usually goes by this name in religious studies. In what follows I want to use some of my own work that deals with the interaction of various social groups who define themselves in some way as "Jewish" or "Muslim" with the aim of teasing out a second-order set of reflections. My work on these two traditions is not to "compare" a generic or heuristically constructed Judaism with an equally generic heuristically constructed Islam to ascertain some sort of theological or interfaith end based on essentialist categories (e.g., prophecy or messianism). Instead, I find it much more productive to look at the interactions of specific groups at specific times and in specific places—often underdefined groups that speak the same language, create similar social worlds in response to the same political uncertainty, and seek to define themselves in light of the other.

History

Too often comparison has been used phenomenologically to privilege certain religious expressions over others. J. Z. Smith, perhaps the one who has reflected more on comparison than anyone else in our field in recent years, argues that every comparison (x is like y) implies, but rarely receives, a third term (with respect to z) (see his discussion in Smith 1990: 50–53). This means that, for Smith, comparison is not based on natural affinity or even historical process, but personal utility. We must remember and duly acknowledge that it is we who are the ones making the comparison and the idiosyncratic nature of this activity produces artificial if heuristically useful results. Comparison is, again in the words of Smith,

> a disciplined exaggeration in the service of knowledge. It lifts out and strongly marks certain features within difference as being of possible intellectual significance, expressed in the rhetoric of their being "like" in some stipulated fashion. Comparison provides the means by which *we* "revision" phenomena as *our* data in order to solve *our* theoretical problems. (Smith 1990: 52)

For Smith, "the statement of comparison is never dyadic, but always triadic; there is always an implicit 'more than,' and there is always a 'with respect to.' In the case of an academic comparison, the 'with respect to' is most frequently the scholar's interest, be this expressed in a question, a theory, or a model" (ibid.: 51).

The academic study of religion is a field littered with suppressed third terms, self-serving differentials, and hidden meanings. Let me take up an example from my own area of research (Hughes 2017). In his *Jews and Arabs*, Shlomo Dov Goitein, one of the pioneers in research into the Cairo Geniza, coined the term "symbiosis" to refer to the historical interaction between Jews and Muslims, Judaism and Islam.[4] The basic narrative that "symbiosis" structures goes something like this: Judaism helped to give birth to Islam in the late sixth century before Islam returned the favor in the tenth to twelfth centuries by facilitating the rise and florescence of, among other things, Hebrew belles-lettres and Jewish philosophy. Informing this dominant narrative is the fiction of a creative and stable Jewish essence that gives life to Islam (as it had to Christianity several centuries earlier) and that later borrows from a now equally creative and stable Islam what it needs. Both essences are assumed to remain untouched by this encounter. While others have tried to modify this somewhat (e.g., Laskier and Lev 2011a, 2011b), "symbiosis" is still largely our default metaphor (Wasserstrom 1995).

Goitein, it seems, was attracted to the concept of "symbiosis" because it facilitated a conceptual framework that preserved Judaism's unique features, its ahistorical essence, within a dominant culture while still enabling Jews to be full participants within it. Islam, for him, was "from the very flesh and bone of Judaism" (Goitein 1955: 130). Or, again: "Judaism could draw freely and copiously from Muslim civilization and, at the same time, preserve its independence and integrity far more completely than it was able to do in the modern world or in the Hellenistic society of Alexandria" (ibid.: 130).

Like many others, Goitein makes Judaism into something stable, already articulated, and well defined in the sixth-century Ḥijāz (i.e., the westernmost region of the Arabian Peninsula, and the home of Mecca and Medina). This conceit sustains the basic and still largely regnant model wherein Jews shape Islam, and the Qur'an simply recycles midrashim and other Jewish literature of the period. It is a model, however, that always assumes that the influence moves in one direction. Left unasked are a couple of important questions:

- Who were these "Jews"?
- What did "Jew" signify" in sixth-century Arabia?

We have to be cautious of assuming an orthodoxy of stable Jewish identity and practice based upon what the rabbinic academies of Babylonia were producing at this time. What "Arab Jewishness" consisted of, in other words, might have looked considerably different than other forms of Jewishness in the larger context of the Mediterranean basin.

In the second phase, according to Goitein, the direction switches and we now see the influence of medieval Islam upon Judaism. Now "the vital contributions made by the cultural elements inherent in one civilization [that is, Islam] to the autonomous spiritual life of the other" (Goitein 1955: 127). This second-phase of the symbiotic relationship was characterized by:

1 the use of Arabic, which led to Arabic ways of thinking and forms of literature, "as well as of Muslim religious notions" (ibid.: 32);

2 the rise of Jewish philosophy, which reveals "the impact of Muhammadan spiritual life on the Jewish mind" (ibid.: 140);

3 mysticism; and

4 Hebrew poetry, which he calls "the acme of Jewish-Arab symbiosis" (ibid.: 155).

"The Hebrew poet," Goitein writes, "could draw in full measure from a civilization which was closely akin to his own, while at the same time cherishing a strong transcendental belief in the mission of Israel" (ibid.: 167). Sometimes, as with poetry for example, he will argue that the Jews had it first, that is, before the advent of Islam, and that the Muslim interest in ornate speech only reentered Judaism in the high Middle Ages (Goitein 1967–1993: vol. 5, p. 424). The anxiety of influence and the politics of who had what first, are never far from the surface in this literature. And while "Judaism" becomes, on Goitein's reading, a midwife to the birth of Islam, the best that Islam can do for Judaism is to function as a mnemonic, a reminder of its poetic and democratic birthright. It is not at all clear to me, however, that medieval Jewish poets, philosophers, belletrists or others clearly distinguished between what was "Jewish" and what was "Islamic" in ways that we today, post-1948, have no problems distinguishing between.

In this one example we witness a rather traditional description of how comparison has been used: to protect, to assign value, and to envisage normativity. Religions, envisaged as species or organisms, interact with one another and in such a manner that one of them, Judaism, is stable and this stability permits it to transfer its essence of monotheism (see Geiger 1970; Graetz 1956) to the framers of Islam. Judaism gives, Islam receives. A couple of centuries later, Islam returns the favor, but this return in no way impacts Judaism's eternal core. Changes in the latter context are superficial or cosmetic at best, and in no way transform what Judaism is or is meant to be.

When done in such a manner, comparison is completely unhelpful as an analytical method. It tells us nothing that we do not already suspect. It confirms hunches. And it supplies a convenient narrative that reinforces half-truths. The traditional use of comparison, in short, does little to make us uncomfortable precisely because it refuses to destabilize our understanding of "religion." As a model, comparison tends to work on the assumption that religions are "things" that can be reified, disembodied, or removed from distinct social contexts. The results are all around us: twelfth century textual expressions can be compared to fourth century ones, and not infrequently in ways that exist not just temporally, but also spatially or geographically far apart from one another.

Yet, this is why, at least on one level, Goitein's model of symbiosis is potentially interesting. He is interested in specific contexts among two religions that we know interacted historically, religious, intellectually, socially, and economically with one another. There is perhaps no greater testament to this than his six-volume *A Mediterranean Society*, which documents using materials associated with the Cairo Geniza the historical interactions between two local communities, including on the familial and individual level. However, when it comes to speaking about religion, Goitein neither theorizes religion nor is he particularly interested in it.[5] It just seems to be there, amorphously and silently informing the inner lives of those he studies through their written texts and correspondences.

Goitein shows the historian's conceit in his discussion of religion in *A Mediterranean Society*. Rather than show the artificial and unstable nature of the term, he assumes both a normativity and even, dare I say it, a Protestant bias. While he is correct to see a crosspollination of ideas, I remain unconvinced that Goitein's model of symbiosis is at all helpful. Primary is the fact that symbiosis implies the interaction of two fully developed religions that, although sharing certain superficial phenomena (language, literature), retained their separate essences.

But just because Goitein's model, like the models of so many on our field, is faulty does not necessarily mean that we have to jettison certain aspects of the comparative enterprise. Rather than see two separate and fully defined species interact, why not start with the fact—and it is a fact since we have absolutely no idea who the Jews of sixth-century Arabian Peninsula were or what they subscribed to when it comes to doctrine—two proximate social groups developed in tandem with one another and used a common structure and vocabulary. What would eventually become two distinct and discrete religions—Judaism and Islam—took considerable time to coalesce and in such a manner that each gained definition from, with, and by the other. What is decidedly not the case, and this is the assumption of many who reproduce the "symbiosis" thesis, is the interaction of two fully developed religions that, although sharing certain superficial phenomena (language, literature), retained their separate essences.

Possibilities

Using this example, allow me to reflect upon comparison more specifically. We have already seen what traditional comparative models have accomplished when it comes to Judaism and Islam in particular and the comparison of other religions in general. In terms of the former, which is my sole concern, these models have (1) shown us that a fully normative and rabbinic Judaism gave birth to Islam, and (2) that several centuries later, the Jewish contact with Islam (in places like the "golden age" of Muslim Spain) allowed Jews to express themselves using new forms (secular poetry, belles-lettres, philosophy, and so on) that they inherited from Muslims. Much intellectual labor has gone on in the modern period to examine the latter; unfortunately, however, such studies tend to reproduce the assumptions inherent to "symbiosis" even if they do not literally invoke the term.[6] The default model is one wherein distinct species interact and that, while superficial changes (e.g., Jews writing in Arabic) may result, the so-called or self-assumed eternal centers of each religion remain pure and unscathed. Unfortunately such a model retells a set of platitudes. Left unasked are a series of difficult questions: Who, for example, were "the Jews" with whom Muhammad interacted? How exactly did Judaism transform during the so-called "golden age"? What exactly happened to the Jews between these chronological bookends?

Before I address some of these questions in greater detail, allow me to make a larger point about the pitfalls of comparison by examining some recent studies that deploy the method. In his *God is Not One* (2010), Stephen Prothero, as his subtitle makes clear, is interested in comparing "the religions that run the world." Thankfully not just focusing on Judaism, his goal is to show for a general readership how religions does not share the same essence, but instead to showcase how the "world's religious rivals are clearly related, but they are more like second cousins that identical twins" (Prothero 2010: 13). His goal is to illumine how to understand religions in order to understand the world's problems: "It is impossible to understand politics in India and the economy of China without knowing something about Hinduism and Confucianism" (ibid.: 11). The religions of the globe, for Prothero, are not reducible to politics, social formation, or ideology. Rather there seems to be some element to each religion that remains untouched by such concepts. He comes up with the following model, into which he situates his eight world-running rival religions:

- a *problem*;
- a *solution* to this problem, which also serves as the religious goals;
- a *technique* (or techniques) for moving from this problem to this solution;
- an *exemplar* (or exemplars) who chart this path from problem to solution (ibid.: 14).

An example should suffice. In Christianity, at least for Prothero, the problem is sin; the solution is salvation; the technique is faith and good works; and the exemplars are saints in Catholicism and ordinary people of faith in Protestantism (ibid.: 14). And, with this model, we thereby understand Christianity and presumably something of American politics (ibid.: 11). That is it. There is little or no nuance. A religion can be reduced to a few slogans or soundbites with no appreciation of historical, textual, or geographical diversity.

Prothero offers us a not particularly helpful model for engaging in comparison at the current moment. Each religion (note the singular) articulates a different, but related, problem, and seeks to solve it different ways. While his goal is to show the diversity among the world's religions, he unfortunately provides none *within* each religion. The result is a completely superficial presentation that hinders actual analysis instead of helping it.

In her *Bringing the Sacred Down to Earth*, Corinne G. Dempsey provides us with another model. Rather than examine monolithic religions, she instead examines local interactions in specific places, and then compares these to other local contexts in disparate geographical contexts. She argues that comparison is primarily about "naming and claiming the sacred from different angles and a variety of settings" (Dempsey 2012: 5). She further claims that the goal of comparison is "to shed light on angles and contours otherwise obscured within particular religious contexts and, in the process, suggest possibilities for bridging human contingencies and perceptions across religious, cultural, and disciplinary divides (ibid.: 5). While aware of comparison's potential to reify and abstract, and its historical use in privileging certain forms over others, Dempsey contends that the way to overcome these pitfalls is "the resolve to take seriously the religious experiences and expressions of those we study" (ibid.: 10).

For Dempsey, comparison is contemporary and not textual. She primarily deals with localized traditions supplied by South Asian and Euroamerican contexts (e.g., Indian neo-Vedanta and Icelandic spiritualism, or Indian and Irish Catholicism). What makes comparison possible for Dempsey is the illusive nature of "the sacred," something that, according to her, functions "as a category that implies to transcendent meaning and power yet is not limited to or divided against the unempirical or the metaphysical" (ibid.: 15). Comparison, in other words, allows us to get at the so-called sacred just as the so-called sacred facilitates comparison. This circle, however, ultimately reproduces and reifies what it seeks to discover in the first place. Dempsey's notion of comparison thus takes us back to an earlier time in its deployment, one seen in the likes of Eliade albeit now more in vogue by using the contemporary category of lived religion."

In his *New Patterns for Comparative Religion* (2016), William E. Paden wants to take Dempsey's localized comparative endeavors and translate them onto the level of the human species. Moving from, in his own words, nouns to verbs, his interest is how groups "do" things such as transmit mythic pasts and ritualize life passages. So, while there might be "thousands of things humans and human groups do in common, and while many might seem obvious or trivial, they could still serve as points of comparison within the rich cultural examples that encompass them" (ibid.: 4). Paden, then, wants to move beyond the rich materiality and textuality that drives Dempsey's analysis and instead examine religions from a cognitive or evolutionary model. Again, in his words,

> with our global, historical perspective, we in comparative religion are positioned to point out that patterns of religious behavior are themselves part of the subject matter when exploring how we have evolved as social beings. For instance what if, for our human species, transmitting accounts about the sacred foundations of one's world is itself a natural niche-building behavior for holding one's group together—and thus apiece with survival-fitness? (Paden 2016: 8)

For Paden, unlike Dempsey, the comparative study of religion is a natural and desacralized activity. It ought to look for the general behind the particular. Unlike comparativists of an earlier generation, however, this general is not some amorphous notion of the sacred so much as it is evolutionary behavior. However, there is still something behind diverse cultural forms that certain people might find problematic. Yet the pattern, what he calls "big concepts,"

> need not suppress diversity and from an evolutionary perspective they are balanced out by the powerful role of diverse environments prompting diverse behaviors and versions of behaviors. So that does not reduce the human mind to sameness, or religion to a single trait, or override the role of cultural and gendered differences ... Quite the opposite: the evolutionary outlook tends to carve up or fractionate "religion" into its individual dispositions in settings where human actions are typically and variously generated from learned cultural skills and not just from simple default, uniform instinctual reactions. (Paden 2016: 230)

Paden tries to walk a very fine line, one that takes social activity seriously while simultaneously trying to be responsible to the cognitive science of religion. In so doing, however, I dare say that he risks offending practitioners of both. The attention to the specific means he only obtusely engages in research in the cognitive study of religion; and the attempt to get at the "big concepts" behind cultural specifics and his superficial engagement with actual religious traditions potentially alienates those interested in historical and textual study.

What do these three models of comparison—for lack of better terms, let us call them the simplistic, the lived, and the cognitive—tell us? Well, for one thing that comparison—despite claims to the contrary—is alive and well in the academic study of religion. This should not be surprising given the fact that, as mentioned earlier, comparison forms a natural part of our cognitive processes. It is only natural that if we want to understand one thing we compare it to something else. This comparison, however, can either be superficial (e.g., Prothero) or more complex (e.g., Paden).

These three models show us that comparison is something that, like beauty, exists solely in the eyes of the beholder. While the comparativist wants us to believe that the act s/he is undertaking is as natural as can be, it is not. Prothero wants a novice to understand why religions are different, whereas Dempsey, writing for other specialists, wants to imagine "the sacred" in the bodily and ritualistic actions of religious believers in different localized contexts.

I want to suggest another model, one that will preoccupy me in the following section. Unlike the aforementioned three models, for me comparison must involve immersion in languages, texts, traditions, and only then theory. One cannot compare unless one knows the languages *in their original*. One cannot compare, say, Arabic and Judeo-Arabic sources from the tenth century unless one actually can read these two languages. We have all seen the extremes to which grandiose comparative frameworks that pay precious little attention to actual sources can lead us. Here the work of Eliade might well be the most egregious example (other examples include Prothero 2010; Henderson 1991, 1998). Such examples provide little to no reflection on what it means to compare. It is simply done either to show the "morphology of the sacred" in the case of Eliade or similarities between reified entities in the case of the others.

Standing at the other end of the continuum is the model supplied by the likes of Paden. While theoretically sophisticated, it provides us with very little practical examples or, when it does, they are never followed through. The comparativist interested in data, then, has to use Paden's suggestive model in a piecemeal fashion. But this is the importance of Paden's work: everyone interested in comparison ought to be able to learn from it and to find a way into it. In between Paden and Prothero is the work of Dempsey, which may actually be the most problematic. Her framework is too idiosyncratic. We do not know if her findings are either repeatable or testable. We must take, in short, take her word for it.

Comparison is a theoretical activity, to be sure. Nevertheless, for it to be an effective theoretical activity, it must be able to account for the data. Comparison must be able to interpret data, and not simply be a clever or poetic activity. This means that we must be self-conscious, self-reflexive on the one hand, and possess all of the historical, literary, and textual skills on the other. We must thus speak to two discrete audiences: other comparativists, that is, scholars that work in different religious traditions but who deal with a similar problem; and non-comparativists who often work solely in one field, but not both. This is not an easy task. In fact, one might well say that it is impossible. How can one write for both specialists in history or area studies *and* scholars who work on religions other than one's own specialty? Whether or not we can actually do so, we must strive to accomplish this. If we do not then we risk either irrelevance or, even worse, charges of oversimplification.

Let me give an example of what I have in mind. I formerly edited a book series with Oxford University Press and I still recall a glaring problem with one of the first submissions to my series—though I did not realize it at the time since I do not work in this particular area. The author in question desired to engage in a comparative study of Asian fire rituals based not on their formal characteristics (which would have been fine), but instead on specific rituals called "*homa*." This author's entire thesis was based on the "fact" that the *homa* rituals encountered across Asia, generally assumed to derive from Indic prototypes, actually came from an Iranian/Zoroastrian model. The key piece of evidence for this author was that the Avestan word *haoma* was the equivalent to the Sanskrit *homa*, and that there was a (Proto-)Indo-Iranian, pre-Vedic, word *homa* underlying both the

Avestan and the Iranian fire rituals. When I sent the ms. out for review, I did what I always do: I sent it to a religionist working in the area and to an expert in the same area but not in religious studies. In this case, the religionist loved it, but the specialist informed me that the MS was based on a fundamental error, namely, that the Avestan *haoma* could never be cognate to Sanskrit *homa* since the former was instead a direct cognate to Sanskrit *soma*, both deriving from the Proto Indo-Iranian *sauma. If Avestan did have a cognate to Sanskrit *homa*, my expert reader informed me, it would be *zauma, which does not exist (or at least is not attested). The anonymous reviewer concluded that "The whole work is based on a fundamental—and embarrassingly elementary—error, and the author seems not to know any of the languages and textual sources on which his/her work rests."

This, framed simply, is the danger of comparison, at least in the academic study of religion.

Contexts

An essay on comparison would not be worth its salt if it did not actually engage in some kind of comparative enterprise, and to provide some practicality to a set of overriding theoretical concerns. This section derives from my recent study (Hughes 2017) on the relationship between, for lack of a better term, "Jewish" and "Muslim" social groups in the century after the death of Muhammad. The period emerging after late antiquity, from roughly the death of Muhammad in 632 CE to the death of Saadya Gaon, one of the most important framers of rabbinic Judaism and someone who wrote primarily in Arabic, in 942, are equally obscure. Despite Goitein's earlier confidence in the contours and contents of Arabian Judaism, even he was forced to admit that "the centuries both preceding and following the rise of Islam are the most obscure in Jewish history" (Goitein 1955: 95). This, however, did not stop him or others from projecting later ideas onto this darkness. More often than not this has involved positing a normative rabbinic Judaism, defined by what was going on in the later caliphal center of Baghdad, and then assuming that it somehow existed at the time of Muhammad and in such a manner that it was either removed from or developed untouched by its immediate Arabo-Islamic environment (Bulliet 1994: 8).

Despite the fact that well over three-quarters of world Jewry lived within Islamic lands until the tenth century, there is no getting around the disconcerting fact that our understanding of Jews during the late antique period is minimal at best (Wasserstrom 1995: 18). Perhaps the one thing that it is possible to say with some confidence is that Judaism, not unlike Islam, was poorly or under defined, with many groups—later written off as "heterodox"— exploring different paradigms of leadership and structures of authority (Grossman 1984: 15-44; 1988). Through later rabbinic and Muslim sources, it is possible to glean the existence of several of these paradigms, which ranged from the highly messianic and apocalyptic to what would eventually become normative. We also learn the names of individuals, groups, and institutions—Isawiyya, Karaites, Exilarchs, Khazars, Geonim—but since the latter carried the day and often treated their ideological enemies using *argumenti ex silentio* (Feldman 1993: 35–38), we know very little about them. While this study examines the contours of these groups, it certainly does not seek to provide histories of them. Rather, I use them as discursive sites to reveal a porosity between numerous Jewish and Muslim social groups responding, often in the same way, to the social, religious, and intellectual turmoil brought about by the rapid spread of Islam and the concomitant process of Islamicization.[7]

One such group is the Isawiyya. Here it is important to acknowledge that the late antique period was awash in messianic and apocalyptic speculation (Howard-Johnston 2011; Bowersock 2012; Stroumsa 2015a: 59–100), into which the originary message of Muhammad undoubtedly tapped and against which it must be situated.[8] As the likes of Friedlaender, and more recently Wasserstrom have argued, there was a common semantic matrix from which emerged various groups—Jewish, Muslim, Jewish-Muslim, or Muslim-Jewish—many of which would later be written off as some version on the theme of heterodox pietism (Wasserstrom 1995: 47–48). Such groups, as Pines argued, would have existed alongside Jewish–Christian communities in places such as Jerusalem at the time of Muʿāwiyah (r.661–680), the founder of the Umayyad Caliphate (Pines 1985). Before all these groups were subsequently written off as heterodox, however, it is important to remember that they were mainstream. The messianism that produced Muhammad and that would undoubtedly have led a large number of Jews, whatever this term might have meant in the early- and mid-seventh century notwithstanding, to accept his apocalyptic message gave way in the coming centuries to a variety of Jewish messianic movements that only make sense within the larger context of the sectarianism associated with early Islamic history. To use the words of Averil Cameron (1991: 287), "Islam took shape within a context of extreme religious and cultural tension." To this we must certainly add that so, too, did Judaism.

The Isawiyya's emergence corresponds to the fall of the Umayyad caliphate, the rise of the Abbāsid one, and the existence of a plethora of loosely connected and largely underdefined proto-Shīʿite *ghulāt* groups (most recently, see Asatryan 2016). Pines, for example, argued that Abū ʿĪsā al-Iṣfahānī (late seventh/early eighth century), the leader of this—for lack of a better term—"Jewish sect," was most likely influenced by a combination of Jewish and Christian beliefs and that his movement, the Isawiyya, bore certain family resemblances to other apocalyptic texts such as the *Doctrina Iacobi*, a seventh-century Greek Christian text that records the existence of a prophet in Arabia at the time of the birth of Islam.[9] But, again, note that Pines falls back on the language of "influences" and "borrowing." Moreover, he also wants to make this into an intellectual movement based on the reading of texts, when, if anything the Isawiyya seem to have been the apocalyptic rebellion of a lower class. My brief analysis here relies on the important discussion of Wasserstrom, who has done more than anyone else to show not only the filiations between the Isawiyya and various sectarian Muslim groups but also the far-reaching consequences of this group. For Wasserstrom, following the earlier study by Israel Friedlaender (1910), the similarities between these *ghulāt* groups, some of whom would be eventually folded into what would emerge as normative

Twelver Shīʿism, and the Isawiyya, are more than coincidental, and most likely based on real historical interactions. For Wasserstrom,

> The early Muslims did not borrow their Messiah from Judaism, nor was Jewish Messianic imagery lent by a Jew to a Muslim in the sense that a lender lends to a debtor. Rather, Muslims consciously and creatively reimagined the Messiah. These Islamic rereadings, consonant with the decentralized pluralism of the Jewish redeemer myths, never pronounced one image of the Messiah as definitive, There were, of course, no councils of Judaism or Islam to rule on the officially proper Messiah. (Wasserstrom 1995: 57)

With no monolithic or monothetic sense of what or who a Messiah was or should be, Jewish groups could rely upon a prophetic vocabulary supplied by Muslim sectarian groups (some of which would eventually be labeled as "Shīʿi"), just as Muslim groups recycled Jewish motifs without necessarily knowing their origins. Neither, of course, were historians and neither were interested in ascertaining what was authentically "Jewish" or 'Muslim." Nor were either interested in saying who had what first or borrowed from whom. The result is that it is extremely difficult to untangle these messianic threads neatly from one another. What we do know, however, is that Abū ʿĪsā's quasi-political, quasi-religious sectarian creation, the Isawiyya, remained one of the most important sectarian movements in Judaism, along with the Karaites (to be discussed presently) until the seventeenth century. According to the Muslim heresiographer, al-Shahrastānī (1086–1153), writing much later, Abū ʿĪsā claimed that

> He was a prophet [nabī] and a prophetic messenger [rasūl] of the awaited Messiah [al-masīḥ al-muntaẓar]; that the Messiah has five harbingers [rusul] who precede him one after the other ... that the Messiah is the best of the children of Adam; that he is of a higher status that the foregoing prophets [anbiyāʾ]; and that since he is his own apostle, he is the most excellent of them He enjoined faith in the Messiah, exalting the mission [daʿwa] of the harbinger; he believed that the harbinger is also the Messiah. (Wasserstrom 1995: 68)

It is worth noting that many of the Arabic terms in this paragraph have decidedly proto-Shīʿi valences. Abū ʿĪsā thus combines "Jewish" and "Muslim" messianic vocabularies in such a manner that he is comprehensible to other groups on both sides of the Jewish-Muslim hyphen. Rather than say that one "influences" the other, it might be more apposite to imagine them as intimately linked. Again, according to Wasserstrom,

> They could be recognized as Jews by (Rabbanite and Karaite) Jews because they seemed Judaically orthopraxy, and could be recognized as believers (by Karaite and Shīʿite) Muslims because they seemed Islamically orthodox. This was, perhaps, and unwieldy if not spurious symmetry. (Wasserstrom 1995: 79)

It is this paradox, the hyphen separating Jew and Muslim, which makes groups such as the Isawiyya—and perhaps even other groups that have not yet come down to us—so interesting. Both Muslim and Jew, neither Muslim nor Jew, they occupy the margins of history. They become the groups that give definition to the center while at the same time subject to further marginalization. So while the Isawiyya will rarely appear in so-called normative histories of Judaism or in classes on Jewish history, at the time they provided a valid socioreligious framework that only in retrospect became labeled as heterodox.

Abū ʿĪsā, for example, claimed to be the last of the five heralds from God announcing the arrival of the Messiah and the end of days (see Pines 1966; Wasserstrom 1995: 84–88; Stroumsa 2015a: 76–77). He acknowledged Jesus and Muhammad as true prophets, but only to their own followers—and here he seems to have been part of the same environment that produced works such as *Doctrina Iacobi* and the *Secrets of Rabbi Shimon bar Yoḥai*, to be discussed presently, though I do not want to reduce this simply to borrowings or influences. Abū ʿĪsā was not an antinomian and seems to have believed in some notion of Jewish law (*halakhah*). In so far as it is possible to reconstruct his doctrines from later Muslim heresiologists (he was after all ignored by later Jewish sources), he forbade meat, fowl, and wine, and instituted a cycle of ten prayers (which includes the *shimoneh esrei*) in a twenty-four hour cycle. It is interesting to note that the early Karaites made similar pronouncements. Also, at least according to al-Shahrastānī, members of the Isawiyya were allowed to marry rabbinic Jews because they shared a similar commitment to the *halakhah* and holy days.

After his messianic claims, Abū ʿĪsā led some sort of messianic uprising before perishing in battle. This, however, was not the end the Isawiyya. Indeed, according to Wasserstrom, the Isawiyya existed as a discrete Jewish sect for at least another three centuries (Wasserstrom 1995: 89). They were not, as some later scholars of Jewish-Muslim relations want to make out, a short-lived or anomalous messianic movement (see Cohen 1974). Indeed, they show up frequently in subsequent Muslim literature, especially heresiologies, where they receive a larger treatment than both Rabbanites and Karaites. However, as mentioned, one searches contemporaneous rabbinic literature in vain for any mention of the Isawiyya despite the fact that they represented the largest messianic movement between the Bar Kokhba revolt in the second century CE and Shabbetai Zvi in the seventeenth century. Though the Isawiyya are frequently left out of the "Jewish" curriculum, the exemplar of rabbinic Judaism, Maimonides, writing in the twelfth century, could still write of Abū ʿĪsā and the Isawiyya that there

> was an exodus of a multitude of Jews, numbering hundreds of thousands from the East beyond Iṣfahan, led by an individual who pretended to be the Messiah. They were accoutered with military equipment and drawn swords, and slew all those that encountered them. According to the information I have received, they reached the vicinity of Baghdad. This happened at the beginning of the reign of the Umayyads. (Maimonides 1985: 127)

Despite the fact the he mentions the revolt, Maimonides nowhere gives us the name of Abū ʿĪsā. Although Maimonides puts the date of the uprising earlier than al-Shahrastānī does, the messianic forces—on Maimonides' reading—are stopped by the caliph on the outskirts of Baghdad with a group of (normative?) Jewish sages, who ask the leaders of rebellion who their instigator was? They replied, "This man here, one of the descendants of David, whom we know to be pious and virtuous. This man whom we knew to be a leper at night, arose the following morning healthy and sound" (Maimonides 1985: 128). The sages subsequently inform Abū ʿĪsā's followers that they are incorrect in their interpretation and that, to them, he possess none of the marks of the Messiah. The caliph then made them to return home and "ordered them to make a special mark on their garments, the writing of the word *cursed*, and to attach one iron bar in the back and one in the front" (ibid.: 128).

Maimonides's retelling of the story neatly encapsulates the tensions between centers and margins in the Jewish world under early Islam. It is a rebellion, too, that neatly foreshadows the Abbasid revolution—an armed and messianic rebellion based on still inchoate Shīʿi doctrine then developing the Eastern provinces of the burgeoning Empire (see Sharon 1983: 17-28; Arjomand 1994). Unlike the Abbasid revolution, which did succeed in gaining power at the center, Maimonides presents the Isawiyya as ignorant of rabbinic sources—which by the twelfth century are certainly normative—and when informed of their ignorance, they politely agreed with the rabbis whom they acknowledge to be in the possession of the corrected understanding. It is a retroactive story to be sure, one that portrays Jewish sectarian movements as ignorant of rabbinic Judaism and as easily correctible. The situation, on the ground, however, was probably much more complex.

We get yet another glimpse of this Jewish-Islamic milieu in the apocalyptic *Secrets of Rabbi Shimon bar Yoḥai*, also composed in the mid-eighth century, apparently in a Persian environment.[10] This work, written at the end of the Umayyad caliphate and at the beginning of the Abbāsid one—to wit, a time of increased messianism and apocalypticism—identifies Muhammad as the fulfillment of Jewish messianic speculation. The work ends with the hope for the restoration of the Temple in Jerusalem and the beginnings of the Abbasid revolution that will usher in an apocalyptic battle between Israel and Byzantium, followed by the Final Judgment. Near the beginning of the text, Metatron—an individual who figures highly in both Jewish and Islamic angelology (see Wasserstrom 1995: 181-205)—informs Rabbi Shimon that

> because of their oppression of Israel, the Holy One, blessed be He, sends Ishmaelites against them, who make war against them in order to save Israel from their hands. Then a crazy man possessed by a spirit arises and speaks lies about the Holy One, blessed be He, and he conquers the land, and there is enmity between them and the sons of Esau. (Lewis 1950: 313)

The *Secrets of Rabbi Shimon bar Yoḥai* is remarkable in the sense that an ostensibly "Jewish" document recycles Muslim apocalyptic speculation, some of which had already been paradoxically recycled from Jewish sources by early Muslims. Again, rather than imagine this as borrowing or influence, we should see it as collective worldmaking in an environment wherein ideas moved freely between porous boundaries. The result is that it is impossible to know with any degree of precision what is "Jewish" and what is "Muslim."

Sectarian groups like the Isawiyya and those responsible for the *Secrets*, if in fact they are different form one another, represent, what Wasserstrom calls, "a comparatively long-lived reaction to Islamicization" (Wasserstrom 1995: 89). I wish to challenge this thesis and to argue instead that rather than react to Islamicization, such groups were instead caught up in the very processes of Islamicization. The eastern reaches of the growing Islamic empire were a hotbed of messianic fervor and apocalyptic speculation, and in participating in this environment, Jews and Muslims, on the margins, did not differ from one another. Indeed, if anything they seem to have been indistinguishable since they both saw the other as invested in the same apocalyptic drama that focused on Jerusalem and the coming End of Days.

We see this clearly in the *Secrets of Rabbi Shimon bar Yoḥai*, which shares a vocabulary of political uncertainty, messianic revolution, and armed revolt. Many of these motifs find expression in *ghulāt* narratives that revolve around the Shī'ī Mahdī-figure. Again, this was not a conscious borrowing in the sense that no one cared or even knew who had what first. It was the case of a well-worn stock of themes, vocabularies, and motifs crossing porous boundaries. If the Muslim become part of the messianic redemption of Jews in the Holy Land (Shoemaker 2011: 248–258), not infrequently Jews are cast as the enemies of Islam in the cataclysmic upheavals associated with End of Days (e.g., the figure of the Dajjāl or anti-messiah).[11] Alongside such prophesies, there also exist those volumes like the *Secrets of Rabbi Shimon bar Yoḥai* that portray Muslims as part of the larger story of the deliverance of the Jews, just as we possess Shī'ī messianic topoi that link the Mahdī as emerging from the House of 'Alī, itself imagined as related to the House of Aaron (on the latter, see Wasserstrom 1995: 57). Groups on each side of the imaginary hyphen thus seem to be using those on the other side for their own purposes and ultimately their own self-definition.

I have used this example as a concrete way to show how I conceive of the task. It is meant to be historical, sensitive to the textual tradition, and, at the same, theoretically sophisticated. I am not interested in speaking about how a reified and monolithic "Judaism bumps up against a reified and monolithic "Islam." We have all witnessed the results of such unhelpful comparisons. Instead, I tried to taxonomize and analyze specific and localized interactions between messianic movements groups who either identify as or are identified by others as "Jewish" (e.g., the Isawiyya) with those identify as or are identified by others as "Muslim" in the context of early eight century Iran. These social groups, certainly undefined or underdefined compared to later centuries, shared a common messianic vocabulary that took shape in response to the political instability associated with the rapid expansion of a still inchoate Islam.

Future

What is the future of the comparative enterprise? In the brief time remaining, I would like to address this issue by means of the previous discussion. While I admit that there are various types of comparisons and comparative models, I think it is imperative that, no matter what model one chooses, there are certain features that must be at the heart of the modern comparative enterprise. At the risk of repeating myself, these are:

1. *Sensitivity to the historical record.* One cannot use history as a plaything upon which one can transpose modern virtues and ideas. Presentism always lurks in the shadows of scholarship in religious studies—used when necessary or convenient and marginalized or truncated when not—but it cannot.

2. *Linguistic dexterity.* One must know the languages in which one ostensibly works. One, quite simply, cannot do comparative work with English translations. If one does not want to learn languages, then, at the risk of sounding overly exclusive, the only option is to work, as many increasingly do, in the idiom of religion/s in America.

3. *Be theoretically sophisticated.* This is what differentiates—or ought to differentiate—the scholar of religion from the historian, the philologist, and the scholar of area studies. This means being aware of the conceit of comparison while simultaneously engaging in it.

These three elements ought to form our collective enterprise. They are what allow us to talk to one another while also being able to talk to those who work on our data but do so outside the disciplinary confines of religious studies.

Aaron W. Hughes holds the Philp S. Bernstein Chair of Jewish Studies in the Department of Religious Studies at the University of Rochester. Recent books include *Rethinking Jewish Philosophy: Beyond Particularism and Universalism* (Oxford University Press, 2014), *Jacob Neusner: An American Jewish Iconoclast* (NYU Press, 2016), and *Shared Identities: Medieval and Modern Imaginings of Judeo-Islam* (Oxford University Press, 2017). Along with Hava Tirosh-Samuelson, he is co-editor of the Library of Contemporary Jewish Philosophy.

Acknowledgment

This chapter provides a microcosm of my *Comparison: A Critical Primer* (Sheffield: Equinox, 2017).

Notes

1   If they be two, they are two so
    As stiff twin compasses are two;
    Thy soul, the fixed foot, makes no show
    To move, but doth, if the other do.

   And though it in the center sit,
   Yet, when the other far doth roam,
   It leans, and hearkens after it,
   And grows erect, as that comes home."
        From John Donne, "A Valediction: Forbidding Mourning" (online at www.poetryfoundation.org/poems-and-poets/poems/detail/44131).

2 Jonathan Z. Smith has done more than anyone to bring attention to these extra-scholarly and extra-curricular agendas. His concern, however, is primarily with the first of the two uses I have described. For him, this involves the uniqueness of what one is trying to compare:

> Here the 'unique' is more phoenix-like, it expresses that which is *sui generis, singularis*, and, therefore, *incomparably* valuable. "Unique" becomes an ontological rather than a taxonomic category; an assertion of radical difference so absolute that it becomes "Wholly Other," and the act of comparison is perceived as both an impossibility and an impiety. (Smith 1990: 38)

3 On the problematic use of history in the "history of religions," see McCalla (1994) and Lincoln (1996).
4 And subsequently recycled by the likes of Lewis (1984: xi, 191) and Stroumsa (2011: 3–6).
5 In his "Religion in Everyday Life as Reflected in the Documents of the Cairo Genizah," one of the first collections supported and produced by the newly formed Association for Jewish Studies, Goitein writes:

> The religion of the Genizah people was a stern, straightforward, Talmudic type of piety; concerned with the strict fulfillment of the commandments and with the pursuit of study required for their knowledge. This somewhat jejune character of their religiosity was enhanced by the rigorous rationalism embraced by Jewish orthodoxy in the wake of centuries of sectarian and theological controversies. (Goitein 1974: 8)

6 Poetry: Schendlin, Pagis, Rosen, Philosophy: pretty much everyon who works on this.
7 More generally, see Cameron (2012: 168–190); also al-Azmeh (2014: 1–46).
8 Though, as G. Stroumsa (1985) has duly noted, we must also not forget the messianism associated with Manichaean texts, which also date to this period. This, of course, adds another layer to the puzzle and further attests to the need to avoid easy typologies.
9 See Pines (1966: 237–249). On the Jewish–Christian context of early Islam, see more recently Crone (2015), Stroumsa (2015b), Zellentin (2013: 150–153), and El-Badawi (2013: 138).
10 On the work see Steinschneider (1874) and Shoemaker (2011: 28–31). An English translation may be found in Lewis (1950); and on the place of Jerusalem more generally, see Livne-Kafri (2001, 2006).
11 See, for example, Bashear (1991) and Cook (2002: 92–122; 2005: 1–12).

References

al-Azmeh, Aziz. 2014. *The Emergence of Islam in Late Antiquity: Allāh and His People*. Cambridge: Cambridge University Press. https://doi.org/10.1017/CBO9781139410854

Arjomand, Said Amir. 1994. "Abd Allah Ibn al-Muqaffa' and the Abbasid Revolution," *Religion and Society in Islamic Iran during the Pre-Modern Era* 27(1): 9–36. https://doi.org/10.1080/00210869408701818

Asatryan, Mushegh. 2016. *Cosmology and Community in Early Shiʿi Islam: The Ghulat and their Literature*. London: I. B. Tauris, 2016.

Bashear, Suliman. 1991. "Apocalyptic and Other Materials in Early Muslim-Byzantine Wars: A Review of Arabic Sources," *Journal of the Royal Asiatic Society*, n.s., 1–2: 173–207.

Bowersock, Glen Warren. 2012. *Empires in Collision in Late Antiquity*. Waltham, MA: Brandeis University Press.

Bulliet, Richard W. 1994. *Islam: The View from the Edge*. New York: Columbia University Press.
Cameron, Averil. 1991. "The Eastern Provinces in the Seventh Century: Hellenism and the Emergence of Islam," in Suzanne Saïd (ed.), *Hellēnismos: Queleques jalons pour une histoire de l'identité grecque: Actes du Colloque de Strasbourg. 25-27 octobre, 1989*, 287-313. Leiden: Brill.
Cameron, Averil. 2012. *The Mediterranean World in Late Antiquity: AD 395-700*, 2nd edition. New York: Routledge.
Cohen, Gerson. 1974. "Rabbinic Judaism (2nd-18th Centuries)," In *Encyclopedia Britannica*, 15th edition, vol. 22: 416-422.
Cook, David. 2002. *Studies in Muslim Apocalyptic*. Princeton, NJ: Darwin Press.
Cook, David. 2005. *Contemporary Muslim Apocalyptic Literature*. Syracuse, NY: Syracuse University Press, 2005.
Crone, Patricia. "Jewish Christianity and the Qurʾān." *Journal of Near Eastern Studies* 74: 225-253.
Dempsey, Corinne G. 2012. *Bringing the Sacred Down to Earth: Adventures in Comparative Religion*. New York: Oxford University Press.
El-Badawi, Emran. 2013. *The Qur'an and the Aramaic Gospel Traditions*. New York: Routledge.
Eliade, Mircea. 1958. *Patterns in Comparative Religion*, trans. Rosemary Sheed. New York: Sheed & Ward.
Feldman, Louis H. 1993. *Jew and Gentile in the Ancient World: Attitudes and Interactions from Alexander to Justinian*. Princeton, NJ: Princeton University Press.
Friedlaender, Israel. 1910. "Jewish-Arabic Studies," *Jewish Quarterly Review* 1: 183-215. https://doi.org/10.2307/1450914
Geiger, Abraham. 1970 [1833]. *Judaism and Islam*, trans. F. M. Young. New York: Ktav.
Goitein, Shlomo Dov. 1955. *Jews and Arabs: Their Contact Through the Ages*, 3rd rev. edition. New York: Schocken.
Goitein, Shlomo Dov. 1967-1993. *A Mediterranean Society: The Jewish Communities of the Arab World as Portrayed in the Documents of the Cairo Genizah*. 6 vols. Berkeley, CA: University of California Press.
Goitein, Shlomo Dov. 1974. "Religion in Everyday Life as Reflected in the Documents of the Cairo Genizah," in S. D. Goitein (ed.), *Religion in a Religious Age*, 3-17. Cambridge, MA: Association for Jewish Studies.
Graetz, Heinrich. 1956. *History of the Jews*, vol. 3. Philadelphia, PA: Jewish Publication Society of America.
Grossman, Avraham. 1984. *The Babylonian Exilarchate in the Gaonic Period* [in Hebrew]. Jerusalem: Zalman Shazar Center.
Grossman, Avraham. 1988. "Aliya in the Seventh and Eight Centuries," *Jerusalem Cathedra* 3: 65-94.
Henderson, John B. 1991. *Scripture, Canon and Commentary: A Comparison of Confucian and Western Exegesis*. Princeton, NJ: Princeton University Press. https://doi.org/10.1515/9781400861989
Henderson, John B. 1998. *The Construction of Orthodoxy and Heresy: Neo-Confucian, Islamic, Jewish, and Early Christian Patterns*. Albany, NY: State University of New York Press.
Howard-Johnston, James. 2011. *Witnesses to a World Crisis: Historians and Histories of the Middle East in the Seventh Century*. Oxford: Oxford University Press.
Hughes, Aaron W. 2017. *Shared Identities: Medieval and Modern Imaginings of Judeo-Islam*. New York: Oxford University Press. https://doi.org/10.1093/acprof:oso/9780190684464.001.0001

Laskier, Michael M., and Yaakov Lev (eds.). 2011a. *The Convergence of Judaism and Islam: Religious, Scientific, and Cultural Dimensions*. Gainesville, FL: University Press of Florida. https://doi.org/10.5744/florida/9780813036496.001.0001

Laskier, Michael M., and Yaakov Lev (eds.). 2011b. *The Divergence of Judaism and Islam: Interdependence, Modernity, and Political Turmoil*. Gainesville, FL: University Press of Florida. https://doi.org/10.5744/florida/9780813037516.001.0001

Lewis, Bernard. 1950. "An Apocalyptic Vision of Islamic History," *BSOAS* 13: 308–338. https://doi.org/10.1017/S0041977X00083488

Lewis, Bernard. 1984. *The Jews of Islam*. Princeton, NJ: Princeton University Press.

Lincoln, Bruce. 1996. "Theses on Method," *Method and Theory in the Study of Religion* 8: 225–227. https://doi.org/10.1163/157006896X00323

Livne-Kafri, Ofer. 2001. "The Early Shiʿa and Jerusalem," *Arabica* 48: 112–120. https://doi.org/10.1163/157005801774229949

Livne-Kafri, Ofer. 2006. "Jerusalem in Early Islam: The Eschatological Aspect," *Arabica* 53: 382–403. https://doi.org/10.1163/157005806777900297

Maimonides, Moses. 1985. "Epistle to Yemen," in *Epistles of Maimonides: Crisis and Leadership*, trans. Abraham Halkin, 91–149. Philadelphia, PA: Jewish Publication Society of America.

McCalla, Arthur. 1994. "When Is History Not History?" *Historical Reflections* 20.3: 435–452.

Neusner, Jacob. 1991. *Rabbinic Political Theory: Religion and Politics in the Mishnah*. Chicago, IL: University of Chicago Press.

Paden, William E. 2016. *New Patterns for Comparative Religion: Passages to an Evolutionary Perspective*. London: Bloomsbury.

Patton, Laurie C., and Benjamin C. Ray. 2000. "Introduction," In Laurie C. Patton and Benjamin C. Ray (eds.), *A Magic Still Dwells: Comparative Religion in the Postmodern Age*, 1–22. Berkeley, CA: University of California Press.

Pines, Shlomo. 1966. "The Jewish Christians of the Early Centuries of Christianity According to a New Source," *Proceedings of the Israel Academy of Sciences and Humanities* 2(13): 237–310.

Pines, Shlomo. 1985. "Notes on Islam and on Arabic Christianity and Judaeo-Christianity," *Jerusalem Studies in Arabic and Islam* 4: 135–152.

Pregill, Michael. 2007. "The Hebrew Bible and the Quran: The Problem of the Jewish 'Influence' on Islam," *Religion Compass* 1(6): 643–659. https://doi.org/10.1111/j.1749-8171.2007.00044.x

Prothero, Stephen. 2010. *God Is Not One: The Eight Rival Religions That Run the World—and Why Their Differences Matter*. New York: Harper One.

Sharon, Moshe. 1983. *Black Banners from the East: The Establishment of the Abbasid State: Incubation of a Revolt*. Jerusalem: Magnes Press/Leiden: Brill.

Shoemaker, Stephen J. 2011. *The Death of a Prophet: The End of Muhammad's Life and the Beginnings of Islam*. Philadelphia, PA: University of Pennsylvania Press.

Smith, Jonathan Z. 1982. "In Comparison a Magic Dwells," in his *Imagining Religion: From Babylon to Jonestown*, 19–35. Chicago, IL: University of Chicago Press.

Smith, Jonathan Z. 1990. *Drudgery Divine: On the Comparison of Early Christianities and the Religions of Late Antiquity* Chicago, IL: University of Chicago Press.

Steinschneider, Moritz. 1874. "Apocalypsen mit polemischer Tendenz," *ZDMG* 28: 627–659.

Stroumsa, Guy G. 1985. Gnostics and Manichaeans in Byzantine Palestine," in Elizabeth A. Livingston (ed.), *Studia Patristica* 18, 273–278. Kalamazoo, MI: Cistercian Press.

Stroumsa, Guy G. 2015a. *The Making of Abrahamic Religions in Late Antiquity*. Oxford: Oxford University Press. https://doi.org/10.1093/acprof:oso/9780198738862.001.0001

Stroumsa, Guy G. 2015b. "Jewish Christianity and Islamic Origins," In Behnam Sadeghi, Asad Q. Ahmed, Adam Silverstein, and Robert Hoyland (eds.), *Islamic Cultures, Islamic Contexts: Essays in Honor of Patricia Crone*, 72–96. Leiden: Brill.

Stroumsa, Sarah. 2011. *Maimonides in His World: Portrait of a Mediterranean Thinker.* Princeton, NJ: Princeton University Press.

Wasserstrom, Steven M. 1995. *Between Muslim and Jew: The Problem of Symbiosis Under Early Islam.* Princeton, NJ: Princeton University Press. https://doi.org/10.1515/9781400864133

Yearly, Lee H. 1990. *Mencius and Aquinas: Theories of Virtues and Conceptions of Courage.* Albany, NY: State University of New York Press.

Zellentin, Holger. 2013. *The Qurʾān's Legal Culture: The Didascalia Apostolorum as a Point of Departure.* Tübingen: Mohr Siebeck, 2013.

Chapter 2

He Who Knows One Language Knows None: On the Inevitabilities of Comparison and Translation

Lucas Carmichael

In the same 1870 lecture where F. Max Müller advocates for the comparative study of religion with a reference to Goethe's paradox that "He who knows one language, knows none," the forefather of *Religionswissenschaft* also condemns "those who think that they have a right to speak on the ancient religions of mankind, whether those of the Brahmans, the Zoroastrians, or Buddhists, or those of the Jews and Christians, without ever having taken the trouble of learning the languages in which their sacred books are written" (Müller 1873: 35). Is it surprising that he also recommends the careful historical investigation of all texts, "whether sacred or profane," beginning with "these simple and yet momentous questions: When was it written? Where? and by whom?" (ibid.: 26). If a Müller-inspired replacement of "religion" for "language" in Goethe's phrase has "functioned as the guiding inscription emblazoned upon the entranceway to the temple of religious studies ever since," as suggested by Aaron Hughes in Chapter 1 of this volume, so too have the denizens of this temple long grounded their work in the historical investigation of texts in their original languages.

Rather than evincing undisciplined comparative scholarship, the context surrounding Müller's evocation of "He who knows one language knows none" demonstrates that the principles of comparison Hughes recommends in his conclusion have long been enshrined in religious studies and have yet to prove sufficient to avoid the problems he critiques. I agree with the majority of these critiques, and would like to suggest that as we take this opportunity to reassess "comparison" as a methodological tool we also attend to the ideas of history and translation that Hughes brings up and with which comparison has long been associated in the "scientific" study of religions. Perhaps here we can find additional traction for progress.

In response to Hughes's concluding recommendations of three "certain features that must be at the heart of the modern comparative enterprise," I will argue that (1) while sensitivity to the historical record is a must, it consistently teaches that "presentism" can never be avoided and that the past is interpreted always in relation to the present, that (2) while linguistic dexterity is a must, it is expressed always in and through translation, and translation therefore demands careful attention, and that (3) while "being aware of the conceit of comparison while simultaneously engaging in it" is a must, theoretical sophistication requires incorporating sustained attention to these conceits into our work and not addressing them in ways which might allow them to continue to be overlooked or marginalized.

Revisiting Müller

It is generally easier to note and critique the marks of historical context in scholarship of the past than it is to grapple with our own historicity as scholars, yet the two are intertwined. A brief return to Müller suggests his ongoing influence and the echoes of his aspirations in our current enterprise.

The study of religion that Müller proposed, and which Hughes notes was roundly embraced, was based always in a conjunction of the historical, linguistic, scientific, and comparative. Among other evidence of the connections between these terms, Müller uses the phrases "Science of Religion" and "Comparative Religion" interchangeably, suggesting the evidence-based inductive procedures he thought would correct previous, unscientific speculations on religious texts and their histories. In 1870, he lectures, "If it is said that the character of scientific research in our age is preeminently comparative, this really means that our researches are now based on the widest evidence that can be obtained, on the broadest inductions that can be grasped by the human mind" (Müller 1873: 12). While many of the premises and results of this approach can be critiqued, can we doubt that he aspired to a what he understood to be a "modern," "scientific" comparative method?

Moreover, he did so to correct what he perceived to be previous errors and excesses. Müller opens his 1879 preface to the first of his landmark fifty-volume collection, *Sacred Books of the East*, with an argument against the popular opinion that the included texts are "books full of primeval wisdom and religious enthusiasm," recommending that it is "high time to dispel such illusions, and to place the study of the ancient religions of the world on a more real and sound, on a more truly historical basis" (Müller 1879: ix). It is as part of an evidence-based, textual turn toward "documentary, in opposition to purely traditional, history" (ibid.: xl), that he then proposes, "in order to have a solid foundation for a comparative study of the religions of the East, we must have before all things complete and thoroughly faithful translations of their sacred books" (ibid.: xi–xii). To translations I will soon return, but here stress that Müller understood his approach to be a modern, scientific investigation into the historical record preserved in ancient religious texts. He did so in an attempt to overcome the parochialism he perceived in past research: to move beyond "that peculiar reverence which everybody, down to the mere fetish worshipper, feels for his *own* religion and for his *own* God" (Müller 1873: 9). Comparative philologists (and their use of Goethe's quotation) were held up by Müller as models to encourage scholars of religion to be less partisan and more scientific, to study to understand rather than to endorse or condemn, and to replace speculations on "superficial similarities" with "honest historical" research.

To be sure, Müller also understood comparative philology to suggest universal qualities in religion beyond the specifics of individual traditions—above all, a "faculty of faith" that "enables man to apprehend the Infinite under different names, and under varying disguises" (ibid.: 8–17). That the pursuit of this and other shared features suggests, in Hughes's words, "a model in which specific religions are imagined to manifest timeless and disembodied truths" is as undoubtable as it is problematic. Notwithstanding Müller's concern for historical accuracy, he urged his audience to "draw in every religion a broad distinction between what is essential and what is not, between the eternal and the temporary, between the divine and the human" (Müller 1879: xxxviii). Moreover, despite his appeals to impartial comparisons, in 1879 Müller makes clear the underlying Christian nature of these eternal truths:

> Like an old precious medal, the ancient religion, after the rust of ages has been removed, will come out in all its purity and brightness: and the image which it discloses will be the image of the Father, the Father of all the nations upon earth; and the superscription, when we can read it again, will be, not in Judaea only, but in the languages of all the races of the world, the Word of God, revealed, where alone it can be revealed,—revealed in the heart of man." (Müller 1873: 67)

We see here that Müller's privileging of original languages, historical recovery, and disinterested comparison did not fully insulate him against surrounding European biases of the late nineteenth century. Should we expect them to? Does not all scholarship, good, bad, and otherwise, reflect the contexts of its production?

The remainder of Müller's works and opinions, including his ambivalent relationship to Christianity, exceed the scope of this response. However, this brief treatment has been enough to demonstrate that while he is indeed guilty of many of the problems Hughes notes in his critiques of Comparative Religions, he also embraced the very principles Hughes concludes to be essential to the future of the comparative enterprise: Müller argued in favor of historical accuracy over the concerns of his time (though he could not entirely escape them), in favor of working in original languages over translations (though he published hundreds of translations), and in favor of a modern, scientific, and nuanced theoretical sophistication (though this too showed the marks of its era).[1] Our efforts today are not dissimilar, and we do well to attend to Müller not to follow in his footsteps but to recognize we face many of the same conditions and perils.

Presentism and the Historical Record

How, then, might comparison advance? Below, I offer initial suggests in response to Hughes's three "features that must be at the heart of the modern comparative enterprise." I begin each section by quoting Hughes's descriptions in full:

> (1) *Sensitivity to the historical record*. One cannot use history as a plaything upon which one can transpose modern virtues and ideas. Presentism always lurks in the shadows of scholarship in religious studies—used when necessary or convenient

and marginalized or truncated when not—but it cannot. (Hughes, Chapter 1, this volume)

I fully agree that sensitivity to the historical record is a must, and we should carefully contextualize our materials, but that will not avoid what is here termed "presentism." It will continue to lurk in the shadows, and must be brought consistently to light—not to be dismissed, but to be acknowledged and negotiated as an inevitable and even productive element of all interpretation.

It is all too easy to overestimate our abilities to free ourselves from the prejudices of the present. Certainly, the languages we acquire help, if in part only by showing us different ways of conceptualizing the world and the difficulty of fully inhabiting them. Certainly, the theorist we read challenge our biases and push us to new insights that exceed our immediate circumstances, though they form their own contexts, and the wax and wane of particular theorists continues to mark cohorts of academics. Certainly, the methods we employ can be refined and improved through reflection on past flaws and the debate of new proposals, but if we pursue an objectivity free of contemporary interests through these acquisitions of languages, theories, and methods, we'd do well to revisit the arguments of Hans-Georg Gadamer, among others.

In *Truth and Method*, Gadamer critiques and rejects the notion that a scholar, or any other interpreter, might insulate himself or herself from the prejudices that arise from his or her own historical context and somehow engage in a disinterested, "objective" investigation and recovery of an original text, author, "truth," or practice (Gadamer 1989).[2] For Gadamer, this is a false "historicism," and real historical understanding should be recognized not as the impossible impartial recovery of the past, but rather as the ongoing, historically-situated negotiation of past and present:

> Real historical thinking must take account of its own historicity. Only then will it cease to chase the phantom of a historical object that is the object of progressive research, and learn to view the object as the counterpart of itself and hence understand both. The true historical object is not an object at all, but the unity of the one and the other, a relationship that constitutes both the reality of history and the reality of historical understanding. (Gadamer 1989: 299)

As much ontological as epistemological, Gadamer's hermeneutics suggest that we must have a sensitivity to history, but also to our own historicity, both in appreciating our location in history (with the accompanying prejudices that shape our investigations and interests) and in attending to the history that separates us from our material and through which that material has come down to us today. The latter is the history of effects, or effective history (*Wirkungsgeschichte*), which Gadamer demands should be investigated "every time a work of art or an aspect of the tradition is led out of the twilight region between tradition and history" (ibid.). This investigation is not "a kind of inquiry separate from understanding the work itself," but rather is fundamental to such understanding because the interpreter of the work has already been affected by the history in which the work takes part before his or her investigation even begins (ibid.).[3]

This history of effects is not absent from Dr. Hughes's exposition of comparison. He builds from the evocations of Müller, Eliade, and others to an analysis of the models of Prothero, Dempsey, and Paden. When he turns to an example of comparative work in his area, he begins with the earlier efforts of Gotein, Wasserstrom, and Pines, and details the normative historical interpretations of his materials, including the "retroactive story" of Maimonides. However, while these indications of effective history occur throughout Hughes's presentation, they are framed as counterpoint rather than influence and as ancillary rather than essential to the "correct" interpretation Hughes ultimately advances. All the same, it is not hard to discern how even a concern to correct previous viewpoints brings a presentism to history that has been shaped by its antecedents. Identifying historical influences on the "presentisms" of contemporary scholarship is part of an effort that I imagine would have Hughes's general sympathies: recognizing scholarly interpretations as "discursive sites" to both improve their comparative operations and to destabilize impulses towards the essentialization, objectification, and reification of the complex materials we study.

While our work should always attend carefully to historical context, we cannot through such attention seek to isolate it from its own context of production. I take this to be the thrust of the J. Z. Smith declaration to which Hughes draws our attention: "Comparison provides the means by which *we* 'revision' phenomena as *our* data in order to solve *our* theoretical problems" (Smith 1990: 52). I see no reason to limit this statement only to some scholarship, "poor" comparisons of some sort or another, or any a less comprehensive of a community than Smith's inclusive "*we*." Moreover, the words speak to the present and future of comparative studies in religion as well as the past, and apply equally to the comparisons Hughes critiques, the one he offers, my own work, and that of any other.

Linguistic Dexterity and Translation

We are always at some remove from our materials, and our work is shaped always by the hermeneutics of comparison. By necessity, we construct interpretive bridges across times, languages, and cultures. Our work is marked by both ends of these crossings, but perhaps even more by the process of moving back and forth between them. I have found it useful to think about this movement in terms of translation, which evokes the ghost of Müller and brings us to Hughes's second requirement:

> (2) *Linguistic dexterity*. One must know the languages in which one ostensibly works. One, quite simply, cannot do comparative work with English translations. If one does not want to learn languages, then, at the risk of sounding overly exclusive, the only option is to work, as many increasingly do, in the idiom of religion/s in America. (Hughes, Chapter 1, this volume)

I agree, of course, that we should learn the languages in which we work, but not with the implication I see here that this knowledge insulates us from the vicissitudes of translation both with respect to English and to "the idiom of religion/s in America." Since I am writing in English and in connection with the North American Association for the Study of Religion (NAASR) to an audience who most likely belongs to NAASR and the American Academy of Religions (AAR) among other organizations, I will venture to suggest that a significant portion of all our research, publishing, and teaching relates to "religion/s in America" and is accomplished through "English translation."[4] Most of us, in our backgrounds, training, and employment, are deeply enmeshed in contemporary Anglophone conceptions of religion, even in our efforts to document, articulate, and translate alternative ideas from other times, places, and languages. This is not a claim for any type of superiority for Anglophone perspectives but only for their pervasive influence and ultimate contingency. I worry that inattention to "English translations" and "the idiom of religion/s in America" turns critical attention away from the context in which our scholarship takes place and is transmitted. The contextually bound and linguistically determined nature of even academic interpretations are all too obvious at the remove of only a generation or two, and I see no reason to excuse myself or anyone else from their effects.

Translation is inevitable, and cannot be ignored. It is involved in some fashion in nearly every aspect of every attempt to access and transmit historically and culturally distant materials. At minimum, both knowledge of languages and a nuanced appreciation of translation are therefore necessary to "linguistic dexterity."

Admittedly, Hughes does not suggest knowledge of the original language alone in his recommendations for the comparative enterprise, but he does propose it as a uniquely necessary qualification, while many other qualifications remain unstated and potentially undervalued in our work and training. The preeminence of philology in Religious Studies begins at least as early as the time of Max Müller, and knowledge of an "original" language too often continues to give a false sense of objectivity to historically situated interpretations. Among many examples other than Müller, the excesses Hughes critiques in the work of Mircea Eliade were largely grounded in, and seemingly legitimized by Eliade's thorough knowledge of Sanskrit (not to mention Romanian, Italian, French, German, and English). Outside of academia, generations of religious devotees have devoted themselves to mastering the original languages of their canonical texts, and their endless debates over proper interpretation should give us pause over the sufficiency of the instruction to "know the languages in which one ostensibly works."

Such knowledge did not prevent debate over the texts Hughes presents, nor the materials I research. Among scores of experts on the *Daode jing* (*Tao Te Ching*), no two have been of the same opinion, and their differences inform a large portion of the over three hundred and eighty English translations of this short text (with hundreds more into other languages).[5] Reviewing these texts makes clear the close connections between the authors' historical contexts, interpretations, and translations—connections that no amount of language training has yet overcome.[6] Why continue to pretend at such a possibility? Is it not a thorough knowledge of a language that makes it most clear that there are no "timeless" translations nor interpretations of any texts?[7] Language training does not supplant the hermeneutics of translation, but rather makes them ever more central to conducting and communicating our research.

I am not arguing against language training, but I resist the idea that it results in a fluency whereby we attain unmediated, transhistorical access to the definitive interpretations of our materials, let alone the ability to transmit these interpretations as the "original" texts in a new language. Here, translation theorists are useful, particularly Lawrence Venuti, who critiques a false "transparency" achieved through ideas of fluency that dominate contemporary translation practices in England and America. He writes:

> A translated text, whether prose or poetry, fiction or nonfiction, is judged acceptable by most publishers, reviewers and readers when it reads fluently, when the absence of any linguistic or stylistic peculiarities makes it seem transparent, giving the appearance that it reflects the foreign writer's personality or intention or the essential meaning of the foreign text—the appearance, in other words, that the translation is not in fact a translation, but the "original." (Venuti 2008: 1)

For Venuti, any equivalency between translation and original is impossible. He argues for the necessity of restraining and marking translations' inevitable domestications through a disruptive, "foreignizing" mode of writing that "resists dominant values in the receiving culture so as to signify the linguistic and cultural differences of the foreign text" (ibid.: 18).

A translation, for Venuti, is "imprinted by the receiving culture, assimilated to its positions of intelligibility, its canons and taboos, its codes and ideologies" (ibid.: 14). He allows no room for a hermeneutic that would ignore the situatedness of the translator and the inevitable distortions involved in transmitting a foreign text. This limits even the "foreignizing" strategy that he argues might "restrain the ethnocentric violence of translation" (ibid.: 16). Ultimately, even "foreignization does not offer unmediated access to the foreign—no translation can do that" (ibid.: 19). However, it has the beneficial effect of disrupting the illusion of transparency:

> A translated text should be the site where linguistic and cultural differences are somehow signaled, where a reader gets some sense of a cultural other, and resistancy, a translation strategy based on an aesthetic of discontinuity, can best signal those differences, that sense of otherness, by reminding the reader of the gains and losses in the translation process and the unbridgeable gaps between cultures. (Venuti 2008: 264)

Following Venuti, we might consider disrupting the apparent naturalness of our comparisons by maintaining our visibility as scholars who make comparisons always for particular ends and always from historically situated contexts with their own "positions of intelligibility," "canons and taboos," "codes and ideologies."

To dispel the illusion of transparency, Venuti recommends that we attend to and remind our readers of "the unbridgeable gaps between cultures." Here I think he errs. It is not that these gaps are "unbridgeable" to which we must

attend—they are all too frequently crossed on bridges both robust and flimsy—
but rather that even bridged they always remain and cannot be collapsed. Here
we can return briefly to Gadamer, who stresses the historical distance between
text and reader as at once unavoidable and productive:

> In fact the important thing is to recognize temporal distance as a positive and
> productive condition enabling understanding. It is not a yawning abyss but is
> filled with the continuity of custom and tradition, in the light of which everything
> handed down presents itself to us. (Gadamer 1989: 297)

This continuity may be significantly disrupted by the translation of texts into new
contexts, but the resulting gaps are "not a yawning abyss" but are filled always
with the histories through which we encounter and interpret the past. The gaps
across which our various acts of translation move are filled with an uncollapsible
history of effects through which we must always traverse. It is for these reasons
that I find historical translations to be fascinating records of implicit and explicit
comparisons, of the impacts of context on interpretation, and of the mechanisms
through which previous interpretations affect the history of what they pass
down to subsequent generations. Again, I see no reason to excuse contemporary scholarship from what is clear in the historical record: the ever-entangled,
contextually-bound, historically-informed activities of interpretation, comparison, and translation.

Theoretical Sophistication, for Now

Recognizing these dynamics and accounting for them in dexterous scholarship
brings us to Hughes's final requirement:

> (3) Be theoretically sophisticated. This is what differentiates—or ought to differentiate—the scholar of religion from the historian, the philologist, and the scholar
> of area studies. This means being aware of the conceit of comparison while simultaneously engaging in it. (Hughes, Chapter 1, this volume)

I applaud theoretical sophistication, but suspect that this, too, is a quality linked
closely to its historical (and disciplinary) context. Herbert Giles shocked the sinological world when, in 1886, he brought the sophistication of German higher criticism to bear on the dating and authorship of the *Daodejing*, when he aggressively
critiqued the simplistic translation theories of the 1856 "Delegate's Version" of
the Bible in Chinese, and when he modified the pronunciation guide of his predecessor at Cambridge into the Wade-Giles romanization system that became the
standard in his field for generations to follow. By 1955, however, he was largely
forgotten and his work dismissed as "amateur" by a successor to his chair at
Cambridge, Edwin Pulleyblank (1955: 3). This is certainly a sign of the progress
of Sinology, which continues to improve its investigations and expand its libraries, but it also shows that what is "sophisticated" in one day can quickly become
"amateur" in another, and suggests that "sophistication" is measured always in
relation to its context.

Those works in our field that have ranged too recklessly across time, geography, and culture have certainly distorted specifics into generalizations that reveal too much about their authors and too little about the phenomena they purport to explain. However, I fear that some current marks of sophistication have perhaps moved too far in the other direction. For at least a generation or two, most of us have narrowed our research to ever more specific contexts to avoid the inevitable complications of alternative interpretations as we move but steps away from a chosen time, geography, or particular individual or group. That is, we have generally recognized the contextually bound nature of interpretation by carefully delimiting narrow contexts for the interpretations we study (our material) and for our resulting interpretations of them (our scholarship). While this avoids many of the excesses of past comparative work, it generally fails to fully appreciate that insofar as we take up any materials distant from our own historical contexts we still engage in comparison. We are always interpreting and translating our materials in relation to ourselves, and often across vast differences in language, thought, and culture. Reflecting on comparison as method is an opportunity that is little served if we continue only to narrow the targets of our research and analysis, ignore the history of effects that informs the "presentism" of our interests, and dismiss the importance of translation in our negotiations with texts in their original languages.

Perhaps the biggest difference between Hughes's approach and that for which I advocate is not what he places at the "heart of the modern comparative enterprise"—features I have elaborated on while leaving largely intact—but in the prioritizing of the aspects of comparison he describes. For Hughes, "comparison must involve immersion in languages, texts, traditions, and only then theory" (Chapter 1, this volume). I would maintain that theoretical sophistication is indeed key to the future of the comparative method and that attention to theory must be foregrounded and sustained or we can too easily fall into variations of the past. Contemporary theory offers a host of new ideas and approaches we might bring to history and translation among other key concepts long central to the Science of Religion and long articulated in relation to the activities of comparison. It seems the task of our current era of theoretical sophistication, therefore, not only to narrow our foci and to critique the flagrant essentializing, objectifying, and ahistorical comparisons of the nineteenth and early twentieth century, but also to reconsider the connections between a network of foundational concepts and approaches in our field with which comparison continues to be linked.

Among other departures we might make from Müller and company, Hughes's chapter suggests to me that we might add sustained reflection on our own place in history to the ongoing production of historical research. To the study of original languages, we might add more recent inquiries into the operations of communication and translation. To the narrow topics of our research, we might add the wider history of effects through which we encounter them. To comparison itself, we might add sustained reflection on the twin observations to which Hughes alerts us: that comparisons are inevitable and that they are shaped by the too often unacknowledged interests of their makers. Comparison, like all methods, must be understood in relation to ourselves: to those who compare and not just to that which is compared. It is an activity we engage always from our own context and always across gaps which we must *translate but not collapse* if we are to do justice to the complex histories of our materials and discipline.

Lucas Carmichael holds a PhD in religion and literature from the University of Chicago Divinity School and is a lecturer in religious studies at the University of Colorado at Boulder. His research focuses on the translation and reception of Chinese classics in Europe and America.

Notes

1. Among other signs of "sophistication," in his preface to the *Sacred Books* series, Müller cautions his readers against judging a tradition from without rather than within (Müller 1879: xxxvii), the dangers of over generalizations (ibid.: xxiii), and ignoring "that very important intellectual parallax which, no doubt, renders it most difficult for a Western observer to see things and thoughts under exactly the same angle and in the same light as they would appear to an Eastern eye" (ibid.: xvi).
2. See "The Connection between the Historical School and Romantic Hermeneutics" (Gadamer 1989: 194–212); "Dilthey's Entanglement in the Aporias of Historicism" (ibid.: 213–233); and, on prejudice and correcting historicism, "The Elevation of the Historicity of Understanding to the Status of a Hermeneutic Principle" (ibid.: 267–276).
3. This point is often lost in interpretations of Gadamer that take his notion of understanding to be a fusion of two separate horizons. While Gadamer does speak heuristically of two horizons, he is also very clear that there is only "the one horizon, whose bounds are set in the depths of tradition" (ibid.: 305). He explains that "Projecting a historical horizon, then, is only one phase in the process of understanding," and that "Historical consciousness is aware of its own otherness and hence foregrounds the horizon of the past from its own. On the other hand, it is itself, as we are trying to show, only something superimposed upon continuing tradition, and hence it immediately recombines with what it has foregrounded itself from in order to become one with itself again in the unity of the historical horizon that it thus acquires" (ibid.).
4. Here I follow Hughes's equation of work in English translation with the "American idiom," though I am happy to include the national idioms of other English speakers or any other idioms associated with the modern languages in which all contemporary scholarship is published, exchanged, and taught. The point is that scholarship is deeply conditioned by the linguistic, national, and cultural contexts in which it occurs and is transmitted.
5. Knut Walf has provided the most comprehensive bibliography to date, with 206 English translations and 437 translations into other languages (see Walf 2010: 11–66). My own count and corrections to the English portion of this bibliography lists 380 English translations (Carmichael 2017: appendix).
6. Such a review is infrequently undertaken, but Norman Girardot has produced an excellent analysis of at least one translator (Girardot 2002). For an analysis of four additional translators, see Carmichael (2017).
7. This is, of course, not a universally held conclusion. The most famous statement to the opposite effect—or at least the possibility of context-less translation—is Walter Benjamin's "The Translator's Task," first printed in 1923.

References

Benjamin, Walter. 2012 [1923]. "The Task of the Translator," trans. Steven Rendall, in Lawrence Venuti (ed.), *The Translation Studies Reader*, 75–83. London: Routledge.
Carmichael, Lucas. 2017. "The *Daode Jing* as American Scripture," PhD dissertation, University of Chicago, Chicago, IL.
Gadamer, Hans-Georg. 1989. *Truth and Method*, revised translation by Joel Weinsheimer and Donald Marshall. New York: Crossroads.
Girardot, Norman. 2002. *The Victorian Translation of China: James Legge's Oriental Pilgrimage*. Berkeley, CA: University of California Press.
Müller, F. Max. 1873. *Lectures on the Science of Religion*. London: Longmans, Green, & Co.
Müller, F. Max. (ed.). 1879. *The Sacred Books of the East*, vol. 1. Oxford: Clarendon Press.
Pulleyblank, Edwin George. 1955. *Chinese History and World History: An Inaugural Lecture*. Cambridge: Cambridge University. Press.
Smith, J. Z. 1990. *Drudgery Divine: On the Comparison of Early Christianities and the Religions of Late Antiquity*. Chicago, IL: University of Chicago Press.
Venuti, Lawrence. 2008. *The Translator's Invisibility: A History of Translation*, 2nd edition. New York: Routledge.
Walf, Knut. 2010. *Westliche Taoismus-Bibliographie*. Essen: Die Blaue Eule.

Chapter 3

Comparison and the Production of Knowledge

Thomas J. Carrico, Jr.

Introduction

In Chapter 1 of this volume, Aaron Hughes suggests that "comparison" occupies a tenuous, troublesome, and often unexamined status as a viable method within the academic study of religion. He rightly illustrates the pitfalls that come with these types of research programs, moving from a broad conception of comparison as simply "the way people interpret the world" to a narrower discussion of comparison as an academic enterprise. These pitfalls include, but are not limited to, reductionism, idiosyncratic readings of overly broad categories, lack of familiarity with the language and history of all groups under study, and a lack of sustained reflection on the theoretical assumptions made when explicitly comparing one group to another. Hughes provides a typology of comparative models before offering his own comparative analysis of the Isawiyya followed by perceptive insight into what, explicitly, makes this analysis a compelling model for comparative work. Groups like the Isawiyya, he argues, do not fit neatly into rigidly defined or otherwise inherited notions of religions as stable groups. He goes on to clarify that "Abū 'Īsā thus combines 'Jewish' and 'Muslim' messianic vocabularies in such a manner that he is comprehensible to other groups on both sides of the Jewish-Muslim hyphen." He continues, noting that

> it is this paradox, the hyphen separating Jew and Muslim, which makes groups such as the Isawiyya ... so interesting. Both Muslim and Jew, neither Muslim nor Jew, they occupy the margins of history. They become the groups that give definition to the center while at the same time subject to further marginalization. (Hughes, Chapter 1, this volume)

Hughes uses his analysis of the Isawiyya to illustrate and outline the necessary "features that must be at the heart of the modern comparative enterprise," namely, "sensitivity to the historical record," "linguistic dexterity" and theoretical sophistication (Hughes, Chapter 1, this volume). Both Hughes's study of the Isawiyya as well as his threefold prescription raise an issue which is essential to any methodological reflection on comparison: should we conceive of comparison as a widespread method or as a specific program of study?

The session index of this year's American Academy of Religion annual meeting,[1] includes one explicitly comparative *section*, "Comparative Studies in Religion," and five explicitly comparative *groups*, "Comparative Approaches to Religion and Violence," "Comparative Religious Ethics," "Comparative Theology (#aarcomptheo)," "Latino/a Critical and Comparative Studies," and "Religions in Chinese and Indian Cultures: A Comparative Perspective." Within the program book of this meeting, there are a large number of papers whose abstracts and titles suggest comparative themes that are not being presented within these comparative groups.[2] In short, if this year's AAR annual meeting is any indication, there are far more comparative projects than there are formal arenas of comparative inquiry. Given this apparent dichotomy between comparative work and recognized fields of comparative inquiry, the question becomes "in what setting should the academic labor of comparison produce a particular kind of knowledge?"

If comparison is an activity that is limited to trained, professional comparativists, then disciplinary boundary maintenance becomes a, if not the, primary issue. If, however, we construe comparison more broadly as a method that may be employed across and within existing disciplinary boundaries, then we need to reflect on its function within processes of scholarly production: what are the existing social and institutional constraints on comparative inquiry? What is the intended product of this particular form of academic labor? How does this form of labor contribute to, participate in, reproduce, or challenge existing hierarchies? To put the point in more explicitly Marxist terminology, how do we conceive of this methodology as a bridge between the concrete labor of academic production and the abstract labor of imbuing the label "comparative" with recognizable significance? Drawing on recent debates in the academic subfield of comparative religious ethics, I will suggest that Hughes's central claims should be clarified by a more explicit differentiation between comparison as a methodology and comparison as a discipline or a formal field of study. Casting the net more broadly, I will argue that to critique the scholarly act of comparison amounts to demystifying the process of scholarly production. Comparison requires attention not only to the ways that we juxtapose new knowledge to old, information to assumptions, or the circulation of power in more than one social formation but also to the institutional setting that makes a particular comparison possible.

Comparison

In an analysis that is, itself, rather laborious Marx begins *Capital* by describing the production process of a coat. From procuring raw materials to investing them with value through human labor by weaving and tailoring, Marx attempts to show how a single commodity embodies different types of value and connects disparate elements of society. The coat is a product presented as singular, but which represents the convergence of all the moving parts of socio-economic production. Regarding the value of the coat specifically, he discusses several elements: the use-value of the coat as a piece of clothing, the exchange-value of the coat as the price that a consumer might pay for the coat, and their reflection of the human labor constitutive of the production process. But, for Marx, all human labor is not created equal. He states that "the body of the commodity ... always figures as the embodiment of *abstract* human labor, and is always the product of some specific useful and *concrete* labor" (Marx 1990: 150; emphasis added).

Using the example of weaving and tailoring this hypothetical coat, Marx shows that both are examples of human labor in the sense that the weaver weaves linen and the tailor crafts a coat from it. However, the linen and coat are recognized differently: a coat holds a different use value than that of a length of linen, giving the labor of weaving and tailoring different values as wel. Concrete labor is the act of expending physical energy to invest any product with value—working to make a product. Abstract labor, however, consists of labor specific to a particular product and is the work put in (both physically and ideologically) to create a product that will gain social recognition as valuable. Both are present in the work of making a product, and illustrate the social nature of producing goods. Although academic labor is fundamentally different from weaving and tailoring, the production of scholarship necessarily entails both concrete and abstract labor. On the one hand, the concrete labor of scholarship involves research, writing, and editing. On the other, abstract scholastic labor involves arranging our research, writing, and editing in a form that is socially recognizable as having both use and exchange value through recognition by an established body as "legitimate scholarship," be it a field of inquiry, scholarly journal, or academic publisher.

As an example, with regard to formalized fields of inquiry, organizationally "comparative religious ethics" exists as a "group" within the American Academy of religion and is otherwise recognizable in articles printed in the *Journal of Religious Ethics* (*JRE*). This group has a statement of purpose, a chair, and a steering committee. It includes a broad range of scholarship and its disciplinary history is typically traced from the 1973 founding of the *JRE* as well as David Little and Sumner Twiss's 1978 work *Comparative Religious Ethics*. Both projects sought to break from the hegemony of "Christian ethics" as an academic field while utilizing comparison as a form of cross-cultural analysis that would also provide the comparativist with opportunity for social and cultural self-reflection. However, after a series of debates arising from Little and Twiss' work settled on a broad methodology, there was little that unified works in the field (see especially Little 1981 and Stout 1980, 1983). There are many works from the subsequent decades that compare the ethical reasoning of different groups but that is about all that tied them together. There isn't a specific mode of comparison, a common comparative vocabulary, a stipulated set of groups, or other overarching theme other than a broadly construed methodology. Current debate, therefore, seeks to provide a more cohesive vision of the field as a unified scholarly enterprise. On the one hand, scholars like Elizabeth Bucar and Aaron Stalnaker argue that comparative religious ethics "is and should be practiced as a field of study in active collaboration with other fields that consider human flourishing, employing a variety of methods borrowed from multiple disciplines" (Bucar and Stalnaker 2014: 360). In short, its lack of specific norms of scholarship is its strength. John Kelsay, however, is "specifically interested in the accounts we are able to give to colleagues who ask about our work, especially with an eye toward procedures of evaluation or affecting the distribution of resources" (Kelsay 2014: 357). What, specifically, does this group contribute to the overall academic enterprise? Kelsay clarifies that he means an account of the field intelligible not only within the bureaucratic decisions of a university or department but also intelligible within debates in the field of religion about what does or does not constitute good scholarship. To return to Hughes's chapter, the debate centers around the process of how to recognize work as comparative.

Hughes states that "though I have never called myself a 'comparativist' or someone who engages in the task of 'comparative religion,' I guess I am and I do" (Hughes, Chapter 1, this volume). While the type of comparative work Hughes advocates fits into a more broadly conceived method, both Kelsay and Bucar argue that "comparison" constitutes a specific mode of inquiry undertaken by an organized group of scholars to produce an organized body of knowledge; they disagree on the organization of scholars, breadth of inquiry, and method of organization. In short, they agree that there ought to be a formal comparative field of inquiry before developing arguments about what ties that field together. Hughes's tri-fold prescription elucidates one framework within which these studies should be done to constitute good scholarship. Yet, the question of the role of disciplines in academic production remains. The purpose statement of the comparative religious ethics group in one sense builds on Hughes's insight, but also relies on a conception of scholarship and the use of academic authority that warrants further examination. According to this statement, the central aspects of comparative ethics are as follows:

- Describes and interprets particular ethics on the basis of historical, anthropological, or other data
- Compares such ethics (in the plural) and requires searching reflection on the methods and tools of inquiry
- Engages in normative argument on the basis of such studies, and may thereby speak to contemporary concerns about overlapping identities, cultural complexity and plurality, universalism and relativism, and political problems regarding the coexistence of divergent social groups, as well as particular moral controversies. (AAR undated)

It's difficult to read the first two aspects without levying critiques at the third: engaging in normative argument. At this point, one might object that scientific inquiry is not normative or that, as scholars, we are to be critics rather than caretakers of our data, or that we shouldn't enter into debates we purport to study. Within the study of ethics, particularly, we may recall Pierre Bourdieu's indictment of the professional ethicist when he situates academic ethicists within a system characterized by "the flagrant inequality of access to what is called 'personal opinion' regarding concepts such as 'the good' or 'the virtuous'" (Bourdieu 1997: 68–69). The moral judgment of one who studies morals carries an institutionalized authority to which many do not have access—an authority that is a direct product of the production of knowledge.

Authority and the Production of Knowledge

When we discuss academic comparison, we are discussing the production of a specific type of authority. In Bourdieu's analysis, it is the social position of the scholar—and her subsequent right to legitimate opinion—rather than the intrinsic goodness of the virtues being studied that enables these norms to be reproduced as "good." Within a particular social field, some people's reason counts more than others; some people are able to appeal to types of authority (personal opinion combined with institutional consecration) that others simply don't have access to; and some people are able to reach a wider audience than others. This access to an institutionally objectivized form of rationality, the ability to mobilize larger amounts of capital, and the authority granted to some actors and not others are all mis-recognized under the authority of scholarship. This is to say, when one cites "scholarship" one is citing the authority of the institutions that produce scholarship and the authority that institutions grant to particular actors. For Bourdieu, the production of knowledge entails the production of the ethical neutrality, authority, and expertise of the scholar. Knowledge and authority are both produced within the social arrangement of the academic field and by the labor required to maintain the standing of those who are consecrated as members. It's worth asking, then, where does the scholarly method of comparison fit in with these processes? What value does it add?

If concrete academic labor produces scholarship, then the abstract labor of creating or reproducing an organized body of scholarship contributes to a social arrangement within which certain positions afford different amounts of authority. Bruce Lincoln helpfully differentiates between these two different kinds of academic products—texts and fields—when he aims to "transcend a distinction often made between executive and epistemic authority: between the authority of those who are "in authority' (e.g. political leaders, parents, military commanders) and that of those who are "an authority" (e.g. technical experts, scholars, and medical specialists)." For Lincoln, authoritative speech

> is best understood in relational terms as the effect of a posited, perceived, or institutionally ascribed asymmetry between speaker and audience that permits certain speakers to command not just the attention but the confidence, respect, and trust of their audience, or—an important proviso—to make audiences act *as if* this were so. (Lincoln 1994: 3-4)

He goes on to describe "discursive authority" as

> (1) an effect; (2) the capacity for producing that effect, and (3) the commonly shared opinion that a given actor has the capacity for producing that effect...the result of the conjuncture of the right speaker, the right speech and delivery, the right staging and props, the right time and place, and an audience whose historically and culturally conditioned expectations establish the parameters of what is judged "right" in all these instances. (Lincoln 1994: 10-11)

So, a work of academic comparison, in order to display its authority, must adhere to recognizable indicators of good scholarship—sensitivity to the historical record, linguistic dexterity, and theoretical sophistication, as Hughes prescribes. But what authority does the comparative element of a study add? Further, we might consider how this raw material of a methodological tool establishes an asymmetry between speaker and audience. We also ought to inquire about its role in producing knowledge that gives the enterprise a specific form of authority? Is there a specific authority granted to a work of comparative scholarship that is recognized by an institutionalized body like the comparative religious ethics group? Or is there a broader type of authority produced by the "various types of comparisons and comparative models" to which Hughes alludes (Chapter 1, this volume)?

Concluding Thoughts

Hughes's study of a group that might be recognized as either Jewish or Muslim opens up many possibilities for scholarship—he is able to critique not only the methodological tools used to study them (a reified conception of a group) but is also able to actively critique the subtle use of comparative language between these reified groups ("borrowing," "influencing," in Hughes's words). This provides a standing from which his study is able to complicate simplified pictures of society, challenge dominant paradigms of scholarship, and discuss the social processes within which actors are caught up" (Hughes, Chapter 1, this volume). Comparison, then, can serve as an excellent tool in the service of critique and, as a method, has the potential to provide a more robust account of social dynamics than other modes of inquiry.

Beyond this, though, reflections on comparison ought to entail reflection upon institutional dynamics within which comparative scholarship takes place. Comparative studies claim to produce a particular type of expertise—not only in producing scholarship on a particular topic, but developing a methodology for comparing it to other topics. Hughes's work demonstrates the authority invoked by this multifaceted expertise by challenging the rigidity of categories like "Islam," "Judaism," and other reified groups. The comparative religious ethics group demonstrates that the authority of comparison is located in institutions as well as individual projects. Within these institutions, conferences, edited volumes, and journalistic roundtables are some ways that a enable such scholarship (and authority) to be more readily reproduced. Both individual and institutional instances of authority speak to the value of a label—Hughes's analysis in a more informal way and comparative religious ethics in a more traditional, institutionalized way. However, both instances of authority illustrate clearly the labor that this enterprise entails: as Hughes states, "*while the comparative act might be natural, specific comparisons are not*" (Chapter 1, this volume). The abstract labor that differentiates "comparative scholarship" from "scholarship" ought to draw our attention to ways that the label "comparativist" is employed, the ways that comparativists differentiate themselves from other scholars, the social position of these scholars, the status of knowledge as it relates to claims to power, the modes of authority these processes rely on and reproduce (especially with regard to Lincoln's "asymmetry between speaker and audience"), and the specific types of resistance that the comparative enterprise makes possible.

Thomas J. Carrico, Jr. is a PhD candidate at Florida State University. He previously earned a Master of Arts in Middle East and Islamic studies from the American University of Paris, a Master of Divinity from Columbia Theological Seminary, and a Bachelor of Arts in philosophy from Christopher Newport University. His research areas include method and theory in the study of religion, religious ethics, political economy, and Victorian England. His dissertation examines the moral dilemmas raised by "lucifer" matchstick production in the nineteenth century and, more broadly, the ways that social factors impact moral reasoning.

Notes

1 As of November 10, 2016, this year's list is located at https://papers.aarweb.org/Session_Index.pdf; however, full lists, in hierarchical order from largest-spanning to smallest, are available at the following sites:

- Program Units: www.aarweb.org/annual-meeting/program-units
- Sections: www.aarweb.org/node/260
- Program Unit Groups: www.aarweb.org/node/261
- Program Unit Seminars: www.aarweb.org/node/262
- Program Unit Clusters: www.aarweb.org/node/927

2 Whether the groups labelled "interreligious" or "interfaith" ought to be included in this taxonomy is a debate for a different project. For the purposes of the present chapter, I will focus on the process by which the label "comparative" is invested with a particular type of academic authority (and the extent to which such efforts are successful and problematic).

References

AAR. Undated. "Comparative Religious Ethics Unit." Retrieved from https://papers.aarweb.org/content/comparative-religious-ethics-group (accessed March 7, 2018).

Bourdieu, Pierre. 1989. *The State Nobility*. Stanford, CA: Stanford University Press.

Bucar, Elizabeth M. and Aaron Stalnaker. 2014. "On Comparative Religious Ethics as a Field of Study," *Journal of Religious Ethics* 42(2): 358–384. https://doi.org/10.1111/jore.12060

Kelsay, John. 2014. "Response to Bucar and Stalnaker," *Journal of Religious Ethics* 42(3): 564–570. https://doi.org/10.1111/jore.12070

Lincoln, Bruce. 1994. *Authority: Construction and Corrosion*. Chicago, IL: University of Chicago Press,

Little, David. 1981. "The Present State of the Comparative Study of Religious Ethics," *Journal of Religious Ethics* 9(2): 210–227.

Little, David and Sumner B. Twiss. 1978. *Comparative Religious Ethics: A New Method*. New York: Harper & Row.

Marx, Karl. 1990. *Capital, Volume One*. London: Penguin.

Stout, Jeffrey. 1980. "Weber's Progeny, Once Removed," *Religious Studies Review* 6(4): 289–295.

Stout, Jeffrey. 1983. "Holism and Comparative Ethics: A Response to Little," *Journal of Religious Ethics* 11(2): 301–316.

Chapter 4

On Z-Factors and Empires

Andrew Durdin

Aaron Hughes's essay on "Comparison" (Chapter 1, this volume) offers a thoughtful analysis of this usually uncritical method in the study of religion. Hughes starts from the fact that while there may be some degree to which comparison is endemic to human cognition, no comparisons are natural or even inherently useful. Drawing two things together in order to appreciate their similarities is a contrived undertaking, done for certain reasons, whether these are made explicit by the comparer or not. That I might compare thee to a summer's day or even assert vigorously that love is a battlefield, these are poetic meditations intended to evoke powerful images and emotions and make sympathetic connections between things considered dissimilar. Yet as Hughes notes, a poetic register is not appropriate for scholars. Indeed, for all that "postmodernism" has made us rethink whether our scholarly work is better thought of as "science" or "art" (or even "magic"; see Patton et al. 2000), I would hope that it's uncontroversial to agree with Hughes that the job of the scholar involves more rigor than the caprice of the poet: i.e. thorough training in languages, texts, and historical traditions that generate the data sets from which we draw our theoretical interpretations and make our comparisons. Or, to put it in a different idiom: if the only thing separating our narratives from other myths is footnotes, then these notes should be packed with dense and carefully considered philological, ethnographic, and historical detail.[1]

By now it's a truism that the field of Religious Studies traditionally has not opted for carefully considered comparisons. Scholars of religion have taken perceived similarities (and, for that matter, differences) as *explanans* rather than *explanandum*. As Hughes puts it, comparison in our field has been complicit in "a host of apologetical and often highly ideological ends," which reify certain cultural objects and the relations between them, rather than attempt to account for the production of these as part of larger ideological processes by which social groups come to see certain social configurations as common sense, natural, or even sacred.

Hughes (via J. Z. Smith) reminds us that comparison is never just dyadic but triadic; *x* and *y* are alike "in reference to" *z*. If *x* and *y* are the manifest units of comparison, then scholars of religion have tended to take these simply and unproblematically as religions—i.e. phenomenologically consistent, sui generis entities or "traditions" that seem stable enough (or share enough "family resemblances") to serve as units of comparison on a global scale and across space and time. As Hughes rightly points out though, comparisons undertaken with these units have proven "superficial," and I would add, that's at best—at worst, they distort and deceive. From his own field of Jewish-Muslim relations in Late Antiquity and the Middle Ages, Hughes shows how the dominant metaphor of "symbiosis" controls both how religions are conceived and how they are thought to interact with one another. On this metaphor, Islam and Judaism, despite a certain amount of internal diversity, are monolithic and enduring traditions, which "bump up" against each other periodically in space and time. Such moments of contact might result in mutual borrowing and exchange among these traditions but ultimately such moments leave their essences intact.

But the metaphor of symbiosis is not isolated. And this brings me to the third term in Smith's comparison equation above: z. The symbiosis metaphor stipulates Judaism and Islam as more or less like each other in reference to essences and moments of borrowing, but this metaphor is not the only suppressed z framework that naturalizes its units of comparison. Hughes briefly points up other models that frame recent comparative projects in religious studies. For example, he highlights Stephen Prothero's attempt to rework the "World Religions" edifice around liberal notions of diversity and globalization, where Prothero simultaneously critiques Huston Smith's Cold War-era "all religions are one" sentiment while at the same time he merely produces a more updated version of it. Along with Hughes's examples (he also mentions Corinne G. Dempsey's revamp of "the sacred" and William E. Paden's cognitive evolutionary model) we could list any number of other Z factors that have operated behind the scenes in the history of the History of Religions to produce and reproduce the normalcy of comparing the units of religions: e.g. evolutionary or functional notions of the human mind or society, or more particular schemas like tripartite ideology, *homo religiosus*, or *la mentalité primitive*—to name a few.[2]

There are several constructive ways to engage Hughes's essay, but here I want to present two loosely related issues. Both revolve around the suppressed Z terms, which have "littered" the field and have silently framed the conditions of comparison but also defined its units. First, I wish to explore the factor of empire that persists in the background of Hughes's remarks on his chosen exemplum. I want to bring to the fore the way Hughes positions the nascent and trans-regional Islamic empire in his case study of the Isawiyya in order to raise questions about the status of the categories of the "global" (or "universal") and "local" for comparative method, and how these get identified and circumscribed in such scholarly endeavors (and perhaps even how we might do this better). Second, I want to ask after the transition Hughes indicates from a situation of local, underdefined groups using a shared common vocabulary to the emergence of reifying and proprietary claims made by later writers that trade said common vocabulary for a more rigid discourse of heresy. In other words, in thinking about comparative method, I'm interested both in accounting for such a common vocabulary and the different groups that draw on it (like the Isawiyya), but also for the terms and concepts in this vocabulary that end up getting weaponized, that is, those picked out and used to divide and create stark oppositions, and the motivations and aspirations that inform this selection and re-signification. While there is not space to deal with either of these issues at length or in detail, my hope here is to effectively raise engaging questions about these issues by way of Hughes's essay. To this end, I approach these issues of comparison by posing a few general questions: What are the presumed units of any given comparison? How does one account for these historically, or from what historical factors do they emerge? And, what (if anything) entitles us to speak of them as discrete entities? To illustrate these matters, and since I'm no expert in Hughes's field, I will offer examples from my own research in the ancient Roman world.

Instead of phenomenological and global comparisons, which were favored by a previous generation of comparativists, Hughes favors comparisons arising from more local and situated interactions. At first glance, in his case of the Isawiyya, the units of comparison are putatively "underdefined" groups of "Jews" and "Muslims," who exist in close proximity to one another, who share "the same literal language and think with the same metaphorical language," and who are responding to similar social and political stressors. In such a context, these groups assert self-defining cultural differences by drawing from a shared conceptual environment framed by a common set of terms, tropes, metaphors, metonyms, and narratives. More specifically, on the eastern end of the burgeoning Islamic empire in the seventh through tenth centuries CE, there was a "hotbed of messianic fervor and apocalyptic speculation" based on a "common semantic matrix," a shared "prophetic vocabulary"—e.g. the Messiah—that self-identifying "Jews" and "Muslims" (in quotes), or maybe Jews-Muslims/Muslims-Jews (with a hyphen), could take up, fashion, and refashion to their own purposes. Sticking with the idea of Messiah, it's not so much that the Jews had their own traditional and native concept, which Muslim groups had co-opted as Mahdī in this way or that, but rather that the notion of Messiah was ready-to-hand for "[g]roups on each side of the imaginary hyphen" for imagining themselves and construing others. The comparative process for Hughes, then, is to follow these shared concepts in the nuances of how they were "consciously and creatively reimagined" in the different projects of these underdefined groups who drew on this vocabulary. Thus on Hughes's model we are not comparing discrete groups that represent instantiations of stable traditions easily identified as "Judaism" or "Islam" but rather tracking a set of cultural indices common to particular groups of Jews and Muslims in a socially contiguous relationship and tracing the discursive forms of power exerted to make rather than imitate social and culture distinctions between these groups. Notions of borrowing, influence, and diffusion, then, are replaced by "intimate links" and "common environment."

My interest here is in the broader social and historical contexts that created the conditions for such common vocabularies and the underdefined groups that drew on and contested them. Specifically, my research in the so-called "religions" of the ancient Roman world has attuned me to the context of empire and how Rome's military violence toward and administrative restructuring of conquered populations recalibrated social and culture indices of political belonging, creating new and different ways for such communities to (re)imagine ties of cultural affiliation and estrangement. Or, to put it another way, I'm interested in how different social groups, including groups we might call "religious" or "religions," are the effects of, and not just affected by, empire.

Admittedly, my knowledge of the historical situation that Hughes evokes is limited and I do not assume the Islamic empire was a priori the same political entity as the high Roman Empire that occupies my time. But nonetheless, an important z factor here is not simply the more local messianic context, but also the trans-regional (and perhaps uneven) spread of Islam, or the process called Islamicization, that created the even wider background of "political uncertainty" and "turmoil" against which Hughes sees the creation of these groups and to which their messianic imaginings were responding. In other words, "Jews" (x) and "Muslims" (y) are alike in their common messianic lexicon in reference to the larger and less local imperial ambitions of something called "Islam" (z). Of course, based on Hughes's own suspicion of such a category, we might ask, what's the nature of this imperial Islam? What were the more the sociological and material effects of its military and administrative actions? And how do these relate to the creation of a common discourse of messianism and apocalypticism he describes? To my mind, the background picture we get from Hughes's essay is suggestive: it is not only one of political instability caused "by the rapid expansion of a still inchoate Islam" but also a context of the transition from one regime (the Umayyads) to another (the Abbasids) and (therefore?) a destabilization of the center and what counts as marginal versus normative discourse. In this transitional moment, one gets the impression of a social vacuum where alternative, sectarian, and, in this case, messianic groups could provide "a valid socioreligious framework that only in retrospect became labeled as heterodox." While Hughes's suggestion in terms of margins and centers is intuitively appealing to me, I'm unclear on how the margins affected the center, especially when marginal messianic groups like the Isawiyya were uninterested in authenticity and proprietary claims to their shared vocabulary. Now to be generous (but not too generous), I suppose such factors might be an issue for specialists in the field. But nevertheless, I'm interested in how such factors inform the situation of contiguity Hughes describes. I find Hughes's statement that the Isawiyya were doing more than reacting to Islamicization—that "such groups were instead caught up in the very processes of Islamicization"—quite instructive and would like to hear more.

To illuminate my motives for raising these issues, let me draw from my own field of the ancient Roman world, where the dizzying array of cults under the Roman Empire has been an obsession (at least since the Enlightenment) for historians of this period. While this situation of plurality is often observed, and even emplotted to support various narratives, only recently have there been rigorous efforts to explain it.[3] Worse still, too often explicit emic explanations for such plurality have been taken up by scholars and recast as models for second-order analysis. For example, as Clifford Ando has recently pointed out, scholars' tendency to study ancient cults by tallying and inventorying them is a legacy of early Christian polemics, which pioneered the strategy of emphasizing the multitude and unwieldiness of "pagan" cults in order to underwrite the uniqueness of Christian cult from its contemporaries (Ando 2013b: 89, n. 11). Yet, as scholars of Roman antiquity have abandoned familiar triumphalist narratives of the ancient world, controlled by Christianity's inevitable rise and paganism's fall, they have exchanged it for an equally problematic "marketplace" model of religion.[4] Here the specters of modern economic capitalism linger as the plurality of "cults," or its frequent synonym "religions," become fetishized and commodified units in competition for customers, vying as so many choices available for the newly individualized ancient individual (acting as something of a *homo economicus*) and "bumping up" (to use Hughes's language) against each other in the self-regulating, decentralized religious marketplace of the late republican and Principate periods.[5] Such a model dehistoricizes the conditions for the situation of ancient pluralism, and, as Ando has argued in response, a preferable question might be to ask what "entitles" scholars "to speak of plural 'religions' and to understand them as historically autonomous and thus in competition in the first place"—or further, as discrete units of the same kind able to be compared with one another (Ando 2013b: 85). In fact, we might even ask if "religions" is a useful term to characterize these various collective affiliations that both interested ancient commentators and committed insiders described with a range of terms (e.g. *religiones, collegia, disciplina, factiones, secta*—to say nothing of the many Greek terms)? To my mind, the most interesting contemporary scholarship focuses on plurality and diversity in its social and historical contingency: both the sociological conditions and as a social problem ramified in different ancient sources. As I mentioned above, such a view emphasizes the intense pressures of Roman violence and how their subsequent refiguring of various political and administrative structures upset traditional communal dynamics in the Mediterranean world. One effect was an increase in human mobility, which in turn brought theretofore isolated groups, their gods, rituals, literatures, and the various technologies of cult into more sustained contact with one another and invited new cultural forms that could bind members of communities as they interacted with and represented themselves to other groups (see Ando 2013a).

This is broadly construed to be sure, but this model, it seems to me, might contribute to a plausible account for the existence of common vocabularies among underdefined groups. In fact, this sets into relief the quite post-colonial insights that have lately framed a great deal of useful scholarship on the origins of Christianity: namely, an acknowledgment that Christian cult was not so clearly distinct from its contemporaries. I think Daniel Boyarin's *Border Lines* is a reasonably good example illustrating how in the first few centuries CE "Christians" and "Jews" discursively shored up their own collective boundaries from a common biblical and philosophical vocabulary (Boyarin 2004). The concept of *logos* was not diffused or borrowed between monolithic traditions of Judaism or Christianity (or especially Paganism), but rather available and drawn on by Jews and Christians (and others) rather freely in various efforts to distinguish their similarities and dissimilarities and define the boundaries of their groups in situations where they weren't perhaps so different. Here Hughes's approach complements Boyarin's.

But still too often the context of empire and the diversity it fostered are merely treated as Umwelt, an "environment," and much analysis still starts from a baseline of Christian diversity (and Hellenistic Judaism), and then draws in, at will, various but often isolated aspects of the wider (non-Christian) culture, utilizing various metaphors of influence and adaptation.[6]

This leads me to my second point. Although Hughes wants to emphasize the situations of historical contiguity and shared vocabulary, he notes that for his selected case, this fluid and underdefined situation eventually gave way to a desire among some to reify these groups, to round them out into much more discrete entities, and to partition out the common conceptual trove into legitimate and illegitimate discourses along the stricter binary of us versus them. In other words, these later parties were interested in heresiology. From Hughes's comments it seems that in order to see the fluid situation he emphasizes, he rightly must read against the grain because in some sense the information on the Isawiyya comes to us in sources that have already re-signified them as a defined group against which the Rabbis, or say, Maimonides could assert the normativity of rabbinic Judaism. Again, turning to my own interests in Roman antiquity, I've found it a useful endeavor to analyze, in different ways, how ancient Roman intellectuals both conceived of the religious diversity mentioned above and generated conceptual schemas to make sense of it. While this may not be considered heresiology *in stricto sensu*, it does reveal how the Romans adapted mostly Greek paradigms of thought to anatomize, classify, and construe themselves and others in a landscape of increased religious plurality that their own imperialism produced. This endeavor involves redescribing the nature of particular sources by bringing out certain social and theoretical underpinnings of them. For example, we might see Cicero's late republican treatises *On the Nature of the Gods* or *On Divination* and Marcus Varro's *Divine Antiquities* as not just interventions into debates spawned by Hellenistic philosophical theology, but rather some of the first "substantial theorizing on religious diversity" in Roman antiquity (Ando 2010: 59), incited by a new cognizance of human difference, even if Roman writers still utilized a number of well-worn ethnic and religious stereotypes to represent what in reality were complex constituencies. Or, a century later, Pliny the Elder attempted to give a history of the *magicae vanitates*, which modern scholars have so often seen unproblematically as a history of magic. Instead, I would argue we could take this text as an attempt to construct the radical otherness of the non-Roman, or perhaps the anti-Roman, and the closest pre-Christian precursor to something like heresiology. Pliny takes the Latinized form of the relatively narrow Greek word *mageia* and expands it to account for and harshly condemn, on a global scale, all manner of suspicious and marginal peoples and practices in interpreting Greek history as well as contemporary Roman history (Pliny, *Natural History* 30.1–18).

We are, by now, used to saying that so-called elite or orthodox texts are overly aggrandized in their claims to universality and normativity. In their discursive practices, authors of such texts frequently misrepresent their partial perspectives and values as if these constituted some sort of comprehensive whole coextensive with the social itself; in other words, they portray their work as representing some normative state of affairs rather than as an attempt to produce this state of affairs. With heresiology in particular, the compiling of lists of names, beliefs, and practices of heretical groups, and differentiating, taxonomizing, and evaluating them tends to illuminate more the desire of certain writers to eliminate ambiguity and clearly demarcate collective boundaries of perceived "others," fortifying their own normative position, while telling us precious little about how, if at all, these groups self-organized. Recognizing these pretenses has incited scholars to a great deal of useful research both into alternative historical sources and alternative methods for (re)reading traditional sources. Indeed, I take the general lesson of Hughes's essay to be that, though some source may make claims that there are stark divisions between certain groups, these claims are often made in a context that presumes contiguity and commonality and are intended to do away with such a context—that is, these are assertions of difference rather than an innocent report of some real difference. Such attempts at strict bifurcations rarely diminish the complexity "on the ground"—they may hide it, or divert attention from it—but it is always useful to throw such would-be normative texts back into the wider contextual fray (as framed by the historian) and see how successful or not these texts were in their stated persuasive aims.

But my question is: where does this will to power, this desire to dominate tradition through reifying one's own group and others into manageable units, emerge? Human nature? This seems unsatisfying, although at times critical theory has—for all its dislike of larger-than-life narratives—given the impression that human nature disposes us most basically to self-interested power grabs of which creating simple binaries of us/them are indicative. In Hughes's example, where do the heresiological impulses emerge that incite later, retrospective accounts to turn "underdefined" Jewish groups into well-defined groups that reinforce rabbinic authority? Does it come from the appropriation of some element in the previously shared vocabulary among such groups? Or elsewhere? Indeed, in the context of the ferment of margins and centers that Hughes emphasizes, this location seems up for grabs in the centuries between the Isawiyya and those who are writing about them. The larger methodological implications for comparison might be that not only must one attempt to account for shared vocabularies, but one must also account for those terms, concepts, and themes that end up being reversed, revamped, and re-signified, in order to create distinctions and cauterize these as differences.

One last time I turn to the Roman Empire. I mentioned above a shift in models for ancient religion from those dominated by teleological narratives of Christian triumph to a marketplace model that attempts to spurn these by asserting paganism's continued vitality even up to the early Middle Ages. For all the problems and unforgivable flaws of "rise of Christianity" narratives, what these narratives did offer were various explanations (again deeply problematic) of why Christianity developed as a cultural form so militant against others. More recent market models are less equipped to account for this. Again quoting from Clifford Ando: [W]hat our fear of teleology will apparently not permit us to say is that religion in the Roman empire has a history; that one religion, armed not least with a polemical understanding of what religion is, sought successfully to eradicate its peers but that its victory must have deep historical roots existing in intricate connection to this disembedding of religion" (Ando 2013b: 87–88). In other words, that Christian hegemony and Christian claims to exclusive normativity had deep roots in how the superordinate structures of empire came to disrupt more local and traditional forms of social and political belonging, including peoples' imagined relationships with their gods and the interpretive lines along which these groups refashioned themselves.

I belabor this last point because the retrospective positions of heresiologists often produces a comparative situation that we as scholars of religion find all too familiar: i.e. a set of atomized units of comparison, one of which represents an authorized or idealized tradition versus any number of deviant, or more politely, alternative traditions. For the sake of provocation, I would say that the discursive practices of heresiology produce a situation that looks a great deal like the comparative situation that Hughes is trying to move us away from. Following the considerations of David Chidester, I raise the question of where such dominating, or—to put it in our Religious Studies idiom—such essentializing impulses emerge both to implicate scholars of religion as heresiologists and to make strides to reverse these measures in order to more easily recognize and exist in the fluid and "frontier" domains that Hughes outlines (Chidester 1996). These heresiological impulses have been diagnosed to some extent, but only shifted around, as Masuzawa has shown us is the case with world religions. Nevertheless, they haven't yet been expunged from our field (Masuzawa 2005).

In conclusion, I would like to return to my initial point on empire. We may be done with universal schemas in making our comparisons (good riddance), but we cannot be done with recognizing the power of universalizing claims and the apparatuses that make them seem like more than just local, situated claims. Relatedly, we may also need to interrogate a bit more carefully just what we mean by local. The disjunct of universal versus local wrongly implies distinct conceptual realms. My emphasis on empire, to my mind, illustrates that larger trans-geographical and trans-regional political institutions not only affect whatever we might construe as "local," but in some degree also create the conditions for them and constitute their dynamics. These can function as z factors which naturalize a set of items and options that appear ready and willing to be compared. Conversely, we might fully affirm that universality is always a socially situated, local claim, but this does not diminish the power of historically situated groups, organizations, and coalitions to claim universality and set the terms of debate while backing it up with a material (read: coercive) and immaterial apparatus that operates over spans of space and time.

I'll leave the matter at this: one of the central ironies of the mid to late twentieth century was that while academics celebrated postmodernism and the death of totalizing systems, placed a premium on area studies, and scholars of religion specifically expressed horror at the excess of global comparativism, at almost the same time the so-called global market seemed to bound to the forefront, with its proponents claiming it as (and here I quote David Graeber) "the single greatest and most monolithic system of measurement ever created, a totalizing system that would subordinate everything—every object, every piece of land, every human capacity or relationship—on the planet to a single standard of value" (Graeber 2001: xi). Indeed, the dominance of our current "neo-liberal" empire has set and tried to normalize its terms, including its own marketplace of religions (e.g. Prothero), and, as I see it, the value of Hughes's insights are precisely to invite us to look to the margins, the interstices, and crevasses where, as Hughes has pointed out, we can recover a sense of the contingency and fragility of such universalizing claims to power, disrupt their units of analysis, and confound the choices these lay out.

Andrew Durdin is currently a lecturer in the humanities at the University of Michigan-Dearborn, and, beginning fall 2018, will join the Florida State University Department of Religion as Assistant Teaching Professor. His research focuses on Roman religion, magic and religion in the Roman Empire, and scholarly historiography of ancient religions.

Notes

1 Here my allusion is to Bruce Lincoln's (in)famous quip in *Theorizing Myth: Narrative, Ideology, and Myth* (Lincoln 1999: 209).
2 See Bruce Lincoln's "Theses on Comparison" (Lincoln 2012).
3 Clifford Ando has, in my opinion, done the most to investigate this matter, and he has done so across a few different publications (e.g. Ando 2010, 2013a, 2013b). For a related argument see Rüpke (2014). These essays have heavily influenced my thinking in the following pages.
4 For the most interesting articulation of this view see Andreas Bendlin's "Looking Beyond the Civic Compromise: Religious Pluralism in Late Republican Rome" (Bendlin 2000: 115–135). Also see North (1979: 85–103; 1992: 174–193). Related to this metaphor (as evinced in these articles) is also the continuing debate over the utility or not of the "civic model" of religion or "polis religion," and how it adumbrates the trajectory of ancient Mediterranean (religious) history.
5 For this recent problematizing of the individual in the ancient Mediterranean world (which does not necessarily suffer from the problems I perceive in the marketplace model) see Rüpke (2013), esp. Rüpke's own introductory remarks in "Individualization and Individuation as concepts for Historical Research" (ibid.: 3–18).
6 See Rüpke (2009) for this critique and his application of it to a recent overview of early Christianity.

References

Ando, Clifford. 2010. "The Ontology of Religious Institutions," *History of Religions* 50(1): 54–79. https://doi.org/10.1086/651726
Ando, Clifford. 2013a. "Cities, Gods, Empire," in Ted Kaizer, Anna Leone, Edmund Thomas and Robert Witcher (eds.), *Cities and Gods: Religious Space in Transition*, 51–57. Leeuven: Peeters.
Ando, Clifford. 2013b. "Subjects, Gods, and Empires, or Monarchism as a Theological Problem," in Jörg Rüpke (ed.), *The Individual in the Religions of the Ancient*

Mediterranean, 85–111. Oxford: Oxford University Press. https://doi.org/10.1093/acprof:oso/9780199674503.003.0004

Bendlin, Andreas. 2000. "Looking Beyond the Civic Compromise: Religious Pluralism in Late Republican Rome," in Edward Bispham and Christopher John Smith (eds.), *Religion in Archaic and Republican Rome and Italy: Evidence and Experience*, 115–135. Edinburgh: University of Edinburgh.

Boyarin, Daniel. 2004. *Border Lines: The Partition of Judaeo-Christianity*. Philadelphia, PA: University of Pennsylvania Press. https://doi.org/10.9783/9780812203844

Chidester, David. 1996. *Savage Systems: Colonialism and Comparative Religion in Southern Africa*. Charlottesville, VA: University of Virginia Press.

Graeber, David. 2001. *Toward an Anthropological Theory of Value: The False Coin of our own Dreams*. Basingstoke: Palgrave Macmillan. https://doi.org/10.1057/9780312299064

Lincoln, Bruce. 2012. "Theses on Comparison," in his *Gods and Demons, Priests and Scholars: Critical Explorations in the History of Religions*, 121–130. Chicago, IL: University of Chicago Press.

Lincoln, Bruce. 1999. *Theorizing Myth: Narrative, Ideology, and Myth*. Chicago, IL: University of Chicago Press.

Masuzawa, Tomoko. 2005. *The Invention of World Religions: Or, How European Universalism was Preserved in the Language of Pluralism*. Chicago, IL: University of Chicago Press. https://doi.org/10.7208/chicago/9780226922621.001.0001

North, John. 1979. "Religious Toleration in Republican Rome," *Proceedings of the Cambridge Philological Society* 25: 85–103. https://doi.org/10.1017/S0068673500004144

North, John. 1992. "The Development of Religious Pluralism," in J. Lieu, J. North, and T. Rajak (eds.), *The Jews among Pagans and Christians in the Roman Empire*, 174–193. London: Routledge.

Patton, Kimberley C. and Benjamin C. Ray (eds.). 2000. *A Magic Still Dwells: Comparative Religion in the Postmodern Age*. Berkeley, CA: University of California Press.

Rüpke, Jörg. 2009. "Early Christianity Out of, and in, Context," *Journal of Roman Studies* 99: 182–193. https://doi.org/10.3815/007543509789744774

Rüpke, Jörg (ed.). 2013. *The Individual in the Religions of the Ancient Mediterranean*. Oxford: Oxford University Press. https://doi.org/10.1093/acprof:oso/9780199674503.001.0001

Rüpke, Jörg. 2014. "How Does an Empire Change Religion, and How Religion an Empire? Conclusion and Perspectives Regarding the Question of 'Imperial and Provincial Religion'," in his *From Jupiter to Christ: On the History of Religion in the Roman Imperial Period*, 271–284. Oxford: Oxford University Press.

Chapter 5

Complicating "Comparison": On Perspective, Rhetoric, and Recognition in the Study of Religion

Stacie Swain

Aaron Hughes's essay on comparison (Chapter 1, this volume) is rich with potential directions for analysis and dialogue. In response, I will revisit a number of statements that Hughes makes about how comparison is or ought to be done. These statements enable me to tease out some broader implications not only for comparison, but also for method more broadly within the study of religion. I will explore what I deem to be three interrelated matters of importance in any comparison: perspective, rhetoric, and recognition. These matters relate to questions and tensions that I encounter within my own work, which consists of examining interactions between state actors and those who have come to represent the category "Indigenous" within Canada.

I will begin by addressing the conceptualization of "comparison" as an object of study and focus for dialogue. The program for "Method Today" explicitly asks panelists to consider, "four key tools that all scholars of religion surely employ, regardless their approach to the study of religion" (NAASR 2016). Such a statement identifies comparison as a method or tool within *any* approach. Framed thusly, comparison is not seen to be exclusive to the subfield of comparative religion. Hughes notes of his own work upon early Jewish and Christian groups, "Though I have never called myself a 'comparativist' or someone who engages in the task of 'comparative religion,' I guess I am and I do. I imagine this is because I do not see myself as doing the type of essentialist comparative work that usually goes by that name in religious studies" (Chapter 1, this volume). Rather than essentializing religion(s), Hughes characterizes his work as focusing upon "the interactions of specific groups at specific times and in specific places" (ibid.).[1] In other words, he takes his own recommendation to destabilize "religion" as an object of study that our field purportedly revolves around, in order to perform responsible and productive acts of comparison.

The above statements by Hughes are demonstrative of the entanglement of theory and method with which scholars must grapple, however self-consciously they choose to do so. These statements show that Hughes's three criteria for a responsible comparison—sensitivity to the historical record, linguistic dexterity, and theoretical sophistication—are unavoidably conditioned by his theoretical perspective, which is comprised by his academic interests, his conceptualization of religion *as* an object of study (or not), and how he believes that we ought to go about studying religion. As Jeppe Sinding Jensen notes, "conceptual objects are not given, but produced. 'Religion' is such an abstract conceptual object and the seeing (etc.) of 'it' will depend profoundly on the observer's preconceptions and predispositions" (Jensen 2015: 2). Given Hughes's focus on specific groups, places, and times then, that he locates an ideal comparison at the nexus of social theory and historical, linguistic, and cultural expertise should come as no surprise. For those who destabilize "religion" similarly, mastering these skills should should make our comparisons not only responsible and interesting, but intelligible to others who engage our theoretical perspective.

Intelligibility is or ought to be the primary purpose or goal of comparison, academic or otherwise. For example, consider Hughes's use of an analogy, a form of comparison, to open his essay and make his perspective on comparison intelligible. This analogy, which compares scholarship to poetry, provides an example of the triadic nature of comparison as conceptualized by J. Z. Smith. Within Smith's triadic configuration, there are always two objects or examples along with an "in relation" or "with respect to." As he puts it, "In the case of an academic comparison, the 'with respect to' is most frequently the scholar's interest, be this expressed in a question, a theory, or a model" (Smith 1990: 51). The interest, model, and question in Hughes's analogy is the act of comparison, while his two examples are poetry and religious studies scholarship. Hughes's analogy allows him to draw upon the language and imaginaries of two domains to make, his model for comparison intelligible. His analogy also plays with the boundary between two domains, perhaps resulting in the poetically academic statement, "One must explicate the logic that comprises the comparison and try to illumine the gossamer threads that are perceived to hold [two different or contradictory objects] delicately together" (Chapter 1, this volume). Hughes also points out the apparent paradox of comparison: that it is at once a natural cognitive process that we perform when we wish to understand something, yet can simultaneously be an artificial academic endeavor that serves a particular set of interests. As he emphasizes, "*while the comparative act may be natural, specific comparisons are not*" (Chapter 1, this volume; emphasis original). While I agree that some comparisons *seem* more natural than others, I am less convinced that framing comparison as paradoxical enables one to avoid what Hughes calls apologetics or ideological ends. What (or whose) purposes might the distinction between natural and artificial acts of comparison serve? And, why do some comparisons seem more natural than others?

Hughes states, "while there are good comparisons and bad comparisons, common to both is the sheer artificiality of the enterprise" (Chapter 1, this volume). If generic comparison is natural while specific (good or bad) academic acts of comparison are artificial, how do we know when we're doing one or the other? This distinction appears to be predicated upon either intent or distance, both of which are matters of perspective. Both intent and distance are contingent upon the scholar and their motives or positioning—but, these are not qualities solely attributed to those in the position of "scholar." Perhaps then, the naturalness or the artificiality of an act of comparison can be understood as a matter of degree. One's perspective—one's interests, intent, and distance—matters whether you are an academic or not.

What if one were instead to grant the supposition that all scholarship is *more* discourse on discourse in the same way that some scholars claim to study discourse on discourse?[2] What sets an academic comparison apart from any other is who performs it, the context in which it takes place, and the intended audience. A comparison performed by a scholar of religion—or from another field or discipline—may certainly be assessed by additional demands for clarification, as Hughes prescribes (Chapter 1, this volume). But, academic comparison is also subject to the scrutiny that we apply to our own sources of "data" wherever similarities and distinctions are drawn. When we compare, how do we participate in the co-constitution of contexts, identities, and ideas through our academic discourse? Shifting the terms of analysis to account for the supposition that scholarship is discourse on discourse (on discourse) results in a more porous boundary between primary and secondary sources and thus a broadening of the scope of analysis, including in such a way that scholarship can be more easily considered within the category that we tend to call "data."

A statement by noted Māori scholar Linda Tuhiwai Smith serves as an example that illustrates why we might loosen the descriptive hold of "primary" and "secondary." In her landmark work *Decolonizing Methodologies*, she states, "Concepts of spirituality which Christianity attempted to destroy, then to appropriate, then to claim, are critical sites of resistance for indigenous peoples. The values, attitudes, concepts, and language embedded in beliefs about spirituality represent, in many cases, the clearest contrast and mark of difference between indigenous peoples and the West." (Smith 2012: 143) If, as it seems fair to say of both myself and Hughes, one is interested in how the discourse on religion and related categories is used by one group to define itself in opposition to another, does one treat this statement as a primary or a secondary source? Situating it as a perspective within a more comprehensive approach to discourse allows it to serve as both. It must be noted though, that *all* academic claims are subject to this scrutiny and flexible status; to claim differently reveals not only othering at work but its opposite, the presumption of a normative voice.

Scholarship is merely one more context in which discourse occurs, even if it is one that often produces claims of critical distance (less often nowadays, objectivity) from that upon which it centers. In thinking about comparison, to what extent might we consider how context shapes perspective, which in turn produces and conditions the comparisons that we make? In the context of scholarship, as Hughes highlights with his requirement of linguistic expertise or dexterity (Chapter 1, this volume), comparisons take place, are produced and conditioned, through language. Scholarship provides a discursive site as much as we claim to study the "discursive sites" of others (Chapter 1, this volume). This is how new models, theories, and methods are produced; they are not simply "tools" that are picked up and used, but are discursively reconstituted whenever cited. We do, however, have preconceptions and make choices regarding how we describe that which we claim as objects of comparison and our redescriptions of those objects. The field of religious studies, while not internally homogenous by any means, provides a context in which objects compared are made intelligible not only through each other (i.e. their respective domains), but also through various redescriptive idioms. Linguistic dexterity is therefore as much a requirement for engaging in scholarship as it is for scholars to, as Hughes puts it, "account for our data" (ibid.). Scholars give *an* account *of* their data in addition to attempting to account *for* their data in an explanatory sense.

To return to Hughes's essay, his theoretical approach and the idiom in which he chooses to work—social theory intermixed with history—make his example of comparison intelligible to me, despite the fact that I have very little background in the times, places, and peoples within his research. While I may not be able to vouch for the accuracy of the detailed content of Hughes's comparison,[3] due to the form and language of his analysis I do understand the nature of the work that he performs. Indeed, due to my familiarity with the approach and idiom that Hughes espouses (historical, social), I could even import some of his statements into my own analyses if I were to change sundry nouns and adjectives. Our work becomes mutually intelligible not through a comparison of the content of each, but because of the academic idiom that we both utilize: the language of social groups, self-identification, identity definition in relation to an "other," groups on either side of a social imaginary, shared vocabularies, porous borders, collective world-making, a common semantic matrix, and so on. Hughes and I share not only a comparative model, but also a comparative idiom.

I have drawn this correlation between Hughes's work and my own in order to highlight the role of academic rhetoric. When I say "rhetoric," I do not imply insincerity (or artificiality), but persuasive language used for the purpose of argumentation. Although speaking of comparative literature and not religion, Gayatri Spivak shifts the focus to content and form by depicting these disciplinary expressions as "moves of languaging" (Spivak 2009: 612). The languaging moves, the rhetorics, idioms, or vocabularies that we use in our scholarship, constitute not only our descriptions and acts of comparison, but also the extent to which they will be intelligible to those who encounter our work (whether within the study of religion or outside of it). By mastering languaging moves within our work, we perform the role "scholar of religion" and reproduce the collectives and contexts that produced us as scholars.

As scholars we are, to approximate the terms of Louis Althusser (1971), hailed by an apparatus in relation to which we materialize as scholar-subjects. At the same time, we are within that apparatus and reproduce it. This apparatus can be understood as research, scholarship, and/or the academy. That which hails us constitutes our "apparatus of recognition" (Radhakrishnan 2009: 464). Before we can compare, we must know how to recognize our examples and transform them into "data." As Rich King puts it, "the kind of object one considers 'religion' to be and the kinds of claims that one makes about that object is significantly determined by the disciplinary lens and formative assumptions that ground that analysis in the first place" (King 2013: 142). On the same theme, David Chidester describes his engagement with "comparative religion": "I needed to know about the material conditions, possibilities, and constraints in which my knowledge was being produced and I was producing knowledge" (Chidester 2014: xviii). Working within an academic and disciplinary apparatus, these conditions, possibilities, and constraints configure how we recognize our objects of study (and how they relate to the concept of religion), and subjectivate them through our critical scrutiny. Comparison is one method through which we make so-called objects into our subjects; we do so discursively, producing discourse on discourse.

As a provocative question then, while the terms of our comparisons may have changed to eschew former essentialisms, have the conditions, possibilities, and constraints of our scholarship changed as well? To be clear, I do not think that there is a type of scholarship that can get outside of context and perspective (or ideology and apparatus) to attain some pure objective position. I do, however, wonder if the current context of scholarship reproduces the aspiration to do so. Contemporary scholars call this a "critical distance," placing ourselves *in relation to* rather than *outside of* that which we make the "subjects" of our study through our gaze. This critical distance, I believe, is meant to be attained through what Hughes considers, "theoretical sophistication" (Chapter 1, this volume). As he defines, "This means being aware of the conceit of comparison while simultaneously engaging in it" (Chapter 1, this volume). Emphasizing the artificiality of academic comparison seems to serve a similar purpose as emphasizing "critical distance." Such statements construct our perspectives as our conditions, possibilities, and constraints allow.[4]

To conclude with a question regarding "Method Today" more broadly, what are the implications of the statement that *all* scholars of religion surely employ comparison, regardless of their approach to the study of religion? The answer, of course, depends upon how one conceptualizes "scholar," "religion," "comparison," "approach," and "the study of religion." These elements are neither self-evident nor isolable from one another, not unlike the "tools" selected for us to hone our collective intellects upon: description, interpretation, comparison, and explanation (NAASR 2016). Comparison, or *a* comparison, is only as natural or artificial as one claims it to be, with both claims susceptible to scrutiny. While we cannot help but compare, perhaps one comparison seems more natural than another when an act of recognition is taken for granted. However, as R. Radhakrishnan states:

> If the world is one in its reality but irreducibly plural in its knowability, where and how should the project of comparison be situated: in the one, the many, or in an ecstatic mode that constantly reorganizes the apparatus of recognition? (Radhakrishnan 2009: 464)

While I eschew the possibility of ecstasy as in the Greek *ekstasis* or "standing outside of oneself," in this response I hope to have drawn attention to the apparatus of recognition. A responsible comparison within the academic study of religion entails deciding where comparison is situated, considering who or what one is responsible to, and acknowledging the conditions, possibilities, and constraints that produce us as scholars of religion.

Stacie Swain is a doctoral student in political science at the University of Victoria. She completed a Master's degree in religious studies from the University of Ottawa in 2017. Stacie's research examines the politics of Indigenous ceremony in relation to Canadian settler colonialism, sovereignty, and jurisdiction. She is broadly interested in interdisciplinary theories of place, public institutions, and the nation-state.

Notes

1 I found myself echoing both of these statements with respect to my own work upon interactions between indigenous and non-indigenous (settler) groups in contemporary Canada rather than anything classified as indigenous religion, spirituality, or tradition.
2 Andie Alexander (2016) suggests that we consider primary sources as "discourse on discourse," and I think the same should go for scholarship that we consider secondary; while a secondary source is commonly understood as a commentary upon a primary source, this operational binary is often taken for granted and can obscure as much as it reveals.
3 My admitted lack of specialized knowledge in Hughes's area of research somewhat echoes an episode that Hughes points out of himself, in which he belatedly learns that a comparative study of fire rituals is problematic due to an error in translation (Chapter 1, this volume).
4 Including, for example, as per those institutions, educators, and mentors who have socialized us as scholars of religion.

Reference

Alexander, Andie. 2016. "The Problem with the Primacy of Primary Sources," *Studying Religion in Culture* September 26. Retrieved from https://religion.ua.edu/blog/2016/09/the-problem-with-the-primacy-of-primary-sources (accessed February 26, 2018).
Althusser, Louis. 1971. "Ideology and Ideological State Apparatuses," in his *Lenin and Philosophy and Other Essays*, 127–186. New York: Monthly Review Press.
Chidester, David. 2014. *Empire of Religion: Imperialism and Comparative Religion*. Chicago, IL: University of Chicago Press. https://doi.org/10.7208/chicago/9780226117577.001.0001
Jensen, Jeppe Sinding. 2015. "Closing the Gaps—Some Notes on the *Making* of Perspectives," *Method and Theory in the Study of Religion* 28(4–5): 465–477.
King, Richard. 2013. "The Copernican Turn in the Study of Religion 1." *Method and Theory in the Study of Religion* 25(2): 137–159. https://doi.org/10.1163/15700682-12341280
NAASR. 2016. "Call for Papers: Method Today." Retrieved from https://naasr.com/2016/01/17/call-for-papers-method-today (accessed February 26, 2018).
Radhakrishnan, R. 2009. "Why Compare?" *New Literary History* 40(3): 453–471. https://doi.org/10.1353/nlh.0.0100
Smith, Jonathan Z. 1990. *Drudgery Divine*. Chicago, IL: University of Chicago Press.
Smith, Linda Tuhiwai. 2012. *Decolonizing Methodologies: Research and Indigenous Peoples*, 2nd edition. London: Zed Books.
Spivak, Gayatri Chakravorty. 2009. "Rethinking Comparativism," *New Literary History* 40(3): 609–626. https://doi.org/10.1353/nlh.0.0095

Chapter 6

Response

Aaron W. Hughes

Comparison, perhaps more than any other method in our field, has been much used and even more abused. It has been used to show uniqueness, and it has been used to demonstrate sameness. However, nothing is unique, at least in the taxonomic sense of the term, and things cannot be the same or else they would be identical. This has not stopped many, however, from persevering. In like manner, comparison has been used to assign value and it has been used to demean. Comparison, then, is a highly charged political and ideological tool, yet it is often done or presented as if it were as natural as can be. This is because comparison, at least in the academic study of religion, has been the vehicle par excellence to access the "sacred"—the so-called "really real," and that which many perceive to be the raison d'être for the professional religionist—since it is assumed that the sacred can only be known through the discovery of its many manifestations. This is the traditional phenomenological model that we do not need to rehearse here, the one that has done a lot of damage to our self-respect, and it is the model that my main paper tried to leave behind, far behind.

There is, however, no getting around comparison. It is a natural component of our epistemological framework. "I am taller than you," for example, or "Messi is a better footballer than Ronaldo." Even if we resign ourselves to area studies or the study of one tradition, we still use comparison, as Carrico well reminds us. When I try to make a critical edition of a text, for example, I must compare various manuscripts. Comparison, then, is not going anywhere. As a result, we have to ask ourselves what it can do and what it cannot, how we ought to undertake it and how we ought not to, and what constitutes a good comparison and what does not.

Within this context my argument is rather simple and, I would hope, not even controversial. It is that comparison has to be small-scale, attuned to contexts (note the plural), and highly self-conscious or self-reflective. By "small scale," I mean the micro level, what historians now call "micro-history"—I think as a way to register their displeasure with "big data." It is ridiculous to compare, say, Judaism and Islam with one another. It makes much more sense, however, to compare localized Jewish and Muslim social groups—note I am not saying religious traditions here, but *social* groups and *social* actors—who interacted with one another in particular times and in particular places. By "contextual," I mean that if one does not have an intimate familiarity with the requisite linguistic, historical, intellectual, social, and other settings, one might as well forget it. The results will be facile at best or just plain wrong at worst. But, I quickly hear the refrain of the anthropologists in the room: who cares about texts any more? To whom I respond simply, "I am who I am"—a medievalist who has spent the past twenty years reading texts and is here thinking about comparison as a way to account for and help understand those texts. This means that I call upon the comparativist to know the languages as well as the philologist, history as well as the historian, and social theory as well as the social theorist. Perhaps an impossible task! As for "self-conscious" or "self-reflective," I mean several things. These include:

1. we must rationalize to ourselves (and to our readers) why we are doing what we are doing;

2. that our results should be independently verifiable (with no *dei ex machina*);

3. we should realize that our interpretations are confined or localized to particular places and not representative of either timeless truths or essentialized reifications.

On one level my argument is certainly old-fashioned. For those interested in comparison, go and learn the languages and the various historical contexts of that which you purport to compare. On another level, it may be revolutionary in the sense that I also argue that the old comparison no longer holds and we must look for other paradigms aligned with other fields like history, philology, or, perhaps even cognitive science.

I think that all my interlocutors here are correct to note just how problematic the term "comparison" is and can be. As Carrico (Chapter 3, this volume) duly notes, although comparison is invoked but rarely at the institutional level at the AAR, its virtual omnipresence seems to be solidified by its apparent absence. Whether explicit or implicit, comparison structures so many of the various papers and panels that comprise the AAR's Annual Meeting. Yet, it is absent because no one reflects on just when, why, how, where, or by whom the comparative act takes place. He asks, "in what setting ought the academic labor of comparison produce a particular kind of knowledge?" While certainly important, I might add that I am not at all sure that comparison produces a "particular kind of knowledge" other than idiosyncratic guesses or hunches. As a result, I remain to be convinced that there can really be an "academic labor of comparison." Although my sense is that Carrico wants there to be in order to locate the field of comparative religious ethics therein, yet we still have to ask ourselves what job the modifier "comparative" is doing when appended to "religious ethics." I am not sure then if comparison is or can be an activity that is limited to trained, professional comparativists because there are no professionally trained comparativists, at least in the way I define the term. If Carrico wants to ask, "what are the existing social and institutional constraints on comparative inquiry?" I prefer to ask what are the intellectual and cognitive constraints on comparison?

As the ancient rabbis would ask, "to what is this similar?" Carrico says it is similar to comparative religious ethics—a field that my own work in medieval Islamic and Jewish philosophy rubs up against every now and then. I appreciate his comparison of my informality to their formality. I will take the compliment, but allow me to say why I take it as such. Comparison, I maintain, cannot or should not be institutionalized, and this is why I see myself as an "accidental comparativist." While comparative religious ethics emerges historically, as he informs us, out of the desire to make the study of ethics a little less Christian and a little less theological, that field—and I am happy to be corrected—still risks an ahistorical, cross-cultural analysis that is centered on normativity of which my original paper is largely critical. For me, comparison cannot be cross-cultural, comparing texts or phenomena from different times and places. Whereas I try to make sense of social groups without recourse to religious traditions, comparative religious ethics, to use his locutions, engage in "normative arguments" and "may thereby speak to contemporary [social and political] concerns." I put the proverbial cart before the proverbial horse: not only am I not interested in normativity, I am not interested in contemporary concerns, which I argue are actually responsible for our inability to place and map non-normative groups, and their texts and concerns, in the first place. It is ultimately institutional bodies, to reiterate, that keep marginal groups at bay even though such marginal groups have helped to define what is orthodox at the center.

Carrico asks, "Should we conceive of comparison as a widespread method or as a specific program of study"? My sense is neither, to wit, that comparison has to be specific and localized. I do not know if there can be "comparativists" in light of the damage that the likes of Eliade and other phenomenologists had done to the term. Someone like Daniel Boyarin, whose work I admire and respect for the reasons that I list in my paper—his expert sense of the historical record, his exceptional linguistic and textual skills, and his knowledge of critical theory—certainly does not call himself a "comparativist" or a "comparative religionist."

I am especially grateful to Andrew Durdin (Chapter 4, this volume), who, while not a specialist in the social groups of the Eastern Islamic Empire in the eighth and ninth centuries, nonetheless spends considerable time—unlike the others—thinking through my example, albeit from the perspective of his own material that he works on in the ancient Roman world. What he has done is use my discussion of empire, society, and religion to think about his own material. Sometimes my framework works for him and sometimes it does not. But, reading his response, the point is that we find common ground with which to illumine one another's work. This, for me, is comparison—again, I am not even sure how comfortable I am using this term—done properly. We are both attuned historically and textually to our respective exemplars, but share a common methodological ground with which we can learn from one another.

Let me now look at some of his specifics. Let me begin with the z-factor. I'm not sure if my z-factor is, as Durdin intimates, "normative Islam" precisely because there is no such thing at the point at which my comparison begins. Maybe it is "rabbinic Judaism," something that these overlapping social groups struggle with and with whom rabbinic Judaism must struggle. This is why I think groups like the Isawiyya effect the center—on the outermost edges of Empire they represent the genealogical precursors to other groups—the Karaites in Judaism, the Shiʻa in Islam—that will most decidedly influence the production of normativity in the caliphal center. Groups like the Isawiyya, then, and without getting into all the technical details, create orthodoxy because before they become marginalized as heterodox they are, for all intents and purpose, in the proverbial center. I concur about Durdin's invocation of Boyarin's work, which I have used as a torch to try and bring some nuance to me data. But I do hear his (Durdin's and not Boyarin's) insistence that we take Empire seriously from an analytic perspective and not just as the stage on which our characters act and perform.

This is related to his second point, namely, what do we do with heresiology, a genre—as Steven Wasserstrom pointed out years ago with respect to medieval Islam or Boyarin has done more recently for late antique Christianity and rabbinic Judaism—represents the genealogical antecedents to what we do now. We create, we draw lines, we mark territory—all based on some imagined sense of orthodoxy or normativity. Durdin is rightly cautious of the heresiological impulse that remains at the core of the academic study of religion, but I would respond that we have to do for the modern heresiologists what we do for the ancient ones: treat them—as I think Swain does—as "secondary sources" that expose precisely the kinds of wills to power and totalizing discourse that Durdin, correctly, abhors.

Now for Stacie Swain's response (Chapter 5, this volume). I have to admit I am as into "meta" as anyone in a NAASR panel, but I think there are two ends of the comparison continuum—the one that is phenomenological and the other that analyses comparison without comparing. Swain provides us with astute example of the latter and informs it with a sensitivity to, in her own words, "perspective, rhetoric, and recognition." I think we are in agreement, and I assent positively to her analysis and attention to theoretic and methodological detail.

Swain asks, "what purpose might a distinction between natural and artificial acts of comparison serve? And, why do some comparisons seem more natural than others?" I would reframe the first question since all comparison are ultimately artificial, and with an eye to my own actual work in late antique Arabic and Judeo-Arabic texts, as "what purpose might a distinction between a good and a bad comparison serve?" The second question, then, for me at least, becomes why do some comparisons seems better than others? I like to think that good, not natural, comparisons account for the microhistorical historical processes in group identity, formation, and patrol. Indeed, the microhistorical might not even be comparative, but only accidentally so since the field of religious studies has told us we must talk about religions and the way to do so is ostensibly through "comparative" frameworks.

So, if earlier I referred to myself as an "accidental comparativist," allow me now to refer—I do not want to say define—myself as a "post-comparativist." How to chart what a post comparative framework might look like is our task. On one level I might argue that the example I supplied is not even "comparative" since I am looking at groups that define themselves—or are defined by others—as both/neither Jewish and/nor Muslim. So, again, it is the field that turns this into a comparative project because whenever we see the invocation of two or more "religions," there we must surely have comparison.

This means that I have no problems with answering some of her other questions, again, by simply agreeing with her. "What if one were instead to grant the supposition that all scholarship is discourse on discourse in the same way that we study discourse on discourse?" Agreed. "Is there a difference between primary and secondary data? Of course not.

In this vein, Carmichael (Chapter 2, this volume) actually seems to use theory to argue against learning the languages in which we work. I suspect that this is because he is an Americanist and, like most who work in that field, he has not bothered to learn other languages and immerse himself in other cultures because he does not have to. Though, I can honestly not imagine what graduate school would look like without language work and seminars devoted to reading philology, codicology, and epigraphy. Perhaps to overcompensate, he writes:

> Since I am writing in English and in connection with the North American Association for the Study of Religion (NAASR) ... I will venture to suggest that a significant portion of all our work is conducted "in the idiom of religion/s in America," just as a significant portion of our research, publishing, and teaching is accomplished through English translation. (Carmichael, Chapter 2, this volume)

This, for me, is just plain wrong, especially to this Canadian. While we certainly work with translations in the classroom, anyone who works on another area and uses English translations upon which to base their arguments will be a laughing stock.

We can wax theoretical all we want and invoke Gadamer's *Horizontverschmelzung*, but if we cannot read languages from the traditions in which we purport to work, we have failed as scholars. I am not sure why Carmichael is so worried about this since he works on English translations of the *Daoede Jing*—as he correctly notes these are his data and, as such, they are his primary sources. No one is asking him to go learn Chinese. But if he was to work, say, on the *Daoede Jing* in its immediate historical and intellectual context, I would assume that he would agree with me—or, at least, admit to himself—that he ought to learn Chinese. This would not give him "unmediated" or "transhistorical" access to the work, whatever that might mean (even though he accuses me of arguing for this), but it would give him the skills and confidence to say what interpretations the text can support and what it cannot.

In the final analysis and after all our theoretical posturing, we must ultimately return to the data—we must be able to read it in the original, and we must be able to contextualize it. And this is my point: theorizing the data without recourse to situating the data and its alternative, simply situating the data without recourse to theorizing, represent two sides of the same coin. What is necessary is both. That means speaking to and showing disciplinary competence to specialists in one's area (for Durdin, for example, presumably this means Classicists and other experts in Roman Religion in its various imperial contexts) and being able to come here and speak to us. No easy feat. Indeed this is the potential impossibility that comparison—be it of the accidental or post variety—sets for itself, and indeed for us.

Aaron W. Hughes holds the Philp S. Bernstein Chair of Jewish Studies in the Department of Religious Studies at the University of Rochester. Recent books include *Rethinking Jewish Philosophy: Beyond Particularism and Universalism* (Oxford University Press, 2014), *Jacob Neusner: An American Jewish Iconoclast* (NYU Press, 2016), and *Shared Identities: Medieval and Modern Imaginings of Judeo-Islam* (Oxford University Press, 2017). Along with Hava Tirosh-Samuelson, he is co-editor of the Library of Contemporary Jewish Philosophy.

Part II

Chapter 7

Forget about Defining "It": Reflections on Thinking Differently in Religious Studies

Naomi Goldenberg

When my department of Classics and Religious Studies was tasked by the university administration with drawing up a list of "learning outcomes" for honors students in the religious studies program, the following three goals were proposed:

1 To understand the concept and human reality of the religious in diverse contexts.

2 To analyze phenomena and events related to the religious as they arise in everyday life.

3 To identify key dimensions of human religiosity throughout human history.

These pedagogical objectives support some common assumptions. Among them are: that there is something that can be pointed to as "the religious" that exists as both a "concept" and as "human reality"; that "the religious" is sufficiently ubiquitous that it occurs "in everyday life"; and that "human religiosity" (which might or might not be synonymous with "the religious") possesses "key dimensions" that appear "throughout human history."

The description of our religious studies program on the departmental website continues in a similar vein:

> Our program offers a scientific study of religions, not theological studies within any given religious tradition. Religion always had a central place in virtually all civilizations and cultures. The program examines profound existential questions that human beings have asked themselves since the dawn of time. Students will reflect on several of these questions. Technology and science have radically changed our view of the world, but we still find religion in our contemporary society. In fact, religions are key elements in every culture, they play a fundamental role in the life of billions of people. Every day, we can see the central place of religion in politics. Religion will continue to be a critical factor in public life around the world.
> (Department of Classics and Religious Studies, University of Ottawa 2017)

In these sentences, "religions" are posited as phenomena that are amenable to "scientific" study. "They" are present everywhere and always have been. They are linked to deep and timeless human perplexities. They are beyond major modification by more recent types of expertise. And, not only are they now basic to contemporary life throughout the globe, but they always will be.

My departmental colleagues who composed these learning outcomes and the website description are a highly intelligent, accomplished group of religious studies scholars. They are familiar with the substantial body of critical scholarship in the discipline that, for two decades at least, has argued the following: that "religion" is a modern concept that operates as a distorting anachronism when applied to the study of earlier epochs; that "religion" has roots in European colonial ambitions and intellectual history; that "religion" is a citation of Christianity as idealized prototype and thus the claim that "it" is timeless and universal promotes Christian hegemony; that whatever is considered not religious (i.e., that which is labeled secular or political) in any given context is a function of dynamics of power; and that continuing to treat "religion" as an unproblematic descriptor or as a coherent analytic category at best impedes clarity of study and at worst obscures operations of political ideology. I do not expect my colleagues to refrain from disagreeing with some or even all of these general tenets of the sub-field of "critical religion." Rather, what I find disconcerting is their choosing to ignore critical approaches to fundamental terms when they are describing religious studies as a discipline.

The inattention paid to critiques of religion as a category of thought and language is not only typical of a large part of the academic study of religion but also permeates discourse about religion in popular culture, law, and government. Those scholars and theorists who, like me, would like the academic study of religion to disturb conventional understandings of the term have set ourselves a massive task of deconstruction whose scope and difficulty can be as daunting as it is exciting. Nevertheless, the very complexity and protean quality of the topic make taking apart "religion" a compelling, intense and far-reaching project.

In this chapter, at the invitation of NAASR, I want to try to push the project of deconstruction in the field of religious studies further by framing the following methodological suggestions for improving academic practice and building more adventurous and consequential theory:

1. Explore the politics of representing "religion" in popular culture
2. Analyze "religion" in relation to governance.
3. Keep gender in mind.
4. Argue against "redescription" and the slippery use of "it" as a pronoun for an abstract and mystified "religion."
5. Use more specific vocabulary in the practice of religious studies scholarship.

I offer these proposals in the hope of generating discussion and debate that will render passé descriptions of "religious studies" characterized by reification and mystification.

Explore the Politics of Representing "Religion" in Popular Culture

In the introduction to their collection titled *Stereotyping Religion: Critiquing Clichés*, Brad Stoddard and Craig Martin write that "clichés sometimes have political effects and thus deserve serious consideration" (Stoddard and Martin 2017: 1). Stoddard and Martin cite the dissemination of anti-Semitic propaganda in 1930s Germany as an example of how material from common and widely available cultural products became a justification for violent and racist government policy over time. The authors see the mission of their work in the volume as confronting a series of common clichés about religion, all of which, though lesser in authoritarian effect than those from proto-Nazi times, do have political impact. "Before we can produce critical, sophisticated scholarly work," they write, "we must become conscious of the stereotypes we hold and set them aside. Clearing away the clichés that clutter our minds is quite possibly the first and most important step to doing sophisticated academic work" (ibid.: 3).

Stereotyping Religion: Critiquing Clichés focuses academic attention on the task of unraveling "religion" as term and concept in popular culture. By contextualizing and historicizing broadly circulated opinions about "religion" such as "religion makes people moral," "religion is intrinsically violent," and "religion is a private matter," the authors in the collection demonstrate the type of analysis that will be necessary to declutter in order to make space for more incisive critical work.

Stoddard and Martin are correct in pointing to the "political effects" of clichés about religion. I want to continue to demonstrate the connection of politics and the popular representation of religion by describing two specific cultural events that were staged in Ottawa, Canada. The first is a museum exhibit sponsored by the Canadian federal government and the European Union; the second is a music and dance performance underwritten by the municipality of Ottawa. My analysis of both cultural productions relates to the first two suggestions for improving theory in religious studies that I outlined above—namely (1) to dissect "religion" in popular culture and (2) to connect the citation of "religion" with government.

"God(s): A User's Guide" is the title of a major international exhibit that appeared in Gatineau, Québec, a district within the national capital region of Ottawa, Canada, in 2011–2012. The large collection of artifacts, explanatory texts and audio-visual displays was ensconced in the city for nine months as part of a tour of capitals in Europe and North America. Other stops included Brussels—at the Museum of Europe—an institution financed by the European Parliament and Quebec City, the seat of government in the province of Quebec.

The venue for the exhibit's stint in the Ottawa region is spectacular. The Canadian Museum of History is an elegant curvilinear building designed by the architect Douglas Cardinal—on a dramatic cliff bordering the broad and churning Ottawa River on the Quebec side of the national capital area. Directly opposite the museum near the edge of an equally impressive cliff's edge on the Ontario side of the river, rise the magnificent Gothic revival buildings that house the Parliament of Canada. The Peace Tower, an impressive and imposing edifice modeled with reference to Big Ben, gives the skyline a focal point in the phallic architectural style often favored by governments.

The splendidly positioned museum is a major tourist destination. Its glorious site, the succession of its two ambitious titles—The Canadian Museum of Civilization and the Canadian Museum of History—as well as its proximity to Parliament operate to give the impression of weighty national and international importance to whatever exhibit takes place there. Such grandiosity of presentation and expectation was apparent during the tenure of "God(s): A User's Guide." An energetic and well-funded publicity campaign brought the exhibit to the attention of the inhabitants of Ottawa and its environs through newspaper ads, internet announcements and a uniquely designed and widely distributed poster.

The exhibit was given a great deal of space in the museum. Many large rooms containing glassed-in display cases radiated outward in circular rings around an even larger room of more glass display cases. Visitors walked through room after room of photographs, placards, objects, graphics, videos, interactive games and audio recordings selected to relate to the words religion and/or gods.

Here is a sampling of the panoply of images and texts displayed in the exhibit:

1 Diaphanous white fabric sculptures resembling oversized cotton balls were attached to the ceilings of some of the rooms to represent clouds.

2 A replica approximately 3 feet high of the Notre-Dame Cathedral Basilica was displayed in a plastic case. (The church itself is within easy walking distance across a bridge on the Ottawa side of the river.)

3 Brightly painted plastic and wooden images of chimerical figures from various mythological traditions, geographical locations and chronological periods were placed in cabinets adjacent to one another. Wings, teeth, claws and swords were prominent features.

4 Depictions of traditional celebrations and holidays abounded. Highlights were grinning skulls and multicolored costumes representing the Mexican Day of the Dead.

5 Familiar words and phrases were emblazoned in large letters on floors and walls. Some were: "light," "places," "life cycles," "birth," "marriage," "death," "body," and "food."

The impression the exhibit conveyed was colorful and kaleidoscopic. That this effect was deliberate and in accord with how the principals wanted religion to be understood is clear from a text printed on a placard that visitors were invited to pick up and read. Elie Barnavi, scientific advisor for the Museum of Europe, asks: "But what is religion?" He answers:

> [It is] too many things, in fact, to be confined to one definition: beliefs and myths; practices and institutions; texts and traditions; places and itineraries; the cruelty of sacrifice and the consolation of prayer; the fraternity of the faithful and the war

against infidels; figures of gods and saints, heroes and villains. It is also a power structure, a trade network, a grid for interpreting the world, a balm for the existential angst of the individual and the collectivity. Lastly, it is a symbolic system, a purveyor of meaning, hope, values and identity ... (Barnavi 2010)

He goes on ... but I'll pause here to state what I think is an obvious conclusion to be drawn from both the exhibit and Barnavi's reflection about religion: there is nothing that anyone can point to that "religion" is not. Whatever "it" is, at one time or another and/or in one place or another, anything and everything that exists in the world and/or that pertains to human beings can be encompassed by the term.

It is important to stress that the exhibit "God(s): A User's Guide" is not atypical of efforts to define or represent "religion." The event in the museum exemplifies the comprehensive, lavish and amorphous nature of popular discourse about religion that also characterizes a perplexing fluidity and lack of boundaries attached to the term in academic writing. A pertinent observation from a well-known essay by Jonathan Z. Smith titled "Religion, Religions, Religious" is "not that religion cannot be defined, but that it can be defined, with greater or lesser success, more than fifty ways" (Smith 1998: 281). Because "religion" is such an open-ended, enormous grab-bag of a category, it can be cited to refer to almost anything as Barnavi's description above demonstrates.

Nevertheless, the European and Canadian governments that sponsored the creation and transatlantic travels of "God(s): A User's Guide" depicted religion as pan-cultural, all-encompassing and largely harmless in order to reflect specific contemporary goals and interests of Western democracies. What can be observed about the strategies and related to presenting "religion" in this particular example can, I think, be generalized to characterize efforts by such governments to both master and employ the category.

The black and white poster used to advertise the exhibit quite literally all over Ottawa was carefully wrought to depict a citizenry that is both diverse yet curiously the same. In the art work, we see photographs of the heads and shoulders of four middle-aged adults: two men, and two women whose clothing and hair styles seem to represent four different but nevertheless identical attitudes toward "God(s)." One woman wears a cross; another a hijab. Both men sport thin beards: one appears to be Asian in some sort of robe; the other, wearing a black hat and a tie is apparently Caucasian. *All have their eyes closed.* Other details are worth noticing: for example, the woman in the hijab, in contrast to the woman wearing the cross is sexualized along conventional lines: she is younger than the other three and free of wrinkles, has thicker lashes along with heavier eye shadow and opens her mouth ever so slightly. The Asian man is clearly smiling; while the assumedly Jewish man is not. An interpretation of the reasoning behind the choices made in composing the subjects as differing from one another would be interesting. However, it is the depiction of their similarity with eyes shut and attention presumably turned inward that I think serves the major didactic purpose of the artwork. The poster seems to say that being a "user" of "God(s)" means that one is a quiet and peaceful meditator who keeps her or his eyes shut.

The photographs' theme of sameness that underlies variation was implied with a remarkably effective technique in an installation of the images in the long, narrow hallway that led from the ticket booth into the exhibit. Four huge copies of the photographs were displayed on the right as visitors entered. The images were constructed to visually morph into one another as one walked past. They were literally presented as being interchangeable with one another. However—the shape shifting had limits: while the Asian and Jewish man changed into one another as did the Muslim and Christian woman; at no time did any man change into a woman or vice versa. A strict gender dimorphism was maintained.

Thus, one central didactic purpose of the exhibit was well-portrayed through the poster and photos extracted from it: all ideal "users" of "God(s)" are alike in being quiet, serene and focused on inwardness; they meld into one another as long as the separation of genders is maintained. Visitors to the exhibit were thus subtly presented with the connection of the category of religion to the delineation of male/female difference.

Another ideological tenet promoted by the exhibit relates to the quality of peacefulness and harmony depicted on the poster. Discordant parts of the history and current practices of various traditions were barely mentioned: the inquisition, the torture and burning of witches, controversies about male and female genital alteration, specific examples of inter-group denunciations and vendettas were absent from the displays as well as any reference to male privilege and domination upheld by "religious" hierarchies throughout the world.

In keeping with the downplaying of any reference to unpleasantness associated with the concept of "God(s)" and religion, tight control and discipline exercised at four panel discussions with "experts" insured that discordant or provocative issues were not allowed to disturb the positive and harmonious atmosphere cultivated by the museum at events arranged to coincide with the exhibit.

At the first panel, an open microphone was set up to allow audience members to ask questions to the presenters. Someone asked whether Islam and women's rights were in conflict. Panelists seemed uncomfortable and, at the next three public discussions, the open microphone was gone and the audience was not permitted to address speakers directly. Instead, bits of paper were circulated on which questions could be written down. These queries were then given to a discussion moderator who chose a few questions to pose to the panel. Controversy was thus suppressed.

In summary, the exhibit was an elaborate example of a popular representation of religion that conveys at least three ideological points that are currently favored by Western democratic governments. *One* is that all religious traditions are basically similar because all are examples of the generalized abstraction known as "religion." *Two* is that all legitimate religions are chiefly concerned with peace, comfort and good order. And *three* is that although men and women might have separate roles, basically all bona fide religions, when practiced as they should be, treat the sexes equally and appropriately.

Another way to describe the entire saga of "God(s): A User's Guide" is that the exhibit exemplifies what is referred to in the field of religious studies as "world religions discourse." This vague but widespread approach to religion emphasizes the sameness of religions, their basic goodness and their common yearning for justice, harmony and compassion (Masuzawa 2005: 320). Since 9/11, versions of world religions discourse have been mined by Western governments as a source of platitudes about unity amid diversity. Once again, my city of Ottawa provides an example.

Each January 20, World Religion Day is hailed in Canada's capital as an affirmation of multiculturalism. One particularly inclusive celebration officiated by Ottawa mayor Jim Watson at City Hall featured musical presentations by a French-Catholic choir, a Mormon Trio and a Jewish pianist. Also highlighted in full color newspaper photos of the event was an Indian dance performance using green saris and jingling bells to signify what Fiona Buchanan (2013) writing in the *Ottawa Citizen* termed "the Hindu faith." The mayor hoped that World Religion Day would make people feel more kindly about the building housing municipal government. "Last year alone," he said, "140,000 people came to visit Ottawa City Hall—mostly to pay taxes and parking tickets. We want to change that."

Other speakers at the ceremony also expressed good will and good wishes. Francois Couillard from the Baha'i Community observed that despite differences in beliefs and practices, religious groups at their core, all "want to live in peace and harmony, and improve the world we live in." Waubgeshig Rice, a representative of a First Nations group, said "our goal today is to share a message of unity and diversity with the hope for a beautiful future" (quoted in Buchanan 2013).

Like the exhibit, World Religion Day, presents "religion" as an amorphous yet benign and unifying force that promotes feelings of benevolence and even a subdued sense of fun in relation to differences among ethnicities that are represented in carnivalesque fashion. Unlike the parking tickets mentioned by Mayor Watson that can stir up resentment toward local officialdom, "religion" as conjured by the city of Ottawa on World Religion Day is a balm that can promote a positive attitude toward municipal authority.

In order for governments to employ references to "religion" to cast the power they wield in a beneficent light and thus to function as a public relations enhancement, the term must be shorn of any connotations about aggression or violence. The foreclosure of violence to groups or institutions that Western governments recognize as "religions" is, I think, key to understanding how the category has come to be used in contemporary statecraft.

Analyze "Religion" in Relation to Governance

Perhaps Jonathan Z. Smith's most quoted sentences are these from *Imagining Religion*: "Religion is solely the creation of the scholar's study. It is created for the scholar's analytic purposes by his imaginative acts of comparison and generalization. Religion has no existence apart from the academy" (Smith 1982: xi). Rarely, in his long and distinguished career, has Smith pointed researchers and theorists in the field of religious studies in a wrong direction. I think he does so here. Although I agree with William Cavanaugh that "Smith's main point ... is that religion is not simply found, but invented" (Cavanaugh 2009: 58), Smith names both the wrong agents of the invention and the wrong place of origin. Instead of thinking of the academy as the site of the discursive production of "religion" and professional academics as primary creators, I suggest that scholars of religious studies ought to be looking at institutions of governments as progenitors of "religion" as both term and concept.

For the last several years, with the collaboration of colleagues and students, I have been developing a theory that links "religion" to ideas about government, jurisdiction, and sovereignty (Goldenberg 2013a, 2013b, 2015, 2017). I understand this effort as a stepping stone to better theory in the field. It is my hope that other scholars will find aspects of my thinking useful in their own work and turn their attention to considering religions as the evolving products of governance.

My argument is framed around the hypothesis that it is useful to think about religions as what I term vestigial states within more dominant jurisdictions. I draw on the idea of "state" as described and utilized in international law as a locus of authority exercising effective jurisdiction over a territory and/or population (Crawford 2007). By "vestigial state" I am referring to sets of institutions and practices that reference former governments as historically based and/or imaginatively elaborated sovereign powers. In general, vestigial states are both tolerated and encouraged as attenuated and marginalized governments within more comprehensive states. However, because they are always ambitious (sometimes I use the term "once and future" state to describe this quality) they compete in varying degrees with dominant ruling orders and therefore tend to be problematic—especially if a vestigial state challenges the exclusive right of the government in which it is situated to control violence.

The locus of management of legalized violence is key to the distinction I am drawing between a religion as a marginalized authority and a dominant state. I draw on Max Weber's work to support this point. In "Politics as a Vocation," he writes:

> It is ... the case that in the final analysis the modern state can be defined ... by the specific means that are peculiar to it ... namely, physical violence ... we must say that the state is the form of human community that (successfully) lays claim to the monopoly of legitimate physical violence within a particular territory ... All other organizations or individuals can assert the right to use physical violence only insofar as the state permits them to do so. (Weber 2004 [1919]: 33)

Weber's observation clarifies what it is that dominant governments (generally) foreclose to what they identify as religions in their midst. Although states vary in regard to what is permitted to the religions they license in their jurisdictions, the right to initiate violence through police or military actions or to enforce a court decision is reserved for the prevailing ruling order. If a religion commits or sanctions acts of physical violence, it is longer unproblematically referred to as a "religion." Adjectives such as "terrorist" or "militant" are used to distinguish it from what are considered proper forms of religion as a classificatory genre of institution, behavior and ideology. The fact that the accusation that "all religions are violent" is used to disparage and discredit religions is, I think, an indication that the legitimacy of whatever is labeled "religion" can be undermined by being linked to violence. Because power over violence is so basic to dominant governments, state-sponsored representations of proper "religion" always stress a connection between true religion and peacefulness. The poster I described above that depicts four calm harmless people with their eyes closed typifies such a policy of disassociating religion and violence; while paradoxically reinforcing the connection in this very disavowal.

While reserving power over violence for themselves, contemporary governments often cede other functions and responsibilities to what I am calling the vestigial states in their purview. Religious authorities will routinely be placed in charge—at least partially—of the regulation of marriage and family life. In contemporary democracies such as the United Kingdom and India, "faith-based" courts pertaining to matters of family law can be permitted to grant divorces, allot marital property and determine custody of children. Economic arguments are often used to support such franchising of judicial services: money is saved when some legal proceedings are handled outside taxpayer-funded institutions. In the current climate of neo-liberalism, activities related to social welfare are increasingly downloaded to state-recognized religions whose leaders are usually eager to increase their spheres of influence by accepting responsibilities for under-resourced populations.

* * *

The hypothesis that religions are usefully theorized as vestigial states has to be tested in reference to specific contexts and histories. Jewish history demonstrates the theory particularly well. I draw on work by Leora Batnitzky (2011), Daniel Boyarin (2004) and others to argue that the production of "Judaism" as religion is a result of the machinations of successive empires in dealing with a conquered ethnic group within their territories. I test out the argument that religion evolves as a technology of governance to a wide range of ideologies and institutions pertaining to Greek mythology, the Bible, Druids, Christianity, and Buddhism (Goldenberg 2015). Although such a panoply of texts, phenomena and time periods makes careful historians, textualists and ethnographers shudder, I contend that because "religion" as a descriptor is being applied to all these contexts, an effort ought to be made to theorize what common process might lie behind the word.

Groups aspiring to have the status and privileges of religions often use narratives that identify with former sovereignties both real and/or semi-fictional. Contemporary forms of Wicca, for example, posit an ancient history in which governments were organized according to the principles Wiccans now follow. Thus, Wiccan covens are imagined in part at least as vestigial embodiments of previous sovereign governments. In a somewhat similar vein, some groups conceive of themselves as harbingers of a better, more exalted government that will arrive in future time. Thus, either a venerated past or a glorified world to come can function as the chronological site for an anticipated alternative governing order.

Nostalgic mention of a deity (that I interpret as a reference to a former idealized though superseded sovereignty) is commonly used to support and justify current governmental power. An example is the 1982 Canadian Constitution, which begins with this phrase: "Whereas Canada is founded on principles that recognize the supremacy of God and the rule of law ..." Thus, just as Canada was marking its independence from Britain by replacing the British North American Act with a home-grown constitution, "God" was invoked to justify the newly claimed authority perhaps in place of Britain as previous colonial master. Another example of the citation of religious vocabulary in a ritual performance of the nation is President Dwight Eisenhower's 1954 addition of the words "under God" to the U.S. Pledge of Allegiance. In this case, the mention of a mystified, more exalted sovereignty was being hailed to bolster and validate the American form of government in contrast to competition from "godless" communism.

The theory I have briefly outlined circumvents the barrier to thinking that is presented by assuming consistent and definable differences between "the secular" and "the religious." Instead of persistent and circular debates about the essence of "secularism" and "secularity" in contrast to that which is "religious," by thinking of religions as forms of contained sovereignty, the terms of discussion about what is religious and what is not are moved to considerations of jurisdiction and authority over law and regulation that place among competing institutions authorized by appeals to venerated and abstract principles. (I understand ideals such as "freedom," "justice," and "equality" to function theistically as the stated purposes of governance.) Some will label the trajectory of this theory "reductive." My answer is an assertion of *au contraire*. After years of immersion in books, papers, conferences, and panels about the supposed differences between "religious" and "secular" that always conclude with some kind of commonplace about similarities, overlapping qualities, shifting meanings and fluid contexts, religious studies scholars should be looking for alternatives. Theories that avoid the secular/religion logjam are necessary at this moment in the history of the discipline.

Keep Gender in Mind

The present critical analysis of religion and attendant categories has, I think, been influenced by decades of feminist theory that has succeeded in politicizing issues that were once considered too private, too personal, and too intimate to be assessed politically. By insisting that "the personal is political," feminism stretched the understanding of "politics" (i.e. the shifting dynamics of power among groups) to include spheres of life that had been seen as somehow natural and non-political. Such a direction in popular and academic thought is likely contributing to the deconstructive trajectory now at work in religious studies: "religion" as term, concept and category, heretofore largely accepted as a given of social life, starts to seem less concrete and more constructed.

In addition to this methodological expansion of the range of subjects considered fair game for political analysis, feminist thought also stirs controversy about "religion" in another way. Because the spheres of life that have been both most relevant to women have also evolved as those most frequently accorded to "religion" as areas of guidance and governance, feminist activists have been compelled to evaluate religion as a central mechanism of social control for over a century (Stanton 1974 [1895]). I suggest that conflicts around and within subject areas identified as "women and religion," "sex and religion," and/or "gender and religion," can be productively seen as related to issues of jurisdiction.

Although dominant states have largely taken away or severely curtailed the military, economic, police, and juridical powers of groups they now designate as "religions," limited governments defined as religions are generally allowed to retain a measure of authority over their adherents in domestic and familial spaces, i.e. those spheres of life considered to be "private." Thus, it is that institutional practices, behaviors and regulatory codes related to women, reproduction, children, sex, gender come to constitute core zones of religious influence.

Notably, an exception to Weber's observation about a state's jealous control of legalized violence, is the regulation of violence in varieties affecting women and children that states are inclined to turn over to religious oversight. For example, faith-based court proceedings in democracies such as the United Kingdom, Canada and India have been allowed from time to time depending on shifting policies to decide cases pertaining to domestic abuse in particular communities. In addition, the cutting of the genitals of both male and female infants and children as religious practice is widely permitted, vociferously defended and inconsistently regulated throughout the world (Arora and Jacobs 2016; Baldas 2017; Otterman 2015). Were it not for the classification of male and female circumcision as "religious," many—if not all of these types of acts—could be described as criminal in regard to the medically documented dangers to children's health and well-being.

The current trajectory of theorizing about the subject areas touching on issues of "religion" and terms such as gender, women, and sexuality is often described in conference titles and edited collections as a "rethinking" of what is presented as feminist orthodoxy that is unduly critical of religion and insensitive to the feelings and convictions of devout women. Probably the text most often cited as inspirational for delivering feminists a much-needed comeuppance is Saba Mahmood's *Politics of Piety: The Islamic Revival and the Feminist Subject*. Mahmood's book focuses on groups of ardently pious women in Egypt who are shown to be highly intelligent people displaying agency and self-awareness. She writes that her work shows "we need to rethink with far more humility than we are accustomed to, what feminist politics really means" (Mahmood 2005: 38).

Unfortunately, Mahmood's work can be interpreted as meaning that feminist criticism of religion ought to be abandoned and replaced with a proper attitude of respect for traditions and ideologies that accord women theologically defined roles and positions. There is a great deal that can and should be said about such revisionism. I understand it in part as exemplifying what Aamir Mufti has named "the emergent orthodoxy" of postsecular ways of thinking (Mufti 2013: 7). In order to keep to the purpose of this paper (i.e. to put forward suggestions for more aggressive deconstructive theory about "religion") I want to call attention to what I see as a new direction Mahmood's work.

In *Religious Difference in a Secular Age: A Minority Report*, Mahmood reflects on how "religion" in the Middle East was placed in charge of family life and sexuality as a result of colonialism. She writes that "religion-based family law is a modern invention that did not exist in the premodern period" (Mahmood 2015: 63). Her extensive analysis of how religion got to be accorded the jurisdiction of sex, gender and family goes a long way to showing how religion and secularity are artifices of government. Unfortunately, as Lama Abu-Odeh points out, Mahmood tends to reify "secular" and "secularity" as stable and coherent concepts in history (Abu-Odeh 2017). I would extend this observation to Mahmood's essentialized understanding of "religion" and "religious." For example, she understands "religious differences" under colonial rule as being "intensified and proliferated" but stops short of reflecting on them as created (Mahmood 2015: 62). Nevertheless, her more recent work demonstrates that the connection of women with "religion" is the result of an extensive political history that goes beyond the contemporary piety movements she extolled previously. By doing so, Mahmood opens the possibility of serious feminist critique about the placement of women's lives and concerns under "religious" jurisdiction.

Although I have focused here on the evolution of Mahmood's work because reference to *Politics of Piety* has become commonplace in the contemporary disparagement of critical feminist approaches to religion, I see the destabilization of religion as a category because of a putative connection with the "private" as becoming more generally prevalent in venues and texts that engage the topics of women, sex and gender. The justly lauded collection titled *Religion, the Secular and the Politics of Sexual Difference* (2013), edited by Linell Cady and Tracy Fessenden, serves as an example. Several essays in this popular book, that announces itself on its cover as a "contribution to the new feminism" argue against the discursive positioning of religion as apolitical and private even though none of the authors extensively engage with work that deconstructs "religion" or "secular." Although this lacuna is lamentable, the authors nevertheless demonstrate how sustained thinking about religion, women, gender and sex inevitably challenges perceptions of religion as a discrete, consistent and coherent concept.

Argue Against "Redescription" and the Slippery Use of "It" as a Pronoun for an Abstract and Mystified "Religion"

Surprisingly, even among astute contemporary theorists whose work explains the inadequacy of the terminology that has so far characterized Religious Studies as an academic field, there is a tendency to defend the continued use of the same vocabulary, albeit in an enlightened manner. Brent Nongbri, in his insightful book *Before Religion: A History of a Modern Concept*, writes powerfully and convincingly about the need for "students of the ancient world ... to work on generating a better vocabulary for talking about the various ways that ancient peoples conceptually carved out their worlds, a better means of describing the clusters of practices and beliefs outlined by ancient authors" (Nongbri 2013: 53). He says that it would be "a very healthy practice" for scholars of antiquity, like himself, to "force ourselves to think outside our usual categories" (ibid.). As the first step in that direction, he continues "it is crucial to understand that this is not simply a problem of finding another concept or word that covers the same ground as "religion," of finding a better word for it. The whole point is that, in antiquity, there never was any "it" there to begin with." Yet, inexplicably to me, Nongbri also states that "I do think the use of religion as an explicitly second-order or redescriptive concept has a place in the study of antiquity" (ibid.: 158–159). Say what?

Nongbri's undermining of his own argument in *Before Religion* is brief and unsustained in his text that builds a cogent case for directing historians to purge their intellectual toolbox of a distorting anachronism. His explanation of why the production of "slightly tweaked" books using misleading vocabulary should be superseded by more focused studies is the central message he conveys to his readers. This direction is effectively advanced in *Imagine No Religion: How Modern Abstractions Hide Ancient Realities* by Carlin Barton and Daniel Boyarin, who state that a central purpose of their critiques of their predecessors is "to emphasize how bound up the very project of defining 'religion' understood as a *project of redescription* is in Christian concepts and categories—and how difficult it is for a Western scholar to escape those concepts and categories" (Barton and Boyarin 2016: 8). Barton and Boyarin recognize that if "religion" is continually reiterated in scholarship even though its utility as a "first order" analytic category is discounted, it will persist in distorting perceptions. They quote Wittgenstein that "uttering a word is like striking a note on the keyboard of the imagination" to emphasize that words are not easily distinguished what they habitually convey. To strive for a more accurate understanding of groups in antiquity, it is necessary to try to use the language of those groups, "and thus to imagine no religion" (ibid.).

As important as is the task of dropping "religion" is from the lexicon used by scholars of the ancient world, the case for curtailing its uncritical use in contemporary theory is perhaps more urgent. Consider this assertion from the concluding chapter of *The Impossibility of Religious Freedom* by Winnifred Sullivan: "religion has proved to be not an irrational, private, and authoritarian premodern relic destined to fade away, but has proved remarkably vital and ubiquitous, refusing the place assigned it by the modern consciousness" (Sullivan 2005: 152). Sullivan's text carefully shows that there is no consensus about what "religion" means in courts of law or among academics. Yet, in the sentence quoted above, she continues to write about religion almost as if it were a living thing, a pervasive, energetic "it" that (anthropomorphically) refuses to stay where it has been put by a reified agent she names "the modern consciousness." Like the effect of Nongbri's work, the impact of Sullivan's writing encourages the deconstruction of religion and attendant categories; however, glitches like this one in her text that seemingly reinstate religion as a coherent and independently animated phenomenon, undercut her own analysis.

If we continue to cite and recite "religion" as if it were a word that identifies something distinct yet paradoxically unidentifiable in human life, we do more than hamper our understanding of epochs of the past. We also impede our ability to see through the veils of ideologies that currently surround us. In order to lift these veils, or, at least, make them less opaque, we should, gently perhaps, point out lacunae in foundational key and current texts and apply a critical rigor to our own writing as theorists and scholars. As I have argued here, part of that rigor will involve a cessation of acrobatic "redescriptions" of religion and the persistent conjuring of the term as a revenant "it."

Use More Specific Vocabulary in the Practice of Religious Studies' Scholarship

"What is above all needed," writes George Orwell in "Politics and the English Language," "is to let the meaning choose the word, and not the other way around. In prose, the worst thing you can do with words is to surrender to them" (Orwell 1968 [1946]: 138).

How could scholars working in departments of religious studies and related disciplines cease surrendering to "religion," "secular" and attendant vocabulary, if they are at all convinced that our field ought to be mindful of the type of arguments to which I have referred and presented in this chapter? One practice I have adopted is to avoid the uncritical and rote use of the terms on which I am commenting. For example, instead of citing "religions" as if the word named a distinct genre of phenomena, I identify the traditions and ideologies that pertain to the particular issue I am discussing. I refer to Christianity, Judaism, Islam, Buddhism and Hinduism even though I realize that these are also problematic generalizations. Whenever I can, I attempt to be even more precise: Lutherans, Evangelicals, Catholic, Baptist, Hasidic, Lubavitch, Sunni, Shiite, Theravada, Hindutva, etc. Perfection is impossible. I acknowledge that all words are to some degree ambiguous—as those who want to surrender to our field's usual vocabulary tirelessly explain to me. Yes, of course. The practice I am advocating does not aim to completely dispel the nebulae which surround all meanings. By naming groups more specifically as Jews, Catholics, and Hindus, rather than as "religions," I momentarily stop propagating the idea that "religion" exists as an abstraction of which there are only examples. The more specific the name of the group, the greater will be the gesture toward particular histories, behaviors and polities.

Relatedly, I make an effort to circumvent phrases such as "religious law," "religious teaching," and "religious differences." Depending on the topic at hand, I try for more precision not only by naming the groups involved in specific conflicts but also by identifying the subject matter of distinctions and disagreements: are we talking about rules concerning Jewish divorce, arguments about zoning, Catholic tenets related to birth control, institutional autonomies, exemptions from taxes, or public policies about holidays?

Perhaps one of the most misleading generalizations in common usage at present is the phrase "religious violence." These two words have the effect of covering over the distinct circumstances and histories that give rise to particular instances of conflict, hostility and brutality. Consider this example from the *New York Times* in an article titled "The Inspiration of Ample India" by Roger Cohen:

India is ample. Soon to be the most populous country on earth, it is home to close to a billion Hindus, some 172 million Muslims and tens of millions of Christians. Cochin is dotted with churches and mosques. Nobody cares too much. There's room for multiple truths. It is this that makes the country such a source of hope. Whatever the errors of policy, and whatever the occasional flaring of terrible *religious violence* [italics mine] as in Gujarat in 2002, the nation's basic alchemy is good–with or without large-denomination bank notes. (Cohen 2017)

In Cohen's language, "religious violence" is depicted as something that can "flare" up perhaps like a forest fire or an outbreak of measles. He separates off "errors of policy" as if the mistakes of governments might be a different genre of causation. The Gujarat riots involved Hindu and Muslim communities with a long history of tensions about property, resources and power. Fatalities suffered from a fire at the Godhra railway station stirred calls for revenge. Narenda Modi, Gujarat's chief minister at the time, faced extensive allegations of complicity; and local police forces were accused of both inaction and incitement. Cohen's thoughtless, offhand reference to Gujarat does nothing to so much as gesture toward such complex and specific circumstances and contestations. If he had used no adjective at all for the word "violence," the text would have been less misleading. By employing the clichéd adjective "religious" to describe the riots, he is implying that there is an agreed-upon explanation for the bloodshed. His practice as a journalist should be critiqued and modified so as to avoid giving the impression that an ahistorical, decontextualized cause for such viciousness might exist. And perhaps if more precise academic discourse were to become widespread, educated and well-read journalists like Cohen would become aware of the need for attending to their vocabulary with greater care. As scholars and teachers who have occasion to refer to phenomena like the violence in Gujarat, we ought to feel some responsibility for urging our students and readers of our work to think beyond formulaic phrases.

Postscript (Slightly Optimistic)

At the beginning of this chapter, I wrote about the bureaucratically driven effort in my department to create "learning outcomes" for our courses. One of the suggested outcomes that caused me to cringe was to "identify key dimensions of human religiosity throughout human history." On the day I started writing, I sent an email objecting to the apolitical language and clichéd reification expressed in this and other goals. I did not hold out much hope for change. But I was wrong. I recently received an email in reply stating that the committee charged with designing the outcomes did, in fact, amend the original text. One of the purposes of our courses will now be "to critique theories that posit, describe, or explain human religiosity as an identifiable phenomenon." This is a minuscule victory that possibly might also be a harbinger of the larger discursive shift I am advocating. Time will tell. Nevertheless, this small, revised text testifies to the type of incremental success that consistent nagging about the theme of this chapter can achieve.

Naomi Goldenberg is professor of religious studies in the Department of Classics and Religious Studies at the University of Ottawa in Canada. She has edited *Religion as a Category of Governance and Sovereignty* (Brill, 2015) with Trevor Stack and Timothy Fitzgerald, and is currently at work with Kathleen McPhillips on *The End of Religion: Toward a Feminist Re-invention of the State* (Routledge). Her book elaborating the argument that religions ought to be thought of as vestigial states is in progress.

References

Abu-Odeh, Lama. 2017. "Secularism's Fault," *Feminist Dissent* 2: 148–161.
Arora, Kavita Shah, and Allan J. Jacobs. (2016. "Female Genital Alteration: A Compromise Solution," *Journal of Medical Ethics* 42: 3.
Baldas, Tresa. 2017. "Religious Defense Planned in Landmark Detroit Mutilation Case," *Detroit Free Press*, May 20. Retrieved from www.freep.com/story/news/2017/05/21/female-genital-mutilation (accessed May 5, 2017).
Barnavi, Elie. 2010. "Conflicts and Coexistence," placard distributed at exhibit "God(s): A User's Guide" exhibition, December 2011 to September 2012, Canadian Museum of History, Ottawa, Canada.
Barton, Carlin A. and Daniel Boyarin. 2016. *Imagine No Religion: How Modern Abstractions Hide Ancient Realities.* New York: Fordham University Press.
Batnitzky, Leora. 2011. *How Judaism Became a Religion: An Introduction to Modern Jewish Thought.* Princeton, NJ: Princeton University Press.
Boyarin, Daniel. 2004. *Border Lines: The Partition of Judaeo-Christianity.* Philadelphia, PA: University of Pennsylvania Press. https://doi.org/10.9783/9780812203844
Buchanan, Fiona. 2013. "Religions Share Unity Message," *Ottawa Citizen* January 21. Retrieved from https://pressreader.com/canada/ottawa-citizen (accessed July 14, 2017).
Cady, Linell E. and Tracy Fessenden (eds.). 2013. *Religion, The Secular, and the Politics of Sexual Difference.* New York: Columbia University Press.
Cavanaugh, William T. 2009. *The Myth of Religious Violence: Secular Ideology and the Roots of Modern Conflict.* Oxford: Oxford University Press. https://doi.org/10.1093/acprof:oso/9780195385045.001.0001
Cohen, Roger. 2017. "The Inspiration of Ample India," *The New York Times* April 14. Retrieved from www.nytimes.com/2017/04/14/opinion/the-inspiration-of-ample-india.html?smprod-nytcore-iphone&smid-nytcore-iphone-share (accessed April 15, 2017).
Constitution Act. 1982. The Constitution Act. Retrieved from www.solon/org/Constitutions/Canada/English/ca_1982.html (accessed July 14, 2017).
Crawford, James. 2007. *The Creation of States in International Law*, 2nd edition. Oxford: Clarendon Press. https://doi.org/10.1093/law/9780199228423.001.0001
Department of Classics and Religious Studies, University of Ottawa. 2017. "Why Religious Studies—What is Religious Studies?" Retrieved from https://arts.uottawa.ca/cl-srs (accessed July 14, 2017).
Goldenberg, Naomi R. 2013a. "Theorizing Religions as Vestigial States in Relation to Gender and Law: Three Cases," *Journal of Feminist Studies in Religion* 29(1): 38–50. https://doi.org/10.2979/jfemistudreli.29.1.39
Goldenberg, Naomi R. 2013b. "Demythologizing Gender and Religion within Nation-States: Toward a Politics of Disbelief," in Niamh Reilly; and Stacey Scriver (eds.), *Religion, Gender and the Public Sphere*, 248–256. New York: Routledge.

Goldenberg, Naomi R. 2015. "The Category of Religion in the Technology of Governance: An Argument for Understanding Religions as Vestigial States," in Trevor Stack, Naomi Goldenberg and Timothy Fitzgerald (eds.), *Religion as a Category of Governance and Sovereignty*, 280–292. Leiden: Brill. https://doi.org/10.1163/9789004290594_013

Goldenberg, Naomi R. 2017. "Queer Theory Meets Critical Religion: Are We Starting to Think Yet?" In Richard King (ed.), *Theory/Religion/Critique: Classic and Contemporary Approaches*, 531–543. New York: Columbia University Press. https://doi.org/10.7312/king14542-050

Mahmood, Saba. 2005. *Politics of Piety: Islamic Revival and the Feminist Subject*. Princeton, NJ: Princeton University Press.

Mahmood, Saba. 2015. *Religious Difference in a Secular Age: A Minority Report*. Princeton, NJ: Princeton University Press.

Masuzawa, Tomoko. 2005. *The Invention of World Religions: Or, How European Universalism was Preserved in the Language of Pluralism*. Chicago, IL: University of Chicago Press. https://doi.org/10.7208/chicago/9780226922621.001.0001

Mufti, Aamir. 2013. "Why I am Not a Postsecularist," *boundary 2* 40:1: 7–19.

Nongbri, Brent (2013. *Before Religion: A History of a Modern Concept*. New Haven, CT: Yale University Press. https://doi.org/10.12987/yale/9780300154160.001.0001

Orwell, George. 1968 [1946]. "Politics and the English Language," in Sonia Orwell and Ian Angus (eds.), *The Collected Essays: Journalism and Letters of George Orwell. Vol. 4 of In Front of Your Nose, 1945-1950*, 127–140. New York: Harcourt Brace Jovanovich.

Otterman, Sharon. 2015. "Mayor de Blasio and Rabbis Near Accord on New Circumcision Rule," *The New York Times* January 15. Retrieved from www.nytimes.com/2015/01/15/nyregion/mayor-de-blasio (accessed May 30, 2017).

Smith, Jonathan Z. 1982. *Imagining Religion: From Babylon to Jonestown*. Chicago, IL: University of Chicago Press.

Smith, Jonathan Z. 1998. "Religion, Religions, Religious," in Mark C. Taylor (ed.), *Critical Terms for Religious Studies*, 269–284. Chicago, IL: University of Chicago Press.

Stanton, Elizabeth Cady; and the Revising Committee. 1974. [1895]. *The Original Feminist Attack on the Bible: "The Woman's Bible"*. New York: Arno Publishing Co.

Stoddard, Brad and Craig Martin (eds.). 2017. *Stereotyping Religion: Critiquing Clichés*. London: Bloomsbury Academic.

Sullivan, Winnifred. 2005. *The Impossibility of Religious Freedom*. Princeton, NJ: Princeton University Press, 200.

Weber, Max. 2004. [1919] "Politics as a Vocation." In David Owen and Tracy B. Strong (eds.), *The Vocation Lectures*, trans. Rodney Livingstone, 32–94. Indianapolis, IN: Hackett Publishing Co.

Chapter 8

Preaching to the Choir?
Religious Studies and Religionization

Ian Alexander Cuthbertson

In Chapter 7 of this volume, Goldenberg calls for scholars to pursue "pushier critique" and to build more adventurous theory to "disturb conventional understandings" of the term "religion." At the NAASR panel at which her paper was originally presented, Goldenberg expressed her hope that we use the panel to investigate our vocation as scholars with expertise in religion. In this response, I take up Goldenberg's call for pushier critique and consider the nature of the expertise to which religious studies scholars lay claim. I argue the academic study of religion ought to limit itself to investigations of how the term "religion" is deployed by social actors with varied social, political, and academic agendas as a means of reifying a presumed but thoroughly artificial distinction between apparently separate religious and secular spheres. I conclude by suggesting that religious studies scholars should reconsider not only the ways we describe "religion," but also and perhaps even more importantly, the audience to which these descriptions are directed.

Religion is a powerful term. The world apparently contains dozens of religions—both "major" religions (those worthy of inclusion in introductory textbooks and university syllabi) as well as "minor" ones. In its adjective form, the term "religious" can apparently be used to describe billions of human beings: the world's 2.3 billion Christians, 1.8 billion Muslims, 1.1 billion Hindus must surely be described as "religious," after all. Given religion's apparent ubiquity, it is perhaps no wonder there are many specialized university departments devoted to the study of religion around the world. Each year, ten thousand or so scholars of religion convene at the annual conference of the American Academy of Religion to discuss religion along with the religious individuals, texts, practices, and objects these religious "traditions" apparently include. But in describing these individuals, texts, practices, and objects as "religious" and in viewing these as windows into "religion" more generally, these scholars engage in a long-standing tradition of their own: the isolation and reification of "religion" as a discrete, unique, bounded, and *sui generis* sphere of human activity that warrants university departments, tenure-track positions, specialized journals, and international conferences devoted to its study (McCutcheon 1997). The academic study of religion often assumes, in other words, that religion is an *object* of study: some discrete and self-evident *thing* that can be described and is therefore amenable to academic study and analysis.

Religion is Not an Object of Study

Before any object of study can be described, it must first be defined. A scholar intending to describe religion or religious texts, practices, objects, etc., must first decide "what things from among the stuff of the world" the word "religion" picks out (Martin 2009: 160). But in defining a particular person, text, practice, or object as "religious," scholars necessarily make normative claims. Whenever the labels "religion" or "religious" are applied, scholars indicate that this particular individual or document or activity or object *ought* to be studied and analyzed as one species of the larger and mysterious genus "religion." These normative claims have consequences. For while, as J. Z. Smith argues, religion "is a term created by scholars for their intellectual purposes and therefore is theirs to define" (Smith 1998: 281), the term "religion" is ineluctably tied to other sources of social and political power (Arnal and McCutcheon 2013: 57). In Canada, for instance, freedom of religion is enshrined in the Canadian Charter of Rights and Freedoms. Decisions concerning what counts as religion (and what does not) can therefore contribute to efforts to determine which individuals and practices ought to enjoy the freedoms set out in Canadian law.

Although decisions concerning the official status (religious or not religious) of individuals or groups are, as Timothy Fitzgerald notes, "policed by forces beyond the academy" (2007: 40), scholars also occasionally contribute directly to assessments of whether a particular individual or group ought to be considered "religious" and ought therefore to benefit from the legal protections and privileges set out for religious groups. In their successful attempt to gain charitable status under UK law, for instance, The Druid Network commissioned a statement by Graham Harvey, Reader in Religious Studies at the Open University in support of their application. As Suzanne Owen and Teemu Taira note in their excellent description of this process, Harvey's report had a "major impact" on the decision made by the Charity Commission of England and Wales (Owen and Taira 2015: 102). Yet scholars contribute to the question "what counts as religion?" in more subtle ways as well. Regardless of whether or not a particular individual or group secures "religious" status under law, in continuing to divide the world into "religious" and by extension "non-religious" persons, texts, practices, and objects, scholars engage in the broader normative work of enforcing and securing inherited distinctions between apparently sacred and apparently secular spheres. While scholars are free to determine which things from among the stuff of the world earn the designation "religion," because this term is "laden with cultural and ideological assumptions and interests" (Fitzgerald 2007: 40), these determinations are consequential.

Recent work in critical religion has revealed some of the cultural and ideological assumptions and interests that underlie the apparently natural division between those individuals, institutions, and practices that typically earn the designation "religion" and those that do not. Critics have argued that the category "religion" depends upon a particular Western post-Protestant understanding of religion's relationship to its constitutive others (the state, the secular); that the term has been imported into geographical, cultural, and historical contexts where no such straightforward distinction between religion and nonreligion exist; and that "religion" is used by a variety of social actors as an "ideological weapon" to further their own particular colonial, political, and academic agendas (Schilbrack 2010: 1115). According to these critiques[1] the category "religion" does not "pick out" or describe an existing, if abstract, sphere of human activity but actively *constructs* this sphere in the service of particular theological, political, social, or academic agendas. Religion is not an *object* of study. It is complex *idea* constructed by individuals and institutions that use the term "religion" to describe their beliefs and activities; by governments and other political actors; and by scholars themselves.

Scholars working under the rubric of critical religion have suggested a variety of ways to address the ideological baggage the term "religion" necessarily includes from abandoning the category "religion" entirely (Fitzgerald 2000); to replacing "religion" with a term that is less shaped by Western distinctions between "religion" and the secular (Balagangahara 2005; Dubuisson 2003); to shifting our focus to the ways the label "religion" is claimed and defended along with the practical consequences these claims and defenses entail (Arnal and McCutcheon 2013). To my mind, the debate concerning the usefulness of "religion" as an analytical category employed to describe a separate sphere of human activity or a coherent and stable object of study is over. No such separate sphere or coherent object exists apart from our categorizations. While tracing the genealogy of the category "religion" is a worthwhile and interesting academic endeavor, attempts both to define and describe religion as a general feature of human life inevitably reinforce the largely taken for granted normative view that religion ought to be both separate and unique.

Let Me Be Specific

How might scholars strive, as Goldenberg urges, to "disturb" the conventional understanding of religion as a discrete object of study that is somehow both separate and essentially different from apparently non-religious spheres? In Chapter 7 of this volume, Goldenberg argues convincingly that increased specificity may help to curtail the reification and mystification that scholarly discussions of "religion" so often involve. Goldenberg suggests that by refusing to refer to "religion" and by referring instead to particular traditions (i.e. Christianity, Judaism, Islam, Buddhism), scholars can "momentarily stop propagating the idea that "religion" exists as an abstract of which there are only examples." As Goldenberg argues, discussions of *religious* freedom rather than freedom of speech and of *religious* violence rather than simply violence reify the religious/secular binary and the interests this binary serves. But perhaps Goldenberg does not go far enough in this productive direction. While I agree that scholars ought to replace "religions" with the most specific terms available and write about Catholics or Lutherans instead of Christians, these more specific categories nevertheless depict Catholicism or Lutheranism as coherent and stable social groupings or objects of study that are worthy of scholarly attention and about which meaningful generalizations might be made.

Generalization is perhaps an unavoidable consequence of our vocation as scholars and funding agencies are typically more interested in what our work reveals about religion or Catholicism or Lutheranism than what it reveals about the particular texts, individuals, or practices we actually investigate. But in drawing general conclusions from our limited data we perpetuate the myth that Catholics or Lutherans constitute coherent and stable social groupings about which generalizations might usefully be made. Even if we only employ denominational categories, I think it likely that our audience (academic or otherwise) will extend our generalizations from Lutherans to Protestantism, from Protestantism to Christianity, and from Christianity to religion in general. By refusing to generalize even to the level of specific denominations we may better avoid the reification of the general category "religion." In doing this we may also severely limit the relevance of our scholarship.

Yet perhaps the social relevance of religious studies scholarship is itself an illusion. The writings of Martin Luther, the sermons of a particular Lutheran minister, and the idiosyncratic beliefs of a middle-aged woman who claims the label "Lutheran" are not relevant to any understanding of the imagined stability of Lutheranism as a thing in the world. Like "religion," "Lutheranism" is a constructed category deployed by various social actors for their own particular interests and agendas. To return to Goldenberg's focus on vocation: unless we understand our vocation to involve supporting and reifying constructed categories while ignoring the messiness and ambiguity these categories conceal, we have no business generalizing from our limited data as we so often do. This argument implies that the work of many religious studies scholars should be classified instead as history, literary studies, or sociology. I return to this point below.

Religionization

What, then, is left for religious studies scholars? The term "religion" cannot be usefully employed to describe a unique sphere of human existence or to describe individuals, institutions, texts, beliefs, practices, or objects as "religious," but it is perhaps not altogether useless. The category "religion" can also be used to describe the ways some humans conceptualize their world. In this sense, "religion" does not describe the essence of an object or an existing sphere of human activity but rather a dominant conceptual or rhetorical strategy: one aspect of our shared "social imaginary" (Taylor 2007). In this usage "religion" does not describe (and thereby reify, naturalize, and promote) a separate sphere of human activity either by asserting this sphere's existence or as a consequence of using the descriptor "religious" to pick out particular phenomena (texts, individuals) or apparently stable social configurations (religions, denominations) that exist apart from their categorization as "religion." In referring to an *imagined* distinction, the category "religion" can be used instead to describe intellectual strategies used for separating human existence into discrete spheres along with the specific consequences these strategies entail. Although religion may not exist as a self-evident object in the world, discursive strategies that rely on "religion" and the distinctions this category implies clearly do. These strategies are not objects, however: they are ongoing processes or *events*.

I am not arguing that the meaning of religion ought to be distilled from its popular uses in contemporary discourse. Timothy Fitzgerald (2003) has already provided a thorough critique of this approach. Nor am I arguing that we ought to develop a general notion of what religion is with reference to the ways this term is cited by various individuals or institutions. Although the idea of "religion" is reproduced through continual bodily, affective, intellectual, and institutional citations, focusing on the ways "religion" is cited risks further essentializing that which is being cited.

In his paper "Thinking the Concept Otherwise: Deleuze and Expression" (1998), Peter Cook differentiates between descriptive and expressive concepts. Relying on a distinction between bodies and events, Cook argues that whereas bodies can be described, events are ongoing and immaterial and are therefore indescribable. A key problem of description in religious studies concerns the ways "religion" is understood to describe a stable existing reality—a *body* in Cook's framework. By investigating the deployment of the concept "religion" as an *event,* scholars can avoid materializing the immaterial and resist reification by denying religion any bodily describable form. By shifting focus to the active, ongoing, and fluid rhetorical processes of "religioning" or "religionization" rather than religion, scholars can resist discussing and thereby reifying religion as some *thing* or body that might be described with varying degrees of accuracy.

Malory Nye (2000) has already coined the term "religioning," but Nye employs this term in a way that undermines what I take to be its greatest strengths. While Nye's transformation of the noun into a verb emphasizes fluidity, Nye also suggests that religioning ought to involve the study of *religious* practices and the ways individuals *manifest* their religiosity (ibid.: 467). Like citation then, religioning might therefore be understood to refer to and depend upon an essentialized body: religion as revealed in religious practices; religiosity as manifested in religious individuals. I agree with Nye that scholars ought to focus on active processes but not as expressions of some pre-existing body.[2] While religioning in Nye's usage describes the ways religious individuals *do* religion, I propose scholars employ the term "religionization" to describe instead the event or process of imagining religion to be both separate and unique. Arvind-Pal Mandair (2015) uses the term religionization in this sense in his exploration of the ways Sikhs engage in "religion-making" or the "reification and institutionalization of certain ideas, social formations, and practices as "religious" in the conventional Western meaning of the term" (ibid.: 120). For Mandair and myself, then, religionization describes the ongoing discursive processes involved in constructing religion as a separate sphere of human activity, one modeled on an inherited Western distinction between religion and the secular. Yet I am interested both in the ways groups religionize themselves (e.g. Sikhs reimagining their lifeworld as religion; Druids re-framing their practices as explicitly religious) and also the ways religious studies scholars religionize those individuals and groups that already typically earn the designation "religious."

Events involve bodies. The study of fluid processes of religionization would therefore involve studying and describing these bodies (texts, individuals, objects). But a focus on religionization alters the presumed relationship between these bodies and the events in which they are involved. Rather than presume that texts, individuals, or objects are somehow instances or manifestations of a stable (if constructed) thing in the world, a focus on religionization frames these instead as discrete components of a larger event that are significant only to the extent that they are imagined to be significant. Rioting also involves bodies. But it would be absurd to imagine that the individuals we label rioters or the actions, discourses, objects etc., that we take to be components of this event are themselves riotous or constitute instances or manifestations of "riot" as an essentialized category. In fact, actions that might be described in very different terms (as protest, assembly, or theft) only gain their significance as "riotous" by virtue of their being "riotized" by participants, politicians, or media commentators.

The practical consequences of this semantic reconfiguration might help to further clarify what it is that scholars of religion actually do. According to this reconfiguration, scholars who describe "religion" as a separate sphere of human activity are *religionizing* and are in this sense no different from individuals who self-identify as religious and make these same distinctions or from government agencies (e.g. the Charity Commission of England and Wales) that adjudicate what gets to count as religion and what does not. Scholars who study instead human attempts to imagine a separate sphere of human activity and to label this sphere "religion" are doing what I take to be the only legitimate avenue left for scholars of religion: the study of religionization as a social project that is caught up with a variety of other social, political, economic, and scholarly agendas. According to this proposed semantic shift there are no religions and no religious texts, individuals, or objects. There are only processes of religionization that refer to *imagined* bodies ("religions," "religious" texts etc.) in their attempts to frame ambiguous phenomena and events as religion.

Non-Religion and Object-Construction

While scholars religionize every time they uncritically label an individual or group "religious," the dynamics of scholarly religionization are best illustrated (somewhat ironically, perhaps) through an examination of recent work on non-religion. For the most part, recent work on nonreligion has proceeded along inductive lines. Lois Lee (2015), for instance, draws on fieldwork and qualitative interviews to describe what she refers to as nonreligious individuals and practices. Lee is interested in exploring secular or non-religious subjectivities in an attempt to determine "what it means to be secular" (ibid.: 2). In her exploration of "the different things that anchor 'secular' experience," Lee proposes secular subjectivities may be "substantial" and may therefore constitute coherent (if fluid) ways of being in the world (ibid.: 58). Lee is careful to note that her research findings are not necessarily representative of nonreligious individuals more broadly (ibid.: 11). Nevertheless, her project attempts to actively construct nonreligion as a coherent object of scholarly scrutiny. This kind of object-construction happens in religious studies as well but because the term "nonreligious" is not used as frequently as "religious" to group together disparate individuals or practices into a supposedly coherent and describable whole, Lee's groupings bring her scholarly "imaginative acts of comparison and generalization" (Smith 1982: xi) to the fore.

In *The Nonreligious: Understanding Secular People and Societies* (2016), Phil Zuckerman, Luke W. Galen, and Frank L. Pasquale draw on a number of quantitative studies to "compile, in one cohesive volume, what existing social scientific research reveals about nonreligious men and women in the world today" (ibid.: 223). Zuckerman et al. take the term "secular" to denote "an enduring attribute or particular *kind* of individual" (ibid.: 23; italics original). Zuckerman et al. describe how and why people become secular (ibid.: 89–106); the personality, cognition, and family behaviors of secular individuals (ibid.: 107–127); secular morality and ethics (ibid.: 146–173); and secular social and political attitudes and values (ibid.: 174–196). Like Lee, Zuckerman et al. offer only tentative generalizations about their constructed object of study. Although they group secular individuals together and make generalizations about their personalities, ethics, and political views, they recognize that "lumping people together waters down or obfuscates important differences between types of nonbelief" (ibid.: 7). Yet while Zuckerman at al. are (at least momentarily) hesitant to lump together secular individuals in order to make general claims about the ways secular people raise their families or vote, this necessary hesitation is far less apparent religious studies. Generalizations about religious individuals or about Christian practices are commonplace even though these too obfuscate not only the differences between individuals who claim the label "religious" or "Christian" but also the scholarly tradition of assuming these labels to refer productively to real and coherent objects of study.

As Lee admits, nonreligion and religion are semantically parasitic categories (Lee 2015: 25). Apparent nonreligious subjectivities are not self-evident objects of study but instead depend upon the *imagined* religious subjectivities against which they are defined and in reference to which they are constructed. But while recent work on nonreligion sheds light on the kind of object-construction that occurs when religious studies scholars religionize, it also involves processes religionization. Discussions of nonreligion (and secular individuals and practices) also refer to the imagined distinction between nonreligion and religion on which processes of religionization depend. Lee admits that it may be necessary for her to defend the study of nonreligion from "critics who fear that it will reify the problematic notion of 'religion'" (ibid.: 26). But while Lee cites Fitzgerald (2000) and McCutcheon (2007) to assert that the category "religion" serves religious interests, she ignores the ways both "religion" and "nonreligion" also serve scholarly interests and agendas. I think that Lee is correct when she argues that the study of nonreligion is legitimate and necessary, not because, as Lee suggests, the study of nonreligion will "provide a way of interrogating the concept of 'religion' itself" (Lee 2015: 27), but rather because work on nonreligion sheds light on the imaginative processes of object-creation and religionization on which the study of both "nonreligion" and "religion" depend.

Preaching to the Choir

My own enduring interest and engagement with the insights raised by critical religion have often been met with mild confusion or disdain. Colleagues in the religious studies department where I teach will often listen attentively whenever I insist that religion is not a self-evident *thing* in the world and then shrug their shoulders and proceed with the serious academic business of studying various individuals, texts, and practices in an attempt to determine what these might reveal about religion as a coherent object of study or thing in the world. Yet If J. Z. Smith is mistaken, as Goldenberg argues (Chapter 7, this volume), in claiming religion is solely the creation of scholars' imaginative acts of comparison and generalization and has no independent existence apart from the academy (Smith 1982: xi), perhaps this widespread reluctance on the part of many religious studies scholars to take seriously the critiques that critical religion provides is inconsequential. But while I agree the academy is not the *only* site for the "discursive production of religion" and scholars ought to interrogate the ways governments work both to produce and police the idea of religion as an apparently separate sphere (Stack et al. 2015), because scholars are also educators they have unique opportunities to disturb conventional understandings of the term "religion."

Scholars are sometimes accused of writing for mostly for one another. Yet as Arnal and McCutcheon note, although scholars working under the rubric of critical religion have contributed much to the project of disturbing conventional understandings of the term "religion," "troublesome assumptions persist despite the so-called advances" (Arnal and McCutcheon 2013: 7). Critical religion scholars, like all scholars, may sometimes be guilty of preaching to the choir; but when it comes to interrogating the category religion, our colleagues in the choir often seem to be too caught up with their own particular academic projects to pay much serious attention. As Goldenberg remarks, the academic study of religion is often inattentive to "critiques of religion as a category of thought and language." The insights generated by critical religion belong, perhaps, where they can most effectively disturb the largely taken for granted notion that religion constitutes a separate sphere of human activity and a self-evident object of study: in undergraduate classrooms.

While scholars may only infrequently intervene in official government assessments of what constitutes religion, as instructors we can help ensure that the next generation of scholars with expertise in religion frame this expertise not in terms of individuals, texts, and practices that somehow manifest an inherent self-evident religiosity but rather in terms of the complicated rhetorical strategies employed by various self-interested social actors along with the consequences these strategies entail. While our colleagues may forever respond with mild confusion or disdain, it seems (at least somewhat) more likely that our students will take these insights seriously. Luckily, some excellent introductory textbooks already exist for instructors interested in disturbing conventional understandings of religion in their classrooms (Nye 2015; Martin 2017). Perhaps the insights generated by critical religion will be most effective not only if we strive for pushier critique, as Goldenberg suggests, but if we remember that our critical approaches belong not only in volumes such as this one but also in our classrooms.

Ian Alexander Cuthbertson is a Baker Postdoctoral Fellow at Queen's University in Kingston, Ontario and an instructor in the Humanities Department at Dawson College in Montréal, Québec. Ian is broadly interested in exploring how the modern category "religion" is deployed to legitimize certain beliefs, practices, and institutions while delegitimizing others.

Notes

1 See Schilbrack (2010: 1112–1138) for an apt summary of critical approaches to the category "religion."
2 Nye seems to have revised his position. In a blog post Nye asserts, "I don't think religion is a 'thing' to be studied. 'It' is not an entity in itself" (Nye 2017).

References

Arnal, William E., and Russell T. McCutcheon. 2013. *The Sacred is the Profane: The Political Nature of "Religion"*. New York: Oxford University Press.
Balagangadhara, S. N. 2005. *"The Heathen in his Blindness …": Asia, the West, and the Dynamic of Religion*. Daryaganj, New Delhi: Ajay Kumar Jain for Manohar Publishers & Distributors.
Cook, Peter. 1998. "Thinking the Concept Otherwise," *Symposium* 2(1): 23–35. https://doi.org/10.5840/symposium19982126
Dubuisson, Daniel. 2003. *The Western Construction of Religion: Myths, Knowledge, and Ideology*. Baltimore, MD: Johns Hopkins University Press.
Fitzgerald, Timothy. 2000. *The Ideology of Religious Studies*. Oxford: Oxford University Press.
Fitzgerald, Timothy. 2003. "Playing Language Games and Performing Rituals: Religious Studies as Ideological State Apparatus." *Method and Theory in the Study of Religion* 15(3): 209–254. https://doi.org/10.1163/157006803322393378
Fitzgerald, Timothy. 2007. *Discourse on Civility and Barbarity*. New York: Oxford University Press.
Lee, Lois. 2015. *Recognizing the Non-Religious: Reimagining the Secular*. Oxford: Oxford University Press. https://doi.org/10.1093/acprof:oso/9780198736844.001.0001
Mandair, Arvind-Pal. 2015. "Sikhs, Sovereignty and Modern Government," in Trevor Stack, Naomi Goldenberg, and Timothy Fitzgerald (eds.), *Religion as a Category of Governance and Sovereignty*, 115–142. Leiden: Brill. https://doi.org/10.1163/9789004290594_007
Martin, Craig. 2009. "Delimiting Religion." *Method and Theory in the Study of Religion* 21(2): 157–176. https://doi.org/10.1163/157006809X431015

Martin, Craig. 2017. *A Critical Introduction to the Study of Religion*, 2nd edition. London: Routledge.
McCutcheon, Russell T. 1997. *Manufacturing Religion: The Discourse on Sui Generis Religion and the Politics of Nostalgia*. New York: Oxford University Press.
McCutcheon, Russell T. 2007. "'They Licked the Platter Clean': On the Co-Dependency of the Religious and The Secular." *Method and Theory in the Study of Religion* 19(3): 173–199.
Nye, Malory. 2000. "Religion, Post-Religionism, and Religioning: Religious Studies and Contemporary Cultural Debates." *Method and Theory in the Study of Religion* 12(1): 447–476. https://doi.org/10.1163/157006800X00300
Nye, Malory. 2015. *Religion: The Basics*, 2nd edition. London: Routledge.
Nye, Malory. 2017. "I Don't Study Religion: So What am I Doing in the Study of Religion?" *Medium* April 21. Retrieved from https://medium.com/religion-bites/i-dont-study-religion-so-what-am-i-doing-in-the-study-of-religion-be2653682feb (accessed April 25, 2017).
Owen, Suzanne, and Teemu Taira. 2015. "The Category of 'Religion' in Public Classification: Charity Registration of The Druid Network in England and Wales," in Trevor Stack, Naomi Goldenberg, and Timothy Fitzgerald (eds.), *Religion as a Category of Governance and Sovereignty*, 90–114. Leiden: Brill. https://doi.org/10.1163/9789004290594_006
Schilbrack, Kevin. 2010. "Religions: Are There Any?" *Journal of the American Academy of Religion* 78(4): 1112–1138. https://doi.org/10.1093/jaarel/lfq086
Smith, Jonathan Z. 1998. "Religion, Religions, Religious," in Mark C. Taylor (ed.), *Critical Terms for Religious Studies*, 269–284. Chicago, IL: University of Chicago Press.
Smith, Jonathan Z. 1982. *Imagining Religion: From Babylon to Jonestown*. Chicago, IL: University of Chicago Press.
Stack, Trevor, Naomi R. Goldenberg, and Timothy Fitzgerald (eds.). 2015. *Religion as a Category of Governance and Sovereignty*. Leiden: Brill.
Taylor, Charles. 2007. *Modern Social Imaginaries*. Durham, NC: Duke University Press.
Zuckerman, Phil, Luke W. Galen, and Frank L. Pasquale. 2016. *The Nonreligious: Understanding Secular People and Societies*. New York: Oxford University Press. https://doi.org/10.1093/acprof:oso/9780199924950.001.0001

Chapter 9

Religion and Description

Daniel O. McClellan

I am grateful for the opportunity to engage with Naomi Goldenberg's thought-provoking essay, "Toward a Pushier Critical Analysis of 'Religion' and Attendant Categories" (Chapter 7, this volume), and for the chance to be able to make a small contribution to this volume. I find myself in agreement with the broader strokes of her essay—and particularly her concern for religion's conceptualization as a mechanism for social control—and so, rather than critique her essay directly, my goal in this space will be to supplement it to some degree by sharing a cognitive perspective on how conceptual categories such as "religion" form and are used, and by discussing how I believe this bears on how religion is and could be described. Central to this discussion is the observation that description is frequently understood as definition, which, I contend, is too often precisely prescription. The overlap of these approaches strikes me as a significant methodological stumbling block for the study of religion today, and engaging it directly will hopefully shed some additional light on the conventional concern for "consistent and definable differences between 'the secular' and 'the religious'" (Chapter 7, this volume) that Goldenberg laments in her essay, and perhaps raise some possibilities for moving beyond it.

I would like to start, however, with an observation regarding Goldenberg's framing of the category of religion. Following her description of the "God(s): A User's Guide" exhibit, she references Jonathan Z. Smith's famous assertion that the issue with religion as a category is "not that religion cannot be defined, but that it can be defined, with greater or lesser success, more than fifty ways" (Chapter 7, this volume; Smith 1998: 281). Goldenberg cites Smith in order to show the category is "an open-ended, enormous grab-bag of a category" that, as a result, can be employed to describe almost anything.[1] While there are certainly many scholars, government entities, and others who exploit both the vagaries of the category as well as the boundaries that have been asserted in ways that serve their interests, these are features of numerous conceptual categories, and religion's "perplexing fluidity and lack of boundaries" (Chapter 7, this volume) is more a function of how our minds seem to construct and use categories than of any kind of problem with this particular one.

In light of this, what I would like to challenge in this response is the notion common in various corners of the study of religion that a legitimate conceptual category ought to be amenable to definition. In the conventional sense, a dictionary definition of a concept, term, or category provides a list of features shared by all the accepted members of that category in a way that distinguishes those members from those of other categories. These features are generally referred to as "necessary and sufficient features" (or "conditions"). They are *necessary* for membership in the category and they are *sufficient* for distinction from other categories. As an example of how this informs dictionary definitions, the *Oxford English Dictionary Online (OED Online)* currently defines the most salient sense of the word "bird" as:

> Any feathered vertebrate animal: a member of the second class (Aves) of the great Vertebrate group, the species of which are most nearly allied to the Reptiles, but distinguished by their warm blood, feathers, and adaptation of the fore limbs as wings, with which most species fly in the air. (OED 2017a)

Here the first segment of the definition provides the broadest set of features *necessary* and *sufficient* to distinguish birds from all other categories: (1) feathered (2) vertebrate (3) animal. Possession of those three features absolutely determines membership in the category. The rest of the definition fills out a clearer picture of the relationship of the category to others, adding other features that are not sufficient for distinction, such as warm blood and "adaptation of the fore limbs as wings" that help "most species fly in the air." Because it is both naturally occurring and biologically discrete, the category "bird" is more amenable to delineation by means of necessary and sufficient features, but the assumption underlying most dictionary definitions—namely that this approach to categorization can adequately delineate all concepts—is untrue. It presupposes a conceptual substructure of necessary and sufficient features governing the formation and use of categories. This, however, is not how categories form, are learned, or are used.

To illustrate this, consider the word "furniture." If you're reading this, you've probably used the word before. Did you have to look it up in a dictionary to understand what it meant? Do you keep a list of the necessary and sufficient features for "furniture" in your head and compare the features of a potential piece of furniture to that list every time you need to decide if something's furniture? The answer to both questions is most likely no (but let me know if it's not!). None of these things are natural because that's not how people learn and use categories. If we look up "furniture" in the *OED Online*, it reads, "Movable articles, whether useful or ornamental, in a dwelling-house, place of business, or public building" (OED 2017b). By this definition, a telephone, rug, laptop, pillow, pen, or coffee cup could be furniture. It's "an open-ended, enormous grab-bag of a category." Someone might say a box of push-pins is "technically" furniture, which in this case would be a way of saying we should "technically" include them because the framework we use for definition forces us to, even though nobody ever uses the word that way. Dictionary definitions are supposed to derive from usage, though, which highlights a pretty significant flaw in that framework and contributes to the prescriptive use of definitions.

So how do we form and use categories? Psychologists in the late 1960s and 1970s who were studying the perception of color noticed that colors tended to have natural focal areas shared by languages and social groups around the world, despite the fact that the color spectrum lacks natural boundaries (e.g., Berlin and Kay 1969; Heider 1971; Mervis and Rosch 1975). Cognitivists began to investigate the possibility that this phenomenon extended to other kinds of categories, and a series of experiments conducted in the 1970s by Eleanor Rosch and her colleagues provided empirical evidence that it did (Rosch 1973a, 1973b, 1975a, 1975b, 1975c, 1976; Rosch and Mervis 1975; Rosch et al. 1976). In one early experiment, Rosch asked psychology students to rate different items according to how well they represented a given category term (such as furniture, fruit, bird, sport, and other broad level categories). The results showed a high degree of consistency in the way the different items were ranked by the subjects, and particularly with those items considered most prototypical of the categories. An apple was consistently ranked as a good example of "fruit"; a strawberry was consistently a slightly less good example; a fig was consistently a poor example (Rosch 1973a).

This led to a great deal of subsequent research that resulted in a model for understanding how categorization works called prototype theory (Rosch 1978, 2011; Lakoff 1987; Geeraerts 1989; Taylor 1995). According to this theory, membership in conceptual categories can be graded. There are better and poorer members of most categories. If I ask you to think of a bird, few, if any, are going to think of a penguin or emu. They're at the periphery. They're even qualified as "flightless birds." We don't call robins "flight birds," they're just birds, without qualification. The focus of category development and usage is the exemplars, or prototypes. Rosch described the process of category formation in the following way (Rosch 2011):

> [P]eople form and use an idea and/or image of the category that represents the category to them, and which is more like (or more easily generates) the good than the poorer examples of the category. That representation often serves as the reference point to which people refer when performing tasks relevant to the category, such as identifying something as a member of the category or using the category in some other way.

Category usage and cultivation is thus focused on the center of the category, not on the boundaries. Boundaries are actually not inherent to most conceptual categories, and so often don't develop until a rhetorical need arises for them, at which point they are often rather arbitrarily established, and on the basis of necessary and sufficient features. Russell McCutcheon has popularized the following example of how this can have real-world consequences (McCutcheon 2013: 122). The Nix family was a late-nineteenth century family in New York that made their living importing tomatoes into the United States. At the time, vegetables were taxed, while fruits were not. Collectors at the port of New York sued the Nix family for back duties, and the case went to the US Supreme Court, where the court ruled in 1893 that although tomatoes are botanically a fruit, they are eaten during the "principle part of the repast, and not, like fruits generally, as dessert" (149 U.S. 304). Tomatoes, they determined, were to be considered a vegetable. So the classification of the "common language of the people" was used to establish a highly arbitrary boundary that rendered the taxes due.

Finally, we learn about categories through experiencing the classification of items in speaking, reading, and in all kinds of non-verbal communication. Categories do not precede usage; they are formed through it. Because that process is based on subjective experience, it is relative and contextual. If I ask an American in San Antonio to think of a boot, most are going to think of something approximating a cowboy boot. If I ask a UK citizen in London to think of a boot, most are going to think of something approximating an army boot, if not the trunk of a car. Our prototypes are different from person to person, from time to time, and from place to place because we develop them ourselves through our own experiences with the world and with language.

From the perspective of prototype theory, then, category boundaries are fuzzy and negotiable, and are often a function of discourse about the category and individual experience with it, and not of anything inherent or native to the category itself. Going back to the "furniture" example, if we assert that the *OED Online* adjudicates meaning and categorization, virtually anything placed in a room or space to be used within that room or space could "technically" qualify as furniture, no matter how ludicrous it would sound for someone to call it furniture in a conversation. Additionally, any furniture not confined to a "dwelling-house, place of business, or public building" would not "technically" qualify as furniture. Definitions can and do sometimes include many entities not usually considered part of the category, and can often exclude entities that usually *are* considered part of it.

This *should* sound a lot like the concerns that people express with attempts to define religion, but that resistance to definition is not necessarily a product of the illegitimacy of the category. It's a result of the fact that the practice of definition requires the imposition of a conceptual framework upon categories that are not always amenable to that framework. So, returning to Goldenberg's discussion, the fact that the category is an open-ended grab-bag is really not unusual, we just normally aren't aware of just how open-ended and fuzzy many of the categories we use are. Ludwig Wittgenstein observed long ago:

> [H]ow is the concept of a game bounded? What still counts as a game and what no longer does? Can you give the boundary? No. You can draw one; for none has so far been drawn. (But that never troubled you before when you used the word "game.") (Wittgenstein 1958: 33)

I would argue that to expect or require definitions or boundaries for concepts like religion and secularism is to depart from the realm of description and to enter prescription. The production of a list of necessary and sufficient features for a concept will focus on those features thought to essentialize the category, and that process is often quite arbitrary and subjective, as Goldenberg's discussion of the "God(s): A User's Guide" exhibit demonstrates. (I might highlight here Brent Nongbri's assertion that scholars tend to define religion as "anything that sufficiently resembles modern Protestant Christianity"; Nongbri 2013: 18). A more consciously descriptive approach, I think, ultimately serves Goldenberg's goal of dismantling the secular/religious dichotomy, but I think it also raises the question of how much prescription is going into the work that we do as scholars. In line with Jonathan Z. Smith's rhetorical point addressed above, it has been recently argued within the social-scientific study of religion as well as within the cognitive science of religion that we need some kind of clear definition of religion in order just to be able to delineate what it is we're studying (Schaffalitzky de Muckadell 2014; Franek 2014). In addition to appealing to distorting conceptual frameworks, these scholars betray a concern for structuring the field in a way that empowers *scholars* to declare where the boundaries of a discursively reified conceptual category are to be drawn.

Yes, such boundaries would certainly serve to more clearly delineate the broader subject of our study, but on a level that fundamentally impedes our ability to gain insight to the experiences and worldviews of individuals, who become relevant within this framework only insofar as they index our delineation of the category. For our conceptual frameworks to serve the data, they must be amenable to the diachronic and synchronic variability of those data, which is not commensurate with the prescriptive foundations of the practice of definition (and particularly in a field so concerned for transhistorical and transcultural definitions). The conceptual category of "religion" did not form upon, and is not governed by, underlying conceptual substructures, but rather is continuously reified within discourse about it.

I think a proposal for moving forward that merits consideration is that of Kocku von Stuckrad, who has advocated in recent publications for a discursive approach to religion (von Stuckrad 2003, 2010, 2013, 2014, 2015). A few principles he develops are particularly relevant to my comments. First is his suggestion that we treat definitions not as tools for discursive analysis, but as *objects of* discursive analysis. Next, instead of defining religion and its constituent parts, he recommends we analyze the definitions constructed within discourse about religion. Von Stuckrad yields to the gravitational pull of the definitional enterprise in trying to delineate the field of study, but he hands the keys to the objects of study, defining RELIGION as "the societal organization of knowledge about religion" (von Stuckrad 2013: 17). Now, he distinguishes the word being defined from the word within the definition by putting the former in small caps, explaining that the small caps "RELIGION" is the discourse itself—the object of our study. The word within the definition ("religion") refers to contributions to a discourse on religion—the "definitions, meanings, and communicational practices" provided by agents engaged in that discourse, including scholars. This is a moving target.

This approach allows scholars of religion to function in a much more descriptive capacity and allows the description of the object of study to accommodate all the fluidity and variability that is realized within discourse about religion in all the different registers in which it occurs. Now, my own specialization is Hebrew Bible and Second Temple Judaism, and I try to avoid using "religion" in relation to those fields precisely because no such concept or term occurs within the literary corpora, but when engaging communities that construct their self-identity around a specific conceptualization of "religion," a descriptive approach, I believe, can and should acknowledge as well as interrogate that usage. Perhaps sustained engagement with the way the use of the term aids specific groups' structuring of values and power within and between communities would even be a helpful topic of study in and of itself that could make it more relevant to discourse communities within the other language registers. That may facilitate greater awareness of the problems with the term and its usage and move—or push—the discussion toward breaking down the dichotomies decried by Goldenberg.

Daniel O. McClellan is a doctoral candidate in theology and religion at the University of Exeter writing on Hebrew Bible, cognitive linguistics, and the cognitive science of religion. He currently works as a scripture translation supervisor for The Church of Jesus Christ of Latter-day Saints.

Note

1   Of course, this is not how Smith reasoned about the category. For him, religion is the proprietary product of scholarly discourse, and its definitions exist in order to establish a "disciplinary horizon," without which "[t]here can be no disciplined study of religion" (Smith 1998: 281–282). The rhetorical goal of Smith's assertion is the scholarly arrogation of the category and its stewardship. As I will discuss below, however, there can absolutely be disciplined study of religion without asserting the sole right to define it.

References

Berlin, Brent, and Paul Kay. 1969. *Basic Color Terms*. Berkeley, CA: University of California Press.
Franek, Juraj. 2014. "Has the Cognitive Science of Religion (Re)defined 'Religion'?" *Religio* 22(1): 3–27.
Geeraerts, Dirk. 1989. "Introduction: Prospects and Problems of Prototype Theory," *Linguistics* 27(4): 587–612. https://doi.org/10.1515/ling.1989.27.4.587
Heider, Eleanor Rosch. 1971. "'Focal' Color Areas and the Development of Color Names," *Developmental Psychology* 4: 447–455. https://doi.org/10.1037/h0030955
Lakoff, George. 1987. *Women, Fire and Dangerous Things: What Categories Reveal about the Mind*. Chicago, IL: University of Chicago Press. https://doi.org/10.7208/chicago/9780226471013.001.0001
Lech, Robert K., Onur Güntürkün, and Boris Suchan. 2016. "An Interplay of Fusiform Gyrus and Hippocampus Enables Prototype- and Exemplar-Based Category Learning," *Behavioural Brain Research* 311: 239–246. https://doi.org/10.1016/j.bbr.2016.05.049
McCutcheon, Russell T. 2013. "'They Licked the Platter Clean': On the Codependency of the Religious and the Secular," in William T. Arnal and Russell T. McCutcheon (eds.), *The Sacred Is the Profane: The Political Nature of "Religion"*, 114–133. Oxford: Oxford University Press.
Mervis, Carolyn B., and Eleanor H. Rosch. 1975. "Development of the Structure of Color Categories," *Developmental Psychology* 11(1): 54–60. https://doi.org/10.1037/h0076118
Nongbri, Brent. 2013. *Before Religion: A History of a Modern Concept*. New Haven, CT: Yale University Press. https://doi.org/10.12987/yale/9780300154160.001.0001

OED. 2017a. "Bird, n2," *Oxford English Dictionary Online*. Retrieved from www.oed.com/view/Entry/19327?rskey=qXu1yf&result=1&isAdvanced=false#eid (accessed March 2017).
OED. 2017b. "Furniture, n7a," *Oxford English Dictionary Online*. Retrieved from www.oed.com/view/Entry/75684?redirectedFrom=furniture#eid (accessed March 2017).
Rosch, Eleanor H. 1973a. "On the Internal Structure of Perceptual and Semantic Categories," in Timothy E. Moore (ed.), *Cognitive development and the Acquisition of Language*, 111-144. New York: Academic Press.
Rosch, Eleanor H. 1973b. "Natural Categories," *Cognitive Psychology* 4(3): 328-350. https://doi.org/10.1016/0010-0285(73)90017-0
Rosch, Eleanor H. 1975a. "Cognitive Reference Points," *Cognitive Psychology* 7(4): 532-547. https://doi.org/10.1016/0010-0285(75)90021-3
Rosch, Eleanor H. 1975b. "Cognitive Representations of Semantic Categories," *Journal of Experimental Psychology: General* 104(3): 192-233. https://doi.org/10.1037/0096-3445.104.3.192
Rosch, Eleanor H. 1975c. "Universals and Cultural Specifics in Human Categorisation," in Richard W. Brislin, Stephen B. Bochner, and Walter J. Lonner (eds.), *Cross-cultural Perspectives on Learning*, 177-206. New York: John Wiley.
Rosch, Eleanor H. 1976. "Structural Bases of Typicality Effects," *Journal of Experimental Psychology: Human Perception and Performance* 2(4): 491-502. https://doi.org/10.1037/0096-1523.2.4.491
Rosch, Eleanor H. 1978. "Principles of Categorization," in Eleanor Rosch and Barbara B. Lloyd (eds.), *Cognition and Categorization*, 27-48. Hillsdale, NJ: Lawrence Erlbaum.
Rosch, Eleanor H. 2011. "'Slow Lettuce': Categories, Concepts, Fuzzy Sets, and Logical Deduction," in Radim Belohlavek and George J. Klir (eds.), *Concepts and Fuzzy Logic*, 89-120. Cambridge, MA: MIT Press.
Rosch, Eleanor H., and Carolyn B. Mervis. 1975. "Family Resemblances: Studies in the Internal Structure of Categories," *Cognitive Psychology* 7(4): 573-605. https://doi.org/10.1016/0010-0285(75)90024-9
Rosch, Eleanor H., Carolyn B. Mervis, Wayne D. Gray, David M. Johnson, and Penny Boyes-Braem. 1976. "Basic Objects in Natural Categories," *Cognitive Psychology* 8(3): 382-439. https://doi.org/10.1016/0010-0285(76)90013-X
Schaffalitzky de Muckadell, Caroline. 2014. "On Essentialism and Real Definitions of Religion," *Journal of the American Academy of Religion* 82(2): 495-520. https://doi.org/10.1093/jaarel/lfu015
Smith, Jonathan Z. 1998. "Religion, Religions, Religious," in Mark C. Taylor (ed.), *Critical Terms for Religious Studies*, 269-284. Chicago, IL: University of Chicago Press.
Taylor, John R. 1995. *Linguistic Categorization: Prototypes in Linguistic Theory*, 2nd edition. Oxford: Clarendon Press.
Von Stuckrad, Kocku. 2003. "Discursive Study of Religion: From States of the Mind to Communicative Action," *Method and Theory in the Study of Religion* 15(3): 255-271. https://doi.org/10.1163/157006803322393387
Von Stuckrad, Kocku. 2010. "Reflections on the Limits of Reflection: An Invitation to the Discursive Study of Religion," *Method and Theory in the Study of Religion* 22(2-3): 156-169. https://doi.org/10.1163/157006810X512347
Von Stuckrad, Kocku. 2013. "Discursive Study of Religion: Approaches, Definitions, Implications," *Method and Theory in the Study of Religion* 25(1): 5-25. https://doi.org/10.1163/15700682-12341253

Von Stuckrad, Kocku. 2014. *The Scientification of Religion: An Historical Study of Discursive Change, 1800-2000*. Berlin: de Gruyter.
Von Stuckrad, Kocku. 2015. "Discourse," in Robert A. Segal and Kocku von Stuckrad (eds.), *Vocabulary for the Study of Religion*, 429–438. Leiden: Brill.
Wittgenstein, Ludwig. 1958. *Philosophical Investigations*, trans. G. E. M. Anscombe. Oxford: Basil Blackwell.

Chapter 10

Perhaps Action Enough

Emily D. Crews

In Chapter 7 of this volume, Naomi Goldenberg tackles two central issues in critical religious studies:

- What do—and what should—scholars do with and about the category of "religion?"
- How do we interact with the ways in which other peoples or institutions treat this category?

To answer these questions she investigates various realms of discourse about "religion"—the scholarly, the popular, and the judicial or governmental—and asserts that, within each, religion is generally understood to be a term with a constant and identifiable referent. In these discourses, religion is treated as "a concept and a human reality" that must be considered and evaluated to properly understand the functioning of any society. Goldenberg resists this reading and insists, following the work of other critical scholars, that rather than understanding "religion" as something essential, "timeless, and universal" scholars must undertake a project of "deconstruction" that makes apparent its constructed, amorphous, and contingent nature. Goldberg's own approach to undertaking this deconstructive project relies on five primary moves: exploring "the politics of representing 'religion' in popular culture;" analyzing "'religion' in relation to governance;" arguing against re-descriptions of "religion;" and using "more specific vocabulary" in scholarship in religious studies.

Each of Goldenberg's major "deconstructive" moves offers valuable contributions to the project of "taking apart 'religion'."

However, it is her second goal—"to analyze religion in relation to governance"—and its connection to scholarly and popular discourses that I most want to discuss in my response. Goldenberg argues that, in the matter of the origins of the concept of "religion," the venerable Jonathan Z. Smith has "pointed researchers and theorists in the field of religious studies in a wrong direction":

> Smith names both the wrong agents of the invention and the wrong place of origin. Instead of thinking of the academy as the site of the discursive production of "religion" and professional academics as primary creators, I suggest that scholars of religious studies ought to be looking at institutions of governments as progenitors of "religion" as both term and concept. (Goldenberg, Chapter 7, this volume)

Thus, in her chapter, and in the book project of which it is a part, Goldenberg is at pains to collapse the boundaries between the conceptual categories of "the secular" and "the religious," and to re-orient critical scholars of religion toward new origin stories for these concepts.

She does so by highlighting the discursive and material imbrication of various structures of governance. She is specifically interested in the ways in which the supposed fixedness of "religion" is exploited by neo-liberal Western governments, and how institutions identified as "religious" in turn make use of narratives of sovereignty. She argues that governments produce, nuance, adjudicate, and obscure definitions of "religion" to "cast the power they wield in a beneficent light" and that "groups aspiring to have the status and privileges of religions" legitimize their power by identifying (or being identified as) "vestigial states"—"sets of institutions and practices that reference former governments as historically based and/or imaginatively elaborated sovereign powers." Religious institutions as vestigial states are given allowance by the dominant government to legally preside over certain aspects of its citizens lives, particularly those that deal with social welfare, while the government maintains for itself the employment and management of legalized violence. Together these seemingly differentiated spheres perform a common function: the control of a membership base through ideological manipulation.

Goldenberg uses, inter alia, the case of the Canadian Museum of History in Ottowa to illustrate this inseparability (indeed, the non-existence) of the secular and non-secular. In an exhibit entitled "God(s): A User's Guide" the museum curates an image of religion that echoes the one crafted and sanctioned by organs of the state, in which all the world's religions are (1) similar, (2) chiefly concerned with peace, comfort, and good order, and (3) characterized by a division of gender. It accomplishes this central goal by presenting both on the museum's promotional materials and at the exhibit's entrance an image of four devotees of world religions in which the clothing, posture, and spatial relations of the figures are nearly interchangeable. Issues of difference, conflict, violence, and exploitation are elided in the face of sameness. This archive is meant to inculcate in its viewers/participants a kind of vague, pleasant orientation toward religion that, in turn, produces these same feelings toward the state—or at least a muted response to its activities. Thus, the Canadian government has attempted a double sleight of hand: first, purporting that the term "religion" refers to some coherent, definable essence and second, exploiting that assumption to argue that religion is a pleasant, peaceful phenomenon, thereby obscuring its deeper and more questionable ideologies and actions.

Goldenberg has provided a rich set of data and questions on which a conversation about method might be built, and our options for how to proceed are many. I would suggest, of these options, that we pursue three directions in particular (none of which are at all original, but which seem to have continued relevance for the work we, as scholars of "religion," do together). First, let us considering Goldenberg's critique of Jonathan Z. Smith. Second, let us think through two questions: is there a way to define "religion" without assuming an inherent substance? That is, do categorization and definition necessarily require essence? And how can projects like Goldenberg's help scholars of religion think about the relationship between the descriptive method and assertion of normative claims?

Goldenberg on Smith, or Scholars versus Governments

As I reference early on in this response, Goldenberg takes to task scholars she feel have failed to critically address the issues she lays out in her "pushier" critique. Among those is Jonathan Z. Smith, whose assertion that religion is solely a scholarly creation is rejected by Goldberg in favor of her argument that "scholars of religious studies ought to be looking at institutions of governments as progenitors of 'religion' as both term and concept" (Chapter 7, this volume). It seems to me, however, that both Smith and Goldenberg are correct. Even if we are to take Smith at face value, as Goldenberg does, it does seem to me that her argument in fact validates Smith's, to some degree, and vice versa. Her insistence upon the imbrication of the discourses on "religion" produced by various institutions of governance shows the ways in which the scholarly is necessarily inseparable from the popular and especially the national or judicial. Smith's point—that the category of religion as it appears in scholarship is not one lifted wholesale from texts or groups accounts of their own behaviors, but rather created in the mind of the scholar—is easily applied to or seen as working in concert with Goldenberg's governments. I have seen this process endlessly illustrated in the work of early scholars in my own specific areas, religions in African and the African diaspora, who provided data and theories about "religion" at the behest of colonial governments, and whose local informants' ideas about such notions were the raw materials for what became foundational studies in the humanities and social sciences. In this instance and in so many others, each of these discourses—the scholarly, the governmental, or the popular—was crafted and refined in relation to one another. In giving dominance to one as a corrective to Smith, Goldberg fails to realize the full power of her own argument.

Can We Categorize without Assuming Essence?

As someone who has been forged in the fires of the History of Religions subfield at the University of Chicago Divinity School, I am particularly predisposed to think that defining what I mean by "religion" is a crucial—and, indeed, necessary—part of my project. In doing so I make it clear to readers and, perhaps more importantly, to myself, what it is I mean when I write, for instance, that my dissertation analyzes "the religious lives of Nigerians immigrants living in the United States." To define and constrain our objects of inquiry seems, at the very least, a responsible scholarly enterprise.

What Goldenberg's essay rightly suggests, however, is that this attempt at clarity might create the possibility of the very problem she outlines—that, by defining religion, we assume, or at least we imply to readers, that there is such a thing as "religion" that we can apprehend, and on which we can pin a definition. She points to a number of scholars, Winnifred Sullivan and Brent Nongbri among them, whose recent work has fallen victim to this kind of failure to realize the full potential of critiques of the category of religion.

I wonder, though, if what many of us intend when we seek to define and explain "religion" is not something close to what Goldenberg is arguing for. That is, to define something as it exists in the discursive constructs that order our world does not mean that we necessarily understand it to be an actual thing in itself. Rather, it is only a reality in so much as the people, communities, and institutions with which we work think of it as a reality, and it is thus our responsibility as scholars to work with (and, of course, against) those realities, producing evaluations that help us to understand the greater functioning of ideas, practices, groups, etc. that take or are given the label "religion" or "religious." I think here of Durkheim and his notion that the sacred exists only in the sense that it is a notion brought to life, as it were, by the assumptions and actions of the social group. The sacred—or in this case, religion—has no ontological status outside the social, and the ways in which it is understood and realized vary immensely depending on that social group and sub-divisions within it. The same might be said, for instance, of gender. To say that we live in a gendered society is not to imply that the gender norms are themselves correct or based in some kind of essential "gendered-ness," but that naturalized assumptions about gender variously, opposingly, and often time problematically animate our actions and convictions.

I agree with Goldenberg that there is a rash of scholarship that operates blindly when considering "religion," failing to parse the many layers of problematic meaning the category has accrued. I likewise agree that this blindness has led to a greater failure to identify and critique the uses and abuses of this category by various authoritative bodies, and that Goldenberg's deconstructive efforts are one step in a corrective direction. However, the task facing scholars of religion, it seems to me, is not to attempt to replace this thing we think we are studying, or even necessarily to follow each of Goldenberg's (or others') specific guidelines, but rather to state clearly for our readers, interlocutors, and selves our own understandings of the term and the way in which those histories and ideas are born out of or conflict with the scholarly genealogies and sets of data on which our work is built. All this to say: perhaps close reading, honest self-reflection, and the interrogation of others who "think religion" in its many forms are action enough. Thus, what I mean when I say that I study "religion" in Nigerian immigrant communities in the United States is that I study an set of ideas, practices, discourses, and dispositions that are understood in a particular way by a particular group of people in a particular place and time, and that my own evaluation of this concept is informed by this and many other communities' evaluations of the term.

Descriptive/Prescriptive

Through its engagement with the category of religion and its role in both scholarship and neo-liberal politics, this paper provides a valuable opportunity to consider anew the descriptive method, which Goldenberg employs to great success and which is, after all, the topic of this section of this book.

Scholars of religion are no strangers to the formulation in which claims produced by the descriptive method are set in direct opposition to those produced by the prescriptive. For critical scholarship on religion, the former constitutes an appropriate scholarly claim, while the latter does not. Most of us are also aware of the numerous critiques of this stark binary of description and prescription, which attend to the many normative values underlying seemingly objective claims and ultimately argue that descriptive observations are never free from normative judgments, try as some scholars might to read, write, and think them as such.

In the first portion of the paper in particular, Goldenberg is acutely attentive to the observable. She treats with care and precision the museum and its "God(s)" exhibit, describing in detail not simply the displays and their contents, but also placards, audio recordings, public relations materials, and even the museum building itself and its location in the Ottawa cityscape. In doing so she is able to convincingly argue for the existence of a normative conception of religion advanced by the exhibit, the museum, and the government. Paradoxically, however, it is this using *description* to unveil *prescription* that she is led to make her own normative judgments about the uses and abuses of religion and its definitions. That is, the treatment of religion as a: a term with a stable, universal referent and b: an instrument of the neo-liberal agenda is highly problematic for Goldenberg, and her suggestions are in themselves deeply normative.

As I see it, this helps to illuminate a major challenge facing religious studies: how to insist upon a general method of description that also allows for the validity of certain normative claims, such that critical scholarship is able both to understand its own frailty and to make normative claims in service of its greater critical project. Goldenberg's paper can serve as an example of such a project, wherein the author advances normative claims (or statements informed by normative values) about how scholars of religion *should* behave vis-à-vis their objects of study and the work they produce about those objects. The normative status of these claims does not invalidate their rigor or that of the scholarship of which they are a part. Rather, they exist in close and generative relation, the normative powerless without the descriptive to bear it up and the descriptive made more powerful by its normative implications.

Emily D. Crews is a PhD candidate in history of religions at the University of Chicago Divinity School. Her dissertation examines the role of religion in its many forms in the lives of Nigerian immigrants in Chicago.

Chapter 11

In Pursuit of a Pushier Study of Those Words We Like to Put in Quotes

Neil George

I warmly welcome Naomi Goldenberg's call for a "pushier" study of religion (Chapter 7, this volume). By and large I agree with most of her stated goals. Attempting to understand the politics of how "religion" is represented in culture is a task that I consider to be at the heart of the field as I understand it, although I find myself disagreeing with some of the claims and suggestions that she makes in service to this agenda. I certainly agree that gender, as well as a range of other socially constructed and heavily loaded concepts, needs to be an important part of how we view the various purposes that "religion" is put towards achieving. Redescription and vague abstractions of "religion," I suspect, make scholars complicit in the maintenance of the systems they purport to study. I also support the use of the most specific available language. Given her wonderful overview of these topics, I want to focus instead on the areas with which I find myself most in disagreement:

1. I disagree with her assessment that it is "institutions of government" that should be seen as the progenitors of "religion."

2. I disagree with any broad application of "religions as ... vestigial states."

3. I disagree that violence is a uniquely defining attribute in navigating religion-secular discourse.

Goldenberg and I are both united in disagreement with J. Z. Smith's suggestion that "religion" "is a term created by scholars for their intellectual purposes and therefore is theirs to define" (Smith 1998: 281). Undoubtedly Smith's legacy has stood the test of time better than most, yet in this instance he goes astray. Although academics may be notable for the sheer quantity of definitions they construct for "religion," there is little evidence that they have ever held much sway in terms of how others have deployed it but Goldenberg is absolutely correct to deny the privileged place that Smith grants to the scholar in the construction of the category of "religion." Scholars of religion may have created more definitions for "religion" than anyone else, but the very fact of quantity reveals little about the word's history or its political implications.

Even such a seemingly straightforward claim as the one made by Smith, however, is open to interpretation. For example, Goldenberg highlights William Cavanaugh's (2009) generous reading that attempts to bring out the "main point" Smith was trying to get at, while other examples of justifying Smith can easily be found, as when Russell McCutcheon zeroes in on a very specific meaning/use of "religion" that he believes would justify Smith's statement (McCutcheon 2007: 188). Without denying that Smith's statement could impart some level of wisdom or be valid in some narrower sense, Goldenberg seems entirely correct to dispute his understanding of who the agents are and where this work occurred.

Instead of the self-reflective focus of Smith, Goldenberg argues that scholars of religion should be, "looking at institutions of governments as progenitors of 'religion' as both term and concept." This move towards a governmental focus is an empirical claim, but Goldenberg justifies it here only in terms of its theoretical usefulness. Assessing this claim requires some sense of what is being referenced by "institutions of governments." In this case I understand the suggestion to be that "religion" is first and foremost a tool created by the government for the propagation and maintenance of government power by arranging social hierarchies in particularly advantageous ways. In a secondary sense, however, Goldenberg may also be using this to reference vestigial states, which could broaden what counts as "institutions of government" somewhat further, but I will deal with this in a moment.

Historical records, however, would suggest a more complex and nuanced history for the category "religion" than as a tool of government. Government is not the same thing, however, as governance. This is an important distinction. Undoubtedly "religion" is a category primarily concerned with the othering of certain people from others, of creating, maintaining, and justifying social stratification. In this sense, "religion" is absolutely about governance. The issue comes instead in the matter of *who* is engaged in the discursive processes of classifying people, behaviors, beliefs, institutions, etc. as religious--nonreligious, religious-secular, religious–political, religious–scientific, etc. This is not as top down of an approach as Goldenberg has formulated it.

When the science–religion binary joined what might be called the pantheon of religion-secular binaries, it was not at the hands of "government," but rather at the hands of those who by some measures might be considered outsiders. The shift occurred almost overnight, going from an essentially unheard of expression to one of the most discussed topics of the closing decades of the nineteenth century with little to no input from anything that would be productively considered an institution of government. The early formulations of religion and science as being in conflict were largely spread by the scientific naturalists and their allies. That is to say, men trained to study the natural world who had trouble getting jobs, especially in specifically academic employment, who spent much of their early careers without any prospects for professorships, leadership roles in academic societies, or funding for their work. Indeed, many historians have followed the lead of Frank M. Turner in suggesting that the rhetoric of conflict was spurred on at least in part by the unequal social and economic standing these men faced in comparison to part-time clergy-naturalists who dominated the faculties, membership roles, and funding opportunities during most of the nineteenth century (Turner 1978; Harrison 2015: 161–162). Without going as far as to suggest that a group of cisgendered white men were underdogs in every sense of the word, it seems hard to suggest that the scientific naturalists, who were clearly interested in the redistribution of authority, privilege, and money, were in any sense government actors. Indeed, it is more plausible to suggest that their rhetoric was spurred on by their status as outsiders to the institutions relevant to their interests, being designed to create rather than being dependent upon the type of authority Goldenberg has in mind. If they are classified as having acted on behalf of "institutions of government," then it would be hard to see that label as anything other than meaningless.

Yet Goldenberg potentially has a way to meaningfully expand the sphere of what counts as government by the inclusion of vestigial authorities existing within the conceived boundaries of the broader states. What Goldenberg here frames as a core tenet of her argument is in my mind one of the least useful things on offer in her generally excellent essay, namely, "that it is useful to think about religions as ... vestigial states" (Chapter 7, this volume). Although offered in a format that would lead many of her readers classify it as yet another definition of religion, this was undoubtedly not Goldenberg's intention, with her stated goal being to create "a stepping stone to better theory in the field," offering thoughts others might find useful rather than wading into the more rigid implications of a "definition." Such a rhetorical distinction, however, may not make much of a practical difference. Regardless of her intentions and desires, inasmuch as the "religions as vestigial states" formulation *resembles* a definition, it suffers many of the same pitfalls that a definition would. In doing so, Goldenberg walks down a path similar to the one she criticizes Nongbri for taking by failing to live up to the implications of her own theoretical rigor. After all, if we are to avoid, "citing 'religions' as if the word named a distinct genre of phenomena," why should we theorize "religions" *as* anything? Indeed, given her stated intention to use more specific language when possible why should we be willing to get bogged down in the vagaries of "religion(s)" rather than focus on more specific statements such as "Group X may be usefully thought of as a vestigial state"?

As Goldenberg has pointed out, there is almost nothing that has not been called "religion," or as she puts it, "there is nothing that anyone can point to that 'religion' is not." By all accounts this seems to be a fairly strong argument in favor of treating the word "religion" as entirely incoherent. Despite this, she makes the suggestion, "that because 'religion' as a descriptor is being applied to all these contexts, an effort ought to be made to theorize what common process might lie behind the word." Whether intended or not, this seems to promote a degree of exceptionalism in regards to "religion," for which there is little warrant. I am not certain that Goldenberg would disagree with me when I say that there is no process behind the word "religion" that is unique to the word religion. Rather, what becomes clear is that it matters what classifications people use, which holds true whether the word is "religion," "politics," "secular," "economics," "science," "culture," etc. Like the rest of the words listed as well as many others, "religion," when used, may confer advantage or disadvantage. In this sense, it may be and, "has been so useful for creating a certain type of social order in Europe and North America" (McCutcheon 2007: 189).

In this sense, Goldenberg is correct to associate "religion" with "governance," although this is just one example of the broader connection between discourse and governance. This, it seems to me, is, in part, a matter of using the correct word, and Goldenberg has not given sufficient justification for focusing on "religion" or "religions" as concepts that scholars should be using to label things. When Goldenberg asks us to consider "religions as ... vestigial states," things become problematic. Either "religions" is a placeholder for "everything that has ever been called 'religion,'" or else "religions" is here being taken to mean a very specific set of groups/beliefs/etc. that undoubtedly bears a closer resemblance than she would care to admit to the "world religions discourse" of which she is so critical. The former is absurd for the fairly obvious reason that "vestigial state" loses all meaning if applied to the incalculably broad range of things that have been called "religion." The later imposes boundaries on what gets to count as "religion," which, to say the least, are difficult to justify.

So how then are we supposed to use "religion(s)"? The simple answer: don't do it. In *The Ideology of Religious Studies*, Fitzgerald (2000) questions its utility, asking, "What extra meaning does 'religious' add?" What is the difference between a ritual and a *religious* ritual? Between culture and *religious* culture? Belief and *religious* belief? As a descriptive tool, "religion" holds no use for the scholar, because the addition of "religion" as an adjective in these cases speaks not to any quality of the thing being described but rather it reveals something about the individual performing the act of identification. This can be seen in Teemu Taira's recent work on Karhun kansa (People of the bear) in Finland, where they fought for and won the right to legal recognition as a "religion," earning certain legal protections as well as economic benefits regarding taxation. Of course, conflict over terminology for advantaging and disadvantaging various positions is not new. One only needs to think back to the popular example of the 1893 case before the Supreme Court of the United States, *Nix v. Hedden*, whereby tomatoes, despite being the fruit of a vine, were declared to legally be vegetables, making their import subject to different rules of taxation.

Yet the concerns here are not simply of the implications of how classifications are applied at the level of group identity. The famous Jeffersonian phrase, "separation of church and state," is part of this rhetoric, which does not just apply at the institutional level. Of course, this separation is a highly productive fiction, which Craig Martin has observed is essentially impossible to achieve, because, "unless the state forbade churches to produce and distribute ideology, to produce conditions of persuasion, to socialize subjects into regimes of normalization and privilege, and so on" (Martin 2010: 164). Separation fails in countless ways, yet acknowledging that a group engages in political behavior is not the same as identifying that group as a vestigial state. There must be a meaningful distinction between those who are directly or indirectly involved in a discourse of governance and groups that resemble vestigial states, with the latter being a very specific type of involvement with governance. There is, I would suggest, plenty of reasons to want to consider "religion" in relation to governance inasmuch as it is used by people seeing to organize society in specific ways to label individuals who are involved in the production and distribution of ideology that helps socialize people into specific political behaviors. There is far less reason to think that most or all individuals/groups labeled "religion" deserve to be called vestigial states.

I am not then suggesting that Goldenberg abandon her work on vestigial states. Rather, I am only concerned to see it reframed, because "classification matters" (McCutcheon 2007: 174). Of course, because the words we use matter, reframing it does necessitate at least some degree of change. I would propose that Goldenberg may find it useful to untether her work on vestigial states from "religion," to move from claiming that "religions" may be productively considered as vestigial states to the alternative claim that some groups existing within the perceived boundaries of "modern" governments may be productively theorized as vestigial states. One might reasonably expect that some but not all of the groups that fit this picture would have fallen under a "world religions" framework, while other "world religions" would not fit as neatly. This makes sense, as it seems it would only undermine her work to suggest that there was anything specifically *religious* about vestigial states.

Goldenberg's approach to examining "religion" in relation to governance also falls short in part because of a degree of myopia in her focus on violence. Although absolutely correct to consider the role of violence in the discursive connection between "religion" and governance, there is ample reason to believe that it is a mistake to follow Max Weber's century-old *Politics as a Vocation* (2004 [1919]) in placing such a strong emphasis on the role of violence, as it wrongfully shifts the focus away from a range of concepts that are important within "modern" discourse.

Goldenberg argues that, "Because power over violence is so basic to dominant governments, state-sponsored representations of proper 'religion' always stress a connection between true religion and peacefulness." Although the absolute nature of this formulation whereby this *always* happens may be up for debate, it is entirely reasonable to suggest that a religion-violence binary plays an important part in mediating the role of "religion"-identified groups. Examples such as "God(s): A User's Guide," are incredibly common and can be found almost anywhere. Of course, not all representations suggest that "true" religion is necessarily distinct from violence, but rather "true" religion is inherently violent and therefore illegitimate. Although a far less common position, it nonetheless reinforces the same suggestion that "true" religion can be legitimate only insofar as it is not violent. Goldenberg, then, is not wrong to give emphasis to the role of violence in the discursive construction of the religion-secular dichotomy, but rather the assumption that violence is somehow unique or more essential than a range of other terms such as "politics," "economics," or "science."

A quick examination of the rhetoric present in discourse on the intersection of "religion" which each of these categories quickly reveals significant similarities.

Identifications of "true" religion as something separate from the pursuit of monetary gain are hardly rarer than those discussing "religion" and violence. After all, money is a fairly direct and clear symbol for the supposedly "secular" world that "true" religion is supposed to be removed from (see Arnal and McCutcheon 2013: 67). One may also consider the strong reactions against creationism/intelligent design within the scientific community, the general public, and the opposition such perceived incursions on "true" science have received from the courts, who have been willing to help police these boundaries.

These similarities are more than surface deep and point to similar functionality in how all of these terms, like violence, are constructed so as to continually reinforce the more basic religious-secular distinction. In other words, violence is just one pillar of a far more robust discursive construction that creates a taken-for-granted appearance to "religion" as a private and apolitical domain that has little purchase on the day-to-day of human life. If this is true, then it is undoubtedly overstating the case to say that, "the foreclosure of violence to groups or institutions that Western governments recognize as 'religions' is ... key to understanding how the category has come to be used in contemporary statecraft" (Goldenberg, Chapter 7, this volume). Indeed, rather than violence serving as a unique way of distinguishing, "a marginalized authority and a dominant state," it may be the case that the authority of these "vestigial states" is actually undermined by the types of responsibilities that governments are sometimes willing to download onto these groups, rather than by the ones that they withhold, but that is somewhat more speculative.

To stay grounded in a concrete example, let us further consider the rise of the science–religion binary as a way of fleshing out its similarity to religion–violence discourse. The so-called "conflict thesis," also known as the warfare thesis, the military metaphor, and the Draper–White thesis, arose primarily in the 1860s and 1870s, with few doing more to spur it on that John William Draper and Andrew Dickson White, who published their massive retellings of history in terms of a seemingly cosmic struggle between "science" and "religion," which often rang a slightly different note than their previous work, suggesting how new the distinction was even to them. It is likely that its popularity was in part dependent upon how well it was absorbed into the broader discourse on the "religious" and "secular."

In the preface of his *History of the Conflict Between Religion and Science*, Draper wrote:

> The history of Science is not a mere record of isolated discoveries; it is a narrative of the conflict of two contending powers, the expansive force of the human intellect on one side, and the compression arising from traditionary faith and human interests on the other. (Draper 1875: vi)

Despite this statement, he had written his lengthy *History of the Intellectual Development of Europe*, where, despite a similarly Whiggish view of history, the binary construction of religion–science is entirely absent. It was not until he wrote his *History of Conflict* as part of the *International Scientific Series*, a book series designed to promote the ideas of the scientific naturalists that the science–religion dichotomy reared its head in his writings.

He succeeded, however, in using the distinction to great effect, connecting it with the anti-Catholicism of his day, and arguing that there was a meaningful distinction between the "dogmatic theology" of Catholicism and the "private interpretation" of Protestants. He cashes in on the notion of *private* interpretation in ways that were unacceptable to most Christians, using it to dismiss miracles, revelation, and political or scientific involvement, yet nonetheless created a discursive strategy that would elevate "science" while delegitimizing "religion" within another discursive domain. Likewise, according to White, the problem arose because in the past, more primitive societies required that their, "moral and spiritual teachings ... be inclosed in myth, legend, and parable" (White 1955: 263). It is this encasement, these cultural entrapments, that cause the problem. Fortunately, White suggests, these have nothing to do with "true" religion. Both of them embrace this concept of "true" religion, a core essence that could not be touched by the advancing tide of scientific discovery and which was perfectly acceptable for all. This "true" religion amounted to a vague moral code that had few concrete principles and even fewer ways to lead to action.

Even those who opposed their framing of "religion" and "science" as being in conflict embraced the idea of an essential core that was simultaneously invaluable and innocuous. For example, the Canadian geologist and former president of McGill University, John William Dawson (1820–1899), denied conflict by claiming that, "true religion, which consists in practical love to God and to our fellow-men, can have no conflict with true science" (Dawson 1876: 73). The ultimate outcome was that many people, whether they believed "religion" and "science" existed in conflict, harmony, or independence, accepted the notion that "true" religion was private, untouchable by the knowledge claims of science because it had no knowledge claims of its own at its "core." Such language might not have been entirely unique to discussions of "science" and "religion," but science–religion discourse did much to advance the privatization of "religion" and the "secularization" of the "scientific" and the "public." When thought of in relation to the discursive relationship between "religion" and violence, little difference emerges. Indeed, when thinking about Goldenberg's example of "God(s): A User's Guide," its portrayal of "religion" as otherworldly works equally well to show religion as something separate from violence, science, politics, and economics. There is nothing particularly unique about the place of violence in sustaining the religious-secular dichotomy.

There is a rich legal history surrounding the policing of the boundaries of the science–religion dichotomy. The most notable of these cases was the so-called "Monkey Trial" of 1925, where John Scopes was convicted for supposedly teaching evolution in a Tennessee classroom, which inspired the play (1955) and then movie (1960) *Inherit the Wind*. Especially notable in the legal history of "science and religion" was the 1981 case *Seagraves v. California*. In writing his decision, Superior Court Justice Irving H. Perluss wrote that no religious rights were infringed by the teaching of evolution because, "science emphasizes 'how' and not 'ultimate cause' for origins" (June 12, 1981). *McLean v. Arkansas Board of Education* offered a detailed definition of "science" and explanation as to why "creation science" does not meet the criteria for true "science," failing on at least four of the five benchmarks laid out in the decision: guided by natural law, explanatory, testable against the empirical world, and falsifiable.

None of this, however, should do much to diminish Goldenberg's well-thought-out attempt to advance a "pushier" study of "religion." In large part the issues present are often a result of a myopic focus that needs expanding rather than comprehensive change. Such expansion, however, does offer the potential for a far richer picture of how the concept of "religion" has been used and abused for the benefit of some over others, even if it may also mean that some of her suggestions that she hoped would be helpful turn out to be less important than may have been thought. All that said, it is becoming increasingly clear that the study of "religion" will be just fine without "religion," and Goldenberg should be applauded for her work towards that end.

Neil George is a Ph.D. candidate at York University. His research focuses on discourses of "religion," especially as constructed in relation to "science" from the nineteenth century onwards.

References

Arnal, William E. and Russell T. McCutcheon. 2013. *The Sacred is the Profane: The Political Nature of "Religion."* New York: Oxford University Press.

Cavanaugh, William T. 2009. *The Myth of Religious Violence: Secular Ideology and the Roots of Modern Conflict.* New York: Oxford University Press. https://doi.org/10.1093/acprof:oso/9780195385045.001.0001

Dawson, J. W. 1876. "The So-Called 'Conflict of Science and Religion'," *Popular Science Monthly* 10 November: 72–74.

Draper, John William. 1875. *History of the Conflict Between Religion and Science.* London: Henry S. King and Co.

Fitzgerald, Timothy. 2000. *The Ideology of Religious Studies.* New York: Oxford University Press.

Harrison, Peter. 2015. *The Territories of Science and Religion.* Chicago, IL: University of Chicago Press. https://doi.org/10.7208/chicago/9780226184517.001.0001

Martin, Craig. 2010. *Masking Hegemony: A Genealogy of Liberalism, Religion and the Private Sphere.* London: Equinox.

McCutcheon, Russell T. 2007. "'They Licked the Platter Clean': On the Co-Dependency of the Religious and The Secular," *Method and Theory in the Study of Religion* 19: 173–199.

Smith, Jonathan Z. 1998. "Religion, Religions, Religious," in Mark C. Taylor (ed.), *Critical Terms for Religious Studies*, 269–284. Chicago, IL: University of Chicago Press.

Taira, Teemu, and Breann Fallon. 2016. "Categorizing 'Religions': From Case Studies to Methodology," The Religious Studies Project, September 19. Retrieved from www.religiousstudiesproject.com/podcast/categorising-religion-from-case-studies-to-methodology (accessed February 26, 2018).

Turner, Frank M. "The Victorian Conflict between Science and Religion: A Professional Dimension," *Isis* 69. 1978: 356–376. https://doi.org/10.1086/352065

Weber, Max. 2004 [1919]. "Politics as a Vocation," in David Owen and Tracy B. Strong (eds.), *The Vocation Lectures*, trans. Rodney Livingstone, 32–94. Indianapolis, IN: Hackett Publishing Company.
White, Andrew D. 1955. *A History of the Warfare of Science with Theology in Christendom*. New York: George Braziller.

Chapter 12

Response to the Responses

Naomi Goldenberg

The thoughtful and well-crafted responses by Emily Crews, Ian Cuthbertson, Neil George and Daniel McClellan to my essay (Chapter 7, this volume) demonstrate the provocative and wide-ranging analysis that is being done by contemporary religious studies scholars. Each commentary has caused me to think somewhat differently about my current project of theorizing religion in relation to governance; and each is influencing me as I plan future writing. Here is what I have learned:

1. In discussions of description, definition and deconstruction of the category of religion, it is important to emphasize that the concept designates nothing that is unique and separable from spheres of life and thought that can be and are designated with other terms that are more approachable discursively. "Religion" often functions as a word that stops critical thought about history and context. Crews (Chapter 10, this volume) leads me to think that it is necessary to further stress this point. She asks: "is there a way to define 'religion' without assuming an inherent substance?" Whether or not there is such a way I am more concerned with what the label does in current usage—namely to claim and to create an illusory distinction that discourages analysis. To varying degrees, whatever is designated "religion" leads to reification that can paralyze thought. The objective of my deconstructive project is to take apart any discursive walling off of "religion" from the *stürm und drang* of contingencies of struggles for influence, power, and resources.

2. Although, to one extent or another, definitions of all words—such as "bird" or "furniture" to use two of McClellan's examples (Chapter 9, this volume)—are imprecise and mutable, the consequences of such wooliness differ widely. I ought to clarify better that I understand that the ways in which central terms of our discipline are institutionalized and used politically are far more crucial than any linguistic or morphological conundrum. I am concerned that the incoherence of "religion" as a term and concept is particularly significant because "religion" is accorded special status in laws and foundational national documents such as constitutions. Because

the amorphousness and instability of "religion" is to date generally unrecognized in popular, legal and academic discourses, granting exclusive rights, privileges, restrictions and protections to ideas, institutions, practices and texts labeled as "religion" is uniquely problematic. As "religions" proliferate globally and gain influence as authoritative bodies, I think that it becomes ever more important for us as scholars to address the definitional void at the heart of our field. Ornithologists explaining the evolution of similarities and differences between sparrows and ostriches have another calling.

3 Theorizing religions as vestigial states will continue to be a focus of my work despite George's criticism (Chapter 11, this volume). I urge him to give this part of my work a closer reading—particularly as it relates to Weber's insight about a state's interest in maintaining a monopoly on physical violence. Nevertheless, I take George's point that I have not so far addressed the "incalculably broad range of things that have been called "religion." I have been wary of extending my argument about religion as a technology of governance too far. However, despite its protean and kaleidoscopic usages, whenever "religion" is cited, I have begun to think that it is meant as a gesture toward principles of power, regulation and control. In short, the word and its cognates now imply attitudes and practices of making order whether in regard to public institutions or to intimate feelings, habits, thoughts, actions and "ways of living." I might well mine previous scholarship that picks up this theme in order to elaborate the connection of religion understood as a term and concept that has emerged out of the history of statecraft with the idea of governance more capaciously conceived.

4 I intend to cite Cuthbertson's account (Chapter 8, this volume) that explains "religionizing" as a productive direction for religious studies' scholarship. I agree heartily with his proposal for a "semantic shift" that would turn away from treating religions as prediscursive phenomena in favor of exploring how, why and to what ends organizations, behaviors, events, people, texts and objects become classified as "religious." All the work (including my own) that is sometimes called "critical religion" adheres to such an approach.

I find it important that Crews and McClellan appear to voice an unease with the implications of such a method by their mention of communities with whom they interact. Crews writes that the members of the group in which she does her research understand themselves "in a particular way ... in a particular place and time." She and McClellan seem to imply that a critical attitude toward religion as a concept would challenge a group's self-description and perhaps interfere with channels of communication. Yet both opt for transparency. Crews does not want to replace "religion" as a descriptor; but rather recommends being clear about "our own understandings of the term." McClellan raises the possibility that communities' "self-identity" as religions might be questioned as well as acknowledged. I think such suggestions have merit and ought to be elaborated. Self-understandings are the result of the repeated citation of multiple discourses that carry contemporary social, cultural, and political valence. Every particularity of time and space is contingent on history and circumstance. Because we all speak, think and live within ideas that both restrict and enable us, we might think of our work as scholars as articulating as much as we can about the narratives—such as "religionizing" in which we are all enmeshed.

Naomi Goldenberg is professor of religious studies in the Department of Classics and Religious Studies at the University of Ottawa in Canada. She has edited *Religion as a Category of Governance and Sovereignty* (Brill, 2015) with Trevor Stack and Timothy Fitzgerald and is currently at work with Kathleen McPhillips on *The End of Religion: Toward a Feminist Re-invention of the State* (Routledge). Her book elaborating the argument that religions ought to be thought of as vestigial states is in progress.

Part III

Chapter 13

Explanation and the Study of Religion

Egil Asprem and Ann Taves

Introduction

The rise of the evolutionary and cognitive science of religion in the last two decades has sparked a resurgence of interest in explaining religion. Predictably, these efforts have prompted rehearsals of longstanding debates over whether religious phenomena can or should be explained in nonreligious terms. Little attention has been devoted to the nature of explanation, methods of explanation, or what should count as an adequate explanation.

The lack of attention to explanation is further aggravated by a concomitant lack of attention to what we mean by theory in the study of religion. As has been the case in anthropology (Ellen 2010), we routinely discuss theories of religion without discussing what counts as a theory. For some, theory is associated with the range of classical and contemporary theories of religion included in introductory texts (see for example Pals 2014 or Stausberg 2009). For others, including many in the humanities, theory is associated with "critical theory," of either the literary or social science variety.

As Stausberg (2009: 2-3) indicates, there are, however, many competing views of and controversies over the meaning of theory in the different sciences and disciplines. For our purposes, it is enough to note (1) the distinction between the colloquial and scientific definitions of the term and (2) the intimate connection between scientific theories and explanation. The *American Heritage Dictionary* (as cited by Reznick 2010: 220) makes the basic distinction we will presume here. Colloquially, theory typically refers to abstract reasoning, speculation, hypothesis or supposition. In the sciences, however, it refers to "systematically organized knowledge applicable in a relatively wide variety of circumstances; especially, a system of assumptions, accepted principles, and rules of procedure divided to analyze, predict, or otherwise explain the nature or behavior of a specified set of phenomena" (ibid.). Scientific theories, in other words, seek to "explain the nature or behavior of a specified set of phenomena … [in light of] a system of assumptions, accepted principles, and rules of procedure" (ibid.). Whether the theories have been viewed as scientific or not, much of the debate regarding explanation in religious studies has centered on two issues, one explicit and the other not: (1) the debate over reductionism, i.e., whether theories of religion can or should explain religion in nonreligious terms, and (2) a tacit debate over "scientism," i.e., over whether anything resembling scientific methods and lines of theorizing is desirable or possible in the humanities (see for example Stenmark 1997).

In what follows, we assume the legitimacy of attempts to explain religious phenomena in nonreligious terms in light of the assumptions, principles and rules of procedure in the social and natural sciences. Building on Proudfoot's (1985) distinction between descriptive and explanatory reduction, we presuppose the legitimacy and importance of the latter. We will directly engage the issue of "scientism," which we view as a dismissive term typically directed at perceived over-extensions of scientific inquiry, through our discussion of historical and contemporary explanation in the philosophy of science. In doing so, we want to make the point that there are various views of explanation in the sciences, some of which we consider more appropriate for explaining socioculturally-informed human behavior than others. Specifically, we argue that the *new mechanistic-causal approach* commonly presupposed in the "special sciences" (biology, the neurosciences, and psychology), referred to by philosophers of science as "*the new mechanism*," can be extended to the study of religion following the lead of researchers who are extending it to the social sciences.

Our aim in making this case is, first, to move the discussion in religious studies beyond general worries about "reductionism" and "scientism" (or "positivism") and, second, to ground theorizing about human experience in a broadly evolutionary base. We do so recognizing that any discussion of mechanisms in the social sciences and history must take account of complexities typically not encountered (or dealt with) in the natural sciences. Our goal, in other words, is not to subsume or subordinate the humanities to the natural and social sciences, but to connect them in a spirit of consilience (Slingerland and Collard 2011).

In the sections that follow, we will discuss explanation in theories of religion (§1), the nature and limitations of the "old mechanism" and other older approaches to explanation in the philosophy of science (§2), and how the "new mechanism" overcomes these difficulties (§3). Throughout this discussion we will highlight the complexities that will need to be addressed in extending the new mechanist approach to explanation to the humanistic social sciences.

1 Explanation in Theories of Religion

"Explanation" has several different meanings in ordinary English (Craver 2014: 30–35):

1. It can refer to a communicative act. The professor explained (communicates) the material to her students. The text explains (communicates) what you need to know.

2. It can refer to a cause or a factor that produces a phenomenon.

3. It can refer to a mental representation or model of the causes that produce a phenomenon. The model explains (represents) the (causal) explanation.

Explanations in the first and third senses are known as *epistemic* explanations. They involve humans or other intentional creatures trying to communicate ("explain") something to an audience. Explanations in the second sense are known as *ontic* explanations. They presuppose a view of reality (an ontology) which assumes that certain entities and processes exist in the world "whether or not anyone discovers or describes them" (Salmon 1989: 133, quoted in Craver 2014: 31), and assumes that there exist ontic structures (e.g. mechanisms and causes) that explain the production and behavior of various phenomena.

1.1 Theories of Religion

Explanation in the second sense allows us to distinguish between phenomenological and explanatory models. Phenomenological models describe or redescribe (i.e., interpret) a phenomenon "without revealing the ontic structures that produce it" (Craver 2014: 40). We can distinguish three broad types of theories:

1   Phenomenological theories of religion.

2   Supernaturalistic causal theories of religion.

3   Naturalistic causal theories of religion.

Phenomenological theories of religion, associated historically with figures such as Chantepie de la Saussaye, Otto, Kristensen, van der Leeuw and, more recently, with Ninian Smart and Mircea Eliade, are only loosely connected with philosophical phenomenologists, such as Husserl, Heidegger, Sartre, and Merleu-Ponty. All, however, give priority to human experience from the first person point of view (Smith 2013). Some who hold to this approach bracket their own ontological views and limit themselves to describing or interpreting the ontological claims of their subjects. Such theories, typically characterized as *phenomenological or interpretive (hermeneutical)*, describe the causal explanations of those they study, but refrain from offering causal explanations (i.e., ontic claims) of their own.

Phenomenological bracketing has given rise to "methodological agnosticism" (see for example Porpora 2006), which we, like others (Martin forthcoming), find problematic. We do however endorse the idea of a first step in which researchers *temporarily* hold back their own explanations in order to describe the phenomenon one wants to explain and avoid descriptive reduction (see discussion of Proudfoot below).

In so far as the phenomenological is construed as the *only step*, however, it is tied to the notion of religion as a sui generis phenomenon. This view holds that to the extent that religion *can* be explained, it must be explained "on its own terms," that is, it cannot be reduced to something that is not religion. The simplest version of sui generis theorizing holds simply that, in Daniel Pals's words, "one ought to accord them [religious phenomena] a certain independence" from other human activities and experiences (Pals 1987: 259). Thus one can explain religious phenomena in terms presumed to be internal to the religious field (e.g., "the holy," "the sacred," "mana," or "power"), but not in terms of "external" factors, such as social alienation, latent neuroses, or evolved cooperative strategies. We question whether such internal explanations are explanations at all. Worse still, as it seeks such "internal" explanations, the sui generis approach has often developed into forms of crypto-theology that essentially produce supernaturalistic causal explanations.

Supernaturalistic causal theories of religion are premised on the idea that not only is religion a thing apart, but this thing is ultimately rooted in an ontologically real dimension of sacrality, transcendence, or the supernatural. In so far as phenomenological theorists of religion (e.g., Otto, van der Leeuw, Eliade) *embrace* the ontological claims they are describing as sui generis, their theories take on an implicit or explicit supernaturalist quality. These theories postulate the existence of an ontologically real religious reality that humans respond to but do not create. These theories implicitly or explicitly include this ontological reality as a potential factor in their *causal explanations* of events. In a sense, they reverse the order of explanation: Instead of mundane events in the material world explaining the emergence and activities of "religions," the manifestation of "religious" power explains events in the mundane world such as revelations, sacred place, or charismatic authority.

Naturalistic causal theories of religion offer (reductionistic) explanations based on language or discourse (literary and cultural theories), collective processes (social theories), mental processes (cognitive theories), and/or biological processes (evolutionary theories). Some theorists want to limit their explanations to one type of cause or privilege one type of cause over the others. Others view these causes as interacting and want to figure out how they are related. In current practice, however, the boundary between phenomenological and naturalistic causal theories of religion is blurry because, on the one hand, scholars are not clear on the distinction between description, interpretation, and explanation and are worried about appearing reductionistic, scientistic, or positivist, on the other.

Ontologically, there is a divide between those who view (scientific) explanations as being grounded in mind- and language-independent structures in the world (realists) and those that view (scientific) explanations as entirely contingent on communicative processes, with only an arbitrary relation to a language-independent world (constructionists). In light of our definitions of explanation above, realists are after ontic explanations, while constructionists typically insist that epistemic explanations are all we've got and "the best we can do is contribute intelligently to the conversations of our time" (von Stuckrad 2010: 158). While we acknowledge the importance and value of constructionist explanations, we agree with theorists like Engler (2004) and Hjelm (2014), who emphasize that constructionism does *not* preclude realism or entail radical relativism. Thus we prefer to locate constructionist approaches within a critical naturalistic (and hence realist) framework (see Asprem 2014: 80–86), premised on the view that humans evolved. We, thus, presuppose that scientific theories of religion offer causal explanations of human behaviors that are ultimately grounded in an evolutionary (rather than transcendental) framework.

To specify what that means more carefully, we need to clarify our approach to two other widely discussed problems in the study of religion: what is meant by religion and what is meant by reduction and reductionism.

1.2 Defining Religion

In the discussion so far, we have proceeded as if we could shift the ontological ground of "religion" from the transcendental to the social-cultural realm without incurring any difficulties. In fact, this is not the case. Those who ground religion in ontological reality are able to offer *essentialist* definitions of religion based on their understanding of the sacred, transcendent, or supernatural, which they typically derive from tradition or revelation. Scholars who want to treat religion as a socio-cultural phenomenon without grounding it ontologically typically *stipulate* a definition of religion that then constitutes the phenomenon they seek to describe and/or explain (Platvoet 1999; Arnal 2000), which then imposes a scholarly definition on the range of religion-related terms mobilized by different groups on the ground.

As Stausberg (2009: 3–6) points out, theories that take religion as their object of study of necessity make implicit or explicit claims regarding the specificity of religion(s):

> Only if religion can be said to have or to be identified with any specific *properties*, to possess its own *regularities*, or to be communicated as a specific *code*, can one be sure to recognize religion in observation, unless one makes it a point to analyze only instances of religion identified by social actors as "religion." (Stausberg 2009: 3)

As researchers, we are interested in the latter and so choose to analyze the use of religion-related terms by social actors. We view "religion" and related terms (e.g., spirituality, magic, superstition, the esoteric, and the occult) as complex cultural concepts (CCCs), that is, as abstract nouns with unstable, overlapping meanings that vary within and across social formations (see Asprem and Taves 2017).[1] Here, in other words, we are in agreement with constructionist approaches to "religion": *as a CCC*, "it" does not exist apart from human communicative actions, and being "identified by social actors as 'religion'." Given this, we, like Beckford (2003) in sociology and Bloch (2010) in anthropology, question whether it is possible to construct a theory of religion per se.

"Religion" is, of course, not unusual in this regard. Indeed, we think that human experience is typically expressed in terms of complex cultural concepts and embedded in social formations. Because CCCs are embedded in social formations that determine their meaning, we do not think it is possible to explain CCCs (as such) in scientific terms. The emergence of meanings and uses of these concepts is the subject matter of discursive, constructionist approaches. However, studying CCCs is not the only thing we can do. The building block approach (BBA) is premised on the idea that we can explain human experience, by first redescribing phenomena of interest in behavioral terms, and then decomposing them into components (or building blocks) in order to reconstruct how the phenomena emerged and identify mechanisms that interact to produce them. Now we are no longer studying the CCCs (e.g. "religion," "magic," "prayer"), but clusters of observable *human behaviors* that serve as raw materials for the meaning-making processes that result in, and sustain, CCCs.

In so far as the phenomena of interest to us involve knowledge and practices, we share the explanatory agenda that Roy Ellen views as central to anthropology, broadly conceived, as concerning:

> the mechanisms by which knowledge and practices acquired in previous life-cycles are learned, re-learned, negotiated, re-negotiated, modified, and reinterpreted to allow individuals to function socially and ecologically in shifting contexts and successive generations. Our major concern as anthropologists is to explain how objects, practices, ideas, patterns of interaction, and relationships continue to be transmitted sufficiently accurately to allow for the reproductive continuity, not of each unit of 'culture' or 'society', but of each locally or virtually delineated population. The question is ultimately a Darwinian one, but it requires different kinds of intermediate-level theorizing to answer it. (Ellen 2010: 393–394)

Methodologically, however, we presuppose that any explanation must be based on a careful descriptive analysis of the phenomena of interest to us as researchers in the terms used by those we are studying. This brings us to the issue of reduction and reductionism.

1.3 Reduction and Reductionism

In religious studies, the term "reductionist" has often been used as an epithet to disparage a theory without careful consideration of what is meant by the term (Idinopulos and Yonan 1993). As technical terms, as opposed to epithets, both reductionism and reduction can be used in various ways that need to be specified in any serious discussion (see Brigandt and Love 2015). Here we will use *reduction* to refer to placing the phenomenon we seek to explain (the explanandum) "in a new context, whether that be one of covering laws and initial conditions, narrative structure, or some other explanatory model" (Proudfoot 1985: 197).

As Proudfoot states, reduction in the context of *describing* a subject's point of view is highly problematic. He distinguishes between descriptive and explanatory reduction as follows:

> *Descriptive reduction* is the failure to identify an emotion, practice, or experience under the description by which the subject identifies it. This is indeed unacceptable. [If a person says they had a "vision in which the Virgin Mary appeared to them" and we redescribe the phenomenon of interest as a "delusion with religious content," we are guilty of a descriptive reduction.] ... *Explanatory reduction* consists in offering an explanation of an experience, [including why they interpreted it the way they did,] in terms that are not those of the subject and that might not meet with [their] approval. This is perfectly justifiable and is, in fact, normal procedure. (Proudfoot 1985: 196–197; see also Blum 2015)

The first step, thus, is always to analyze these human efforts to make sense of situations in their own—oftentimes competing and contested—terms and thus, where possible, to reconstruct the process through which meanings emerged and were stabilized in systems of knowledge and social practice. As a second step, we can seek to explain these processes in scientific terms.

As already indicated, we will argue that the best way to produce reductive explanatory theories of various behaviors subjects deem religious is by identifying the various components (entities and activities) that interact to produce the behaviors. This is what the new mechanists mean by a mechanism. As we will see in §3, there is broad agreement in both the biological and social scientific literatures that the identification of mechanisms must begin with a detailed description of the phenomenon or phenomena to be explained before attempting to identify parts. Before turning to the new mechanism, however, we need to have a closer look at how mechanistic approaches—old and new—are situated within philosophical accounts of scientific explanation more generally.

2 Explanation in the Philosophy of Science

In §2, we highlight the following difficulties with traditional scientific approaches to explanation:

1 Aristotle's four *aitia*, which could be translated either as causes or explanations, generated confusion regarding the relationship between causation and explanation. His conception of final cause, grounded in teleological explanations of biological traits and human-made artifacts, led to confusion surrounding the relationship between functions and causes.

2 The extension of the (old) mechanistic theory of causation, which worked well in astronomy and physics, to the biological, psychological, and social sciences, where it failed to address the complexities of living organisms, much less humans.

3 The retreat from all metaphysical claims, causality included, such that scientific explanation was reduced theoretically to deductive-nomological laws, which bore little relation to the way that scientific research was actually being conducted.

4 The embrace of statistical explanations, which are expressed as probabilities based on correlations, but do not identify causal mechanisms.

The philosophy of science has produced a number of different views on what explanation is. Central to these debates is the issue of causation—what counts as a "cause," and what role do causes play in explanations? Here we shall discuss four influential approaches to the question of causes and explanation, each of which had limitations that the new mechanism attempts to overcome:

1. Functional-teleological accounts.
2. Causal-mechanistic accounts.
3. Law-based accounts.
4. Statistical/probabilistic accounts.

2.1 Functional-Teleological Accounts

These accounts typically are derived from *Aristotle's four causes/explanations*. Although Aristotle's philosophy was premised on a now outmoded cosmology, he did much of his thinking about explanation/causation in relation to living things. This gives his approach both major weakness and surprising contemporary strengths, which we will discuss below. Relative to causation, the main thing to note is that, in contrast to some later approaches, Aristotle did not make a sharp distinction between causation and explanation. He was concerned to argue, notably in *Physics* (II.3) and *Metaphysics* (V.2), that there are four different ways to explain "why" something exists. These are typically rendered as his "four causes": the material, efficient, formal, and final cause. However, the word Aristotle used in Greek, *aitia*, is perhaps better translated as "explanation" (see Broadie 2009), since the "four causes" are, in fact, answers to four different explanatory questions. As Broadie explains, to ask about a phenomenon's material causes is to ask what it is composed of (the statue is made from granite). To ask about its formal causes is to ask about its shape and structure (the statue is in the likeness of a man). To ask about its efficient cause is to ask how it was produced (the artisan worked the granite to produce the statue). To ask about its final causes is to relate the phenomenon to the goal that set the production in motion (the king had the artisan make the statue in order to honor the gods). On this view, a complete explanation of a phenomenon thus requires information about how a phenomenon is composed of certain kinds of matter (its material cause) arranged in accordance with a particular structure (its formal cause) by an agent (its effective cause) for the sake of realizing a certain goal or end (its final cause). It is the final causes, meaning the *goals* and *intentions* that underlie some (effective) course of action, that have explanatory priority in Aristotle's scheme (Falcon 2015). In other words, Aristotelian explanations are essentially teleological or functional *in relation to goal directed action*. In contrast, later theories of explanation tend to distinguish clearly between teleology and causation, and to view functions as part of a causal explanation only in a very limited sense.

2.2 Causation and Early Modern Mechanical Philosophy

The basic Aristotelian epistemology laid the natural-philosophical foundations for the many scientific advances of the late-Hellenistic and Islamic cultures of the Mediterranean basin, and contributed greatly to the so-called "renaissance of the twelfth century" in the Latin high Middle Ages (Grant 1996). However, two major disruptions in the view of explanation took place during the early modern period. The first disruption was associated with the development of classical mechanics in physics, and the subsequent expansion of the "mechanical philosophy" to areas such as biology (e.g., Descartes) and politics/society (e.g., Hobbes). Nowadays associated with "the scientific revolution" almost to the point of identity, the mechanical natural philosophy explicitly severed ties with Aristotelian physics in favor of a simpler view of explanation that focused solely on the interaction of empirically observable and quantifiable properties of matter (see for example Clatterbaugh 2009 for an overview).

Much of the motivation for this shift came from the obvious empirical failures of the Aristotelian program to provide accurate prediction of basic phenomena such as motion. The emerging mechanistic research programs thus combined a focus on observation and experimentation with a use of mathematical measurements and formalizations. The mechanistic view held that there is no need to invoke intentions, goals, or reasons in accounting for physical systems; all phenomena can be explained in terms of quantifiable properties related to inert matter in motion. In contemporary philosophy of science, this view of causality is generally known as *conserved quantity accounts* (Salmon 1971): a causal mechanism is characterized by "the conservation of inertial motion through contact action" (Descartes, paraphrased in Craver and Tabery 2015: 5). Gone are Aristotle's final causes—exchanged instead for chains of causal interactions whereby pieces of inert matter transfer observable physical qualities to one another.

The successes of the mechanistic program in astronomy, physics, and eventually also in chemistry, inspired natural philosophers to attempt to apply this model of explanation to other fields of inquiry, including biology and moral philosophy (the founding discipline of the social and psychological sciences). In these fields, it generated much controversy that has retroactively shaped the reputation of the mechanistic program. From Descartes's view of animals as mindless automata to Hobbes's bleak view of human society and La Mettrie's robotic humans, the attempt to subsume all of nature to a mechanistic explanatory scheme in which mechanisms are understood as closed interactions of conserved quantities continues to provoke a strong negative reaction (Asprem 2014: 50–67). It is our impression that much of the present-day opposition to bringing scientific methods to bear on humanistic phenomena tacitly views contemporary science through this anachronistic lens.

2.3 Empiricism and the Decline of Causation

A second disruption in theories of explanation is associated with the rise of empiricism, and especially with the work of David Hume. While philosophers today differ on how to interpret Hume's accounts of causation in the *Treatise of Human Nature* and *Enquiry Concerning Human Understanding* (see for example Garrett 2009), one particularly influential interpretation sees Hume as a skeptic about the very concept of causality. On this view, the empiricist philosopher does not see any evidence of causality *as such*—all he has access to is regularities of experience. Thus, while a mechanist might say that billiard ball *A* striking billiard ball *B causes* ball B to move and A to stop, the Humean skeptic would counter that all we see is a *tendency* of A–B collision and B acceleration to follow each other in a certain temporal sequence. We do not see the "cause"—only a correlation of two behaviors. To the extent that the Humean variety can be called a theory of causation, it is what philosophers of science today call a "regularity theory." All things considered, when we say that A is a cause of B, we mean that there is a statistical relationship between their occurrences.

While much of the rapidly advancing science of the nineteenth century followed closely on the mechanistic philosophy, the empiricist skepticism toward causation made a remarkable comeback in the twentieth. Coupled with the increasing mathematical sophistication of the mechanistic theories and the rise of statistical analysis, Humean-style empiricism led to the decline of the concept of causation in modern philosophy of science—a decline from which causation is only now starting to recover.

2.4 Logical Positivism, Covering Laws, and the Decline of Causation

Despite the popular view that "modern science," and physics in particular, is all about discovering causes and effects, both philosophically minded physicists and philosophers of science of the past century tended to view the concept of causation with much suspicion (for an early example, see Russell 1912). In the first half of the twentieth century, the influential logical empiricist (or logical positivist) school, formed primarily in the Vienna circle, followed Hume in questioning all metaphysical claims, causality included. According to them, a scientific theory must only contain statements that refer directly to specific sense data (the empirical or positivist part), and a formalized system of logical and mathematical relationships that connect such observational statements (the logical part) and allows for the derivation of *new* observational sentences (hypotheses) that can be tested against experience. Coinciding—and partially interacting with—the rise of logical positivism, an ambitious generation of young physicists working to define the new quantum mechanics occasionally emphasized the uselessness of the old mechanistic view for their discipline: Werner Heisenberg even went so far as to state that the new physics "establishes the final failure of causality" (Heisenberg 1983 [1927]: 83; cf. Asprem 2014: 114–119). The view of causality under attack here is, of course, the classically mechanistic one of continuous contact-mediated transfer of quantities.

The dominant approach to scientific theorization that emerged from these developments was the so-called *deductive-nomological* (DN), or "covering law" theory of explanation, associated above all with Carl Hempel (1965). According to Hempel, to *explain* an event is to invoke a law that *describes* and *predicts* that event given certain starting conditions. In other words, it must be possible to *derive* the sentence that described the behavior to be explained (the *explanandum*) from some broader covering law (the *explanans*). Explanation is a logical relationship between sentences, where one set of sentences is theoretical (laws), and the other is descriptive (describing the behavior to be explained) (see Woodward 2014).

Much like Hume, then, deductive-nomological explanation has no place for causality, only for laws that describe regularities in nature.

The deductive-nomological account of explanation is unabashedly tailored to physics. In the sciences, however, one size does not fit all. The DN theory is not very good at accounting for explanations in the so-called special sciences, such as biology, psychology, or neuroscience, where "general laws" are typically not very helpful. It also has problems with the so-called *historical* sciences—including cosmology, geology, and evolutionary biology, as well as paleontology, archaeology, and history—that seek to explain how *particular* chains of natural events have unfolded to produce the forms and features of the world. In these disciplines, which cover the vast majority of the sciences (and the humanities), explanation is typically *not* about formulating laws as much as finding the relevant, co-dependent factors that help us explain or predict some (typical) course of events. Covering laws theories were still popular when C. P. Snow wrote his influential "Two Cultures" essay in 1959 and during the "positivism dispute" (*Positivismusstreit*) of the 1960s. Because these texts are still influential, the view that "modern science" is all about finding generalizable laws has proved remarkably resilient. Philosophers of science, however, have largely abandoned this view for statistical explanations and accounts that pay closer attention to what scientists in various disciplines *actually do* when they explain phenomena.

2.5 Statistical Explanations

In addition to the fact that the covering law account of explanation makes for a bad fit with actual explanatory behavior among scientists, its indifference to causes means that it fails to sift out relevant from irrelevant information. It is easy to construct general covering laws that logically "explain" some outcome, but which, upon closer inspection, appear rather doubtful. Here is an example invented by Wesley Salmon:

> Covering Law: All males who take birth control pills regularly fail to get pregnant.
> Initial Condition: John Jones is a male who has been taking birth control pills regularly.
> Outcome: John Jones fails to get pregnant. (Salmon 1971: 34)

While the outcome can be derived from the general law and the prevailing condition, they can hardly be said to *explain* the outcome. Any explanation worthy of the name needs to specify the relevant properties that make a difference to the outcome. One way of doing this is to look for *statistical dependencies* between individual factors. Salmon (ibid.) formalized this approach to explanation as the "statistical relevance" (SR) model of explanation (see also discussion in Woodward 2014). In this approach, valid explanations are premised on the *homogeneous partition* of the data—a concept that is roughly analogous with what experimentalists call a control group. For example, if we want to find out whether some attribute X is relevant to another attribute Y within some population or class A, we need to partition the class A into subclasses with and without attributes X and Y, and run statistical analyses to figure out whether members of A are more likely to have Y if they *also* have X. If such a statistical relationship can be found, we would say that *X explains Y*.

The statistical relevance model of explanation overcomes the problem that covering law explanations have with determining relevance, and it also has the advantage of tallying with the way that scientists in many fields—not least in the biomedical sciences—produce explanations in practice. It does however leave out some issues when it comes to the question of causation. The explanations provided by the statistical relevance approach are expressed as *probabilities*, and the explaining factors or attributes are linked by *correlations*. Robust correlations do help us predict phenomena and can even provide clues for effective interventions (such as when taking a particular drug correlates with overcoming a particular disease), but they do not really provide answers to *why* and *how* such correlations occur. As Federica Russo and Jon Williamson (2007) have argued, good explanations in the biomedical sciences *combine* a probabilistic strategy of statistical correlation with a search for specific causal mechanisms that account for the dependencies. It appears that statistical relevance explanations, too, only get at one part of what explanations ought to do.

After a century's eclipse, it has become clear to many philosophers of science studying sciences other than physics that a robust account of explanation that is in touch with how the explanatory project of scientific disciplines really does proceed cannot do without some notion of causality. This realization is a starting point for the new mechanism. As we shall see—and somewhat paradoxically considered the connotations of the old mechanical philosophy—this recent movement has allowed for a broadening of the notion of causation even to the extent of reconsidering aspects of the Aristotelian view.

3 The New Mechanical Philosophy

In §3, we discuss the following contrasting features of the new mechanism:

1. It is based on the way that research is actually being done in the so-called "special sciences" (biology, neuroscience, and psychology) where the focus is on the discovery of [causal] mechanisms that describe how particular phenomena work.

2. Mechanisms are defined not in terms of universal and fundamental causes, but in terms of local interactions between entities (or components) specific to the phenomenon in question.

3. In this view, mechanisms can be conceived vertically as nested levels of mechanisms and horizontally in terms of causal chains distributed along spatiotemporal lines.

4. Because it is grounded in evolutionary biology, the new mechanism includes the goal directed actions of animals and the mental abilities required to produce them as potential causal factors.

5   The phenomena to be explained can be specified at any scale and the nature of the constitutive components will differ depending on the scale of analysis. Social scientists are actively engaged in extending mechanistic explanations to the scales at work in human socio-cultural phenomena.

The new mechanism is squarely grounded in the biological sciences and evolutionary theory. This has enabled it to restore Aristotle's focus on goal-directed action as a central feature in the evolutionary development of animal minds, without postulating teleological causes. As Barrett (2015) argues, it is because animals (unlike plants) *move* that they evolved the abilities associated with minds. The new mechanism presupposes and thus creates a framework within which to model the interaction of these two distinctive features of animals—goal directed action and mental abilities (however rudimentary)—at increasing levels of complexity from the single celled organism to complex human societies. Given the space constraints here, we will defer discussion of the issues involved in extending the new mechanism to the social sciences for a later publication (Taves and Asprem in preparation). Here we will focus on the core features of the new mechanism that provide a basis for its extension to the humanistic social sciences.

3.1 The Emergence of the New Mechanism

Philosophers of science have shown an increased interest in mechanisms and causality since the turn of the twenty-first century (see for example Craver and Tabery 2015). Where the covering law theory of explanation was based on ideal cases from the most theoretical branches of physics, and the statistical relevance theory proved successful for dealing with aspects of the biomedical sciences, a newer group of philosophers, who sometimes refer to themselves as "the new mechanists" (e.g. Bechtel and Richardson 2010 [1993]; Glennan 1996, 1997; Machamer, Darden, and Craver 2000; Craver 2007; Craver and Tabery 2015), are developing an approach to explanation based on how research is done in the so-called "special sciences," such as biology and neuroscience. These are sciences in which a large part of the scientific activity and progress over the past half century has focused precisely on uncovering mechanistic interactions within biological organisms. Typical examples include the mechanism of protein biosynthesis in cells, and the mechanism of the action potential of neurons.

In the words of two of its proponents, "the new mechanical philosophy is less a systematic and coherent set of doctrines than it is an orientation to the subject matter of the philosophy of science" (Craver and Tabery 2015: 3). As such, it has been prompted by the observation that, contrary to the logical empiricists' emphasis on logical formalism and theories of justification, scientists have generally been oriented toward the discovery of [causal] mechanisms that describe how particular phenomena work. The new mechanists place this process of discovery at the center of their understanding of scientific activity, and explore what mechanistic explanations consist of, how and why they work, and what metaphysical implications follow.

While the new mechanists borrow the term "mechanism" from early-modern predecessors such as Descartes, Hobbes, or Newton, the way that they understand the term is markedly different. Notably, the new mechanists do not mean to suggest that the phenomenon explained with reference to a mechanism is thereby "merely a machine"; nor do they embrace the metaphysical view of a deterministic "world machine" of the type famously imagined by Laplace (1995 [1820]: 2). Instead, the new mechanists are interested in how scientists explain some behavior with reference to the interactions of relevant entities and processes. Instead of aiming to reduce phenomena to universal and fundamental causes, such explanations are always local and specific to the phenomenon in question.

3.2 What is a Mechanism?

A mechanism *explains* the behavior of a phenomenon in terms of the interaction of various components (entities and activities). According to one minimalistic consensus definition, a "mechanism for a phenomenon consists of entities and activities organized in such a way that they are responsible for the phenomenon" (Illari and Williamson 2011: 120). The term "responsible for" is carefully chosen, because the behavior can vary widely, from how a system changes into another, to how a system remains static or resistant to change. Moreover, the behavior of the system (the phenomenon of interest) can be specified at any scale, from micro to macro.

At this point we want to flag that the new mechanism's emphasis on identifying relevant *components* and their local interactions and organizations makes it congruent with what we call a building block approach to human experience (see bbhe.ucsb.edu). As we present the basic features of the new mechanism, readers should keep in mind that (1) we view the interacting components of mechanisms as analogous to what we call building blocks, (2) components will *themselves* usually be in need of further mechanistic explanation, and (3) the phenomena to be explained as well as the interacting components adduced to explain them can be any process or entity that admits a sufficiently precise description, from the behavior of a person, to a repeated group practice, to a neuromodulatory process, or a sensory phenomenon. Thus, while the new mechanists are mostly using the framework to identify mechanisms in biological and neuropsychological systems, as a general "orientation to the subject matter of the philosophy of science" it is applicable to a host of other domains as well, including the study of religion.

Figure 13.1 shows how some phenomenon (system S engaging in behavior ψ) can be explained mechanistically with reference to how relevant components of the system (X_1, X_2, X_3, X_4, each engaging in their own behavior ϕ_1, ϕ_2, ϕ_3, ϕ_4) are interacting (arrows) to produce the behavior.

Each of these interacting components engages in its own behaviors, as the illustration shows, and each behavior can itself be explained mechanistically. This is illustrated in Figure 13.2. X_1 exerts *causal power* on X_2 and X_3, within the mechanism that explains S. To continue to break X_1 down into further components (P_1, P_2, ... P_n and T_1, T_2, ... T_n) is to *explain* changes in its causal capacity.

Explanation and the Study of Religion • 147

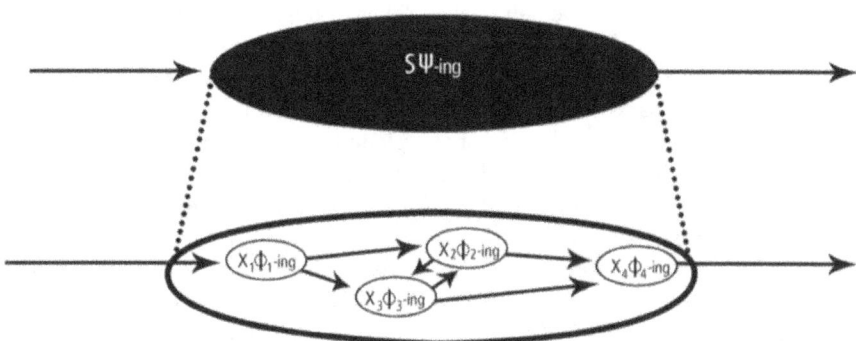

Figure 13.1 A visual representation of a mechanism.

Source: Craver (2007, 121)

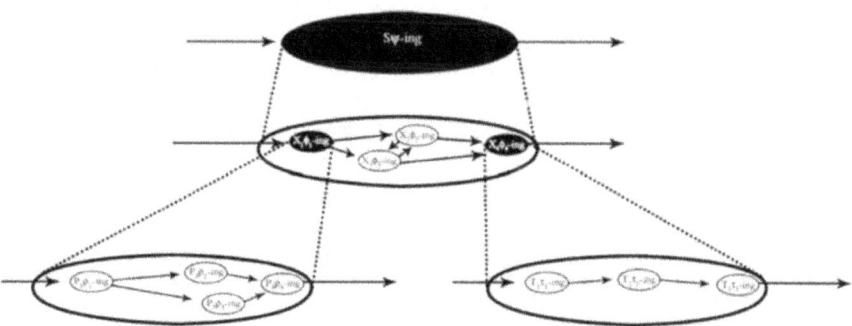

Figure 13.2 A multi-level mechanism.

Source: Craver (2007, 194)

This type of analysis is called *decompositional*. It is *synchronic* as opposed to *diachronic*, in the sense that it considers some phenomenon as a system (S), and analyzes it in terms of component parts that are all interacting synchronously. There are several important things to note here.

First, the cascade of explanations in Figure 13.2 constitutes a "multilevel mechanism" (Craver and Tabery 2015: 20). "Levels of mechanisms" are *not* to be confused with levels of "nature" (ranked according to features such as size and complexity [e.g., atoms, molecules, cells, organs, and organisms]) or "disciplinary levels" (e.g., physics, chemistry, biology, psychology, the social sciences, and the humanities). In the context of a multilevel explanation, "level" simply means that the mechanism (e.g., the interaction of $P_1, P_2, \ldots P_n$ in relation to X_1 or $T_1, T_2, \ldots T_n$ in relation to X_4) that explains any given X is nested within (i.e., a part of) the mechanism that explains the behavior of S. For example, if we make the collapse of WTC 1 on 9/11 as the behavior (S) that we seek to explain, will include the interaction between a building (X_1) and a plane (X_2). The building (X_1) as a whole is constructed of "parts" that in turn explain how the building responded to the impact of the plane. The behavior of the plane (X_2), which contained crew and passengers, some of whom hijacked the plane, can be broken down into interacting individuals with varying intentions and reasons motivating their behaviors (i.e., the interaction of $R_1, R_2, \ldots R_n$).

Second, since mechanisms are nested within mechanisms, such that any particular mechanism is simultaneously both a phenomenon of interest (relative to the mechanism that produces it) and a mechanism (relative to phenomena that it produces), researchers must always specify a phenomenon of interest somewhere in the many levels of mechanisms. For example, a terrorism scholar may be less interested in the chemistry of jet propulsion and the physics of collapsing buildings, stipulating their phenomenon of interest instead as how groups and individuals can become motivated toward behaviors understood as "terrorism."[2]

Third, although there is no causal interaction between levels, there is interaction *at a level*, which takes place *over time*, which may alter the causal capacity of the system in question and, thus, its ability to effect change over time. A single mechanism, thus, links synchronic and diachronic processes.

This double nature means that a mechanism can be elaborated in either of two ways depending on what we want to explain, either synchronically, as we have just discussed, or diachronically. In contrast to the synchronic analysis, comprised of nested levels of mechanisms, we can view mechanisms diachronically as linked into causal chains distributed along spatiotemporal lines (Ylikoski 2013; see Figure 13.3). To have a comprehensive understanding of processes of change, stability, and variation, we need to invoke both these aspects of mechanistic explanation. The analysis of causal chains is necessary to establish which events are related (i.e. whether it is A or B or both that are causally relevant for bringing about C), while a synchronic analysis of nested levels of mechanisms is necessary to answer why, or in virtue of what, A or B has the capacity to act on C.

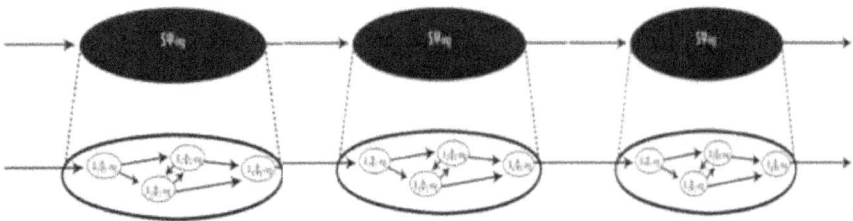

Figure 13.3 A series of diachronic phenomena.

Source: *Authors adaptation of Craver (2007, 121)*

Put differently, one method establishes *causal histories*, the other explains changes in the *causal capacity* of individual entities in those histories.

Although references to "mechanisms" in the natural sciences are often references to constitutive mechanisms, this is an overly narrow view of mechanisms. Here, we are drawing on recent discussions (see Ylikoski 2013; Kaiser et al. 2014) to make a careful distinction between a mechanism viewed constitutively in terms of its component parts and diachronically in terms of causal chains (for further discussion, see Taves and Asprem in preparation). We do so in order to include the diachronic explanations that are more prominent in fields such as cosmology, geology, archeology, evolutionary biology and psychology, and history in the book version.

3.3 Goal-Directed Actions as Causal Powers: From Biology to Society and Back Again

Traditionally, humanists explain events by identifying human actors, attributing mental states, such as intentions and goals, and matching their behaviors with these states. Following the "antipositivist" wave at the beginning of last century, this perspective has also had a strong influence on the social sciences. Taking their cue from thinkers such as Droysen and Dilthey, many scholars assume that there is a fundamental divide between the "natural sciences" (*Naturwissenschaften*) and the "humanities" (*Geisteswissenschaften*) such that the sciences are about explanation (*erklären*) while the humanities seek to *interpret* (*verstehen*).

The split between interpretation and explanation has long since come under severe criticism, not least from theorists seeking to ground our understanding of human behavior in the psychological, cognitive, and biological sciences (for a few paradigmatic examples, see Lawson and McCauley 1990: 12–31; Sperber 1996: 32–55; Slingerland 2008: 2–28). As discussed in §1, we think that the split between interpretation and explanation is best resolved by recognizing Proudfoot's distinction between descriptive and explanatory reduction. We must "interpret" in the sense of uncovering and reconstructing, to the best of our ability, the meanings and points of views of our subjects, but after this, we must reduce in order to explain. This is standard procedure when it comes to identifying mechanisms. Thus, as Illari and Williamson (2011; see also Illari and Russo 2014: 122–124) indicate, there is broad agreement in both the biological and social scientific literatures that the identification of constitutive mechanisms proceeds in three steps:

1 Describe the phenomenon or phenomena;

2 Find the parts of the mechanism, and describe what the parts do;

3 Find out and describe the organization of parts by which they produce, in the sense of bring about, the phenomenon.

We can use these steps to clarify the two ways we can approach the subjective meaning, intention, or beliefs that subjects ascribe to their actions, depending on whether we treat the subjective meaning as the phenomenon of interest (step 1) or as a potential part of a mechanism for a phenomenon (step 2). If we want to study folk explanations as such, they are the phenomenon of interest that we would seek to explain in terms of mechanisms, both causal (diachronic) and constituent (synchronic). We can also consider subjective meaning as a potential component that might interact with other entities or processes to produce a phenomenon. This returns us to a question that the new mechanists are debating, i.e., whether "content-bearing mental states" (i.e., specific beliefs as opposed to believing as a process) can be part of a mechanism (Illari and Williamson 2011: 831). Although the details are not resolved, the new mechanism clearly makes room for this possibility.

From an evolutionary perspective (Barrett 2015), we can understand minds and mental processes as evolving together with organisms' capacity to *move*. As Barrett (ibid.: 18–26) indicates, the foundation of cognition was laid with the mutation that created the first light-sensitive cells: with basic discriminatory powers, such as distinguishing light from dark and hot from cold emerged the basic power to move toward and move away. This is the basis of intentionality. The rest is evolutionary history: With increasing complexity, new discriminatory capacities have been added and old ones overridden, in the constant selection of whatever trait is adaptive in a changing environment. Regardless of whether they are able to reflect on their goals, this means that the goal directed actions of organisms and the cognitive abilities required to produce them must be taken into account as *causal powers* within complex, multilevel mechanisms linked diachronically across evolutionary time.

Moreover, as soon as we ground our understanding of the natural world (and not just biology) in the principle of natural selection, we can reintroduce concepts such as functional design into the explanatory scheme without a return to Aristotelian teleology. This point can be extrapolated to apparently "non-mechanical" phenomena such as goal directed actions and the cognitive abilities that support them. The causal power of intentions, like that of other functional designs, must be approached *diachronically* as well as *synchronically*, and related to *distal* as well as *proximate causes*.[3] In other words: While the traditional, methodological individualist view would be content with relating an action to the intentions of an actor or group of actors, we would proceed to (1) explain those intentions themselves in terms of the interacting constituent parts of the actor or group that produced them (e.g., unconscious mental processing, biologically based drives, psychological biases and heuristics), and (2) explain the general capacity for intentionality—and for pursuing particular kinds of goals—with reference to natural selection as a distal cause.

3.4 A Case Study

We can conclude with an example that demonstrates how this approach to explanation allows us to explain religious claims differently. Joseph Smith's claim to have recovered and translated ancient golden plates buried in a hill in upstate New York provides an apt example. Smith's followers then and today typically explain his actions in supernatural terms, attributing the burial of the plates to an ancient inhabitant of the Americas and the content of the plates to his forbearers who recorded historical events including an actual visit of Christ to his people. Smith's critics then and today view his claims as false and typically explain his actions in terms of deception or fraud. Scholars are generally divided as well. Some—generally Latter Day Saints (LDS) scholars—take Smith's claims at face value, thus opting for a supernatural explanation, while others (generally non-LDS) believe there were no ancient golden plates and conclude from this that Smith was either deceptive or deluded. Both are making claims about his intentions. The former, presupposing the supernatural, claims that his intention was simply to do what an angel of the Lord commanded. The latter claims that he either consciously intended to deceive others or unconsciously deluded himself. Phenomenologically oriented and methodologically agnostic scholars bracket this contentious issue and limit themselves to analyzing what arose as a result of Smith's claims.

Deliberately focusing on a particular aspect of the problem, how might an evolutionary framework allow us to do better job of understanding intentionality? Most crucially, it would require us to remind ourselves that intentionality is a product of evolution. This might lead us to wonder if the competing explanations of Smith's intentions as either real-supernatural or fake-deceptive-deluded might not be a bit too simplistic. An evolutionary perspective on intentionality would situate it in the context of goal directed action, which would remind us that intentions do not have to be conscious in order to result in actions. Many different action oriented systems compete for primacy below the threshold of consciousness (Huang and Bargh 2014). If we also bear in mind that humans have evolved as *social* animals whose mental processes depend heavily on interactions with others, we might wonder if a focus on Smith's intentions alone is sufficient to explain the belief in the existence of ancient golden plates or if group processes might play a significant role.

While scholars have disagreed over whether ancient Nephites or Joseph Smith was the efficient cause of the golden plates (and others have simply opted out of explaining), a mechanistic explanation would seek to explain the behavior (believing in the existence of ancient golden plates) in terms of entities and activities that were responsible for producing it, grounded in an explanation of the evolved capacities that allowed believers to do so. To arrive at a mechanistic explanation, we would have to begin with a careful reconstruction of the phenomenon of interest (the belief) as it developed over time in that particular social historical context, based on the most reliable historical sources. The reconstruction would reveal not only a constellation of relevant beliefs within Smith's family and in his local environment, but also several key points in a historical process of belief formation, which we can think of as a series of diachronic events (as depicted in Figure 13.3; for more detail see Taves 2016).

1 1823—A dream-vision in which an angel appeared and told Smith that ancient plates were buried in a nearby hillside.

2   1827—The recovery of plates

3   1827-1828—Smith and his immediate followers interact with an object that is always covered or hidden in a box per the Lord's instructions to Smith. Witnesses see the ancient plates in vision when delivered/revealed by an angel.

If we focus just on the first event—the 1823 dream-vision—we find that Smith did not attempt to recover the plates until the angel returned, instructed him to tell his father, and he and his family confirmed the reality of the vision. Confirming the reality of the vision confirmed the reality of the angel as an intentional agent and plates as a material object. This crucial initial event can be explained mechanistically as an interaction between an individual (Smith), who had an unusual dream-vision, and others close to him, who believed that contents of the dream-vision were real and not just imaginary. Smith and his family members were the interacting parts that produced the phenomenon of interest (a shared reality in which an external intentional agent [an angel of the Lord] appeared and reported the location of an actual ancient material object).

We can further analyze (decompose) each individual (or component) in this initial 1823 dream-vision event to investigate what they contributed to the interaction in terms of abilities, beliefs, and motivations. It is at this level of mechanism that the family decided whether the reported angel's intention [to get Smith to find and recover the plates] was a product of Smith's imagination or of an independent agent. While the various labels applied to the postulated agent—angel or disembodied spirit, delusional belief, or fictional character—offer explanations, they do not provide mechanisms that explain how the Smith family came to believe an agent was present. An evolutionary perspective on intentionality radically upends our everyday sense of ourselves as unified "selves" and offers an alternative framework in which humans and other animals are understood as comprised of multiple, mostly unconscious impulses directed to different ends that compete for attention and normally gain primacy in serial fashion (Huang and Bargh 2014; McCubbins and Turner 2012: 393-94). From an evolutionary vantage point, we can more easily understand how impulses that surface to consciousness—in dreams or otherwise—may seem self-alien and as a result might easily be construed as belonging to someone else (Wegner 2002: 221-270, Taves and Asprem 2017).

In cases, such as this, where available beliefs about angels lead close associates to conclude that an independent agent has manifested its presence to or through an individual, they may create a shared reality in which this new agent can continue to intervene. The emergence of this shared reality (event 1) enabled Smith and his family to come up with reasons why he was unable to recover the plates when he went to the site, and, in the wake of another appearance of the angel, enabled Smith to come up with a plan for co-creating the plates with the Lord and, thus, to recover them (event 2). The outcome of event 1 thus serves as input into event 2, which in turn serves as input into event 3.

Conclusion

As we hope to have shown, the question of explanation in the study of religion is much more complex and wide-ranging than common dichotomies between explanation and interpretation, or description and reduction tend to convey. This problem already begins in deciding the *explanandum*: are we studying "religion" in the abstract, or are we studying the people who engage in practices that get deemed "religious"? We have defended a naturalistic approach grounded in the new mechanism and evolutionary theory that takes human behaviors—both individual and group behaviors—as its object of study, and seeks explanations that are grounded in evolved capacities that bring together the nexus of bodies, minds, and groups. While this approach may at first sight seem alien to some of our humanities colleagues, we hope to have shown that in *principle* this approach can do justice to a whole swath of cultural, psychological, material, and social elements. To seek an explanation of a phenomenon is, simply, to search for mechanisms that connect individual parts in some causally connected whole, and to embed these mechanisms in causal chains connected over longer time scales. This urges us to expand our explanatory scope in two dimensions: diachronically, we must connect the historical time scales studied by historians to an evolutionary time scale studied by biologists; synchronically, we must deepen our analysis of behavior from the level of conscious intentions, reasons, and goals, to the sub-personal level of evolved drives and tendencies that compete for the control of the body below the threshold of consciousness. Taking this approach may have unsettling consequences for the illusion that an irreducible, "rational" self is in control of the human body, and certainly for the notion that "cultures" and "religions" somehow possess their own inherent teleologies that unfold through history. It does, however, help us pinpoint why and how and to what degree the human capacity of creating niche environments and abstract cultural systems have a real effect in the world.

Egil Asprem is associate professor in the history of religions at Stockholm University. He is the author of *Arguing with Angels: Enochian Magic and Modern Occulture* (SUNY Press, 2012) and *The Problem of Disenchantment: Scientific Naturalism and Esoteric Discourse, 1900-1939* (Brill, 2014), and co-editor with Kennet Granholm of *Contemporary Esotericism* (Routledge, 2014).

Ann Taves is professor of religious studies at the University of California at Santa Barbara where she teaches courses on religious experience, new religious movements, and comparative worldviews and supervises the interdisciplinary Religion, Experience, and Mind Lab Group. She is the author of numerous books and articles, including *Fits, Trances, and Visions: Experiencing Religion and Explaining Experience from Wesley to James* (Princeton University Press, 1999), *Religious Experience Reconsidered* (Princeton University Press, 2009), and *Revelatory Events*, a study of the emergence of three new spiritual movements. She is currently working with collaborators to develop and test a cross-cultural Inventory of Non-Ordinary Experiences.

Notes

1 As we go on to explain: "Due to their instability and variable use, the building block approach does not operationalize CCCs or seek to explain them as such. Rather, it seeks to explain the behaviors to which they refer in the context of specific social formations. So, for example, if we take 'magic' as our point of departure, we must specify the *formation* in which we are studying 'it', redescribe 'it' in behavioral terms, and pose our research questions in *basic concepts* (e.g., what actions are performed?. How are they performed?). The outcome of such a study cannot be a theory or an explanation of 'magic' in general, but of a specific patterned practice, which a given formation may characterize as 'magic,' but which other formations may characterize differently" (see http://bbhe.ucsb.edu/ccc-simple/ccc-elaborate).
2 For a recent example of an evolutionary and (in our sense) mechanistic approach to this very question, see Atran (2016).
3 This discussion is implicitly based on our reading of Tibergen's (1963) "four questions," which will be unpacked in the book version (Taves and Asprem in preparation).

References

Arnal, William E. 2000. "Definition," in Willi Braun and Russell T. McCutcheon (eds.), *Guide to the Study of Religion*, 21–34. London: Cassell.

Asprem, Egil. 2014. *The Problem of Disenchantment: Scientific Naturalism and Esoteric Discourse, 1900-1939*. Leiden: Brill.

Asprem, Egil, and Ann Taves. 2016. "Complex Cultural Concepts." Retrieved from http://bbhe.ucsb.edu/ccc-simple (accessed December 5, 2016).

Atran, Scott. 2016. "The Devoted Actor: Unconditional Commitment and Intractable Conflict across Cultures," *Current Anthropology* 57(S13): 192–203. https://doi.org/10.1086/685495

Barrett, H. Clark. 2015. *The Shape of Thought: How Mental Adaptations Evolve*. New York: Oxford University Press. https://doi.org/10.1093/acprof:oso/9780199348305.001.0001

Bechtel, William and Robert C. Richardson. 2010 [1993]. *Discovering Complexity: Decomposition and Localization as Strategies in Scientific Research*. Cambridge, MA: MIT Press.

Beckford, James A. 2003. *Social Theory and Religion*. Cambridge: Cambridge University Press. https://doi.org/10.1017/CBO9780511520754

Bloch, Maurice. 2010. "Bloch on Bloch on 'Religion'," *Religion and Society: Advances in Research* 1: 4–28.

Blum, Jason N. 2015. "On the Restraint of Theory," paper presented in the NAASR Symposium on "Theory in a Time of Excess," AAR, November.

Brigandt, Ingo and Alan Love. 2015. "Reductionism in Biology," in Edward N. Zalta (ed.), *The Stanford Encyclopedia of Philosophy*, Fall 2015 edition. Retrieved from http://plato.stanford.edu/archives/fall2015/entries/reduction-biology (accessed March 3, 2018).

Broadie, Sara. 2009. "The Ancient Greeks," in Helen Beebee, Christopher Hitchcock, and Peter Menzies (eds.), *Oxford Handbook of Causation*, 21–39. Oxford: Oxford University Press.

Clatterbaugh, Kenneth. 2009. "The Early Moderns," in Helen Beebee, Christopher Hitchcock, and Peter Menzies (eds.), *Oxford Handbook of Causation*, 55–72. Oxford: Oxford University Press.

Craver, Carl F. 2007. *Explaining the Brain: Mechanisms and the Mosaic Unity of Neuroscience.* New York: Oxford University Press. https://doi.org/10.1093/acprof:oso/9780199299317.001.0001

Craver, Carl F. 2014. "The Ontic Account of Scientific Explanation," in Marie I. Kaiser, Oliver R. Scholz, Daniel Plenge, and Andreas Hüttemann (eds.), *Explanation in the Special Sciences: The Case of Biology and History*, 27–52. Berlin: Springer. https://doi.org/10.1007/978-94-007-7563-3_2

Craver, Carl F., and James Tabery. 2015. "Mechanisms in science," in Edward N. Zalta (ed.), *The Stanford Encyclopedia of Philosophy*, Spring 2015 edition. Retrieved from http://plato.stanford.edu/archives/spr2016/entries/science-mechanisms (accessed March 3, 2018).

Ellen, Roy. 2010. "Theories in anthropology and 'anthropological theory'," *Journal of the Royal Anthropological Institute* (new series) 16: 387–404. https://doi.org/10.1111/j.1467-9655.2010.01631.x

Engler, Steven. 2004. "Constructionism versus What?" *Religion* 34: 291–313. https://doi.org/10.1016/j.religion.2004.09.001

Falcon, Andrea. 2015. "Aristotle on Causality," in Edward N. Zalta (ed.), *The Stanford Encyclopedia of Philosophy*, Spring 2015 edition. Retrieved from http://plato.stanford.edu/archives/spr2015/entries/aristotle-causality (accessed March 3, 2018).

Garrett, Don. 2009. "Hume," in Helen Beebee, Christopher Hitchcock, and Peter Menzies (eds.), *Oxford Handbook of Causation*, 73–91. Oxford: Oxford University Press.

Glennan, Stuart S. 1996. "Mechanisms and The Nature of Causation," *Erkenntnis* 44: 49–71. https://doi.org/10.1007/BF00172853

Glennan, Stuart S. 1997. "Capacities, Universality and Singularity," *Philosophy of Science* 64: 605–626. https://doi.org/10.1086/392574

Grant, Edward. 1996. *The Foundations of Modern Science in the Middle Ages: Their Religious, Institutional, and Intellectual Contexts.* Cambridge: Cambridge University Press. https://doi.org/10.1017/CBO9780511817908

Heisenberg, Werner. 1983 [1927]. "The Physical Content of Quantum Kinematics and Mechanics," in John Archibald Wheeler and Wojchiech Hubert Zurek (eds., trans.), *Quantum Theory and Measurement*, 62–84. Princeton, NJ: Princeton University Press.

Hempel, Carl G. 1965. *Aspects of Scientific Explanation and Other Essays in the Philosophy of Science.* New York: Free Press.

Hjelm, Titus. 2014. *Social Constructionism: Approaches to the Study of the Human World.* Basingstoke: Palgrave Macmillan. https://doi.org/10.1007/978-1-137-41396-3

Huang, Julie Y., and John A. Bargh. 2014. "The Selfish Goal: Autonomously Operating Motivational Structures as the Proximate Cause of Human Judgment and Behavior," *Behavioral and Brain Sciences* 37(2): 121–135. https://doi.org/10.1017/S0140525X13000290

Idinopulos, Thomas A. and Edward A. Yonan (eds.). 1993. *Religion and Reductionism: Essays on Eliade, Segal, and the Challenges of the Social Sciences for the Study of Religion.* Leiden: Brill.

Illari, Phyllis and Federica Russo. 2014. *Causality: Philosophical Theory Meets Scientific Practice.* Oxford: Oxford University Press.

Illari, Phyllis and Jon Williamson. 2011. "Mechanisms are real and local," In P. Illari, F. Russo, and J. Williamson (eds.), *Causality in the Sciences*, 818–844. Oxford: Oxford University Press. https://doi.org/10.1093/acprof:oso/9780199574131.003.0038

Kaiser, Marie I., Oliver R. Scholz, Daniel Plenge, and Andreas Hüttemann (eds.), 2014. *Explanation in the Special Sciences: The Case of Biology and History*. Berlin: Springer. https://doi.org/10.1007/978-94-007-7563-3

Laplace, Pierre-Simon. 1995 [1820]. *Philosophical Essay on Probabilities*, trans. Andrew I. Dale. New York: Springer-Verlag.

Lawson, E. Thomas and Robert M. McCauley. 1990. *Rethinking Religion: Connecting Cognition and Culture*. Cambridge: Cambridge University Press.

McCubbins, Matthew D., and Mark Turner. 2012. "Going Cognitive: Tools for Rebuilding the Social Sciences," in Ron Sun (ed.), *Grounding Social Sciences in Cognitive Sciences*, 387–414. Cambridge, MA: MIT Press.

Machamer, P. K., L. Darden, and C. F. Craver. 2000. "Thinking about Mechanisms," *Philosophy of Science* 67:1–25. https://doi.org/10.1086/392759

Martin, Craig. Forthcoming. "Incapacitating Scholarship: Or, Why Methodological Agnosticism Is Impossible," in Jason Blum (ed.), *The Question of Methodological Naturalism*. Leiden: Brill.

Pals, Daniel L. 1987. "Is Religion a Sui Generis Phenomenon?" *Journal of the American Academy of Religion* 55(2): 259–282. https://doi.org/10.1093/jaarel/LV.2.259

Pals, Daniel. 2014. *Nine Theories of Religion*, 3rd edition. New York: Oxford University Press.

Platvoet, Jan. 1999. "To Define or Not to Define: The Problem of the Definition of Religion," in Jan Platvoet and Arie Molendijk (eds.), *The Pragmatics of Defining Religion*, 245–266. Leiden: Brill.

Porpora, Douglas. 2006. "Methodological Atheism, Methodological Agnosticism and Religious Experience," *Journal for the Theory of Social Behaviour* 36(1): 57–75. https://doi.org/10.1111/j.1468-5914.2006.00296.x

Proudfoot, Wayne. 1985. *Religious Experience*. Berkeley, CA: University of California Press.

Reznick, David N. 2010. *The* Origin *Then and Now: An Interpretive Guide to the* Origin of Species. Princeton, NJ: Princeton University Press.

Russell, Bertrand. 1912. "On the Notion of Cause," *Proceedings of the Aristotelian Society* 13: 1–26. https://doi.org/10.1093/aristotelian/13.1.1

Russo, Federica, and Jon Williamson. 2007. "Interpreting Causality in the Health Sciences," *International Studies in the Philosophy of Science* 21(2): 157–170. https://doi.org/10.1080/02698590701498084

Salmon, Wesley. 1971. "Statistical Explanation," in Wesley Salmon (ed.), *Statistical Explanation and Statistical Relevance*, 29–87. Pittsburgh, PA: University of Pittsburgh Press. https://doi.org/10.2307/j.ctt6wrd9p.6

Salmon, Wesley C. 1989. *Four Decades of Scientific Explanation*. Minneapolis, MN: University of Minnesota Press.

Slingerland, Edward. 2008. *What Science Offers the Humanities: Integrating Body and Culture*. New York: Cambridge University Press. https://doi.org/10.1017/CBO9780511841163

Slingerland, Edward, and Mark Collard (eds.). 2011. *Creating Consilience: Integrating the Sciences and the Humanities*. Oxford: Oxford University Press. https://doi.org/10.1093/acprof:oso/9780199794393.001.0001

Smith, David Woodruff. 2013. "Phenomenology," in Edward N. Zalta (ed.), *The Stanford Encyclopedia of Philosophy*, Winter 2013 edition. Retrieved from http://plato.stanford.edu/archives/win2013/entries/phenomenology (accessed March 3, 2018).

Snow, C. P. 1959. *Two Cultures and the Scientific Revolution*. New York: Cambridge University Press.

Sperber, Dan. 1996. *Explaining Culture: A Naturalistic Approach*. Oxford: Blackwell.

Stausberg, Michael. 2009. "There is Life in the Old Dog Yet: An Introduction to Contemporary Theories of Religion," in Michael Stausberg (ed.), *Contemporary Theories of Religion: A Critical Companion*, 1–21. Abingdon: Routledge.
Stenmark, Mikael. 1997. "What is Scientism?" *Religious Studies* 33(1): 15–32. https://doi.org/10.1017/S0034412596003666
Taves, Ann. 2016. *Revelatory Events: Three Case Studies of the Emergence of New Spiritual Paths.* Princeton, NJ: Princeton University Press.
Taves, Ann and Egil Asprem. 2017. "Experience as event: event cognition and the study of (religious) experiences," *Religion, Brain, and Behavior* 7(1): 43–62. https://doi.org/10.1080/2153599X.2016.1150327
Taves, Ann and Egil Asprem. In preparation. *Explanation: A Critical Primer.* Sheffield: Equinox.
Tinbergen, Nikolaas. 1963. "On Aims and Methods of Ethology," *Zeitschrift für Tierpsychologie* 20: 410–433. https://doi.org/10.1111/j.1439-0310.1963.tb01161.x
Von Stuckrad, Kocku. 2010. "Reflections on the Limits of Reflection: An Invitation to the Discursive Study of Religion," *Method and Theory in the Study of Religion* 22: 156–169. https://doi.org/10.1163/157006810X512347
Wegner, Daniel M. 2002. *The Illusion of Conscious Will.* Cambridge, MA: MIT Press.
Woodward, James. 2014. "Scientific Explanation," in Edward N. Zalta (ed.), *The Stanford Encyclopedia of Philosophy*, Fall 2017 edition. Retrieved from https://plato.stanford.edu/archives/fall2017/entries/scientific-explanation (accessed March 3, 2018). https://doi.org/10.1093/acprof:oso/9780195145649.003.0002
Ylikoski, Petri. 2013. "Causal and Constitutive Explanation Compared," *Erkenn* 78: 277–297. https://doi.org/10.1007/s10670-013-9513-9

Chapter 14

"Constitutional God-Given Rights": Explaining Religion and Politics in the Malheur Occupation

Spencer Dew

Description

In January 2016, armed activists calling themselves the Citizens for Constitutional Freedom occupied the Malheur National Wildlife Refuge in Oregon, proclaiming that land and the buildings on it as belonging to "We the People" generally and Hardin County, Oregon, more specifically.[1] The media spectacle/law enforcement standoff that followed was predicated on this claim, justified by—or emerging from, as the activists said—a reading of the Constitution's "Enclave Clause," Article 1, Section 8, Clause 17.[2]

The Citizens for Constitutional Freedom held that the Constitution could not be interpreted—and, therefore, the Supreme Court was illegitimate in any claims made by its members, across history, of interpreting that text. Instead, the Constitution was to be read in line with the original intent of those who wrote it, both the Founders—guiding presences whose words and examples continue to inspire and direct true patriots, those who accept the responsibilities of American citizenship—and God or Christ, who was seen as instrumental in the creation of the Constitution, a text explicitly considered "sacred" and placed in the category of "scripture."

Predominantly Latter Day Saints (LDS), the Citizens for Constitutional Freedom understood history according to an eschatological framework which, in turn, hinged upon the Constitution. This document, the promise of the divinely-inspired American socio-political experiment, was in early 2016 "hanging by a thread" due to the "tyranny" of government overreach and (*illegal, unconstitutional*) claims and actions by that government.

The Citizens, then, were taking part in a simultaneous legal and eschatological drama, the stakes of which were cosmic: restore the rule of the Constitution, save America, free their fellow humans, pave the way for the second coming of Christ. While these themes are not, in the plain or literal sense, mentioned in the text of the U.S. Constitution, the Citizens for Constitutional Freedom found traces of them there, helped by their use of a specific edition—the so-called Skousen Constitution, assembled by W. Cleon Skousen—equipped with a scholarly apparatus including an introduction expressing the hope that this text "will awaken a desire within the inhabitants of this nation to restore to the Constitution the eminence given it by our Founders" and sections of quotations from the Founders ("Observing the Hand of Providence," on God's role in the Founding and the Constitution; "Preserving the Principles," on the responsibilities of citizens in relation to the Constitution; "Guarding Virtue and Freedom," emphasizing the need for citizens to be, in the words of John Adams, "a moral and religious people"; and finally, "Educating the People," emphasizing the need for education in regards to the workings of government and citizens' rights and responsibilities pertaining thereto).[3]

On the front cover of this Constitution—seen sticking out of the breast pockets of those Citizens occupying the Malheur site—is a painting of George Washington offering the viewer a quill pen. On the back cover, Washington's signature appears on a line marked "witness," and a line is left for the owner of each individual edition to sign a pledge "With the original Signers":

> I, as one of *We, the People of the United States*, affirm that I have read or will read our U.S. Constitution and pledge to maintain and promote its standard of liberty for myself and for my posterity, and do hereby attest to that by my signature.

In language at once performative—legally binding?—and referencing a specific register of Mormon teaching on the religion of politics ("standard of liberty" being that flag Moroni, son of Mormon, used to proclaim the freedom of his people in epic LDS sacred history),[4] this pledge, as action, was part of the broader actions of the Malheur occupation, an essential element of the visual rhetoric thereof, where the signed Constitution was displayed, worn next to the heart, gestured toward and with, and offered as proof of claims as well as source of authority.

The question at hand—the question of *method*—is: How do we think about this? What do we *do* with these observations, these facts on the ground?

Interpretation

Asprem and Taves, in a piece dedicated to defining and delineating, tell us that "interpretation" is "uncovering and reconstructing, to the best of our ability, the meanings and points of views of our subjects" (Chapter 13, this volume). Thus, an interpretive approach would note the self-identified folk taxonomical categories in which the Citizens locate themselves—as "armed nonviolent" protesters, for instance—and the historical lineages in which they locate themselves—with Martin Luther King and Rosa Parks as well as Captain Moroni and a broader typological history of Revolution as a repeating event in American identity as well as the political saga chronicled in the Book of Mormon.[5] Likewise, interpretation, as Asprem and Taves present it, would involve acknowledgment of the Citizen's imagined relation to the past—as present—to the text—as "sacred"—to the federal government—as corrupted, in need of an awakening into proper legal understanding and, thus, altered practices. Interpretation, in this vein, would consider the implications—the "meanings"—of the entanglement or overlap of native terms—"citizenship" and "salvation," for instance, and explore, surely, the particular contexts—as a majority Latter Day Saints movement, as a Western movement in the tradition of the Sagebrush Rebellion, as a reaction to recent expansions and policy shift by the Bureau of Land Management—as influences on and important conceptual touchstones for this community.

A promising approach, interpretation, but here we are considering *explanation*, a process Asprem and Taves claim applies to "human experience" "first redescribing phenomena of interest in behavioral terms, and then decomposing them into components (or building blocks) in order to reconstruct how the phenomena emerged and identify mechanisms that interact to produce them" (Chapter 13, this volume). Explanation, thus understood, stands outside "the religious field"— we need not employ language internal to that field (like "the sacred") nor even that contested term itself, "religion."

So, following this rubric: a phenomena of interest, to me, is the use of that Constitution, physically and rhetorically, as practice and belief. A building block, then, would be the act (I almost said "ritual," that work of the scholar's study) of signing the back of the booklet, pledging to serve as the Constitution's "keepers," to join a transhistorical community of fealty to that text believed to be divinely legal. Where does the Asprem and Taves method of explanation take us in regard to this data?

Explanation

Asprem and Taves are to be commended for throwing a gauntlet at NAASR's feet. Their focus on the double need both to delineate "what counts as theory," and then to apply such theory—is both indictment and invitation for this crowd. Moreover, they argue that "the boundary between phenomenological and naturalistic causal theories of religion is blurry because ... scholars are not clear on the distinction between descriptive, interpretation, and explanation and are worried about appearing reductionistic, scientistic, or positivist" (Chapter 13, this volume). They, as I have already noted, create such distinctions, boldly, and eschew worry about—indeed, note the necessity of—reduction. The turn to scientism I'll discuss below, but, in keeping with the spirit of commendation, I appreciate the opportunity of using the Asprem and Taves piece as an invitation to contemporary work I find particularly provoking in its engagement of scientific theories, tools, and data: Robert Fuller's *The Body of Faith: A Biological History of Religion in America*, for instance, T.M. Luhrmann's recent *When God Talks Back: Understanding the American Evangelical Relationship with God*, and Donovan Schaefer's *Religious Affects: Animality, Evolution, and Power*. All three offer exciting, challenging considerations of the consequences of evolutionary thought for thinking about religion. All three represent, moreover, the sort of scholarship I want to speak in favor of: sprawling, erudite but often messy, characterized by an ambition to open questions, to prompt debate and discussion—teachable texts, to be sure, and texts that serve the solitary scholar as something like rambunctious, nudging, occasionally infuriating companions. Books you work *with* and *against* as well as *from*.

I belabor this point because the Asprem and Taves piece has, to me, a very different tone. Here borders are erected and policed; the sense is one of narrowing conversation, understood by Asprem and Taves as a necessary process of clarification, a methodical outlining of terms and processes essential for the articulation of a method of study.

This Asprem and Taves method proceeds via arbitrary selection of data—in the case of the example provided, a moment in the life of Joseph Smith, a foundational claim about LDS history, decontextualized. Next, this data is understood in relation to a supersessionist narrative of history—a vulgar Darwinianism, in the sense of a revisionist cooptation of vocabulary, presented here as a master trope, the theoretical frame through which human behavior can be explained. Theory here is tinged with eschatology, as Asprem and Taves look toward consilience with something resembling utopian longing: a clarity, a correctness of inquiry, possible in the near future. Subjectively delineated data, then, scrutinized under a lens of truth—a real force, moving in the world—puts Darwinism in a position akin to—to use one of those words associated with the "religion field"—"faith." Asprem and Taves are expounding truth claims about "scientific" theory, within and to recognizable communities—us, NAASR, the broader community of believers in "theory" as that which keeps the "academic study of religion" from sliding into "theology" or worse—theory as the critical divider.

Among the rhetoric employed to support this truth claim, perhaps most prominent and forceful is that of *naturalization*—evolution as the way it has always been, as that which is true—though, of course, this claim is bolstered by appeal to recognized authorities as well. Darwin, well recognized as making clever empirical observations about finch beaks, is here the founding father of the one true way to explain human behavior.

As I read Asprem and Taves—from, to be sure, my own specific context—it is almost as if Darwin were reaching out, pen in hand, asking me to sign on and assent to follow Asprem and Taves's prophetic call to action (go forth and explain!), itself at heart an evangelizing mission, for, as Asprem and Taves admit, to consider a given human behavior in light of the evolutionary time frame is primarily useful simply for calling attention back to evolution. "How might an evolutionary framework allow us to do better?" they write. "Most crucially, it would require us to remind ourselves that intentionality is a product of evolution" (Chapter 13, this volume). The earlier draft, presented to the NAASR meeting, stated the issue more broadly: "Most crucially, it would require us to remind ourselves that humans are products of evolution" (Chapter 13, this volume). Explanation reifies and reiterates the master narrative, the truth claim.

Comparison

To what can it be compared? Asprem and Taves, here, give us data, of course—a document composed of "building blocks," emerging from and reflecting certain "complex cultural concepts." Their essay can be not only interpreted, but, via their own system, *explained*.

Explanation of Asprem and Taves—of human desire, striving for certainty of knowledge, of human behavior, enacting rigorous logic in order to render meaningful practices that otherwise would seem absurd, even of a worldview that simultaneously de-centers the human but returns the human—as explainer—back to a privileged position of being able to speak the narrative that shapes all life and that all life follows.

Joseph Smith's unearthing of an ancient chronicle or the prominent placement of a signed edition of the Constitution in the breast pocket of one's prison pajamas as one cross-examines oneself in court—every behavior comes back to evolution. The explainers, then, are in privileged position, their work existing at the latest end of a long trajectory of tool-use and conceptual thinking that makes it so effective. And the purpose doesn't shift so much as the nuance changes: get food, get a mate, establish dominance, prolong life, *survive* (with tenure).

Against Explanation

I feel an urge that, defying traditions of interpretation, I am tempted, now, to call "natural"—an impulse (instinct?) to mess things up a little.[6] There are too many clear lines, too much policing of territory in this Asprem/Taves piece, which seems not just post-hermeneutic but downright hermetic. I want to go ape, rattle if not bust out of the cage, set loose my inner, deep-diachronic monkey, throw—to go vernacular—some shit. A cheap joke:

Q: Why did the monkey throw feces?

A: Because it was available.

Which brings me to the first of three worries with which our signifying Darwinians leave me: the breezy treatment of "available beliefs" (Chapter 13, this volume). Joseph Smith, we're told, could turn to angels—and, presumably, ancient Jewish colonies, buried treasure, alternative gospels and the rest—because such beliefs were available, part of "the cultic milieu," the "mound-haunted landscape" of the Burnt-Over District, as one historian of Mormonism so memorably put it.[7] All that local color, what Courtney Bender calls "specific social contexts and communities" (Bender 2003: 77) and Wayne Proudfoot describes via "reference to concepts, beliefs, grammatical rules, and practices" (Proudfoot 1985: 228), if all of this is relegated to interpretation, then, again, what does explanation do except the only thing it ever can do, which is repeat itself and evangelize for its own master narrative? As I read this piece, there is only ever one ultimate explanation possible, while interpretation—on the contrary—is messy as a chimp pen. Diverse, infuriating, containing such cacophony that sometimes communication seems impossible, interpretation, in the wake of Asprem and Taves's work here, seems to me even more worth of celebration and engagement than before.

I never imagined I'd stand at a NAASR podium and celebrate the Big Tent, but that circus feels so much more *alive*, by which I mean, foremost, generative of questions and conversation but also prompting *responses* to the material consisting of something other than mechanistic or metaphysical frameworks—responses, for instance, of empathy and rage, solidarity and opposition, engagements with the ethical categories voices and/or evoked by the subjects and situations under consideration (see Tweed 2016). *Politics*, to use a euphemism. I see no possibility for politics in the Asprem/Taves method, and I find that absence disturbing. Asprem and Taves, (ironically?) serve to jolt me into an awareness of just how important I find *values* in religious studies (trust me, I gasped at this myself, as I wrote it). But equality, justice: are not such notions core concerns of work in and on human behavior?

O, the Humanities! Before I am excommunicated—ejected from the airtight NAASR bubble—for what sounds too suspiciously like liturgy or some acoustic ballad of "Revolutionary Love," let me flag the second thing that makes me wary in the Asprem and Taves approach: the location of the scholars, their scientific remove. Asprem and Taves "assume the legitimacy" not merely of "assumptions, principles and rules of procedure in the social and natural sciences" but also of the relation of scientist to petri dish or lab rat.

While I get the value of distancing ourselves from the tangle of our not being able to affirm the existence of that which we study, if we follow Asprem and Taves into a view of human behavior as so many compositions of CCCs, with no line between quote-unquote religion and politics, or law (or nationalism, patriotism, citizenship, maybe even also science), aren't we also sometimes *the folk* engaging in folk interpretations and classifications? When some Malheur occupier, whether he calls himself Ammon or Captain Moroni, shakes his Constitution in our direction, even if we don't share the doctrine, don't we share in the larger vocabulary and stakes of the debate; aren't we, here in this room, also "We, the People," simultaneously subjects and signers of the Constitution, for instance, suffering or benefiting from claims made about and actions undertaken in regard to that text?

Must we not take seriously the (conscious) logic of such claims and practices, attempt understanding? And likewise should we not consider such beliefs and behaviors as indictments of our own, perhaps unexamined stances in relation to structures of power, imaginaries, systems of rhetoric, and patterns of action? Explanation sidesteps such questions, avoids—or relegates to some less evolved approach—political awareness.

To make it plain, I think if we're not getting woke by what we study, we're working under illusions, and explanation, as Asprem and Taves has it, facilitates our remove from political considerations and suggests a path of scholarship and teaching eschewing political action which, in the engaging of our subject matter, is always already happening—so the path suggested is one that ignores, that denies, the political.

But here's my third worry, which is that said scientific approach is likewise not without, still, a determining role of *interest*. Asprem and Taves, again, are not measuring finch beaks: they decide what gets selected as data, to what behaviors and experiences, stories and voices, attention is paid. Which strikes me as an incursion of politics into a system that is presented, otherwise, as apolitical, which makes me think that those humanities concerns—things like justice and equality—are at fact in play in this method of explanation, too, just at the level of what gets selected for the explanatory treatment, a treatment that, while it may level out behaviors as all part of the Darwinian master narrative, nonetheless allows for some time spent with specific humans and their behaviors, like the attention, however passing, in the Asprem and Taves piece, to Joseph Smith and his early community of mechanistic relation.

Final Questions Toward Future Theory

My initial interest in this conversation—the project of Method Today—was spurred by both discomfort with and interest in the ways that select experts, particularly through and in the service of popular media, engage in distortive "explanation"—in the vernacular sense—offering accounts of "religion" and religious individuals/communities that reify religion as a distinct force, motivating human action. In relation to the Malheur occupation, Russell McCutcheon published a frequently cited blog post on how such instances of "explaining" express (often implicit) theories of religion—i.e., "does religion cause behavior or does it instead authorize what we do for a variety of other reasons?" (McCutcheon 2016). Expert engagement with Malheur, moreover, reified religion by passing judgment on whether what was voiced and expressed in the occupation was acceptable (legally defendable) religion or not, turning to ridicule and dismissal in order to erect a comfortable distance between the public and those occupiers, motivated either by ridiculous "religion" or some con presented as and copping the name of religion.[8] Across this range of cases, religion is privileged and defended as a universal, even eternal reality in spite of compelling evidence than the category is largely arbitrary. Experts, indeed, are left to wrestle with the fact that the religion and "non-religious" seem inextricable, even indistinguishable in statements and actions from the Malheur occupiers. The "political" or "economic" and "religious" or "non-religious" "goals" and "motivations" blur, requiring more explanation, often taking refuge in the dubiousness purity of any "religion" so deeply invested in the "political," for instance (Marginalia 2016).[9]

As I return to the Asprem and Taves piece after in-person discussion of their larger project at the annual NAASR meeting in San Antonio, I am confused as to the degree to which this essay, too, maintains a position of privilege for the category of "religion." In my reading, Asprem and Taves were offering a method for explaining human behavior across a wide range of complex cultural concepts or CCCs—with no differentiation between the economic and the religious, for instance. But as Taves made clear at the meeting, this is not the case, and revisions to the essay subsequently make clear that Asprem and Taves "choose to analyze the use of religion-related terms by social actors" (Chapter 13, this volume). Asprem and Taves rely on their subjects to call a given behavior "religious" (using that or a term they identify as analogous, which, by way of example, Asprem and Taves offer "magic" and "prayer"). After that point, the behavior is analyzed as if it were any other facet of *human experience*," without explanatory privilege being given to "terms presumed to be internal to the religious field," but I am left unclear on why there is the initial privilege of "religion" (or its supposed cognates) at all (Chapter 13, this volume; italics original). Wouldn't mechanistic explanation, as proposed by Asprem and Taves, apply equally across the range of human experience? While I have voiced reservations about their approach, one promise I saw—and continue, in rereading the essay, to see, despite Taves's comments to the contrary—to this approach was that it artfully (and, to my mind, rightly) side-stepped debate about the category of "religion" by approaching human behavior as human behavior, period. The range of "religion-related terms," as I read the potential of this approach, enter the scholar's consideration at the level of interpretation (as part of the matrix of "available beliefs"), but they are moot and thus remain mute when it comes to explanation.

If I could request a direct response to my response for this volume, it would be this: why limit the model of explanation here to that explicitly identified (by the subject or, through the identification of "related terms," by the scholar) as "religion"? Why not simply lay out a method for explaining human behavior at the level of complex cultural concepts? Such a model of explanation would be liberating not only in its expanse but also in its impartiality to the roiling mess of reification or obsessions over authenticity that consume so many lesser approaches to explaining that which could be called religion. Such a model, moreover, would defy the borders of disciplines and departments and suggest an academic approach to human experience in keeping with the vision of consilience animating the Asprem and Taves project.

Notes

1 Among the best coverage of the occupation and the autumn 2016 trail of the first seven occupiers is Oregon Public Broadcasting's radio series, "This Land is Our Land" (www.opb.org/news/series/burns-oregon-standoff-bundy-militia-news-updates/occupation-trial-podcast-this-land-is-our-land, accessed December 13, 2016) and Anthony McCann's two-part essay in the *Los Angeles Review of Books*, "Sovereign Feelings" and "Ours but Not Ours" (available at https://lareviewofbooks.org/article/malheur-part-i/# and https://lareviewofbooks.org/article/malheur-part-ii-not/#, accessed December 13, 2016). The Bundy brothers, who deferred to the Holy Spirit as actual leader of the occupation but could be seen as fulfilling that role themselves, recorded multiple video addresses explaining their reasoning and goals, including Ammon Bundy's "Dear Friends" recording, ("'Dear Friends:' Ammon Bundy Responds to Stewart Rhodes' Statement Re: The Hammonds," posted by KafkaWinstonWorld, January 1, 2016 at www.youtube.com/watch?v=Zl5rkosu2Ig, accessed December 13, 2016) responding to questions of the righteousness of the occupation. In a December 15, 2015 town hall meeting in Burns, Oregon, the Bundys discussed with the local public their motivation and sought to acquire support for their act of protest against perceived federal overreach. See "Town Hall Meeting Regarding Hammong Family—Burns, OR—12-15-2015," posted by S. Thomas Lewis, December 17, 2015 (in three parts: www.youtube.com/watch?v=0MwcySznHJw, www.youtube.com/watch?v=OPTLXg1fKZ8, and www.youtube.com/watch?v=ACK_nm3oTy8, accessed December 13, 2016).
2 "To exercise exclusive Legislation in all Cases whatsoever, over such District (not exceeding ten Miles square) as may, by Cession of Particular States, and the Acceptance of Congress, become the Seat of the Government of the United States, and to exercise

like Authority over all Places purchased by the Consent of the Legislature of the State in which the Same shall be, for the Erection of Forts, Magazines, Arsenals, dock-Yards, and other needful Buildings."

3 *The Constitution of the United States with Index and the Declaration of Independence*, National Center for Constitutional Studies, 2016 (https://archive.org/details/ SkousenPocketConstitution, accessed December 13, 2016). See also Nigel Duara, "Oregon Armed Protesters Invoke the Constitution—Annotated by a Conspiracy Theorist," *Los Angeles Times*, January 21, 2016 (www.latimes.com/nation/la-na-ff-orego n-standoff-constitution-20160121-story.html, accessed December 13, 2016).

4 *Book of Mormon*, Alma 46:13: "And he fastened on his head-plate, and his breastplate, and his shields, and girded on his armor about his loins; and he took the pole, which had on the end thereof his rent coat, (and he called it the title of liberty) and he bowed himself to the earth, and he prayed mightily unto his God for the blessings of liberty to rest upon his brethren, so long as there should a band of Christians remain to possess the land—"

5 See, in particular, Cox (2014). Shawna Cox was instrumental both in the Bunkerville standoff led by Cliven Bundy and the Malheur occupation, for which she was one of the first seven defendants charged with conspiracy and found not guilty in October of 2016.

6 A feeling emerging from "the sub-personal level of evolved drives and tendencies that compete for control of the body below the threshold of consciousness," perhaps?

7 Origin for the term "cultic milieu" goes to Colin Campbell (1972: 119–136). The phrase "mound-haunted landscape" is Roger Kennedy's (Kennedy 1994: 230, quoted in Givens 2003: 168).

8 One egregious example of this is Goodwin (2016).

9 Dismissal of the Malheur occupiers religion as somehow inauthentic has often been conducted via identification of Mormonism as somehow inordinately political—a Christian theological argument masked as academic observation.

References

Bender, Courtney. 2003. *Heaven's Kitchen: Living Religion at God's Love We Deliver*. Chicago, IL: University of Chicago Press. https://doi.org/10.7208/chicago/ 9780226042831.001.0001

Campbell, Colin. 1972. "The Cult, the Cultic Milieu and Secularization," in *A Sociological Yearbook of Religion in Britain* 5. London: SCM Press.

Cox, Shawna. 2014. *Last Rancher Standing: The Cliven Bundy Saga, a Close-Up View*. Rochester, VA: Legends Library Publishing.

Fuller, Robert. 2013. *The Body of Faith: A Biological History of Religion in America*. Chicago, IL: University of Chicago Press. https://doi.org/10.7208/chicago/ 9780226025117.001.0001

Givens, Terry L. 2003. *By the Hand of Mormon: The American Scripture that Launched a New World Religion*. Oxford: Oxford University Press.

Goodwin, Megan. 2016. "#VanillaIsis, White Tears, and the Adventures of Captain Moroni," *Religion Dispatches*, January 7. Retrieved from http://religiondispatches. org/vanillaisis-white-tears-and-the-adventures-of-captain-moroni (accessed December 13, 2016).

Kennedy, Roger. 1994. *Hidden Cities: The Discovery and Loss of Ancient North American Civilization*. New York: Free Press.

Luhrmann, T. M. 2012. *When God Talks Back: Understanding the American Evangelical Relationship with God*. London: Vintage.
Marginalia. 2016. "Impolite Conversations #8: Oregon Standoff," Marginalia blog of the *Los Angeles Review of Books*, February 2. Retrieved from http://marginalia.lareviewofbooks.org/impolite-conversations-8-oregon-standoff (accessed December 13, 2016).
McCutcheon, Russell. 2016. "So What's Your Theory of Religion?" posted January 6, 2016 to the Studying Religion in Culture blog. Retrieved from http://religion.ua.edu/blog/2016/01/so-whats-your-theory-of-religion (accessed December 13, 2016).
Proudfoot, Wayne. 1985. *Religious Experience*. Berkeley, CA: University of California Press.
Schaefer, Donovan. *Religious Affects: Animality, Evolution, and Power*. Durham, NC: Duke University Press.
Tweed, Thomas A. 2016. "Valuing the Study of Religion: Improving Difficult Dialogues Within and Beyond the AAR's 'Big Tent'," 2015 American Academy of Religion Presidential Address, *Journal of American Academy of Religion* 84(2): 287–311. Retrieved from http://jaar.oxfordjournals.org/content/early/2016/04/12/jaarel.lfw019.full.pdf+html (accessed December 13, 2016). https://doi.org/10.1093/jaarel/lfw019

Chapter 15

Ontological versus Axiological Approaches to Religion

Joel Harrison

One of the primary goals of Egil Asprem and Ann Taves's essay is to show that reductive explanatory approaches to "human" subject matter do not set out "to subsume or subordinate the humanities to the natural and social sciences, but to connect them in a spirit of consilience" (Chapter 13, this volume). This spirit is intended to clear space for the interests of the humanities such that those scholars can and ought to continue their work as they have—though they ought also to acknowledge the consilience of their work with that of the natural sciences,[1] which are united together under the authors' theory of new mechanism. On the authors' view, the work of cultural studies, literary studies, history, etc. gives only a partial account of what the authors refer to as a *mechanism*, which in turn help to explain "complex cultural concepts"[2] (CCCs) such as religion and its related categories. When we explain an event, a cultural concept, an individual's actions, we are breaking these things down into component "parts"—mechanisms—that include cultural context and individual motivations but also psychological, biological, and evolutionary factors. These can be further broken down such that we can explain *anything* in terms of the most complex synchronic mechanistic levels or the broadest diachronic time scales.[3] Indeed the scope of their theory is so broad that it is difficult to see what *wouldn't* fall under its explanatory umbrella.

However, the breadth of the theory also makes it difficult to see what analytic purchase it actually has. Why would one not simply "specify a phenomenon of interest" (Chapter 13, this volume) to be explained, as the authors acknowledge we *must* do, *without* taking the further step of acknowledging its consilience with, say, evolutionary biological accounts? Religious studies scholars do this already. Any cursory scan of the AAR annual meeting catalog will show that myriad phenomena of interest are available for study, and even if two seemingly unrelated phenomena share consilience, they need not be drawn into a unified explanatory theory of cause and effect. The authors admit that the widely varied interests of the discipline ought not be reduced to a single, material principle that would explain them *ultimately*. Yet the theory of new mechanism they advance seems to do exactly that by arguing that while non-reductive approaches can bear fruitful analyses of human phenomena, their fruits are only fully realized when viewed as material mechanisms that are part of a larger mechanical system. It is this particular claim that I seek to contest here. The approaches of the human sciences produce analysis that is valuable on its own terms without the theory of new mechanism.

This is because ideas, beliefs, and actions understood as "religious" by the actors who engage them have their own material effects. One might think that if we view ideas as having causal agency, then we are taking a non-reductive view of religious ideas. However, the authors acknowledge the former while rejecting the latter; they argue that these effects must be understood as mechanisms within their theory that help to explain other mechanisms and CCCs. On my view, the basic failure here is to recognize that an explanation of effects with ideational causes is by definition non-reductive because it requires *not* reducing ideas to their material causes for the sake of analysis. If such reduction is performed, the aims of analysis change. Near the beginning of their essay, Asprem and Taves admit that religion, as a complex cultural concept, "does not exist apart from human communicative actions" and that mechanisms can include "the goal directed actions of animals and the mental abilities required to produce them as potential causal factors" (Chapter 13, this volume). In other words, the ideas of religious adherents can have causal capacities on some level of the mechanism. Coupled with later clarification in the essay,[4] I understand this to be an endorsement of a *kind* of phenomenology of religion as having analytical purchase in their theory. This endorsement comes with the now familiar caution against phenomenology as the *end* of analysis, which would produce a *sui generis* theory of religion where one may only explain the ideas, beliefs, and mental states of religious adherents on the terms that they understand them. The authors move beyond phenomenology, however, by positing religious ideas, belief, and action as nested mechanisms, which help explain complex cultural concepts like "religion" and related concepts.

It is precisely at this intersection of a new mechanistic theory of explanation for complex cultural concepts and the admittance of ideas into such a theory that I would question whether Asprem and Taves' theory (a) is actually completely reductive and (b) provides a compelling case for the unification of synchronic, diachronic, material, and ideational factors into a single coherent theory with sufficient analytical power. To use one of the authors' examples, putting "mechanisms" as academically disparate as "the terrorists who carried out the attack on 9/11" and the study of buildings impacted by planes into causal relationship— which can then *also* be explained diachronically on a time scale as large as evolution—seems to be simply an observation of the facts rather than a theory of how these facts are causally related. While these factors are *in some sense* related to one another, as areas of academic interest, evolutionary biology and cultural studies in the Middle East are extremely diverse areas of interest and thus hard to imagine as part of a single theoretical account in scholarly practice.

I make my case by showing that their theory does not attend to an explanatory *rupture* between particular levels of explanation that they identify; namely between a material-causal explanation of a particular religious belief, idea, or mental state and an explanation of how said belief, idea, or mental state has particular ideational or material effects. These are, in fact, two different kinds of explanation of religion and its related concepts—one *ontological*, the other *axiological*. These represent two different ways of *regarding* a religious phenomenon, idea, belief, action, etc. conceptually.[5] I agree with the authors that these kinds of explanation are not mutually exclusive nor are they necessarily at odds with one another. However, I do not think, as Asprem and Taves do, that accounts of effects produced by ideational causes are reductive explanations that can be placed within a "causal history."[6] To the contrary, I argue that particular "causal capacities," those of religious ideas, beliefs, and actions understood as "religious," can be shown to disrupt attempts at clean causal histories that aim to unite material, ideational, diachronic, and synchronic accounts into one single explanatory account.

A causal explanation of an idea, belief, or mental state, including the concept of religion itself, is an *ontological* explanation. It is an account of what a belief, idea, or mental state *is* in terms of material processes, e.g. explanations through cognitive science, evolutionary biology, or social factors such as economics or politics. In the nineteenth and early twentieth centuries, we find a number of such ontological accounts. Karl Marx, for example, argues that religion *is* a function of the economic mode of production. Tylor, that it *is* an intellectual account of the unknown. Freud, that it *is* psychological neurosis. Each figure is explaining what religion *is* apart from what adherents understand religion to be; they each see themselves as advancing a theory of what religion is "in reality." What has "ontological" status, then, is not religion as such but rather the material processes that give rise to the concept. Asprem and Taves clearly argue for accounts that are not beholden to the explanations and interpretations of the religious adherent. However, they depart from this early form of reduction in two ways. First, they reject the possibility of identifying a single material principle, such as "economy," that would ground a material account of religion. Second, and more pertinent to my argument, is that the ontological status of religious ideas seems to waver between being objects that can be explained in terms of material processes, and thus explained away, and objects that themselves have causal capacities and thus must "exist" in some sense. In what sense they do is not entirely clear; however, in taking an *axiological* approach to religious ideas, beliefs, and mental states, religious ideas need not be "real" in a material sense. That they are held by actors in ways that motivate their behavior and choices is enough to justify their selection as "phenomena of interest." They are real axiologically rather than ontologically in that they generate and are generated by values rather than having reality outside of values.

An axiological explanation, then, is an explanation of effects, material or ideational, which have an ideational cause. This is an account of how particular *values* in the form of ideas, beliefs, and mental states generate particular consequences. In these cases, although the causal ideational components are, at some level, the effect of material factors to which the ideational components are reducible, this reduction does not have sufficient explanatory power to give a *full* account of the effects generated by ideational causes. It is in these cases that we must take religious ideas, beliefs, and mental states as they are represented by those who hold them *not* in order to get at their meaning *as such* (which would actually fall under the ontological approach) but in order to explain their effects.

It is important to clarify that this theoretical account of a division between ontological and axiological explanations of religion is not intended as a course charted *between* phenomenology of religion and material-scientific reductive accounts. Whether the scholar's axiological explanation is conscious to the religious adherent does not have any bearing on such an analysis, which differentiates it from early, problematic phenomenological accounts of religion. I see both phenomenology of religion and explanatory reduction as engaged in the *same* project—namely, an account of what religion *is* (or is not as the case may be)—and thus in contrast with axiological explanations. Robert Segal confirms this in his 1983 essay "In Defense of Reductionism" when he argues that Eliade's phenomenological project is just as reductive as the explicitly reductive approaches he is reacting against.[7] In other words, both projects, Segal argues, seek to explain what religion is. My argument here is not that material explanations of religion or critiques of phenomenology should cease, nor that phenomenology as it has been done in the past should return to its former glory (it should not.) Rather, it is intended to clear the conceptual space for explanations of what religion *does*, which *may or may not* benefit from ontological accounts as supplements to axiological explanations and which would not preclude the axiological from serving as supplements to ontological explanations.

There are hints of a division between the ontological and axiological already embedded in Asprem and Taves's argument, particularly at the admittance of beliefs, ideas, and mental states as units of analysis both as causes and effects and the necessity of identifying a particular "phenomenon of interest" somewhere within the broader scope of the whole mechanism in question.[8] The authors, however, view both as a necessary recognition of the particularities of and distinctions between kinds of data as well as differences between the kinds of objects a scholar might seek to explain, whereas I want to insist on two different ways of conceptualizing the same object of interest. Asprem and Taves acknowledge that, traditionally, these sorts of differences between objects of interest were expressed primarily as a fundamental difference between the human and natural sciences or a difference between interpretation and explanation and identify Wilhelm Dilthey as one of the progenitors of this (Chapter 13, this volume). Like the authors, Dilthey argued the difference was primarily a matter of object or data. Dilthey refers to this distinction in terms of experiences: experience supplied by the senses and "inner experience," which refers to emotions, feelings, and, more broadly cultural attitudes and climates, each provide us different objects at our disposal for explanation. Thus, if we are trying to analyze "Goethe's life" as a conceptual whole, "so long as no one maintains that he can derive and better explain the essence of the emotion, poetic creativity, and rational reflection, which we call Goethe's life, out of the design of his brain or the characteristics of his body, then no one will challenge the independent position of such a science" (Dilthey 1988: 80) by which he means the human sciences. In short, on Dilthey's view, the natural sciences are interested in objects of study entirely different from those of the human sciences, even if both are ultimately interested in "Goethe's life" as a historical phenomenon.

Asprem and Taves generate what I see as an identical division between objects of interest as a marker of difference, e.g. an interest in terrorists rather than jet propulsion in the context of the World Trade Center on 9/11 as a conceptual whole.[9] They reject Dilthey's analysis, however, by maintaining that a better explanation of "Goethe's life" taken as a conceptual whole can be provided by their theory derived from the natural sciences which would emphasize the consilience between the study of Goethe's brain and the study of his writing. In other words, such a whole can and ought to be folded into a theory of new mechanistic explanation where such objects can be elaborated synchronically as nested levels of a mechanism (e.g. Goethe's brain and Goethe's writing) or diachronically "as linked into causal chains distributed among spatiotemporal lines" (Chapter 13, this volume). In the context of the WTC on 9/11, an explanation will "include the interaction between a building (X_1) and a plane (X_2). The building (X_1) as a whole is constructed of "parts" that in turn explain how the building responded to the impact of the plane. The behavior of the plane (X_2), which contained crew and passengers, some of whom hijacked the plane" (Chapter 13, this volume). The hijackers can be broken down further into individuals with motives and reasons that can be explained causally on their own terms, i.e. as part of the cause of 9/11, *and* evolutionarily as an effect on an enormous timescale. Thus, despite maintaining Dilthey's distinction between the objects of interest that might appeal to different types of scholars, the authors intend their theory to be a larger umbrella theory under which all objects of interests and approaches to them serve an explanatory function.

However, there is another way of conceiving the distinction between natural and human sciences not in terms of objects but rather *concepts*, which are constituted by two different ways of regarding the same object. When the object in question is "historical" as in a specific event, person, or text, natural scientific approaches cannot account for it in its totality because the natural sciences are not interested in the unique particularities of specific events but in the adherence of events, persons, etc. to general scientific laws.[10] Conversely, if we are interested in a class of events, persons, or texts, as general concepts, e.g. "wars," "poets," or "novels," the unique particulars of individuals that fit these categories cease to be the element of primary importance. This difference is not intended to subordinate one kind of interest to the other; rather, it highlights the rupture between the two kinds of explanation. If we're interested in natural scientific classification and explanation according to scientific laws and theories, we lose the particularity of the historical event.

The authors' "mash-up" between natural and human sciences in the 9/11 example illustrates this quite well. If we want to understand the physics of buildings impacted by planes, the event "the collapse of the WTC on 9/11" is incidental to that analysis. Even if we want to understand how *these* particular buildings fell, we would still need the general laws of physics that apply to all buildings and planes. Thus, the unique event becomes only one example subsumed under the universal laws of physics. We may say the same for evolutionary biology applied to the actors who carried out the attack. However, if our aim is to analyze the collapse of the World Trade Center on 9/11 in its historical particularity and its particular effects on other phenomena, we must understand this event as a unique, individual conceptual whole. To subsume it to any general concept, e.g. "terrorist attacks," or to general natural processes, e.g. evolutionary biology, forces us to subordinate the particulars of the unique historical event to the characteristics of the general concept or general laws of nature. An historical concept, by contrast, must be unique and individual because, by definition, history itself is composed of an infinite number of unique, individual, unrepeatable events.[11]

If we form general concepts through repetition and the erasure of difference and history, by definition, is unique and without repeated individuals (e.g. there is and will only ever be *one* collapse of the WTC on 9/11) we may wonder how we are to form such "historical concepts" at all. What criteria bring to our attention discrete historical events as conceptual wholes, and how do we justify choosing one event over another for study? Natural scientific methods cannot provide us such criteria because they require repetition. Only an analysis of value, an axiology, which gives us the cultural significance of any historical individual, can justify the selection and conceptualization of any particular phenomenon over another. The sociologist Max Weber gives us a wonderful example of this methodology and historical conceptualization. Weber makes for an interesting case in this context since his method has typically been associated with *Verstehen*[12] and is often characterized as an interpretation of religious belief and action rather than any kind of explanation, especially not like those his contemporaries generated. Placing Weber's work in the framework of my distinction between ontological and axiological explanations, I argue that Weber's work on religion is a type of explanation, namely an axiological one.

In *The Protestant Ethic and the Spirit of Capitalism*, Weber sets out to explain a particular complex cultural concept he calls "the spirit of capitalism" which, he writes in the second chapter, must be understood as "an historical individual; i.e. a complex of elements associated in historical reality which we unite into a conceptual whole from the standpoint of their cultural significance" (Weber 2002: 13). The aim of the text is to give an account of the conditions and primary factors that could have generated "the spirit of capitalism" as a complex cultural concept. Note that Weber is not after the origin of capitalism as such. He does not deny that there are material conditions that contribute to the formation of the spirit of capitalism as a conceptual whole. Instead, he rejects the historical materialist theory that the capitalist mode of production *alone* would be sufficient to explain this particularly efficient, yet peculiarly ascetic type of capitalism. There must be another factor, which he identifies as "inner-worldly ascetic Protestantism," that is itself another historical individual taken as a conceptual whole.

Time does not permit a full treatment of what Weber means precisely by this particular form of Protestant asceticism, but he arrives at the concept through an analysis of a set of theological concepts and their popular circulation among Calvinists in the seventeenth and eighteenth centuries. On Weber's account, the explanatory power of any material explanation of these theological concepts ends at the concepts themselves when considered in relationship to the spirit of capitalism. In other words, the theological concepts cannot be subordinated under any more fundamental material explanation *if* our aim is an account of the spirit of capitalism. The ideas themselves, apart from their material explanation, are the cause of the spirit of capitalism. This does not mean Weber thinks there isn't any material cause that can explain these concepts—only that such causes have no primary explanatory power for the spirit of capitalism. In other words, there is a rupture between the material causes of predestination as a historical-theological concept and the spirit of capitalism. The former cannot explain the latter. Note also that Weber is not simply "bracketing" the material causes of predestination for the sake of a phenomenological explanation of Protestant asceticism. His account of Calvin's theology and its circulation is not an end in itself; rather, it serves to explain the concept at the center of his interest, the spirit of capitalism. This explanation extends well beyond the explicit intentions of those Protestants who helped generate this spirit without reducing their intentions, ideas, beliefs, and actions to material causes.

This difference can be clarified further in my distinction between ontological and axiological accounts. The theological concepts "predestination" and "calling" have ontological explanations apart from their religious meaning; they do not have ontological reality independent of their material causes. One could easily imagine any number of potential psychological or evolutionary explanations, for example, that explain what those concepts are in natural scientific terms. However, such explanations cannot give us a robust account of what those concepts *do* as they circulate among religious populations. This is because these concepts have axiological reality. They are believed, filled with meaning, and applied to action by people who hold them to be true and good. In order to give an account of them in this sense, we need an axiology—an analysis of value—that seeks to understand the cultural significance of these ideas, how such populations understand the concepts and fill them with meaningful content, and how the meaning of that content in turn has effects on other value relationships and the relationships between social institutions.[13] For Weber's analysis of the spirit of capitalism, this entails an explanation of how a commitment to the outward signs of one's election to salvation, understood in terms of purely ethical behavior, becomes rationalized with capitalism such that capitalist production itself, especially if efficient, can serve as one of these signs, and eventually becomes the primary sign.

If we allow that the circulation of religious ideas can have determinative effects on material reality, which Asprem and Taves do, then we must allow that not every element of the authors' mechanistic schema is fruitfully reducible at all times and in all analytical situations. Rather, this kind of reduction seems very much dependent upon the analysis in which one is interested. If my aim is an axiological account of the effects of religious ideas, it is difficult to see why I would *ultimately* subsume that account to a more fundamental new mechanistic theory that puts my account into a cause–effect relationship with factors that I would argue, from the outset, cannot explain the phenomenon I seek to explain. To use another example from the essay, it may be that Joseph Smith's family initiated the acceptance of his account that a supernatural agent gave him instructions regarding the golden plates and that there is a material account of how this could happen, explained in generally natural scientific terms. However, one might also be interested in how the circulation of Smith's account (made possible by the specific cultural values of the populations in which it circulated), the specific theological implications, the formation of a new religious sect in the U.S., etc. had particular determinative effects on social formations in the nineteenth-century Midwest.[14] In the latter case, our interest is specifically in how religious ideas are understood, evaluated, and circulated by a population in order to put that axiology in service of an account of a particular complex cultural concept or historical individual of interest, whether material or ideational.

While I applaud Asprem and Taves's willingness to admit religious ideas, beliefs, and mental states as such as data in an account of complex cultural concepts, it seems less clear how their theory provides any robust analytic purchase at specific levels of interest. In other words, what does the umbrella of new mechanism provide analytically to an account like Weber's? If my interest as a scholar is in the effects of values and ideas, what does my work benefit by putting it into a larger causal schema such as what new mechanism provides? I want to emphasize that this challenge is not a challenge to the legitimacy of natural science in offering explanations of religion. Nor is it a claim that axiological and ontological accounts of religion are mutually exclusive. Rather, it has hopefully signaled that there is room in religious studies for the explanations that I have described because they escape both phenomenological/theological reduction as well as the natural scientific reduction advanced here.

Joel Harrison is a PhD candidate in religious studies at Northwestern University. His work focuses on the intersection of social philosophy, theology, and the emergence of critical theory in the early twentieth century as well as theory and method in religious studies.

Notes

1   "While this approach may at first sight seem alien to some of our humanities colleagues, we hope to have shown that in *principle* this approach can do justice to a whole swath of cultural, psychological, material, and social elements. To seek an explanation of a phenomenon is, simply, to search for mechanisms in causal chains connected over longer time scales" (Chapter 13, this volume).
2   These are defined in the essay as "abstract nouns with unstable, overlapping meanings that vary within and across social formations" (Chapter 13, this volume).
3   "To seek an explanation of a phenomenon is, simply, to search for mechanisms that connect individual parts in some causally connected whole, and to embed these mechanisms in causal chains connected over longer time scales. This urges us to expand our explanatory scope in two dimensions: diachronically, we must connect the historical time scales studied by historians to an evolutionary time scale studied by biologists; synchronically, we must deepen our analysis of behavior from the level of conscious intentions, reasons, and goals, to the sub-personal level of evolved drives and tendencies that compete for the control of the body below the threshold of consciousness" (Chapter 13, this volume).

4 See their explanation of the collapse of the WTC on 9/11 or their example of Joseph Smith and his family (Chapter 13, this volume).
5 The authors treat this distinction as one between objects of analysis rather than two ways of conceptualizing the same object. The difference between these two approaches is detailed more below.
6 "The analysis of causal chains is necessary to establish which events are related (i.e. whether it is A or B or both that are causally relevant for bringing about C), while a synchronic analysis of nested levels of mechanisms is necessary to answer why, or in virtue of what, A or B has the capacity to act on C. Put differently, one method establishes *causal histories*, the other explains the *causal capacity* of individual entities in those histories" (Chapter 13, this volume; emphasis original).
7 "When Eliade imputes to the beliefs and actions of self-professed atheists a significance of which they are not just partly but wholly unconscious and which not just exceeds but outright contradicts their own conscious one, his equation of the actor's point of view with an irreducibly religious one proves entirely arbitrary. Indeed, it becomes hard to see why his interpretation of the actor's point of view is any less reductionistic than the interpretations of religion he opposes as reductionistic" (Segal 1983: 99).
8 Using 9/11 as an example, the authors write, "For example, a terrorism scholar may be less interested in the chemistry of jet propulsion and the physics of collapsing buildings, stipulating their phenomenon of interest instead as how groups and individuals can become motivated toward behaviors understood as 'terrorism'" (Chapter 13, this volume).
9 See note 7 above.
10 This theory comes from the Southwest School of Neo-Kantianism, notably Wilhelm Windelband and his student Heinrich Rickert at the turn of the twentieth century. Rickert views the reality taken in by empirical experience as an infinite barrage of "individuals"—infinite in number as well as individual complexity. This manifold is rationalized by means of the two types of concept under discussion. "Individuals" for Rickert could refer to what the authors call mechanisms, CCCs, or phenomena, e.g. "religion," "the collapse of the World Trade Center on 9/11," "Joseph Smith's claim to have recovered and translated ancient golden plates," as well as the constituent parts that make up these concepts (see Rickert 1986).
11 The neo-Kantian philosopher Heinrich Rickert calls these concepts "historical individuals." He writes: "History can never attempt to represent reality with reference to the *general*, but only with reference to the *specific* and the *individual*. Only the individual and the unique *really happened*, and only a science concerned with the unique, real event itself can be called historical science" (Rickert 1986: 48; emphasis original).
12 Segal, for example, certainly has Weber in mind in his analysis of *Verstehen* and argument for why such allegedly "irreducible" methods are actually reductive: "Advocates of *Verstehen* in history and the social sciences tend to reduce the actor's reasons for his actions to some basic, typically unconscious universal need-for an orderly world, for example" (Segal 1983: 105).
13 For Weber, this entails a new relationship between the spheres of economy and religion such that Calvinists can justify their efficient and successful participation in the economy via an account of their religious value commitments, i.e. outward signs of eternal election. "If any inner relationship between certain expressions of the old Protestant spirit and modern capitalistic culture is to be found, we must attempt to find it, for better or worse not in its alleged more or less materialistic or at least anti-ascetic joy of living, but in its purely religious characteristics" (Weber 2002: 11).

14 Asprem and Taves point out that "Phenomenologically oriented and methodologically agnostic scholars ... limit themselves to analyzing what arose as a result of Smith's claims" (Chapter 13, this volume), but it is unclear if they understand this sort of analysis in the same way that I have explicated, i.e. in terms of irreducible ideas and values.

References

Dilthey, Wilhelm. 1988. *Introduction to the Human Sciences: An Attempt to Lay a Foundation for the Study of Society and History*, trans. Ramon J. Betanzos. Detroit, MI: Wayne State University Press.

Rickert, Heinrich. 1986. *The Limits of Concept Formation in Natural Science: A Logical Introduction to the Historical Sciences*, ed. and trans. Guy Oakes. Cambridge: Cambridge University Press.

Segal, Robert. 1983. "In Defense of Reductionism, " *Journal for the American Academy of Religion* 51(1): 97–124. https://doi.org/10.1093/jaarel/LI.1.97

Weber, Max. 2002. *The Protestant Ethic and the Spirit of Capitalism*, trans. Talcott Parsons. New York: Routledge,.

Chapter 16

Is Explanation Existential?

Paul Kenny

Count me in

My response is to give a resounding cheer for natural theories of religious behaviors that "are located within a critical naturalistic (and hence realist) framework, premised on the view that humans evolved" and presupposing that good explanations (not scientific theories) "of religion offer causal explanations of human behaviors that are ultimately grounded in an evolutionary (rather than transcendental) framework" (Chapter 13, this volume).

My aim in this response is to be a critical friend. I will offer some alternative points of emphasis without demurring from the larger goal and scope of the authors' project.

The first point of emphasis is to prefer the term good explanation to scientific theories in the opening quote from the paper above. I do this because I want to foreground a point made elsewhere in Ann and Egil's paper that the goal is "not to subsume or subordinate the humanities to the natural and social sciences, but to connect them in a spirit of consilience" (Slingerland and Collard 2011, quoted in Chapter 13, this volume).

In my view, no good explanation of religion(s) will be created without inputs from both the humanities and science and furthermore a potential problem of the new mechanistic approach is its overemphasis on scientific method, specifically on analysis into sub components, of which more later on in this response. Following David Deutsche, a natural scientist, I am promoting good explanations by whatever method they are arrived at.

I share the authors' stance in asserting the right to offer explanations of religion in non-religious terms. With them, I reject the, often leveled, charge in SOR, of the "crime" of crude reductionism. Their distinction between descriptive reduction and explanatory reduction, which they use to justify the latter and excoriate the former, helps but, in my view, it does not fully escape the limitations of the reductive method in science and in the new mechanism (Chapter 13, this volume).

The authors celebrate the good, explanatory reduction of the new mechanism. There is an interesting tension throughout in the need both to defend reduction and to limit it. I was left confused as to inter-level causation in the new mechanism. At first sight, the suggestion seems to be that there are no causal, cross level mechanisms, in wider reading it then appears that inter-level causality is possible, for example in the *Stanford Encyclopedia of Philosophy* entry.

My present understanding of the new mechanism is that it holds within it the assumption "that science must or should always explain things by analysing them into components (and hence that higher-level explanations cannot be fundamental)" (Deutsche 2012: 123). Now it may be that my understanding of the new mechanism is still growing and that I have misunderstood, but all the examples that I could find in the authors' paper, on the *Stanford Encyclopedia of Philosophy* website and on the BBA web site seemed to emphasize the reductive method. The writing implies causation flowing upward through a hierarchy of mechanisms and serially through time. The activities and components constitute the phenomenon. I hold that whilst reduction is the preeminent tool for understanding complex phenomena, it is not the end of our explanatory strategies.

My reason for seeking to avoid an overemphasis on analysis into subcomponents is to make the space for the humanities and specifically for the deployment of the abstractions in our explanations that I feel are necessary for the explanations to be successful. The authors' hope is that the new mechanism can be used in order to explain complex cultural concepts (CCCs), such as religion(s) but they are thereby constrained to the reductionist identification of components and activities as "the only method in town" for the provision of the explanations. It is particularly problematic if the target for explanation is an indefinable CCC that can only be brought into the method by a prior reduction of "it" into behaviors or other amenable phenomena that can partake in the new mechanism. Indeed elsewhere Ann and Egil recognize that further work is needed in order to extend the new mechanism into the domains of the social sciences and humanities.

Culture and the New Mechanism

The reason that I am foregrounding culture is because like the authors I see the behaviors in question (religious ones) as being part of human evolution and specifically of the evolved human cognition that underpins those behaviors. In my conception, human cognition is founded in individual ontogeny that in turn is based upon cultural learning, physical biology and personal experience. Of these, the most salient for our explanations of behavior are cultural learning and personal experience.

In this I follow Michael Tomasello's work in *The Cultural Origins of Human Cognition* (1999) and elsewhere. A human child may be biologically equipped but must still develop the meanings, both concrete and abstract, of their culture. Tomasello sees three groups of processes as the basis of that development:

1 cultural learning;

2 discourse and conversation; and

3 abstraction and schematization.

Space and time do not permit their full explication here, but they lead him to the conclusion that "language is a form of cognition; it is cognition packaged for purposes of interpersonal communication" (Tomasello 1999: 150). In support, he quotes Wittgenstein, "We may say that thinking is essentially operating with signs"; George Herbert Mead, "Only in terms of significant symbols is the existence of mind or intelligence possible"; and Lev Vygotsky, "Thought is not merely expressed in words; it comes into existence through them" (ibid.: 201).

This is why, in my view, the direction in which the latest conception of human cognition is traveling affirms the authors' hope for consilience between the humanities and natural science. We have seen "mind" develop from a dualism that posited a transcendent soul as the seat of reason, through a simplistic model of a genetically prepared computing machine that interacts with the objects of reality, to the modern conception of understanding and identity being weaved, in language, out of our joint attentional dialogues with others and via them recursively back through the generations of our cultures.

In my conception, a kind of duality in human experience is real, but is evolved and does not require any supernatural component. The feeling of duality, the normative, outside oneself, (transcendent of the individual?) internal voice is a recurring feature in the phenomenology of religion and a link to the intense emotion often associated with religious behavior. However there need be no supernatural basis to the duality, rather it is the product of the way our minds develop.

At the root of the development of all human cognition are joint attentional scenes which are "are social interaction in which the child and the adult are jointly attending to some third thing, and to one another's attention to the third thing, for some reasonably extended period of time" (Tomasello 1999: 96–98). Tomasello points out two key features that must be present for the transformational effect on human cognitive ontology to be realized:

1. The scene is not primarily perceptual, it only deals with a small subset of the child's perceptual world and it is not only a linguistic event but contains many other [physical] elements so that it becomes "an essential middle ground of socially shared reality—between the larger perceptual world and the smaller linguistic world" (ibid.).

2. The child understands themself and their own role within the scene "from the same outside perspective as the other person and the object" (ibid.). All three are inside the same model and represented to the child in a common format.

This links with Asprem and Taves's insight that any action is embedded in three heuristically different "environments"—normative orders, social dynamics and material conditions where actors are confronted with the challenge to interactively with others interpret, understand, and strategize in concrete situations to solve practical problems (Asprem and Taves 2016).

I wonder how well the new mechanism deals with that duality, with that bifurcation inside each of us between "subpersonal" consciousness (ideally suited to the new mechanism) and "personal" consciousness (founded in cultural learning, attachment and experience). Could the division find a way into the framework? Perhaps this would be a good topic for further debate. In the real successes of the new mechanism in biology we can model how physical and chemical interactions flow in molecular biology and as electrochemical flows as part of minds. However, inside our behavior, inside the human world, there are abstractions that have causal force. Where and how do we account for these in the extended new mechanism?

The paper rehearses the stages (the evolution?) of ideas concerning causes, theory, proofs, etc. The most interesting aspect of the discussion is the omission of the founding phases of human explanation and truth telling. These are the periods of the human journey where knowledge (explanations) could only be constructed in language and out of language itself, experience, memory, told stories, instruction and contemplation. There is little scope in this context for a full discussion of theory making and knowledge building in these eras of human experience but I'll use one of my touchstones, William James, as a shorthand way for getting to a characterization of that phase.

> The old common-sense way of rationalising is by a set of concepts of which the most important are these: things; the same thing; kinds; minds; bodies; one time; one space; subjects and attributes; causal influences; the fancied; the real.
>
> Our fundamental ways of thinking about things are discoveries of exceedingly remote ancestors, which have been able to preserve themselves throughout the experience of all subsequent time.
>
> (For all of us,) new truths thus are resultants of new experiences and of old truths combined and then mutually modifying one another and since this is the case in changes of opinion today, there is no reason to assume that it has not been so at all times. (James 1985 [1902]: 76–77)

Causal factors that people accept, that they act upon determine their behavior. So, in turn, the behavior depends upon what *counts as knowledge* for the individual and their social group. We might re-label these as good explanations that have wide acceptance. We might posit, following James and others such as Daniel Dennett (2013), that humans are unique in being representers of reasons. Why? How did that come about? I will briefly touch on that subject at the end of this response. Humans have always produced explanations, including justifications, for each other, but only in recent history by using scientific method.

If we want to provide scientific theories (good explanations) across the discontinuity between the abstractions of culture and the mechanics of embodied action our method will need to open to both.

Unalloyed Reduction?

The new mechanism seems to imply strongly that we can find the explanation of phenomena *in the parts*. But what if the explanation does not lie *solely* in the parts? Darwin's theory of evolution was only explained in terms of detailed mechanisms in the twentieth and twenty-first centuries.

As the new mechanism and the authors' work discuss, biology is massively complex and diverse. Biology is not just historically situated but is "thrown" in evolutionary and cosmic timescales. Biological phenomena have ceaselessly changed and continue to emerge through time and developmentally in the ontology of the individual organism. Biology is also spatially (geographically) specific, every bit as much as is the case in human cultural diversity and a myriad of human behaviors, including CCCs.

In modern scholarship it is axiomatic that, within the situated, time specific complexities of life forms, at levels below the apparent diversity, very widely implemented biological structures (e.g. eyes, skeletons) or semi-universal instances of organization (e.g. cell structures, DNA) exist.

There are levels of relevant explanation and causation that are not inherent features of the complex biological systems themselves. They are instead part of the physical environment. Then, more abstractly still, there is the most powerful explanatory theoretical tool concerning biology, namely evolution, which is not itself instantiated as a physical entity in the biology or the environment.

Instead, the theory of evolution is a logic process that is expressed through biological entities. Put simply it is, "descent with modification."

Darwin's, good explanation, his theory of evolution, is algorithmic and incredibly simple, yet it is the wellspring of the immense diversity and complexity of biological life forms over time and space. Significantly, in biology neo-Darwinism is not a totalizing theory of life. It addresses certain levels in the overall complexity of biology. The theory of evolution does not, in and of itself, provide a full account of the morphology of a specific organism. In a complete explanation, other factors such as environment need to be invoked. For all that, evolution does provide an incredibly powerful explanatory model from a startlingly simple formulation (Dennett 1996: 48–60).

I am arguing here that the fact that culture and religious behaviors, like biological life, are endlessly diverse and both historically and spatially situated does not mean that the search for underlying patterns in that diversity is futile. It may be possible to identify new, as yet uncovered, structures, quasi-universal and universal processes that are foundational for the emergence of religious phenomena.

The possibility of such discovery is indicated by the genealogy and the experience of SOR scholarship and by the open questions that remain in SOR.

All explanations to date have been partial. There is no shame in a theory (explanation) being incomplete. Both Newton and Einstein's theories have been proved to be so, yet they remain towering achievements. In Michael Stausberg's book *Contemporary Theories of Religion* (Stausberg 2009) great scholarship by Atran, Rappaport and others gave us valuable but incomplete explanations of religion. The same pattern, of partial explanation that contains some truth, is repeated back through the genealogy of scholarship in SOR.

Asprem and Taves argue that

> the *new mechanistic-causal approach* commonly presupposed in the "special sciences" (biology, the neurosciences, and psychology), referred to by philosophers of science as *"the new mechanism,"* can be extended to the study of religion following the lead of researchers who are extending it to the social sciences. (Chapter 13, this volume)

Well yes, possibly, but unalloyed? This seems to be a wholesale adoption of a highly successful methodology from life sciences. What if the broader context requires additional tools beyond the reductive method?

Darwin was not defeated by the diversity, the ever-changing forms, and the temporal and spatial contingency of life. He faced them squarely as the phenomenal stream that required explanation, and found a new way to do so. Can we do the same for the human behaviors that we class as religious?

Abstractions and the New Mechanism

We don't need to think about what is happening at atomic level when we boil a kettle of water. We can achieve things such as predicting how long a kettle will take to boil or how much heat to apply because liquid, bubbles, containers, boiling and so forth can be well explained in terms of each other, without any direct reference to the physical levels below. "That whole class of high-level phenomena is quasi-autonomous—almost self-contained. This resolution into explicability at a higher, quasi-autonomous level is known as emergence" (Deutsche 2012: 108).

Overwhelmingly, high-level physical, inanimate quantities consist of nothing but the behavior of their low-level constituents with most of the details ignored and are thus amenable to reductive analysis. However, that is not always the case, as Deutsche explains:

> Consider one particular copper atom at the tip of the nose of the statue of Sir Winston Churchill that stands in Parliament Square in London. Let me try to explain why that copper atom is there. It is because Churchill served as prime minister in the House of Commons nearby; and because his ideas and leadership contributed to the Allied victory in the Second World War; and because it is customary to honour such people by putting up statues of them; and because bronze, a traditional material for such statues, contains copper and so on. Thus we explain a low-level physical observation—the presence of a copper atom at a particular location—through extremely high-level theories about emergent phenomena such as ideas, leadership, war and tradition. (Deutsche 2012: 109)

Emergent phenomena are essential to the explicability of the world. Slowly developing human knowledge was based around high level regularities among the emergent phenomena encountered by people. Deutsche calls these rules of thumb; William James called them the Common Sense phase of human understanding. Deutsche asserts that "all knowledge creation depends on, and physically consists of, emergent phenomena" (Deutsche 2012: 111). It might be that top-level explanations, in terms of emergent phenomena, are the best, perhaps the only, way to explain other emergent phenomena.

Even if we, as scholars of SOR, go on to explain that religious behaviors are founded in sub-personal level complex bio cultural mechanisms (which is my own project), will society take note? How such explanations come to be accepted and used, if at all, in conducting everyday life will be another matter entirely.

A Conjecture

Here is an, only slightly tongue in cheek, pared down definition of religion. It is expressed in emergent phenomenal terms in order to illuminate a complex cultural construction (i.e. other emergent phenomena). I hope that you will think of it as explanatory reduction and not descriptive reduction! For good measure, it also plays with our chosen topic, explanation.

> Religion(s) are *necessary, explanations of what to do next and why.*

The conjecture is "theory laden"; it is founded upon, and shot through with, a materialist, pragmatist philosophy that has explanatory roots in evolutionary biology, cultural development and in the ongoing complex of systems and processes that comprise human behavior and the cognition that underpins it. It is consistent with the work that I have mentioned in this response.

The conjecture is extreme shorthand for William James's summary of religion, namely that:

1. Religion is rooted in both "thought and feeling."
2. Religious "faith-states" are a "biological as well as psychological condition."
3. Faith-states, due to their "extraordinary influence on action and endurance" are vitally important to human thriving.
4. "Life, more life, a larger, richer, more satisfying life, is in the last analysis, the end of religion."
5. "She [religion] cannot be a mere anachronism and survival but must exert a permanent function, whether she be with or without intellectual content, and whether, if she have any, it be true or false" (quotation marks indicate terms from James 1985 [1902]: 504–507).

In this view, scientific theories *and religions* are *both*

> guesses—bold conjectures. Human minds create them by rearranging, combining altering and adding to existing ideas with the intention of improving upon them ... experience is indeed essential to science [and religions],[1] but its role is different from that supposed by empiricism. It is not the source from which theories are derived. Its main use is to choose between theories that have already been guessed. That is what learning from experience is. (Deutsche 2012: 4)

Learning from experience can disprove and make redundant both scientific and religious explanations.

This still leaves open the question of why humans necessarily give explanations, why they *need* to "represent reasons" (Dennett 2013: 13–47). The first level answer is to justify courses of action to others. But again why? Well, as eusocial animals whose eusociality is founded in cognition, not in genetics as it is for insects, and for whom survival depends upon sustained co-operation and joint action, reason giving and acceptance is nothing less than existential (Wilson 2012). As cognitively shaped eusocial beings, we all need reasons to act in the world (explanations we have embraced), individually *and collectively*. They must encompass all phases and exigencies of life in whatever material, historical circumstance the individual and group are "thrown." Their absence leads to what James would have called "aporia" in the individual and we might call a malaise in society.

This is a conjecture that in the USA and Brexit Britain of November 2016 seems especially relevant to me. It could be that religions always were, and maybe still are, multigenerational complex processes aimed at producing collective action based on commonly held *explanations of what to do next and why.*

Paul is working for his MPhil/PhD at SOAS with a strong interest in theory and method in the Study of Religions. His project title is "An exploration of the foundational role of dialogue in the ontogeny of human minds and some consequences of this in aspects of religious behaviour."

Note

1   My additions. The characterization of religion as a form of explanation is not a part of Deutsche's argument.

References

Asprem, Egil, and Ann Taves. (2016) "Culture." Retrieved from http://bbhe.ucsb.edu/concepts/culture-simple/culture-elaborate (accessed December 29, 2016).
Dennett, Daniel C. 1996. *Darwin's Dangerous Idea*. London: Penguin.
Dennett, Daniel C. 2013. "The Evolution of Reasons," in Bana Bashour and Hans D. Muller (eds.), *Contemporary Philosophical Naturalism and its Implications*, 13–47. Abingdon: Routledge.
Deutsche, David. 2012. *The Beginning of Infinity: Explanations that Transform the World*. London: Allen Lane.
James, William. 1985 [1902]. *The Varieties of Religious Experience*. New York: Penguin.
Slingerland, Edward, and Mark Collard (eds.). 2011. *Creating Consilience: Integrating the Sciences and the Humanities*. Oxford: Oxford University Press. https://doi.org/10.1093/acprof:oso/9780199794393.001.0001
Stausberg, M (ed.). 2009. *Contemporary Theories of Religion: A Critical Companion*. New York: Routledge.
Tomasello, M. 1999. *The Cultural Origins of Human Cognition*. Cambridge, MA: Harvard University Press.
Wilson, E. O. 2012. *The Social Conquest of Earth*. New York: Liveright Publishing.

Chapter 17

Causal Explanations in the Study of Religion

Erin Roberts

Scrolling through the ELI5 ("explain like I'm five") subreddit[1] brings to light a range of explanatory practices. Some questions inspire what we might classify as *descriptive explanations*: *explanations* in that they communicate information and *descriptive* in that they delimit boundaries through definition, classification, and comparison.[2] Other questions attract what we might call *causal explanations*: *causal* insofar as they claim variable set A to be responsible for the existence of phenomenon B and *explanations* in that they aim to demonstrate how it happened that A caused B. Among the causal explanations populating the site, many include both material and non-material entities in their variable sets.

One person, for example, having noticed a difference in the way his dogs communicated with each other as opposed to how they communicated with his son, asked, "Why are dogs not intimidated when a human snarls and shows their teeth?"[3] The most popular explanation was that dogs are "hard wired" to detect intention, to measure possible threat levels posed by other animals (human animals included), and to respond in ways suited to the social context; in other words, the dogs do not growl back because they carry around brains that are able to notice that the boy meant no harm, that he likely could not enact harm anyway, and as a result simply ran around looking happy. Whether or not this explanation could pass muster with an animal communications expert, it is notable in that it is framed not only as a *causal explanation* but, more specifically, as one that accounted for the dog's behavior in terms of its *adapted cognitive features*.

As rightly noted by Egil Asprem and Ann Taves, explanations of phenomena that typically count as "religious" far too often neglect a crucial aspect of humanity: we, like the dogs in the above account, are adapted creatures whose actions result from the convergence of a set of variables including both material and non-material components. Our activities, both individually and socially, are thus well suited for *causal explanations* grounded within the adapted cognitive features that account for our ability to think about other minds, initiate purposive action, and to consider a range of possible outcomes.

By incorporating ideas about the adapted nature of human animals with scientific models for identifying and analyzing *causal mechanisms*, Asprem and Taves make a significant contribution to current discourse about explanatory practices within the Academic Study of Religion (ASR). They draw upon discussions within the philosophy of science in order to describe and compare some of the different aims, assumptions, and models that have been used in scientific explanation. The authors identify one approach—the "new mechanistic-causal approach" (the "new mechanism")—as holding potential for successful application to the explanation of phenomena that we commonly count as "religious." Confidence in the potential of the "new mechanism" seems to be grounded within its capacity for complexity and its understanding of causation.

The flexibility of the causal mechanistic approach allows scholars to model and thus explain phenomena in a manner that reflects the complexity not only of individual human beings but also of their tendency to live in groups. The type of mapping undertaken within this approach to explanation enables the representation of all the moving parts, so to speak, which contribute to the production of any given phenomenon. Taken together, these parts or "interacting components" comprise a "system" that produces the activity under consideration; the model may be extended inward toward even greater complexity by reframing each "interacting component" as itself another phenomenon produced by its own system of interacting components.[4] Although the extended complexity is mapped synchronically with all systems in action at the same time without causal interaction between the nested levels, interaction within a level does take place over time. Mechanisms can be linked together to represent diachronic causal chains that explain events or developments over long periods of time (Chapter 13, this volume).

The importance of causation begins with the idea that principled explanation of any phenomenon requires a degree of theorizing, at least to the extent that one can delimit the boundaries of her object of study. As the authors explain, the field of religious studies famously retains diverse, and sometimes inconsistent (if not contradictory), understandings of what the object of study ought to comprise; while some see themselves to be studying *sui generis* phenomena that transcend the methods and theories of the modern university, others insist that they are studying mundane human phenomena that should be theorized and analyzed as such. Taking the latter perspective, Asprem and Taves look toward other academic fields for recent developments that may be useful; they note that scientific theories aim squarely at explanation, with explanation understood as a practice that accounts for phenomena by identifying their causes. A scholar who seeks to explain religious phenomena by using theories and methods analogous to scientific ones, then, must theorize religion in a way that renders it explainable in terms of the kinds of things that count as scientific causes. While it would be redundant in most other contexts to specify that the kinds of things that count as scientific causes ought to be naturalistic, it is warranted in discussions of method in the ASR as a reminder to distinguish between the supernatural causes claimed by our objects of study and those within our scientific (or at least our analogously scientific) causal explanations.[5]

Asprem and Taves agree with the "new mechanists" that although there are aspects of Aristotle's conception of causation that are not a good fit within an account of explanation grounded in evolutionary theory, there is still much to be retained (Chapter 13, this volume). Of particular value are Aristotle's foci on goal-directed action and functional design (albeit without his notion of teleology). I am in agreement that Aristotle's teleology cannot survive within the context of the "new mechanism" and I also agree that the teleological aspect of his theory may be switched out for the mechanism of natural selection to our own explanatory benefit.

My understanding of Aristotle's account of causation in *Physics* 2, though, runs counter in some respects to that expressed by Asprem and Taves, but not to an extent that calls the essay's conclusions into question. Despite our variant readings, we all seem to agree that Aristotle's teleology is a liability. Nevertheless, I would be remiss not to add further complexity to the reading of *Physics* 2, for it is not a settled issue that it is "the final causes, meaning the goals and intentions that underlie some (effective) course of action that have explanatory priority in Aristotle's scheme" (Chapter 13, this volume). The issue I discuss has to do with the claim about the "explanatory priority" of final causes, especially as there is another claim of similar nature later in the essay:

> The key difference between Darwin and Aristotle lies precisely in the explanation of ultimate causation: Where Aristotle invoked *telos* to explain adaptive designs, Darwin found an economical way of accounting for such designs in the mechanism of natural selection. This new explanation, which essentially offered a new way for Aristotle's imagined opponent to make their case, also involved a crucial shift in how a mechanist deals with the notion of *function* without confusing it with a *cause*. (Asprem and Taves, Chapter 13, this volume)

Aristotle's use of craft analogies alongside his account of causation in the natural world can be famously confusing, as even Aristotle was aware.[6] Asprem and Taves have already described the analogy of the sculptor and the statue, but here I speak more generally about Aristotle's connections between craft and nature.

The causal power of a craftsman does not end up dwelling within an artefact as it would within the souls of living creatures; the craftsman no doubt transforms his chosen material, but the power by which he initiates and completes the transformation does not take on a life of its own. In a living organism, by contrast, the form or essence delivered via the father continues to live within the young creature or, more accurately, it *becomes* the young creature whose natural purposive structures cause growth and behavior.[7] It is crucial to notice that it is the creative causal power of *the efficient (moving) cause* rather than *the final cause* that here turns out to be the cause of purposeful action, as is the case with the builder: "One must always seek the ultimate cause [*to aition akrotaton*] of each thing, as in other matters. For example, a man builds because he is a builder, but the builder builds in virtue of the building craft. This cause, therefore, is prior [*touto toinun proteron to aition*]" (Sedley 2007: 179). As it turns out, the true efficient cause is eternal and pre-existent, lodged within the soul of a craftsman, from whence it is imposed upon the material. While the builder will of course have to involve himself in the production, it is the craft [*hē technē*] that is cause: "It is ridiculous for people not to believe that something is coming about for a purpose if they do not see that the moving cause has deliberated. Yet craft too does not deliberate [*kaitoi kai hē technē ou bouleuetai*]" (ibid.: 177). While his reasons for developing non-deliberative causes are theological, the overall effect is a naturalistic-looking refutation of Plato's insistence that purposeful action must involve intelligent design, creation, and continued administration (ibid.: 167–173). By construing the efficient causes of living organisms as essences embedded within living organisms as purposive structures, Aristotle guards against a theology that requires god to extract itself from its contemplative activity.

If the *telos* does not cause purposive action then it seems that the problem with Aristotle's teleology for the purposes of the "new mechanism" may have less to do with confusion between the *telos* and the cause of goal oriented activity than with the eternal, pre-existent, and un-changing character of the cause. Aristotle's primary cause for natural organisms was impervious to change: it was thought to drive purposeful behavior in the same way through all time. From our perspective, this is simply not the way nature works; the kinds of things that we count as natural causes of goal oriented behavior are not only multiple but also are not unchangeable.[8] In fact it is the changeableness or manipulability of causes, or at least what we take to be causes, that in recent decades has allowed for greater precision in distinguishing causal from correlative or even accidental relationships.

James Woodward, for one, has promoted a theory of causal explanation that includes, among other techniques, something that he refers to as "the manipulation conception" (Woodward 2003). Beginning from the premise that observation alone cannot determine causality or even detect which mechanisms are causal ones, he describes an approach in which "an intervention on some variable X with respect to some second variable Y is a causal process that changes the value of X in an appropriately exogenous way, so that if a change in the value of Y occurs, it occurs only in virtue of the change in the value of X and not through some other causal route" (ibid.: 94). The virtues of manipulability in molecular biology were touted in a 1985 issue of *Scientific American*, which noted that until recent advances in technology, "biologists confronted only the consequences of biological processes, not the causal mechanisms" (Weinberg 1985: 48). Manipulability—a feature that allows for intentional, targeted, exogenous change—can prove useful when one desires to isolate causal factors and clarify the types of interactions going on between components in causal mechanisms and the phenomena in which they are embedded.

How might I apply the "new mechanism" within my own research? The most immediate application that comes to mind is to use the model of the causal mechanism to map out and explain certain phenomena that I am working on in ancient Greek, Roman, and Judean texts on moral psychology. The ancient theories of emotion depend heavily upon claims about causal relationships between a person's overall mental disposition, values, sense perceptions, beliefs, and passions; in several cases, too, the causal relationships involve divine will or the imitation of the gods. In this regard, then, it would be extremely helpful to explain work on various cognitive phenomena (anger, desire, joy) by identifying the beliefs, values, and social situations in which the phenomena were thought to occur.[9] Following upon this, though, it is not clear yet how I would conduct explanatory reduction within the framework of the causal mechanism. It seems that in order move forward after mapping the causal claims of those within the texts of interest, I would need a more robust understanding of causality in order to move beyond what the authors termed "interpretation" of the subjective claims toward explanation in the true sense (Chapter 13, this volume).

A more thorough study of causation could also help me better to understand how the authors populated the causal mechanisms in the case study. The analysis of Joseph Smith's beliefs and his claims about supernatural causes helped illustrate how the "new mechanistic causal approach" to explanation could be applied to phenomena that count as "religious" in manner that can yield new kinds of investigation and analysis, and yet I would still feel underprepared to conduct such an analysis without first having understood a range of options for theorizing causation.

This is the case most especially for the third step of the proposed method: "Find out and describe the organization of parts by which they produce, in the sense of bring about, the phenomenon" (Chapter 13, this volume). Without an understanding of which kinds of entities or activities tend to have causal relationships in the first place, it is not clear how I would go about delimiting a system of components that would count as both "relevant" and "interacting" (ibid.). Without being able to perform variable tests like those conducted by the molecular biologists, I would not be confident that I were populating the systems in a causal mechanism with components whose interactions could be clarified and whose overall configuration could be reliably said to be productive of a phenomenon of interest. There is the possibility of using hypothetical and counterfactual experiments to come closer to distinguishing causes from corollary or associated components, but this of course will require further study on my part.

I close by extending sincere thanks to Egril Asprem and Ann Taves for their work in preparing their paper. My engagement with it has been both challenging and exhilarating; challenging in that the philosophy of science is a relatively new field for me and exhilarating for precisely the same reason. As I stated near the beginning of my response, Asprem and Taves have contributed significantly to current discourse about the theorization and practice of explanation within the ASR. For my part, and I suspect for others as well, this introductory engagement with the philosophy of science provides an excellent starting point for further discussion about scientific theories of explanation.

Erin Roberts is assistant professor in the Department of Religious Studies at the University of South Carolina.

Notes

1 See www.reddit.com/r/explainlikeimfive (accessed February 27, 2018).
2 Descriptions comprising such activities are noted by Willi Braun (2000: 16). For explanation as communicative act see Asprem and Taves, Chapter 13, this volume.
3 See www.reddit.com/r/explainlikeimfive/comments/3p1eee/eli5_why_are_dogs_not_intimidated_when_a_human

4   Phenomena and systems embedded within the components of other systems are referred to as mechanisms "nested" together in a series of non-hierarchical "levels" (Asprem and Taves, Chapter 13, this volume).
5   How one sees fit to populate the category of "supernatural causes" (gods, ancestors, ghosts, angels, fortune, and so forth) will vary according to the claims that emerge from the data set under consideration.
6   It seems in fact that cause and explanation are functional equivalents for Aristotle. In *Posterior Analytics Beta* 1–3, causation plays a crucial role in theories of reasoning and especially in clarifying various kinds of relationships (causal, associative, and so forth) among variables contained within definitions; Aristotle is clearly fond of causal definitions, at least for analytical purposes.
7   I borrow the language of "purposive structures" from Sedley (2007: 167–204).
8   Natural selection and adaptation but also the possibility that DNA can be altered due to trauma.
9   I am already imagining, for example, a set of diagrams representing Aristotle's discussion of emotion in *Rhetoric* 2.

References

Braun, Willi. 2000. "Religion," in Russell T. McCutcheon and Willi Braun (eds.), *Guide to the Study of Religion*, 3–18. London: Continuum.
Sedley, David. 2007. *Creationism and Its Critics in Antiquity*. Berkeley, CA: University of California Press.
Weinberg, Robert A. 1985. "The Molecules of Life," *Scientific American* 253(4): 48–57. https://doi.org/10.1038/scientificamerican1085-48
Woodward, James. 2003. *Making Things Happen: A Theory of Causal Explanation*. Oxford: Oxford University Press.

Chapter 18

To Our Critics

Egil Asprem and Ann Taves

Introduction and Acknowledgements

Our chapter on explanation in the study of religion (Chapter 13, this volume) is part of theoretical work that is still very much in progress. It is therefore not only a privilege, but very useful practice to get this opportunity to test our ideas and arguments on a sharp and critical audience of peers. Our four respondents bring up a fairly wide range of issues, from the historical to the philosophical to the political, marked by the evidently quite different positions from which each is writing. Some of these issues go to the very heart of the explanatory ambitions of our approach, while others are more peripheral to it, yet still important. Some responses enthusiastically endorse our project, while others remain unconvinced. In answering our four respondents, we choose to take the challenge offered us and devote most attention to our staunchest critics. We also give priority to the sorts of issues we find closer to the core of our approach, and which we feel let us explain (in the communicative sense!) aspects that were less evident in the original article.

To ensure that our selectiveness is not mistaken for ungratefulness, however, we wish to acknowledge some of the points we found fruitful but will not discuss at any length here. Erin Roberts's challenge to our reading of Aristotle (Chapter 17, this volume) is, for example, thoughtful and constructive in view of our particular objectives. We will carefully consider her Aristotle interpretation as we work on our monograph. Likewise, we thank Paul Kenny for his constructive remarks (Chapter 16, this volume), most of which do not require a response beyond acknowledging that his points about reductionism, language, and the relations between levels in mechanisms are valuable to us as we continue to refine this framework. While we will return to some of the specific concerns that Roberts and Kenny brought up, we will focus on the responses of Joel Harrison (Chapter 15, this volume) and Spencer Dew (Chapter 14, this volume), which were more critical. Harrison's chapter in particular raises important challenges that not only take us to the heart of the matter, but are also likely to be of interest to other readers in this audience. Before we get to this, however, it appears necessary to revisit the work that "religion" does in our approach.

An Opening Clarification on "Religion"

There appears to be some confusion across the four responses on where we stand with regard to the concept of "religion." While Harrison seems to assume we're in the business of providing "an account of what religion *is*" (Chapter 15, 171, this volume), Dew recognizes that the thrust of our argument is in fact to explain *human behavior in general*. For Dew, however, this prompts the question of why we, according to him, still retain "a position of privilege for the category of 'religion'" (Chapter 14, 164, this volume). We might as well sort this one out at the beginning.

To us, "religion" exists only as a discursive and social reality (what we call a CCC). As such, it is empirically available to us as one among a range of human constructs used to identify and distinguish between complex behaviors. We do not view ourselves as privileging the category of religion over other interpretive categories. Our particular interest is in human efforts to make sense of situations, including experiences, behaviors, interactions and events, particularly those that they find puzzling or out of the ordinary. If such situations are more often than not interpreted in religion-like terms—and we do not assume this is the case—then it is this fundamental interest that leads us to highlight some situations over others. In other words, our object of study is not "religion," but *situations*, particularly those that people find puzzling or out of the ordinary.

The shift we are advocating here is a significant one.[1] It does not eliminate individuals, but dereifies them, allowing us to examine not only what they bring to a situation, but also what subpersonal processes the situation evokes in them. It reconceptualizes individual agency by recognizing that agency is enacted in situations that direct human attention, evoke emotions, precipitate action, and generate interpretations. It thus opens the way to embed discursive constructions in material interactions that are simultaneously bodily, psychological, cognitive, and experiential.

On Ontology and Axiology: Rejoinder to Harrison

Harrison's intention is to "question whether Asprem and Taves's theory (a) is actually completely reductive and (b) provides a compelling case for the unification of synchronic, diachronic, material, and ideational factors into a single coherent theory with sufficient analytical power" (Chapter 15, 169, this volume). In practice, these two questions can be rephrased as being about *what constitutes a (good) explanation*, on the one hand, and *what is the benefit of following the approach we sketch*, on the other. The centerpiece of Harrison's critique concerns the role of "ideas" in our explanatory scheme, which leads him to suggest the need for a distinction between "ontological" and "axiological" explanations. Finally, Harrison illustrates the importance of this distinction by discussing Weber's explanation of the "spirit of capitalism" which, in Harrison's terms, is an axiological one. His challenge, which we will return to, is for us to convince him that our approach adds something useful to Weber's approach.

While we are not convinced that Harrison's distinction between ontology and axiology in this context is as fruitful as he suggests, we can nevertheless use his terms to clarify the place we see for "ideas" in causal mechanisms. We also thank Harrison for inviting Dilthey and Weber to the conversation, as we agree with him that there are interesting similarities and contrasts between our project and theirs.[2] Among the contrasts is that, while the hermeneutical tradition springing from Dilthey argues for a separation between the natural sciences and the humanities—and between explanation and interpretation—on the assumption that scientific explanation is about uncovering *general laws* (a view apparently embraced, through a neo-Kantian lens, by Harrison himself in Chapter 15, this volume), our chapter explicitly rejects such nomological views of explanation in favor of a focus on causal powers. Thus, we think that Weber's methodological project (not only his thesis on capitalism), which treats reasons as causes, provides an excellent context for elaborating how our perspective differs in application to concrete socio-historical problems. We therefore intend to take up Harrison's final challenge of asking what our approach adds to one like Weber's, and what it may entail for scholars like Harrison, whose primary interest is in the effects of values and ideas on historical developments.

Adopting Harrison's terms, we should begin by posing the fundamental ontological question of what "ideas" *are*. From our causal-mechanistic perspective, the meaningful way of formulating this question is to ask "how are ideas constituted" or, even better, "in virtue of what do ideas gain causal power." Rooted in biology and the cognitive sciences, our answer to this question is that ideas are *mental representations*, and that their causal power rests entirely on how biological organisms engage these representations in specific situations.[3] "Ideas" only have effects in virtue of being embodied in culturally embedded animals. The central nervous system encodes and processes representations based on information received from multiple bodily systems. The endocrine system (hormones), for example, can regulate the emotional "gain" on ideas and hence plays an important part in transforming mere representations into subjective hierarchies that shape the organism's response. This, in other words, outlines the shape of a synchronic explanation of ideas as causal powers. It also highlights the sense in which our approach is reductionistic. It does not accept the causal power of ideas on face value, but would look for the material constituent parts of what we call "ideas" that, under certain specific circumstances (situations), give them this power.

One consequence of this view is that the separation of ontological and axiological explanations collapses. Harrison defines an axiological explanation as "an explanation of effects, material or ideational, which *have an ideational cause*" (page 170, this volume; emphasis added). But ideational causes are material causes. To the extent that our interest is in how axiologies have *real effects* (acknowledging that historical actors often act contrary to their confessed values), we must, again, return to their implementation in the actor's biological organism. In two separate papers, we are outlining a theory of *worldviews*, based on but departing from Dilthey's *Weltanschauungslehre*, which aims to do precisely this (Taves and Asprem in press; Taves, Asprem, and Ihm in press). The crucial point is that axiologies are biologically basic in so far as organisms assign value to stimuli in the environment that guide them to adopt one course of action over another. The systems of value that guide this process arise early in evolution, and provide an important basis for more complex organisms to create internal models of self and world, allowing them not only to survive and reproduce, but to transform their material environments by externalizing and objectifying their internal models through repeated action.[4] In other words, human "worldviews" build on a basic ability to create self-models and world-models, shared with a host of other "agents," from bacteria to robots.[5]

An analysis of "values," even in human subjects, must therefore also include a biological and psychological analysis. It is not sufficient to study intellectualized value systems, of the kind expounded in texts of moral doctrine or inferred from the study of political, religious, or philosophical discourse. If, for example, the "religious" idea that "dancing is sinful" causes a Baptist to resist the temptation to join the other moving bodies on the floor (even when the rhythms are compelling and the bodies beautiful), this means that some biological representation related to what we crudely call "the idea of sin" causes the Baptist to override impulses that the other dancers are embracing. Now, a number of different sin related representations might in fact be effecting this override, from an experienced fear of hellfire or a worry that Baptist peers might find out about the dance (emotional responses), to a disciplined, prideful sense of "doing what is right" (Weber's "value-rational action" cast as executive control over impulses). Our point here is that the mechanistic account of how ideas *in fact* impact on behavioral outcomes forces us to think a lot more deeply about the issues. We cannot be content with finding correlations between a behavior and an expressed (or even inferred) belief, but should ask about the emotional, cognitive, and social-psychological components interacting to produce concrete behaviors in specific situations— from individual differences in cognitive ability, to differences in how the belief was socialized and enforced, to environmental factors impacting on executive control and inhibitions, such as alcohol consumption, music, or even stress.

Returning now to Harrison's challenge: What does the new mechanism add analytically to a case such as the role of Protestant ideas in the rise of European industrial capitalism? Setting aside the considerable doubt that has been cast on whether there is any empirically evident causal relationship between Protestantism and capitalism in the first place,[6] the most obvious value of the new mechanist approach is a heuristic one: It provides a way to sort out and order our causal claims, and, importantly, to locate each of these in a consilient nested stack of mechanisms that can be analyzed at different scales according to interest as well as explanatory necessity. So for example, Weber's proposed "rise-of-capitalism" mechanism contains a diverse set of components that interact at a behavioral level: *socio-economic* preconditions (such as the availability of free labor and the separation of work and home), *practices* (such as inner-worldly asceticism and rational book-keeping), and *ideas* (such as the Calvinist doctrine of predestination). The mechanism at this level presupposes the interaction of a large class of people who hold these ideas and engage in these practices in a complex social environment where work and home are separated and free labor is available.

We are not arguing that scholars should always, as a matter of principle, push explanations "downward." For researchers with an interest in macro-sociological comparisons, identification of a proposed mechanism at this level may be sufficient. Weber wanted to see if the components that interacted to produce a specific form of bourgeois capitalism existed in other contexts and, if not, whether their absence could account for those societies' failure to develop the same sort of capitalism. However, by stressing the vertical dimension of mechanisms nested within mechanisms, we insist that it is always a good idea to consider *what gives* each proposed component in a mechanism its causal power. The value of this is particularly evident when an explanatory model (such as Weber's on capitalism) fails to work. Does it fail because the components interact differently than expected, or because there are other unaccounted variables at play, or perhaps because some of the suggested components in fact work differently than one had thought? For example, there is now a consensus that the "Calvinist beliefs" component in Weber's model does not hold up in view of the historical evidence. Examining why this causal component does not work as expected, one should take apart the ideal-type model of what constitutes rational conduct for believers in predestination, and look at alternative explanatory models of belief-formation, its effects on behavior, and interaction with other factors, whether environmental, bodily, or cognitive. In short, troubleshooting a failed explanation does require us to consider lower-level mechanisms, and promises significant theoretical payoffs in the shape of new explanatory models that are more robust and better integrated with other disciplines.

Methodological Challenges: How "Scientific" Do Our Explanations Have to Be?

A sympathetic reader may agree with everything we have said so far, yet still be concerned about how one would go about doing any of this in practice. This is a valid concern, which both Roberts and Kenny raise in their responses. It is tempting to differentiate their versions of this critique into a "soft" (Kenny) and a "hard" (Roberts) critique. In the softer version, Kenny draws a distinction between proposing "good explanations" and using "scientific theories" (Chapter 16, this volume), voicing his preference for the former over the latter. "[N]o good explanation of religion(s) will be created without input from both the humanities and science," he writes, and adds that he sees a danger in the new mechanistic approach of overemphasizing "the scientific method" (page 178, this volume). Being able to carry out explanatory reduction is a good and necessary thing, Kenny agrees, but we should not throw out the baby with the bath water and outright deny the usefulness of humanistic research on such things as the causal relevance of institutions and cultural learning.

Kenny's point is, perhaps, nowhere as clearly stated as when he cites David Deutsche's example of why there is a copper atom at the tip of the nose of the statue of Winston Churchill outside Parliament Square in London (page 183, this volume). Kenny argues, with Deutsche, that a sufficient explanation in this case needs to proceed from the top-down rather than the bottom-up: the copper atom would not have been there were it not for the British cultural institution of erecting statues of wartime leaders, the tradition of casting such statues in bronze (of which copper is a component), and the fact that the Allies won the Second World War. Kenny sees in this an argument for *emergent phenomena*, that is, of causal powers that emerge on a higher level of complexity which, when in existence, have causal force "downwards" to their components. We are sympathetic to emergentism, but think that emergent effects can be accounted for in the new mechanism. This is due to the crucial distinction, explained briefly in our article, between levels of mechanisms and levels of reality. "Classical" emergentism asked how is it that wholes seem to be more than the sums of their parts, but tended to assume that the parts existed at one level of reality and the whole at another "higher" level. This conception of emergence works well enough if we are considering the oxygen and hydrogen atoms that combine to form water. Since mechanisms are defined in terms of the components that interact to produce a phenomenon, levels of mechanisms do *not* necessarily map on to levels of reality. Put differently, we could make a mechanistic model of "how the copper atom ended up on Churchill's nose" that includes all the factors listed by Deutsche as *interacting components* that explain the presence of the atom on Churchill's nose. From a mechanistic perspective, going a level "down" means looking at how each interacting component—the institution of erecting statues, the smelting of bronze, and the outcome of World War II—is, in turn, constituted by relevant causal relationships between yet other components. In other words, the new mechanism is in principle indifferent to the level of reality of the components that comprise a mechanism. It is for that reason we find it particularly well equipped to do precisely what Kenny recommends: Combine scientific and humanistic approaches in mutually reinforcing ways.

The harder critique is, in our view, more serious, but pushing to resolve it also promises to be the most rewarding. The challenge as formulated by Roberts is similar to that of Harrison: "How might I apply the 'new mechanism' within my own work?" While Harrison focused on how it might help him make diachronic causal claims (what he calls axiological explanations), Roberts asks us how, in practice, one could make synchronic ones. The most directly useful way to apply the new mechanism to her own work, she maintains, is as a *model* for "mapping the causal claims of those within the texts of interest" (that is, as a heuristic). She finds it more difficult to see how she would proceed from this mapping and modeling activity to an actual explanatory reduction that would suggest mechanistic causes of the phenomena. This is an important challenge: Roberts worries that the approach we have sketched lacks "a more robust understanding of causality," hinting (and citing James Woodward) that such an understanding could be found along manipulationist accounts that emphasize interventions in causal systems. The challenge here has to do with how one determines which components of a system are (causally) relevant—an issue we discussed at some length in our overview of philosophical accounts of causality. Returning to our non-dancing Baptist, for example, do we really have any way of determining whether in that moment she is motivated by a fear response or in a disciplined manner choosing to ignore the temptation for the sake of a greater purpose? Whether we are reading about her or observing her in the field, the answer is not really. It appears all we have is loose conjecture.

As we discussed in our chapter, one would typically need controlled experiments to determine these sort of causal claims with any meaningful degree of confidence. We do indeed believe experimental methods should be more widely adopted in the humanities. We are enthusiastic about the methodological advances that are currently being made in the psychology and cognitive science of religion toward combining field and laboratory, and devising clever experimental protocols for testing specific hypotheses about the cognitive building blocks of specific religion-related tasks. However, while we wait for experimentalism to get more robust, historians and social scientists of religion already can and should advance the explanatory agenda by attempting to express their theories in causal-mechanistic terms. This, in fact, is a necessary step toward hypothesis-driven research in our field (cf. Bulbulia and Slingerland 2012). In other words, we can use existing theories to hypothesize about the sort of components that *ought* to make a difference, and strive to figure out ways in which those hypotheses could, in principle, be tested. The internally conflicted non-dancing Baptist is a crude illustration of this approach.[7]

Preparing the ground for future experimentalists to test hypotheses is not, however, the only thing that can be achieved by thinking about our subject matter in terms of the new mechanism. We can also learn to test theories by generating computer models and running simulations. The mechanistic models we have been discussing are theories about how a system works. If we convert them into computational (computer-based) models, we can run simulations that produce predictions (or hypotheses) based on the model, and compare these predictions to what actually occurred historically, based on our best historical evidence. Simply specifying a theory precisely enough to produce a model may bring attention to theoretical issues that need to be resolved. Running the model on test data then checks to see if the model is doing what is expected in light of the theory. This may reveal inconsistencies in the narrative version of the theory that need to be corrected or amendments that need to be added. Once the model is working as expected, input parameters can be adjusted to see if the model (the theory) can produce a result that is close to what actually occurred. If it cannot, or can do so only under unrealistic conditions, then the historical data has falsified the theory. Because "manual" efforts to test Weber's theoretical model in light of historical data demonstrated its limitations, we were able to use it to illustrate how testing can lead to refinement of a model's components. Computer modeling and simulation will allow us to perform such tests at much more sophisticated level.[8]

The Value of Scientific Values: A Response to Spencer Dew

Diverging from these core discussions about the nature of explanation and how best to seek them, Spencer Dew's response takes us into a discussion of the ethical and political responsibilities of a scholar. Dew sees "no possibility for politics" in our method, and he finds that absence "disturbing" (page 163, this volume). Dew seems to mean this in two related ways. First, that we appear to be unconcerned with matters of value and are promoting an approach that does not engage with the values or claims of our subjects. Second, that our distancing of ourselves from those we are studying may obscure the fact that we too are prone to "folk" interpretations and classifications and, thus, unexamined biases.

With respect to the first concern, we hold to the disciplinary value of describing and analyzing people's beliefs and practices as evenhandedly as possible, saving our feelings of empathy or opposition for other contexts. As our chapter should make clear, however, we retain the right to explain those beliefs and practices in naturalistic terms, which in many cases conflict with the claims of those we are studying. There is a suitable analogy to be made with the distinction between an opinion piece, reporting, and fact-checking in the context of journalism, where the latter two are crucial to the explanatory process as we conceive of it. Moreover, just as accurate reporting and irreverent fact-checking are of immense value to society and play an important political function, so too should good scientific explanations: in order to take good and effective actions in the world, one must have a good sense of how that world works. Recognizing the value of good explanations is all the more important at times when dominant political forces are becoming increasingly insulated from fact-based critiques.

With respect to Dew's second concern that our approach distances us from those we study, we would argue just the opposite: We have been struck by the thoroughgoing reflexivity of this approach. We have already mentioned that worldviews are rooted in world-modeling activities that are very broadly shared by organisms, ranging from the bacteria in the petri dish to the human primate wearing a lab coat.[9] Taken to its full conclusion, this insight levels the playing field between scientific and folk world-modeling efforts, and emphasizes that both can be essential parts of constructing a worldview. Moreover, it highlights some aspects of scientific explanations that often go unaddressed. On the one hand, acknowledging that organism's world-modeling abilities evolved because they enhanced the organism's chances of survival highlights the limitations of scientific world-modeling. In terms of survival, a painstakingly accurate understanding of one's situation may not be as useful as a quick approximation. The former is essential when it comes to enhancing our survival through medicine and technology, but the latter is still the basis on which we all act in everyday life. On the other hand, the acknowledgment that all human explanations, whether "folk" or "scientific," are unavoidably tied up with worldviews undercuts the distinction between facts and values, highlighting instead how science and scholarship always informs our views of what is valuable and what is right. As a collective world-modeling effort, science remains essentially connected to axiology (what we value), praxeology (what we should do), and to epistemology (what we should believe, and why).

Since how we explain the world is inextricably connected with other aspects of our worldview, we must simply accept that scholarly explanations of any human activity will often lead to an implicit conflict with the worldviews of those we study. However, the appropriate attitude toward this fact is not to downplay the soundness of our own explanations for fear that "our" explanations may reduce away "their" values. We can acknowledge the values that shape our scientific worldviews, as well as the extent to which our actions are for the most part governed by evolved "folk" models of the world, not by science. Any good scientific model of meaning making will need to take all this into account.

Egil Asprem is associate professor in the history of religions at Stockholm University. He is the author of *Arguing with Angels: Enochian Magic and Modern Occulture* (SUNY Press, 2012) and *The Problem of Disenchantment: Scientific Naturalism and Esoteric Discourse, 1900-1939* (Brill, 2014), and co-editor with Kennet Granholm of *Contemporary Esotericism* (Routledge, 2014).

Ann Taves is professor of religious studies at the University of California at Santa Barbara where she teaches courses on religious experience, new religious movements, and comparative worldviews and supervises the interdisciplinary Religion, Experience, and Mind Lab Group. She is the author of numerous books and articles, including *Fits, Trances, and Visions: Experiencing Religion and Explaining Experience from Wesley to James* (Princeton University Press, 1999), *Religious Experience Reconsidered* (Princeton University Press, 2009), and *Revelatory Events,* a study of the emergence of three new spiritual movements. She is currently working with collaborators to develop and test a cross-cultural Inventory of Non-Ordinary Experiences.

Notes

1. This shift is analogous in some ways to the shift in focus from individuals to situations that Randall Collins (2004: 3–6) advocates as the basis for microsociology.
2. We discuss Dilthey explicitly in a separate paper on "worldviews" (Taves and Asprem in press; Taves, Asprem, and Ihm in press). More on this later.
3. Here we must add the caveat that a much broader conception of representations is possible and desirable, taking into account public as well as mental representations—that is, the transmission of ideas in extrapersonal space through material inscriptions and symbolic scaffolding of various sorts. Such public representations are, however, also only effective by virtue of producing representations in the minds of the organisms that interact with them—public representations do not themselves "contain" ideas, as much as evoke them. Due to space constraints, we will limit our discussion here to the essential biological understanding of ideas at the point in time in which they exert causal power (i.e., in a specific action).
4. The choice of the words in this sentence is deliberately meant to suggest a connection to Berger and Luckmann's (1966) theory of socialization, which we think can be updated and amended along these lines.
5. This view is largely based on Metzinger's (e.g. 2003, 2007) theory of self-modeling systems and Clark's (2016) account of predictive coding as a computational strategy.
6. For a substantial critique see, for example, Lehmann and Roth (1993), and see Cantoni (2015) for a recent quantitative assessment.
7. In other work, we have advanced this hypothesis-driven way of thinking about historical source material related to the notoriously difficult topic of subjective experiences. See, for instance, Taves and Asprem (2017), Asprem and Taves (2017: 91–

92), and Asprem (2017). For some of the experimental difficulties involved, see Nielbo, Andersen, and Schjoedt (2017).
8 Currently a team of researchers led by Wesley Wildman at Boston University is collaborating with scholars of religion to introduce these powerful methods into religious studies and other humanities disciplines (for more information, see the Modeling Religion Project and its various subprojects, such as the Modeling Religion in Norway project, run by LeRon Shults: www.ibcsr.org/index.php/institute-research-portals/mrp, accessed February 11, 2017).
9 See Taves and Asprem (in press) and Taves, Asprem and Ihm (in press) for initial attempts at outlining a form of "worldview studies" rooted in our naturalistic perspective.

References

Asprem, Egil. 2017. "Explaining the Esoteric Imagination: Towards a Theory of Kataphatic Practice," *Aries* 17(1): 17–50. https://doi.org/10.1163/15700593-01701002

Asprem, Egil and Ann Taves. 2017. "Connecting Events: Experienced, Narrated, and Framed," *Religion, Brain and Behavior* 7(1): 88–93. https://doi.org/10.1080/2153599X.2016.1150337

Berger, Peter, and Thomas Luckmann. 1966. *The Social Construction of Reality: A Treatise in the Sociology of Knowledge*. Garden City, NY: Doubleday & Company.

Bulbulia, Joseph, and Edward Slingerland. 2012. "Religious Studies as a Life Science," *Numen* 59: 564–613. https://doi.org/10.1163/15685276-12341240

Cantoni, David. 2015. "The Economic Effects of the Protestant Reformation: Testing the Weber Hypothesis in the German Lands," *Journal of the European Economic Association* 14(4): 561–598. https://doi.org/10.1111/jeea.12117

Clark, Andy. 2016. *Surfing Uncertainty: Prediction, Action, and the Embodied Mind*. Oxford: Oxford University Press. https://doi.org/10.1093/acprof:oso/9780190217013.001.0001

Collins, Randall. 2004. *Interaction Ritual Chains*. Princeton, NJ: Princeton University Press. https://doi.org/10.1515/9781400851744

Lehmann, Hartmut, and Guenther Roth (eds.). 1993. *Weber's Protestant Ethic: Origins, Evidence, Contexts*. Cambridge: Cambridge University Press. https://doi.org/10.1017/CBO9781139052467

Metzinger, Thomas. 2003. *Being No One: The Self-Model Theory of Subjectivity*. Cambridge, MA: MIT Press.

Metzinger, Thomas. 2007. "Self Models," *Scholarpedia* 2(10): 4174. https://doi.org/10.4249/scholarpedia.4174

Nielbo, Kristoffer L., Marc N. Andersen, and Uffe Schjoedt. 2017. "Segmentation and Cultural Modulation in Perception of Internal Events Are Not Trivial Matters," *Religion, Brain and Behavior* 7(1): 77–79. https://doi.org/10.1080/2153599X.2016.1150329

Taves, Ann, and Egil Asprem. 2017. "Experience as Event: Event Cognition and the Study of (Religious) Experiences," *Religion, Brain and Behavior* 7(1): 43–62. https://doi.org/10.1080/2153599X.2016.1150327

Taves, Ann, and Egil Asprem. In press. "Scientific Worldview Studies: A Programmatic Proposal," in Andreas K. Petersen, Ingvild S. Gilhus, Luther H. Martin, Jeppe S. Jensen, and Jesper Sørensen (eds.), *A New Synthesis: Cognition, Evolution, and History in the Study of Religion*. Leiden: Brill.

Taves, Ann, Egil Asprem, and Elliott Ihm. In press. "Psychology, Meaning Making and the Study of Worldviews: Beyond Religion and Non-Religion," *Psychology of Religion and Spirituality*.

Part IV

Chapter 19

Interpretation and the Study of Religion

Kevin Schilbrack

In the past few decades, interpretation has become a beleaguered approach in the academic study of religion. Some critics complain that when interpretation seeks to grasp the meaning of religious practices as they are understood by their practitioners, interpretive scholars become little more than mouthpieces for religious communities. Others complain that if there are no criteria for finding a correct interpretation, then interpretations remain arbitrary and never-ending. My goal in this chapter is to clarify and defend the interpretive approach, and I seek to do this by (1) putting on the table what is at stake in speaking of interpretation in the social sciences, (2) identifying the object studied in interpretation, and (3) identifying the limitations of this approach. I therefore structure this paper by asking and answering three questions that have been contentious in the debates about interpretation.

1   Can one understand human behavior independent of the action's meaning?
2   Does interpretation require access to people's mental states?
3   Does interpretation preclude causal explanation?

Asking and answering these three questions provides a guide to some of the controversies raised by interpretation as a method. Though the answers to these questions spill over and connect to each other, I will use the first question primarily to raise ontological issues, the second to raise epistemological issues, and the third to raise methodological issues. Moreover, I have tried to phrase these questions so that there are intelligent positions on both sides of each of these questions, and I give examples of scholars who answer these questions in the opposite way that I do. In short, in this paper I propose what I consider the best answer to each of the questions, but all three are "live," unsettled questions in the study of religion.

1   Can One Understand Human Behavior Independent of the Action's Meaning?

To answer yes to this question is to hold that an observer can grasp what an individual or a group is doing without reference to the meaning of what the people are saying or doing. To answer yes to this question rejects the need for interpretation for the study of human behavior. Call this a non-hermeneutic position. One finds defenders of this non-hermeneutic yes answer among cognitive scientists and philosophers of mind who hold that human behavior is exhaustively explained by the combination of one's genetics and one's physical environment, and no mental entities like manifest or latent desires, beliefs, or goals need to be postulated. According to this position, just as the natural sciences do not include the meaning or purpose of the behavior when they seek to understand, say, the behavior of clouds or the behavior of amino acids (and, in fact, it took centuries for the natural sciences to exclude appeal to such "final causes"), one does not need to include the meaning or the purpose of the behavior when one seeks to understand the behavior of human beings. One therefore does not need interpretation as a method for the study of society that differs from the methods of the natural sciences.

As an example of the yes answer in religious studies, one can consider the work of Edward Slingerland. Slingerland grants that the idea that human behavior is at least partially self-caused by the person's choice of aims is a universal piece of folk psychology. But developments in evolutionary theory (especially the gene-level approach to natural selection) and cognitive science (especially the development of computers that can pass the Turing Test and can defeat chess masters) constitute a veritable "physicalist revolution" that now offers a plausible model of how mind-*like* powers could arise from a purely physical body–brain system, a purely physical system that is as much a product of evolution as the spleen (Slingerland 2012: 78). A physicalist position like this does not include the idea of purposeful behavior and so it does not include the idea of meanings that need interpretation. On the contrary, as Slingerland says:

> As products of a blind process of replication and selection, human beings as whole—body and mind—differ only in degree of complexity from robots or machines; we, like everything in the world, are causally determined, purely physical systems. (Slingerland 2008: 250)

Human beings are automata—"robots designed to believe that we are not robots" (ibid.: 281)—and the emergence of symbolic-cultural systems like religions and people's participation in those practices can be explained in terms of subpersonal processes. To understand what people do does not require one to grasp what they think they are up to.[1]

By contrast, to answer no to this question is to hold that an observer can grasp little or nothing of what an individual or a group is doing without reference to the meaning the action has to the people involved. According to this position, even to identify what the human activity is (as performing a baptism as opposed to giving a bath, for example), one must figure out what the meaning of the behavior to the participants. The meaning that the behavior has for the participants is part of the very constitution of what they are doing. Here, the identity of the action in question is a function of its meaning to the people involved. Those who say no to the first question therefore make "the interpretive turn" (Hiley et al. 1991) and endorse some form of an interpretive social science.

The central claim of those who hold that the social sciences should be interpretive is that some human behavior is meaningful in that it is performed with an aim or purpose. Some human behavior, in other words, is teleological and intentional: a murder is not an accident. Non-sentient behavior (a rock rolling down a hill, or osmosis, for example) is not intentional. Some human behavior (one's heart racing, or the patellar reflex, for example) is not. But the central claim of the interpretive social sciences is that some behavior is constituted by the meanings it has for those who do them and cannot be understood apart from those meanings. On this view, to understand for instance that someone is training his roosters for a cockfight or that he is betting on them requires the observer to include not only the participants' neurons, genes, and physical environment but also local meanings that will be cultural and historically diverse. In religious studies, pilgrimages, sacrifices, spiritual disciplines, and the writing of texts would be in the same category of behavior that cannot be properly identified apart from a grasp of the participants' purposes.

The central claim of the interpretivists in the academic study of religion is not that religious actions have *symbolic* meanings, but simply that, like other purposeful kinds of behavior, religious actions are performed with an aim. And this claim is not merely the phenomenological claim that purposive and non-purposive behavior *feel* different to the person who does them, but that there is an ontological difference between them. The difference may not be empirically visible. As Gilbert Ryle puts it in his famous discussion of an inadvertent blink and a seductive wink, "there remains an immense but unphotographable difference" between the two kinds of behavior (Ryle 2009: 494). Interpretivists often mark this difference by calling an example of meaningful behavior an "action." The choice of which restaurant to go to is typically meaningful in this sense and so the choice would be an action, but digesting would not be. Collective behaviors that we call social practices are also done with a purpose (for example, throwing the ball to first base to put the runner out), and so they also would be considered actions. To mark that human beings act with purposes, interpretivists call them "agents." Human beings are agents if or insofar as they bring about their own actions. Those who answer yes to the first question and reject the interpretivist premise do not speak of human behavior as actions nor human beings as agents in this sense.

Since winks look just like blinks, interpretivists hold that the meaning of an action cannot be captured by visible description alone. Slingerland (2012) argues that therefore the interpretive approach assumes an ontological realm separate and independent from the realm of the physical. The existence of non-physical meanings, he says, makes no sense without mind–body dualism. But most interpretivists do not explicitly endorse mind–body dualism, as Slingerland admits (ibid.: 75). And even if he is right some interpretivists implicitly assume it, they need not. In addition to (i) a reductive physicalism in which the only kind of real things are physical and lack purposes and (ii) the mind–body dualism that Slingerland rightly notes is replete with difficulty, there exists a third option, namely, an emergentist materialism that says when physical entities come into structured relationship with each other, there emerges a more complex whole with properties and powers not possessed by and therefore not reducible to its constituent parts. Think of the water molecule that consists of nothing other than hydrogen and oxygen atoms in structured relation but has properties those atoms do not have, or biological organisms composed of nothing other than molecules in structured relation but have properties those molecules do not. In this way, some argue for the emergence of minds as emergent wholes that are composed of biological parts (themselves composed of molecular parts, composed of atomic parts, and so on), emergent wholes that nevertheless have properties, like intentionality, not possessed by their constituent parts. This emergentist approach produces an ontology that is stratified into levels is but not dualistic. Such an ontology does not require any supernatural elements, and so it fits what many are now calling a "liberal naturalism" according to which actions caused by an agent's intentions are natural phenomena.[2] Given this ontology, interpretivists can avoid dualism by distinguishing between the claim that a wink and a blink are not *visibly* distinguishable, a claim they can make, and the much stronger claim that a wink and a blink have no *physical* difference, a claim that they need and ought not make.[3]

If one answers yes, one approaches the study of human behavior with the idea that no actions are constituted by the self-understanding of the agents, and therefore one does not have to grasp how the actors' intentions to give an accurate account of what they are doing. The yes answer is not merely that human beings are influenced or shaped by non-intentional forces—that moderate claim is made by all interpretivists—but rather that human beings are determined by those forces to the point at which there is no contribution by the agent herself. There are different ways to see human action as determined by forces other than the agent. Some non-hermeneutic scholars argue that human beings are biologically determined; others that human intentions are nothing but the echo of social forces. From the interpretivist perspective, it is true that human actions are influenced by those forces, but false that human activity is completely determined by them.

As noted at the outset, some critics complain that interpretivists privilege the insider's perspective. And it is true that if actions are constituted by their meanings, then one cannot properly identify an action unless one understands what the agents think they are doing. The perspective of the agents involved *is* privileged, then, in that scholars have to take that perspective as foundational. This aspect of the interpretative approach may be troublesome to scholars of religion who do not want their task to be simply repeating what religious people say their practices mean. But the participants' meaning is not privileged in the sense that the task of the interpretive scholar is simply to discover and then repeat what religious practitioners think they do. The task of interpretive scholar goes beyond mere repetition in two senses.

In the first place, the scholar who grasps the meaning of an action understands and can identify the action. But *interpreting* a meaningful action, whether to one's audience or even to oneself, often involves translating that action into one's own language and conceptual categories. For example, if the agents in question understand what they are doing as killing an animal to make an offering to a God, the interpreter who grasps that meaning might judge that this action is accurately translated as "a sacrifice," even if the participants so interpreted do not know that term. This translation uses language unknown to the practitioners and puts their practice into a comparative category. This translation is still an interpretation insofar as it is meant to capture *their* meaning of the action. That is, the claim of the translator to grasp the insiders' meaning presumes that, were the practitioners to know the language and the scholarly vocabulary, they would agree that this translation captures what they are saying or doing. It is for this reason that an interpretation can go wrong: David Frankfurter (2011) argues for example that the Christian theological assumptions of many interpreters of Egyptian religion has led them to interpret as "sacrifices" religious practices in which taking the life of the animal is not the key action but rather only a means to some other end like creating a mummy as a votive sign, warding off evil with pleasant aromas, using its entrails as part of an extispicy divination technique, preparing the animal for an incineration that symbolizes the destruction of enemies, or simply eating it in a feast. In these cases, the interpretation of these actions as "sacrifices" is inaccurate. Since all other scholarly questions presuppose that one has accurately identified the object of inquiry, one might call the interpretive process of understanding and translating religious meanings "first stage" of the academic study of religion.

The interpretivist Wilfred Cantwell Smith (1959: 42) thought that no statement about a religion was valid unless it would be accepted by the practitioners. In effect, he held that the interpretive first stage was the whole of religious studies. But the scholar who grasps what the agents think they are saying or doing may be interested not only in understanding their discourse or action as the agents did and interpreting it in terms that in principle they would accept, but also in explaining those words or actions in terms of causes that the agents in question would not accept. Call this "second stage." The meaning of an action to the participants typically includes their own explanation of the action. The participants may think, for instance, "We make this offering *because* God has told us to." But once a scholar has identified the action in insider's terms in the first stage, the scholar may judge that the participants" explanation of their own action is mistaken, confused, or dishonest, and that the action is better explained in some other way. Making an offering to a God might be explained by a Freudian as an expression of an infantile neurosis or by a Marxist as an example of an opiate for the masses. Explanations like this replace the explanations of the participants, but they still depend on and cannot replace the original description. That is, such explanations claim that in making the offering, the religious participants are moved by forces that they do not know, but the explanations do not claim that the people are not making an offering. In this way, the second stage requires the first one; explanations by external forces wait on interpretation.[4]

2 Does Interpretation Require Access to Someone's Mental States?

If, like Slingerland, one answers yes to the first question, then one rejects the idea that human behavior is purposive or meaningful. But if one answers no to the first question, then one holds that understanding at least some human behavior requires interpretation, in which case the next question one should answer is whether interpretation requires that the interpreter gain access to the agent's mental states.

The movement from the premise that one cannot understand some human activity unless one grasps what it means to the conclusion that one must have access to the mental states of the participants may seem common sense, or even unavoidable. To know what an activity means to the participants, it may seem that one must be able to grasp their intentions, beliefs, or feelings. It seems that one must, so to speak, "get inside their heads." Call the view that interpretation requires access to an individual's mental state "psychologism." Since the job of getting inside someone's head, this mind-reading, is not an empirical task, psychologism entails that the interpreter needs some special non-empirical method to access those internal states.

A famous example of a yes answer to this question is that of Friedrich Schleiermacher. For Schleiermacher, and perhaps still for most people today, understanding what someone means is not a science but an art that involves grasping the mental processes of the person being interpreted. The art of interpretation starts with a linguistic expression and seeks to reconstruct the meaning of its author. To be fair, Schleiermacher did not think that meaning was solely internal. Rather, meaning was two-sided and an interpreter had to deal with both the words written or spoken, which were objective and public, and the author's intention, which was subjective and private. But precisely because Schleiermacher saw a gap between outer language and inner thought, he was led to the view that the empirical sciences alone could not grasp what a text meant and so they required supplementation by the non-empirical method of *Verstehen*, the art of reconstructing the thinking of another person. According to Schleiermacher, one cannot grasp the meaning of the utterance apart from—to cite his infamous term—"divining" the thinking of its author. Here, interpretation seems to require intuition as a method.

Moreover, some interpretivists who answer yes to this second question go further to claim that understanding another person requires not only intellectually divining or intuiting what goes on in that person's mind but also experiencing oneself what that person has experienced. Such a rule is proposed by the comparativist Rudolf Otto who says that religious mental states are *sui generis* and that therefore experiencing what Otto calls a "numinous" state of mind is a necessary precondition of understanding such a state (Otto 1923: 7). A similar claim is made by the scholar of religion Ninian Smart (1973), who speaks of interpretation as empathy or "entering-in." Smart's proposal is that interpretation involves bracketing and provisionally setting aside one's own cognitive and emotional commitments to put oneself imaginatively into the position of those one seeks to understand. As Smart says, "In order to understand what it is like to be say, a Winnebago, one must really make-believe that one is a Winnebago, rehearsing the thoughts and attitudes of a Winnebago" (ibid.:70). Like Schleiermacher, then, Otto and Smart hold the psychologistic view that understanding requires getting access to another person's inner state.[5]

Just as Slingerland warned, psychologistic views of interpretation do assume a mind–body dualism, and they thereby create the epistemological problem of how, apart from what our senses tell us, one can know what another person is thinking or feeling. Interpretive social science as a movement has therefore largely repudiated these views. Already in the nineteenth century, Wilhelm Dilthey, though Schleiermacher's biographer, argued that the meanings sought in hermeneutics could not be grasped through introspection because they were the expressions (*Ausdruck*) or objectifications of a person's life, understood as a social-historical reality.

In the twentieth century, philosophers of interpretation developed multiple paths away from mind–body dualism. Some followed Martin Heidegger's non-dualist ontology of *Dasein* as human being-in-the-world, and for many philosophers the linguistic turn was made precisely to make meaning something inter-subjective and historical rather than, as with Lewis Carroll's Humpty Dumpty, a function of what a speaker wants his words to mean. In this spirit, for example, Hans-Georg Gadamer rejected the idea that the mind of the author is the key to the meaning of a work and instead made practice and language central.[6] Paul Ricoeur used the slogan that what one is seeking when one interprets is not something "behind" the text (that is, not the subjectivity of an individual author), but rather what is "in front of" the text (that is, something to which the texts refers in the intersubjectively constructed and therefore publicly available social world). For Ricoeur, social agreement is precisely what fixes meanings so that they can be studied: the object of interpretation is not a whim or a caprice of an individual, and it is not private or hidden. Thus, even when one person is the author of the text, including actions as a kind of text, the meanings found in that text are a function of collective commitments. Others followed Ludwig Wittgenstein, who argued against the idea of a private language on the grounds that meaning depends not on what an individual thinks but rather on how people publicly use a word. On a Wittgensteinian account, what a word means is neither "in" the word nor "in" the mind of the speaker but is rather hammered out over time as terms are given and taken in particular social interactions (*lebensformen*). In "Interpretation and the Sciences of Man," arguably the most widely read statement on what an interpretative social science involves, Charles Taylor writes:

> Meanings are not just in the minds of the actors but are out there in the practices themselves; practices which cannot be conceived as a set of individual actions, but which are essentially modes of social relations or mutual action. (Taylor 1971: 27)

Rabinow and Sullivan summarize this post-Cartesian view, this no answer to psychologism:

> The interpretive approach emphatically refutes the claim that one can somehow reduce the complex world of signification to the products of a self-consciousness in the traditional philosophical sense. Rather, interpretation begins from the postulate that the web of meaning constitutes human existence to such an extent that it cannot ever be meaningfully reduced to constitutively prior speech acts, dyadic relations, or any predefined elements. Intentionality and empathy are rather seen as dependent on the existence of the prior existence of the shared world of meaning within which the subjects of human discourse constitute themselves. (Rabinow and Sullivan 1979: 6)

In sum, then, those who answer yes to the question of access are interpretivists who hold that the meaning of someone's activity is a mental state, and since it is a mental state, it is not public. Those who answer no to this question are interpretivists who hold that the meaning of someone's activity is not a mental state, and since it is not a mental state, it is not private. As interpretivist social scientists, this latter group agrees that the study of human activities requires one to grasp the meaning of those activities, but they follow Hilary Putnam's slogan that "'meanings' just ain't in the head" (Putnam 1996: 13; emphasis omitted).

The social scientist who best represents this post-Cartesian view of interpretation is Clifford Geertz. Geertz saw it as his task, as he put it, to make sure that the news of the philosophical attack on privacy theories of meaning reached anthropology (Geertz 1973: 12). Stating explicitly his dependence on Wittgenstein and on Ricoeur, Geertz argued that the meanings an interpreter tries to grasp are something external (Geertz says "extrinsic") in that they "lie outside the boundaries of the individual organism as such in that intersubjective world of common understandings" (ibid.: 92). Whereas Ninian Smart focused on grasping inner feelings, Geertz focused on grasping the meaning to the participants of a sheep raid, a funeral ritual, or a cockfight—in short, the meaning of social practices. It is precisely because for Geertz the interpretive the study of human behavior is the study of practices that he says that meaning is "as public as marriage and as observable as agriculture" (ibid.: 91).[7]

Some critics of the interpretive approach have focused on Geertz's statement that religious symbols establish "moods and motivations" (ibid.: 94–98), as if Geertz was, like Schleiermacher or Smart, squirrelling religious meanings away in a private interior realm.[8] But it is not true that "Geertz made interiority the locus of religion" (Lincoln 2003: 1), an accusation that Geertz explicitly and repeatedly rejects.[9] Geertz's talk of moods and motivations reflects his assumption that social scientists are dealing not with robots but with persons, that is, agents who act with purpose. But moods and motivations are for Geertz dispositions to respond and to behave in ways that are at least partially if not fully public. In fact, I would argue that it is not possible to see public social practices as having an effect on people—on mobilizing them in some direction or another—unless those people have moods and motivations. The concept of "inner" dispositions is therefore inexpungeable from the genealogical accounts of how social power forms subjects, and this is why the concept of dispositions is central to the work of social practice theorists like Pierre Bourdieu, Talal Asad, and Saba Mahmoud (see Schilbrack in press).

This no answer, this rejection of psychologism, shifts the work of interpreting meaning away from questions of mental access to questions of translation.[10] Can the interpreter grasp the meaning of the discourse or the practice she studies to the point that she can redescribe that meaning in her own language accurately? This shift involves a distinction between what a discourse or a practice means to an individual and what it means to a collective. The philosopher Margaret Gilbert, for example, argues that any adequate account of groups has to adopt what she calls a disjunction criterion according to which it is not necessary that all, or most, or even any members of a group personally intend what the group collectively intends (Gilbert 2014: 102–106). Think of a jury whose members hear incriminating evidence that is then ruled inadmissible and so the jury finds the accused innocent. One can then accurately say that "the jury collectively believes that the accused is innocent"—even though no member of the jury *personally* believes the accused is innocent. Gilbert illustrates this same disjunction in her analyses of the collective beliefs of friends walking together, the collective guilt of a nation, and so on. Sociality creates groups stitched together by shared meanings, and therefore to grasp those meanings does not require access to the personal feelings, thoughts, or intentions in the group.

One can apply this distinction between group and individual meanings to the study of religions. To interpret the meaning of a discourse or a practice to a group is to provide an account of the practice's collective meaning. For instance, the cultural meaning of a given practice might be that the practice is an offering intended to appease a god. A particular individual might hold that meaning as her own and participate in the practice with the intention of appeasing that god. However, instead she might participate with some other personal intention: of being seen at the event, or capitulating to family obligations, or innumerable other goals. To interpret a collective meaning of the practice does not require access to her mental state.

The sociologist Christian Smith works with exactly this distinction. Smith insists that the task of interpreting collective meaning is distinct from interpreting what participants are thinking. As he puts it:

> In any actual performance of a religious practice, different participants may undertake the same actions for different purposes—from repenting from wrongdoing, to conforming to tribal norms, to struggling against boredom. However, for us seeking to understand religion theoretically, our key point of reference must be the culturally prescribed purposes and meanings of the practices, not primarily the subjective interests or motives of the people performing them. The necessary theoretical starting place for understanding religion is what a religious culture or tradition intends its practices to achieve, not the motivations of people practicing them. (Smith 2017: 30–31; emphasis omitted)

It may turn out that the prescribed meaning that a practice has according to authoritative teachings and the personal meaning it has for an individual participant are the same. The question whether a gap exists between the prescribed and the personal meaning in any instance is an open question, and it is one that is often worth investigating. But the question of what goes on in the minds of individuals is not the same as the question of the collective meaning of a practice.[11] As Smith puts it, to fail to make this distinction is to confuse religion (an analytic concept) with religiousness (an empirical variable) (ibid.: 31).

In sum, then, for the interpretivists who answer no to the second question and adopt an intersubjective account of meaning, to grasp the meaning of a religious discourse or practice does not require some non-empirical method that provides direct access to the mental states of others, but rather the quotidian development of hypotheses that can then be tested according to how well they fit the publicly available evidence.

3 Does Interpretation Preclude Causal Explanation?

Let's take stock of where we are. The first question asked whether one could understand a human action independent of the meaning it had for the agents involved. Though some answer yes and seek to explain human behavior exhaustively in terms of non-intentional material forces, those who answer no to the first question hold that at least some of the actions performed by people differ from the behavior of blind forces precisely because human beings are agents who act with purpose. These scholars hold that this is why the study of human activity, unlike the study of purposeless behavior, requires the interpretation of meanings. To these interpretivists, I posed the second question whether those meanings are the private mental states of individuals and therefore require some non-empirical method of access. Though some answer yes, holding that the interpretation of human action requires the cultivation of empathy or intuition, those who answer no to the second question hold that no special method is necessary for the study of culture because the meaning of text or a social practice is not hidden away from investigation. For these post-Heideggerian and post-Wittgensteinian scholars, "thinking is a public activity," as Geertz put it (1973: 360).

I am now asking the third and last question to those who answered no to both previous questions, that is, to those who hold that the study of human action requires interpretation to identify the public but culturally various meanings that inform them. The third question is whether interpretation precludes causal explanation. The question, in other words, is whether the difference that interpretivists see between purposeless behavior and allegedly purposeful actions implies that human actions are not amenable to the kinds of explanation one finds in the natural sciences. Do the aims of the human sciences differ from those of the natural sciences to the extent that it is confused or inapt to explain human actions in terms other than intentions?

Even when they hold that interpretation does not require a non-empirical method like empathy, several interpretivists have answered yes. Here are two examples, both of which come from classic defenses of an interpretive approach to the social sciences. A clear example comes from Peter Winch, who argued against an idea of "the unity of the sciences" according to which there is no logical difference between explaining a rock rolling down a hill and predicting in what crevice it will land and explaining a student's course though college and predicting in what career she will land. Winch held that any science of human behavior would not be giving mechanical, causal explanations: "I want to show that the notion of a human society involves a scheme of concepts that is logically incompatible with the kinds of explanation offered in the natural sciences" (Winch 1958: 72).[12] The goal of the social sciences was, instead, to interpret and thereby to make intelligible a form of life. A second, less-clear example is that of Clifford Geertz, who also contrasted the methods of the natural and the social sciences: "The concept of culture I espouse ... is essentially a semiotic one...and the analysis of it [is] therefore not an experimental science in search of law but an interpretive one in search of meaning" (Geertz 1973: 5).[13] Instead of explanations, Geertz offered thick descriptions of practices that include their local meanings. In their efforts to go beyond the positivism that dominated the middle of twentieth-century theorizing about social sciences, Winch and Geertz seem to treat the distinction between the natural sciences and the social sciences as a choice that is either/or. On their accounts of an interpretive social science, the study of culture limits itself to understanding practices on their own terms and not seeking causes the participants do not know.

Perhaps the most influential argument against the appropriateness of seeking causal explanations of human behavior in human intentions has been called the logical connection argument.[14] The logical connection argument holds that one cannot plausibly claim that an interpretation of human actions in terms of their meanings is a causal explanation. To say that "The cause of the person performing action X was the person's desire to do X" or "... the person's belief that they should do X" does not explain that action in terms of a contingent scientific law but rather identifies a necessary logical connection between (a) what we call an action and (b) desires or beliefs. Answers like these are no more the application of an explanatory law, and no more informative, than to answer the question, "Why is your brother a bachelor?" by saying "because is not married." In the case of my brother, the answer about his unmarried status is not a causal explanation but a statement of what we mean by the word "bachelor" (the word and its definition being logically connected). In the case of the interpretation, the answer about beliefs or desires is not a causal explanation but a statement of what we mean when we say that a piece of behavior is an "action." The answer may render the behavior intelligible, but it does not explain it in terms of a cause. Thus the interpretivists who answer the third question with a yes are holding that, for the study of human discourse and behavior, interpretation in terms of meanings takes the place of explanation in terms of causes.

I want to end this chapter with a proposal that would be a no to the third question.

It is striking how often one sees the interpretivist position described as insisting that there is a "gap" or a "gulf" or a "chasm" between the natural and the human sciences, as if the claim that human practices involves meanings that require interpretation entails that the object of study in human sciences does not overlap at all with that of the other sciences. But there is a crucial difference between separating the two scientific approaches and merely distinguishing them. It may be that some interpretivists seek to separate the natural and the human sciences in that they argue that it is inappropriate to seek causal explanations for human actions. The quotes from Winch and Geertz suggest exactly this. But if instead interpretivists distinguish the social sciences from the natural sciences without separating them, then one can see this kind of overlap: the natural sciences causally explain but do not interpret the meanings of phenomena they study, and the social sciences both causally explain and interpret the meanings of the phenomena they study. If the yes position regarding separation that we see in Winch and Geertz implies an image of the two kinds of sciences as two non-overlapping circles, then the no argument regarding separation can use an image of concentric circles so that the study of human actions participates in but is not exhausted by the causal explanation of human behavior. Or the interpretivist no argument for distinction-without-separation might develop a more elaborate model that draws on the stratified ontology introduced above and use a three-dimensional image of a layer cake. In a stratified ontology, recall, emergent wholes are composed of nothing other than the physical elements that make them up: water molecules are composed of nothing but hydrogen and oxygen in structured relation, yet those molecules possess properties (like drinkability) that the constituent elements did not have. Given this ontology, the methodological distinctions between chemistry and physics reflect the emergent properties of the objects they study. Explanations at the chemical level are constrained by and cannot countermand what we know from physics, though chemistry concerns properties that physics does not study. There is a parallel distinction (but not separation) between the emergence of organisms and the molecules that constitute them, an ontological distinction that justifies biology as a science constrained by but distinct from chemistry. In this vein, interpretivists can argue that human societies are composed of biological organisms (composed of molecules composed of elements) but that the study of human groups involves new properties and behavior that do not exist at and which are therefore not reducible to the biological, chemical, or elementary levels. Human behavior is thus not independent of biological, chemical, and physical laws. One can therefore endorse an interpretive study of human practices in terms of meanings without removing human minds from human bodies, nor removing those persons from the realm of causes.

Given this view of human intentions as necessarily "embodied and embedded," we can now see not only that interpretation does not preclude explanation, but also that the two methods collaborate so well that they can be hard to distinguish. The interpretation of a practice seeks to grasp the meaning of a practice to the practitioners and, as mentioned above, the meaning of a practice to the practitioners typically includes the reason why they believe they do the action. For the agent, the reason why one does an action is the explanation of the action: "I am going on the pilgrimage to this shrine because I believe that it has healing powers." I judge that people's intentions can be the causes of their behavior (Davidson 1963; Audi 1993; Menzies 2010). As a consequence, in some cases, the reason that people take to be the cause of their action really is its cause. In these cases, the interpretation of the action *is* the explanation.[15] Here, the interpretive and explanatory methods overlap. In other cases, however, the agents are mistaken about the cause of their action. The reason they think they are engaged in the practice is not really its cause. The actual cause of their practice has some other source—some other biological or cultural or unconscious mechanism that the practitioners do not recognize and which they might deny if they heard of it. Here, the two methods diverge.

In those cases where the agents' intentions are the causes of their action, to provide an interpretation of the action is simultaneously to explain the action. In those cases, the scholar provides what might be called an intentional or a reason-giving explanation. In the cases where the agents' intentions are not the causes of their action, by contrast, an interpretation of the agent's intentions does not get at the cause and it does not explain the action. In those cases, the scholar will have to provide an explanation in terms of the social function of the action or some other cause not based on the intentions of the agents. It is important to underline that, even in this second case, when the participants' intentions and the causes of their actions diverge, interpretation is not excluded. Insofar as the action is purposeful, interpretation is necessary to identify the action that is being explained. In those cases when interpretation and explanation diverge, scholars have what one might call a two-stage process. At the first stage, one identifies what the action is in terms of the intentions of the participants: for example, "this is a pilgrimage done in the hope of healing." Insofar as the meaning of an action determines what action it is, this interpretive stage cannot be avoided. Participating in a pilgrimage to a shrine is not an action one can grasp at the level of non-intentional forces, and so to identify such practices requires the interpretation of social meanings. Once the scholar has interpreted the actions accurately, however, she may then explain that behavior in terms of non-intentional causes and causes the participants do not know. Though one cannot identify a practice as a pilgrimage without reference to cultural meanings, one can explain a pilgrimage without that reference. Though scholars have to include the intentions of the participants in order to avoid descriptive reductionism, once those intentions are taken into account, reductive explanations are not precluded by the interpretive method (Proudfoot 1985).

In sum, then, the view on interpretation in the academic study of religion that I recommend is that one should answer all three questions with a no. That is, one should hold that when human beings pursue their goals, these actions require interpretation in terms of what the actions mean to the participants involved. Interpretation requires that one grasp the meaning of the practices in terms of the shared intentions of groups of people, but it does not require access to the mental state of individuals. And meaning cannot be eliminated when an observer seeks to identify what action an agent is doing, but the pursuit of meaning does not preclude explaining what the agents are doing in terms of forces of which they do not know. For this reason, the social sciences should adopt a methodological pluralism. On this compatibilist account, although one particular scholar might focus on interpreting some social practice and another might focus on explaining it, the study of religion as a whole has to include both.

Kevin Schilbrack writes about philosophical questions raised by the academic study of religion. A graduate of the University of Chicago Divinity School, he is now professor and chair of the department of Philosophy and Religion at Appalachian State University. He is the author of *Philosophy and the Study of Religions: A Manifesto* (Blackwell, 2014) and he is presently interested in the relevance of embodied cognition and social ontology for understanding what religion is and how it works.

Notes

1 Slingerland provides a telling response to those who argue that the unpredictability of human choices is a sign that some human actions are caused by novel choice. He writes:

> It is exceedingly likely that, no matter how far the neuroscience of consciousness advances, it will remain impossible—because of sheer computational intractability, quantum randomness, whatever—to accurately predict the future behavior of even a single human being, let alone groups of human beings interacting with one another and with a constantly changing physical environment. It is equally likely that, no matter what advances we make in hydrology and meteorology, it will never be possible to pick out a single molecule of H_2O from the ocean inlet outside my window and predict where that molecule will be one year from now. We never for a minute, though, doubt that molecule's future movements will be fully determined by the laws of physics. By extension, we have no more reason to believe that the cascades of neural impulses in our brains are any less determined and governed by physical causation than the water molecule. (Slingerland 2008: 277)

2 For emergentist accounts of mind, see Clayton (2006) or Deacon (2012). For an emergentist account of personhood, see Smith (2010: ch. 1). For liberal naturalism, see de Caro and MacArthur (2004, 2010).

3 Despite the differences, Slingerland's reductive physicalism is not completely opposed to an emergentist, stratified ontology. Like the non-reductive materialist position I recommend, Slingerland says that consciousness is an emergent property of certain organisms (Slingerland 2012: 80) and he says that we should see "human-level structures of meaning" not as illusory but merely as grounded in and constrained by "the lower levels of meaning studied by the sciences" (ibid.: 81). These claims agree with the non-reductive position I recommend as well. But Slingerland also says that his physicalism allows no new levels for mental phenomena (ibid.: 77n4, cf. 84-5) and he insists that the emergence of mind does not involve any freedom from the determinism of the lower levels. And so he argues that the claim that some organisms are self-caused necessarily crosses a line and represents a form of dualism. This difference between ontologies with and without emergent mental levels can be clarified by attention to the slogan Slingerland quotes that "there are no changes at the mental level without a corresponding change at the physical level" (ibid.: 77, n. 4). Mind-body dualists cannot accept this slogan. But the slogan permits two kinds of materialist readings: a reductive reading like Slingerland's that there are no allegedly higher-level mental events that are not exhaustively caused by lower-level non-mental changes, or a non-reductive reading I endorse that there are no changes at the mental level that happen without effecting a change in the body. The latter, non-reductive view is materialist but also recognizes the possibility of downward causation as emergent realities come to influence their physical parts.

4 The last three paragraphs of this section are indebted to Proudfoot (1985: ch. 6). They also agree with Ann Taves's essay in this volume, which speaks of two "steps" in the study of religions.
5 McCutcheon (2012) mocks precisely this view of interpretation by comparing it to the study of "hunches."
6 For a clear overview of Gadamer's philosophy of "understanding" that focuses on how he seeks to avoid treating it as subjective, see Grondin (2002).
7 For an excellent discussion of Geertz as a Wittgenstein-influenced practice theorist, see Springs (2008).
8 Asad (1993: ch. 1, e.g., 47) was the first to make this influential critique and Asad argues, rightly, that to focus on subjective dispositions like moods and motivations occludes the modes of social power and discipline that instill them. On my reading, however, Asad does not reject but rather keeps all of Geertz's dispositional language. That is, the contribution of the genealogical approach is not to reject the existence or the importance of religious subjectivity but rather to investigate the conditions that give rise to it (see especially ibid.: 33–35).
9 For one example of several, "To undertake the study of cultural activity … is not to abandon social analysis for a Platonic cave of shadows, to enter into a mentalistic world of introspective psychology or, worse, speculative philosophy, and wander there forever in a haze of 'Cognitions,' 'Affections,' 'Conations,' and other elusive entities" (Geertz 1973: 91; cf. Schilbrack 2005).
10 It is an interesting question to ask whether those who argue that interpretation implies a need for access to private mental states (that is, those who identify the interpretative study of religion with the approach of Schleiermacher, Otto, and Smart) are not actually scholars who endorse this approach but rather scholars who take an non-hermeneutic position and want to saddle interpretation with the problem of access.
11 Smith gives this example:

> For example, suppose we observe a religious congregation reciting from a prayer book a prayer for the protection from evil. What matters for our theoretical purpose [of identifying this practice] is that the authors of the prayer, the tradition that adheres to that prayer book, and the culture that prescribes the recitation of those prayers—in short the institution—intend those prayers to be offered to a superhuman power in hopes of receiving their protection form evil. … Whether or not the members of the congregation ware reciting the prayer actually even believe in or fear evil is an analytically separate issue. (Smith 2017: 31–32)

12 Winch was a student of Wittgenstein's, who said: "The very idea of wanting to explain the practice … seems wrong-headed to me" (Wittgenstein 1979: 1e).
13 I say that the example of Geertz is less clear because it is hard to tell whether, like Winch, Geertz holds that explanations of cultural phenomena are wrong-headed *simpliciter* or whether he declines to pursue them himself but allows their value for others. The latter, conciliatory view would not exclude explanation from the study of society. Critiquing Geertz, Talal Asad says the converse—not that interpretation is wrong-headed *simpliciter* but only that it "is not the name of my game" (Asad 1993: 110)—apparently also allowing the both/and position. Analogously, Michael Martin points out that Charles Taylor's "Interpretation and the Science of Man" (1971) "never mentions "cause" or "causality" in connection with interpreting social phenomena or even with explanations" (Martin 1994: 263) and so Martin argues that the most

plausible interpretation is that Taylor, like Winch, sees no role for causal explanation in an interpretive social science. But since, as Martin notes, Taylor's essay never explicitly denies that the social sciences include explanations, I read Taylor, like Geertz, as permitting the both/and position.

14 For a crystal clear discussion of this argument, see Rosenberg (2016: ch: 3). For a brilliant proposal regarding how the generalizations of intentional psychology have the *a priori* character imputed to them by the logical connection argument but can nevertheless support causal explanations, see Menzies (2010).

15 In fact, Mark Risjord (2000) argues persuasively that explanatory coherence is the criterion of a better interpretation.

References

Asad, Talal. 1993. *Genealogies of Religion: Discipline and Reasons of Power in Christianity and Islam*. Baltimore, MD: Johns Hopkins University Press.

Audi, Robert. 1993. *Action, Intention, and Reason*. Ithaca, NY: Cornell University Press.

Clayton, Philip. 2006. *Mind and Emergence: From Quantum to Consciousness*. Oxford: Oxford University Press.

Davidson, Donald. 1963. "Actions, Reasons, and Causes," *Journal of Philosophy* 60(23): 685–700. https://doi.org/10.2307/2023177

De Caro, Mario, and David MacArthur (eds). 2004. *Naturalism in Question*. Cambridge, MA: Harvard University Press.

De Caro, Mario, and David MacArthur (eds). 2010. *Naturalism and Normativity*. New York: Columbia University Press.

Deacon, Terrence W. 2012. *Incomplete Nature: How Mind Emerged from Matter*. New York: W. W. Norton.

Frankfurter, David. 2011. "Egyptian Religion and the Problem of the Category 'sacrifice'," in Jennifer Wright Knust and Zsuzsanna Várhelyi (eds.), *Ancient Mediterranean Sacrifice*, 75–93. Oxford: Oxford University Press. https://doi.org/10.1093/acprof:oso/9780199738960.003.0003

Geertz, Clifford. 1973. *The Interpretation of Cultures*. New York: Basic.

Gilbert, Margaret. 2014. *Joint Commitment: How We Make the Social World*. Oxford: Oxford University Press.

Grondin, Jean. 2002. "Gadamer's Basic Understanding of Understanding," in Robert J. Dostal (ed.), *The Cambridge Companion to Gadamer*, 36–51. Cambridge: Cambridge University Press. https://doi.org/10.1017/CCOL0521801931.003

Hiley, David R., James F. Bohman, and Richard Shusterman (eds.). 1991. *The Interpretive Turn: Philosophy, Science, and Culture*. Ithaca, NY: Cornell University Press.

Lincoln, Bruce. 2003. *Holy Terrors: Thinking about Religion after September 11*. Chicago, IL: University of Chicago Press.

Martin, Michael. 1994. "Taylor on Interpretation and the Sciences of Man," in Michael Martin and Lee C. McIntyre (eds.), *Readings in the Philosophy of Social Science*, 259–279. Cambridge, MA: MIT Press.

McCutcheon, Russell. 2012. "I Have a Hunch," *Method and Theory in the Study of Religion* 24(1): 81–92. https://doi.org/10.1163/157006812X632892

Menzies, Peter. 2010. "Reasons and Causes Revisited," in Mario De Caro and David Macarthur (eds.), *Naturalism and Normativity*, 142–170. New York: Columbia University Press.

Otto, Rudolf. 1923. *The Idea of the Holy*, trans. John W. Harvey. London: Oxford University Press.

Proudfoot, Wayne. 1985. *Religious Experience*. Berkeley, CA: University of California Press.
Putnam, Hilary. 1996. "The Meaning of 'Meaning'," in Andrew Pessin and Sanford Goldberg (eds.), *The Twin Earth Chronicles: Twenty Years of Reflection on Hilary Putnam's "The Meaning of Meaning"*, 3–52. Armonk, NY: M. E. Sharpe.
Rabinow, Paul and William M. Sullivan (eds.). 1979. *Interpretive Social Science: A Reader*. Berkeley, CA: University of California Press.
Risjord, Mark W. 2000. *Woodcutters and Witchcraft: Rationality and Interpretive Change in the Social Sciences*. Albany, NY: State University of New York Press.
Rosenberg, Alexander. 2016. *Philosophy of Social Science*, 5th edition. Boulder, CO: Westview.
Ryle, Gilbert. 2009. *Collected Essays, 1929–1968*. London: Routledge.
Schilbrack, Kevin. 2005. "Religion, Models of, and Reality: Are We Through With Geertz?," *Journal of the American Academy of Religion* 73(2): 429–452. https://doi.org/10.1093/jaarel/lfi042
Schilbrack, Kevin. In press. "Religious Practices and the Formation of Subjects," in David Eckel (ed.), *The Future of Philosophy of Religion*. Dordrecht: Springer.
Slingerland, Edward. 2008. *What Science Offers the Humanities: Integrating Body and Culture*. Cambridge: Cambridge University Press. https://doi.org/10.1017/CBO9780511841163
Slingerland, Edward. 2012. "Mind–Body Dualism and the Two Cultures," in Edward Slingerland and Mark Collard (eds.), *Creating Consilience: Integrating the Sciences and the Humanities*, 74–87. Oxford: Oxford University Press.
Smart, Ninian. 1973. *The Phenomenon of Religion*. New York: Herder & Herder. https://doi.org/10.1007/978-1-349-00114-9
Smith, Christian. 2010. *What is a Person?* Chicago, IL: University of Chicago Press. https://doi.org/10.7208/chicago/9780226765938.001.0001
Smith, Christian. 2017. *Religion: What it is, How it Works, Why it is Still Important*. Princeton, NJ: Princeton University Press.
Smith, Wilfred Cantwell. 1959. "Comparative Religion: Whither—and Why?" in Mircea Eliade and Joseph Kitagawa (eds.), *The History of Religions: Essays in Methodology*, 31–58. Chicago, IL: University of Chicago Press.
Springs, Jason A. 2008. "What Cultural Theorists of Religion Have to Learn from Wittgenstein; or How to Read Geertz as a Practice Theorist," *Journal of the America Academy of Religion* 76(4): 934–969. https://doi.org/10.1093/jaarel/lfn087
Taylor, Charles. 1971. "Interpretation and the Sciences of Man," *The Review of Metaphysics* 25(1): 3–51.
Winch, Peter. 1958. *The Idea of a Social Science and its Relation to Philosophy*. London: Routledge & Kegan Paul.
Wittgenstein, Ludwig. 1979. *Remarks on Frazer's Golden Bough*, trans. A. C. Miles, revised by Rush Rhees. Brynmill: Humanities.

Chapter 20

Homo Interpretans

Jennifer Eyl

Before responding to Kevin Schilbrack's argument in Chapter 19 of this volume, it is important to address the genealogy of the problem of interpretation. Schilbrack observes that, "In the past few decades, interpretation has become a beleaguered approach in the academic study of religion." Why is that? The origins of this problem can be found in the nineteenth-century German romantic hermeneutics of figures like Friedrich Schleiermacher, followed by Wilhelm Dilthey. Schleiermacher in particular argued that accurate interpretation is dependent upon understanding. Hermeneutics is "the art of understanding the discourse of another person correctly" (Ablett and Dyer 2009: 215). And one can understand the other by "feeling oneself" into the other (*sich einfühlen*)—to "disappear oneself" into the context of the other's life and social location. But many twentieth century scholars have observed that this inevitably results in the scholar seeing himself everywhere. Or as Austin Harrington puts it, "self-extinction culminates only in self-projection" (Harrington 2001: 312). As a result, numerous scholars who work in or have been influenced by post-colonial studies rightly critique the Eurocentricity of such essays/attempts toward empathy, understanding and interpretation.[1] Dilthey extends this problem in his attempt to distinguish the natural sciences from the human sciences (Murphy 2010: 15–22; Crowe 2005: 265–283). Today, we would recognize this distinction in the form of, say, chemistry, quantum mechanics, and meteorology versus fields like social psychology, anthropology, social work, or the academic study of religion (to name a few).

To Dilthey, the "natural world" does what is does without intention; there is no teleology in plate tectonics. The processes by which various events and reactions occur in the natural world can be explained if we examine them closely enough. Because there is a lack of intention or teleology, we arrive at understanding through explanation. But in the human sciences—the social sciences—we need the additional step of interpretation, according to Dilthey. The human world includes minds, intentions, and teleology.

One would think that interpretation is useful and necessary. But can interpretation ever be accurate? Habermas would say no. In his critique of Dilthey, he argues, "interpreters cannot abstractly free themselves from their hermeneutic point of departure and simply jump over the horizon of their own life activity, unproblematically suspending the context of tradition in which their own subjectivity has been formed in order to submerge themselves in a sub-historical stream of life that allows a pleasurable identification of everyone with everyone else" (Habermas 1972: 181). While Schleiermacher and Dilthey consider interpretation as a *methodology*, Heidegger and his student Gadamer write of interpretation in *ontological* terms. Gadamer, in particular, "demonstrates the unavoidably social character of the interpretive circle [or, hermeneutic circle]" (Ablett and Dyer 2009: 220). That is to say, "all interpretation takes place within an ongoing history, language, and inter-subjective context … we all inhabit such traditions and are inhabited by them" (ibid.).

This brings us, then, to Schilbrack's observation that "interpretation" is beleaguered. And dually so: On the one hand, there is the problem of determining whether humans stand outside of the natural world in the sense that we are *more than* just a combination of genetics, environment (which triggers epigenetics), and instinct. On the other hand, we have the seemingly insurmountable problem of accurately interpreting others independently of the lenses created and conditioned by our own cultures, practices, interests, experiences, mores, and intersectional "identities" (a term I use with reservation). Added up, these two problems certainly make interpretation suspect. Some of the problems can be addressed (or attenuated) by the introduction of categories of *emic* and *etic*, adopted by anthropologists in the mid twentieth century. But there is no doubt that even participating in the conversation depends on accepting (or at least, knowledge of) a strong nature-culture binary typical of German-Anglo-American scholarship. But what if we do away with this binary? Where does interpretation go?

Schilbrack's chapter circulates around three central questions:

1 Can one understand human behavior independent of an action's meaning (which he classifies as a question of ontology)?

2 Does interpretation require access to people's mental states (which he classifies as epistemological)?

3 Does interpretation preclude causal explanation (a methodological question)?

That Schilbrack distils the problem of interpretation down to these questions makes the larger problem appear less unwieldy, insofar as it cuts through the thickness of the problems generated by traditional Euro-centrism, the remnants of colonialism, and the problems of subjectivity. But I am not sure that this is entirely successful, and my uncertainty has more to do with faults I find in the categories of "interpretation" and "explanation," than with Schilbrack's chapter. Secondly, I resist the notion that each question can be fully answered with a yes or a no; instead, I would suggest a yes *and* a no, insofar as the yes and no are determined by magnitude or proximity to the object (or person, or people) of study.

To answer yes to Schilbrack's first question—"Can one understand human behavior independent of the action's meaning?"—supposes that one can "understand" human behavior solely in light of genetics and/or environment. "Interpretation" in the Schleiermacher/Dilthey sense, is therefore not necessary. This position he calls non-hermeneutic. This question itself is quite old—one of the earliest examples can be found in Epicureanism. While Epicureans were not the first to theorize the existence of atoms, by the time of Lucretius, the philosophical school has a worked out a strong theoretical position on physics: the cosmos is composed only of atoms and void and nothing else (Epicurus, *Letter to Herodotus*; Lucretius, *De rerum natura* 1.419–440). All atoms fall through void at a predictable rate and will fall in the same direction, infinitely, unless bumped by another atom. Here, it would seem that Epicurean physics is in keeping with a non-hermeneutic position, such that all human actions are determined by other actions and determinable (if one traces the chain of prior actions). But Epicureans understood that, left over, is the problem of free will. And to explain that, they theorized that every so often, for inexplicable reasons, an atom may "jump tracks" (which we call the atomic swerve, or *clinamen*; see Lucretius, *De rerum natura* 2.216–224; Lezra and Blake 2016). This inexplicable shift in atomic behavior permits for human free will. Behavior and trajectory are not interminably predictable. Thus, Epicurean physics and Epicurean ethics make room for one another, wherein one may talk about human behavior, choices, intentions, and beyond the sole choices of genetics (had they the concept), environment, or the motion of atoms.

Schilbrack queries whether "human activity is not constituted by the self-understanding of the agents" (Chapter 19, this volume). I see the full answer to this yes *and* no. I will take the example of incarceration and prison recidivism in the U.S. People make choices that entangle them in the criminal justice system, and once entangled it is highly improbable that one will become permanently disentangled. Approximately 76 percent of people currently released from prison in the U.S. will be re-arrested and re-incarcerated within 5 years.[2] If we look closely, we will find that the choices that land a person in prison could be "interpreted" as meaningful actions. Or are they? The social and economic factors that predispose certain people toward entanglement with the criminal justice system are extensive: poverty, racial bias in law enforcement, drug dependence and the so-called war on drugs, stability of home life, access to education, success-affirming role models, etc. Alteration of just one of these many factors impacts a person's predisposition to incarceration. And the recidivism rate is equally subject to social forces: Completion of a secondary degree while incarcerated (high school or GED) moderately lowers the re-incarceration rate. For those who earn a bachelor's degree while incarcerated, however, the re-arrest and re-incarceration rate can drop to less than 5 percent.[3] Completion of a higher education degree decimates the recidivism rate. Is environment a predictor of certain behaviors, practices, and choices? Yes, it undoubtedly is. But this is separate from "meaning," and here I think conversations about "meaning" become tricky. I use this example because it is timely, but also because an observer can zoom in for the intimate picture of the life of an individual and his/her actions (in the full field of possible actions), or pan out to examine social practices, institutional laws and policies, and other social forces that determine the very field of possible choices and actions to begin with. I suspect we do not have access to a view the magnitude of which is great enough for us to ascertain just how much we may be like ants or automatons or moths repeatedly flying into the same hot light bulb. This is not how most of us want to imagine ourselves. There is an ethical dimension in my answer: if we conclude that we are just automatons, ants, moths to the flame, are we also not exculpating ourselves from wrongdoing or personal responsibility?

Schilbrack's second question is an epistemological one: "Does interpretation require access to someone's mental state?" He offers two options: those interpretivists who think meaning is tied to interiority/mental state, and those who do not. For the latter, "meaning" is social and can be read regardless of what the actor's thoughts are. The former position demands an imaginative exercise most likely resulting in the self-projection Harrington warns of. This not to deny that mental states exist, of course, or that they are important. But are they accessible? I agree wholly that "To interpret the cultural meaning of the practice does not require access to [someone's] mental state" (Chapter 19, this volume). Schilbrack holds that the gap between the shared intentions of a group and the personal intentions of each of the individuals who constitute the group shows that groups have causal properties (and therefore exist) in a way that is not reducible to the causal properties (and the existence) of their individual members. A "private language" (à la Wittgenstein), and individual intentions and meanings remain inaccessible. Even for scholars who look at contemporary religious practices and actors, there remains the problem of self-reporting, self-understanding, and misrecognition. This problem is only exacerbated by attempting to access the private thoughts of those removed from us by time, geography, and language. What I find interesting about the former position—that is, the notion that we must have access to mental states in order to interpret a practice—is how it relates to the notion of "spiritual but not religious." This self-designation, which has grown significantly in the past 30 years, valorizes the individual's tastes, aesthetics, and whims above the practices and bonds of more tightly knit family groups, clans, states, etc. To suggest that one needs access to the mental states of others in order to correctly discern the social "meaning" of a practice fits neatly within a highly individualized, privatized, late capitalist idea of the self.

Schilbrack's third question is closely tied to his first, and seems nearly impossible to answer. I will illustrate: when the surface of the earth heats up, moisture on the ground evaporates and rises into the atmosphere. The higher altitudes cool that moisture, condense it, and gravity pulls *most* of it back to the ground in the form of rain. That is how rain happens. It is predictable. Similarly, it is 100 percent predictable that certain economic/political conditions will pull *most* people into social and political strife. We can even manipulate the specifics of the factors and determine the type of strife. What does that mean for the study or religion, though? If we hold with those who would do away with the work of interpretation, we are left with an academic study of religion that essentially boils down to cognitive science and epigenetics. But interpretation itself is part of human cognition: we are nothing if not *homo interpretans*. While cognitive studies certainly have much to offer in the study of religion, we must also be wary of the ways in which interpretation of scientific data is itself conditioned and mediated by language, invisible paradigms about gender and race, etc.

And if we return to my earlier example of Epicurean ethics versus Epicurean physics, we note that no matter how non-teleological human behavior might be, we don't sit well with the notion that human behavior is entirely the result of genetics, environment, and naturally selected instinct.[4] The fact that we cannot sit with this is evident in our theories of justice, personal responsibility, and free will—both writ large and in our day-to-day interactions. So, the two positions are ever at odds, and I see no resolution outside of Kevin's suggestion of paying closer attention to the overlap.

My own question in this conversation pertains to the usefulness of retaining nineteenth-century categories, when perhaps the categories themselves do not get us where we need to go. If our goal is understanding, and the debate concerns the usefulness of interpretation in that endeavor, what happens if we do away with the category interpretation *as defined* by nineteenth-century figures like Schleiermacher and Dilthey? Explanation, as it is, (in my opinion) does so much of the work toward understanding and Schilbrack has just demonstrated that the two overlap. Perhaps interpretation is useful precisely where it overlaps with explanation and the spaces of imbrication are where we should be looking.

Jennifer Eyl is assistant professor of religion at Tufts University. She specializes in early Christianity, religions of the ancient Mediterranean, and theory of religion. She has published in *Method and Theory in the Study of Religion*, the *Journal for the Study of the New Testament*, and in numerous edited volumes. She is the author of the forthcoming book *Signs, Wonders, and Gifts: Divination in the Letters of Paul* and co-editor of *Christian Tourist Attractions, Mythmaking and Identity Formation*.

Notes

1 Tomoko Masuzawa, for example, has examined the emergence of the category "world religions" as a result of European expansion, Protestant theology, and more recent globalization. The emergence of the category ultimately preserves Eurocentric interests and interpretive ideologies about "the Other." See Masuzawa (2005).

2 This statistic according to the National Institute of Justice: see www.nij.gov/topics/ corrections/recidivism/ pages/welcome.aspx. See also Durose, Cooper, and Snyder (2014).

3 This is the recidivism statistic for BA graduates of the Bard Prison Initiative. See New York State Department of Corrections and Community Supervision (2013) and Duwe and Clark (2014).

4 The fact of our discomfort is not evidence against the claim, of course.

References

Ablett, Phillip Gordon, and Pamela Kay Dyer. 2009. "Heritage and Hermeneutics: Towards a Broader Interpretation of Interpretation," *Current Issues in Tourism* 12: 209–233. https://doi.org/10.1080/13683500802316063

Crowe, Benjamin. 2005. "Dilthey's Philosophy of Religion in the 'Critique of Historical Reason': 1880–1910," *Journal of the History of Ideas* 66: 265–283. https://doi.org/10.1353/jhi.2005.0033

Durose, Matthew R., Alexia D. Cooper, and Howard N. Snyder. 2014. *Recidivism of Prisoners Released in 30 States in 2005: Patterns from 2005 to 2010*. Special Report, April, NCJ 244205. Washington, DC: Bureau of Justice Statistics. Retrieved from www.bjs.gov/index.cfm?ty=pbdetail&iid=4986 (accessed February 27, 2018).

Duwe, Grant, and Valerie Clark. 2014. "The Effects of Prison-Based Educational Programming on Recidivism and Employment," *The Prison Journal* 94(4): 454–478. https://doi.org/10.1177/0032885514548009

Habermas, Jürgen. 1972. *Knowledge and Human Interests*. Boston, MA: Beacon Press.

Harrington, Austin. 2001. "Dilthey, Empathy, and Verstehen: A Contemporary Reappraisal," *European Journal of Social Theory* 4: 311–329. https://doi.org/10.1177/13684310122225145

Lezra, Jacques, and Liza Blake (eds.). 2016. *Lucretius and Modernity: Epicurean Encounters Across Time and Disciplines*. New York: Palgrave Macmillan. https://doi.org/10.1007/978-1-137-56657-7

Masuzawa, Tomoko. 2005. *The Invention of World Religions: Or, How European Universalism Was Preserved in the Language of Pluralism*. Chicago, IL: University of Chicago Press. https://doi.org/10.7208/chicago/9780226922621.001.0001

Murphy, Tim. 2010. *The Politics of Spirit: Phenomenology, Genealogy, Religion*. Albany, NY: SUNY Press.

New York State Department of Corrections and Community Supervision. 2013. *College Programs: Educating Those Who Are Incarcerated to Reduce Recidivism*. New York: New York State Department of Corrections and Community Supervision. Retrieved from www.doccs.ny.gov/DoccsNews/2013/College_Programs.pdf (accessed February 27, 2018).

Chapter 21

Combining and Constituting

Mark Q. Gardiner and Steven Engler

The first question that Kevin Schilbrack asks (Chapter 19, this volume) is the most basic of his three: "*Can one understand human behavior independent of the action's meaning?*" The other two questions—about access to others' mental states and interpretation's relation to causal explanation—only arise if we answer "no" to this one. None of these questions have obvious answers. Defending one view or another requires careful groundwork. That this first question is a tricky one is clear from the complexity of the terms that make it up: "behavior," "action," and most especially "meaning." It must be unpacked and re-packed through careful analysis that draws out a range of theoretical, epistemological, and methodological presuppositions.

These kinds of presuppositions are inescapable in the study of religion. Scholars of religion often presuppose implicit answers to these kinds of questions, as they pursue descriptive work and generally ad hoc analyses—"applying" theory A or re-describing their case using concept B in order to salt the gravel for interpretive panning. The value of this volume is to put these issues on the table for more explicit consideration.

When Schilbrack asks, "*Can one understand human behavior independent of the action's meaning?*," we need to arrive at a clearer understanding of just what it is that the question is asking. It can be understood in different ways, each leading to different answers. And, of course, how we answer that first question shapes how we answer the others. Schilbrack is aware of this. His recent book, *Philosophy and the Study of Religion: A Manifesto* (2014), carefully elaborates his philosophical base. By contrast, and appropriately for its length and for its intended audience, this chapter is more a sketch to prime this discussion than a detailed defense of his answers to the three questions.

Rather than dive into debates over philosophical issues, narrowly defined, our response starts from a basic question *about* Schilbrack's questions: how can the issues that they raise be framed in a way that is productive in terms of research? More specifically how do they resonate with the study of religion as a discipline? As we read through the chapter and discussed this general mode of response, it seemed to us that Schilbrack's three questions suggest a prior one: *what are the principal objects that the scholar of religion studies?* The answer he gives is widely accepted, though perhaps that has not always been the case: the principal objects of study are human (religious) behaviors.[1] The trick here is to spell out what constitutes human behavior. Schilbrack has many interesting things to say about this, most of which we agree with. However, many of the points that he raises are seen in a different light when we *begin* with this focus on the discipline itself.

Schilbrack begins by describing behaviors as being composed of, at least in part, things that carry meaning. That is, he makes meanings conceptually prior to behavior. Without getting some sort of handle on the meaning at play in a particular case, we can't even determine whether a certain phenomenon is something that warrants the label "behavior." We want to see what happens when we reverse that starting point, when we begin with an understanding of the subject matter of religious studies and then ask what this tells us about meanings. That offers a useful place from which to ask whether the scholar of religion has to care about meanings. To this end we will begin by re-describing the framework Schilbrack is proposing, stripped of all talk of meanings. We start by looking at what is implied by our taking behaviors as primary objects of study. What emerges, we think, are two frameworks that are not clearly compatible.

Schilbrack hints at a commonsensical distinction. While all human behaviors are paired with bodily movements, not all bodily movements are paired with behaviors.[2] A bodily movement is something that can be described in the "neutral" language of the natural sciences and which can be explained in terms of efficient causation (i.e. in terms of natural laws and the physical movements of other things), in much the same way that a scientist might describe, explain, or predict the action of a rock rolling down a hill (Chapter 19, this volume). Bodily movements are, in principle, fully open to empirical investigation. Behaviors, on the other hand, involve aspects that are not fully open to direct observation. A natural scientific description of the paired bodily movement leaves something out—Schilbrack's use of Ryle's "'immense but unphotographable difference' between a wink and a blink" is a nice, and nicely rhyming, example (Chapter 19, this volume). Social sciences care more about winks than blinks. But what is the difference between a person's behavior and her bodily movements (e.g., between a wink and a blink)?

There are at least two ways to go here. The first thinks of behaviors as bodily movements with something added, and this is a view implicit at various points in Schilbrack's chapter. He often talks of a behavior as a bodily movement combined with a teleological aim, where that in turn is typically cashed out as a purposive intention to achieve some aim or goal.[3] A host of questions suggest themselves. What is the teleological aim that transforms a blink into a wink? Are there different types of winks, depending on the types of intentions—perhaps even a special religious form of wink? Does the intention cause the blink (and consequently, in a circular way, the wink itself)? For scholars, the most pressing question is how we can identify the intention behind the blink as a precursor to taking the blink as paired with a wink. If 'behavior equals bodily movement plus intention,' then we need to be able to identify and characterize the intention as such in order to investigate the behavior. It is this view—that behaviors are bodily movements plus intentional teleological aims—that gives force to Schilbrack's second question, whether the scholar of religion needs to access those intentions, and it guides much of how he answers it. It is not clear from Schilbrack's discussion just how we are to understand these intentional teleological aims, and different views give rise to various methodological problems. We will return to these later.

The second way of distinguishing bodily movements from behaviors does not think of behaviors as composite entities—i.e., bodily movement + intention—but rather as unified things constituted by tightly interrelated aspects. We call this second model "constitutive," in contrast to the first "combinatorial" one. The combinatorial view sees behaviors as composed of two analytically distinct elements: bodily movements describable by natural science and intentions describable by human/social sciences. The constitutive view sees a behavior as a unified phenomenon, one that requires of the scholar a different sort of approach. The combinatorial position is less prominent in Schilbrack's chapter, but there are scattered hints of it: e.g., "To identify what the human activity [i.e. behavior] is ... one must figure out the meaning of the behavior. The meaning the behavior has for the participants is part of the very constitution of what they are doing." On the combinatorial model, one can point to a behavior by pointing to a bodily movement. Of course, full understanding of the behavior will require understanding the implied intention. On the constitutive model, pointing to a bodily movement would radically under-determine identification of a behavior, even if the pointer concedes intentionality to the actor. The bodily movement is not a material substrate that is only contingently related to an intentional teleological aim. Hence, description of the bodily movement and identification of the underlying intention cannot be neatly separated: they are necessarily unified, because they constitute a single thing, the behavior. In the simple example, the constitutive model would not consider a given wink to be a rapid closing and opening of the eye which just happens to be accompanied by the intention, say, to signal romantic interest, but rather as a unified rapid-closing-and-opening-of-the-eye-in-order-to-signal-romantic-interest. Interpreting something as a behavior requires something beyond grasping that a bodily movement has taken place and independently grasping that an intention is lurking underneath it. Behavior is a different sort of thing from the ground up; it is constituted by and recognized as a behavior through a more complex and nuanced process. Winks and blinks are far more different than the first, combinatorial, view suggests. The combinatorial view—"wink = blink + intention"—doesn't do justice either to the frequent inscrutability of intentions or to the complexity of the real world contexts in which behaviors take place.

The key feature of the constitutive model emerges more clearly when we move from such simple examples to the complex ones that are of interest to scholars of religion. A richer, if overused, example will be helpful here. Consider an utterance of "This is the body of Christ" while holding up a wafer. Identifying that a behavior has taken place would require more than just a description of the bodily movements in a neutral language (and a few other things, like the noises made, shape of the wafer, etc.) together with confidence that the speaker is intending to achieve some aim. Stopping there would fail to mark the behavioral differences between the cases of a Roman Catholic priest, a Baptist pastor, someone engaged in host defamation or a performer on a stage. The differences between such actors cannot be captured merely by description of bodily movements in the language of natural science, nor by pointing to a single teleological aim. The various actors' beliefs and whole ranges of other propositional attitudes, such as hopes, desires, predictions, emotions, etc., are needed in the description to even identify *which* behavior is taking place. In other words, on the constitutive model the very conception of a behavior is inseparable from consideration of a much broader range of propositional attitudes than is suggested by the combinatorial one; and these propositional attitudes themselves can only be identified within a larger environmental context including, in this example, social, cultural, and theological aspects. The very use of a term like "priest" or "defamation" in a description takes us well beyond the resources of the language of natural science. Science can describe blinks; but winks require this sort of richly contextualized account, one found, not surprisingly, in the human and social sciences. The very identity of these things called "behaviors" requires thick descriptions, and these thick descriptions inevitably contain terms which necessarily point beyond "bodily movements + actor's intention."

We are now in a good position to ask what conceptions of meaning drop out of each of these different conceptions of the basic objects of scholarly study. Schilbrack's first question asks whether we can understand human behavior independent of the action's meaning. We have paraphrased that as whether we can understand human behavior independent of intentional mental states. Both combinatorial and constitutive models answer "no": whether we focus narrowly on added intentions or more broadly on propositional attitudes in their broad contexts, we cannot escape studying meanings, in this sense. On the surface, the two models differ over the role of mental states quantitatively; for the combinatorial model, understanding one mental state would suffice whereas for the constitutive model many are needed. But the differences are likely much deeper: perhaps reflecting different theories of mind, hence different views of "mental states," or different theories of meaning, hence different views of which things have meanings.

Schilbrack's discussion of the first question, when read though a combinatorial lens, identifies the intentional teleological aim with the behavior's meaning. A bodily movement has no meaning in itself, but an intentional state does, and when put together produces a behavior that is investigable by the social scientist: "wink = blink + intention" and to understand the meaning of the blink, we need merely to understand the intention.

Schilbrack suggests two other important qualifiers at points: that the intentional teleological aims are "owned" by the actors (transforming them into "agents"); and that these aims are transparent to the actors themselves. Thus, meanings are seen as meanings *of* and *for* the agent: "the identity of the action in question is a function of its meaning to the people involved" (Chapter 19, this volume). On this view, because the subject matter of the study of religion is behavior, and because behaviors are semantically charged in virtue of being constituted by meaningful mental states, it follows that the scholar of religion must investigate meanings. Given that, on the combinatorial model, meanings are privately owned, the scholar of religion must try to figure out how the adherents understand their own behaviors. On this view, meanings seem to be "in the heads" of the adherents. As such, Schilbrack's second question—about access to others' mental states—takes on the familiar epistemological problem of a Cartesian social science with the correlated methodological challenge of getting inside other peoples' heads. However, the problem is actually wider than this. On the combinatorial model, there is only a contingent relation between a bodily movement and an intentional mental state: behaviors are bodily movement plus some intentional state, but the model offers no account of why certain intentions and certain movements happen to be combined. As a result, it is difficult to see how the scholar can do her job, if she is limited to an empirical methodology. Schilbrack notes that some scholars of religion, when faced with this problem, have looked for non-empirical methodologies.

Schilbrack does not wish to go down this road, and we and the majority of contemporary scholars of religion would agree. To avoid it, though, given his negative answer to his first question, Schilbrack is forced to consider a very different conception of meaning, one that locates it "outside of the head." Where exactly is meaning, if not linked solely to the intentions of agents? Consistent with the distinction between bodily movements and behaviors, meaning cannot be carried by the bodily movements themselves. It follows from this point, more generally, that meaning cannot be located in anything that is fully describable by the neutral language of natural science. What's left? Here Schilbrack endorses the Taylor/Ricoeur/Wittgenstein/Brandom line that locates it in the "publicly available social world" that is "intersubjectively constructed" (Chapter 19, this volume).

The argument here gets a bit tricky. Schilbrack's negative answer to his second question does not actually deny that there are private and inaccessible-to-the-scholar meaning-bearing intentional states of individuals that combine with their bodily movements to produce their behavior. He suggests, rather, that by shifting attention to social behavior—where the meaning-bearing parts are not located in any particular person's head—the scholar of religion can simply avoid the access problem. Schilbrack seems willing to bifurcate meaning, to accept that there are (at least) two radically different types of meaning. He notes that there is a difference between interpreting the cultural meaning of a given practice and the personal meaning it has to an individual participant. Schilbrack's suggested solution to the access problem is to privilege the social meaning over the individual meaning, at least for the study of religion.

Re-described in terms of our problematic—stripping away mention of meaning and highlighting the agenda of the study of religion—that solution is to take social behavior, not the behavior of individuals, as the proper object of scholarly investigation. This reading is reinforced by Schilbrack's extended description of Christian Smith's privileging of the social. On Smith's account (as cited by Schilbrack), the intentional states of social groups—the "culturally prescribed purposes and meanings of the practices"—can be quite different from "the subjective interests or motives of the people performing them" (Chapter 19, this volume). This makes sense on one level: it seems pretty obvious that an individual may engage in some practice for reasons other than "the practice's authoritative, official, or prescribed" (ibid.) ones. However, this view raises many questions. Is the analogue of an individual's bodily movements in the social case merely the concatenation of the bodily movements of all or some of the participants? This doesn't seem likely, as the description of that analogue has to be more than just a concatenation of descriptions of individual bodily movements. In our example above, it would seem to have to at least make reference to occupational roles (priest, pastor, defamer, performer), and the content of such terms is missed in the purely physical descriptions of the individual's physical makeup and movements. A more important issue is the question of the content and identity of the intentional teleological aims of the collective and their relationship to those of individuals. The collective mental states cannot be a mere concatenation of those of the participants. Some privileging must take place; predominantly those of the elite are taken as definitive. But, why those? Some post-modernists might defend, and so critique, that on the basis that understanding social phenomena is really about understanding power relations. Some "critical" theorists would likely say that the governing mental states that determine the social behavior are just those constructed by the scholar. So, the social behavior version of the combinatorial model needs a lot of theoretical refinement. Similar questions could be raised against any privileging. A whole series of complex questions lie unanswered along this path.

The more important question is whether the social-meaning route succeeds in avoiding the access problem. If meanings are rooted in intentions, moving to a social level doesn't obviate the need to have access to those intentions; if anything, it complicates the problem. How do we study "intentions" at a social level? If the relevant intentional states are those of some elite, say, aren't they just as private and so inaccessible? If they supervene on (some set) of individual intentional states, how are they accessible by a purely empirical methodology? If they are constructs, by whom are they constructed? If by insider participants, they still seem private: how have we left behind the mental states of the Cartesian approach? If constructed by scholarly outsiders, it is difficult to see by what criteria we can have confidence about the correctness or incorrectness of scholarly pronouncements: doesn't the radical constructionist scholar sever the link on which the combinatorial view is based? That is, if the meanings of the behaviors that we study lie in a combination of the intentions and the bodily movements of others, then either the radical contructionist scholar constructs the bodily movements of her subjects along with their intentions, or she severs the two and is left with no way to argue for the validity of her account. It would seem that the only way past this problem is to abandon the combinatorial model of behavior altogether, to hold that behaviors are not combinations of purely physical goings-on coupled with intentional teleological aims transparent to and owned by the actors, whether those actors are understood as individual humans or as social collectives. The social route that Schilbrack advocates, when seen through the combinatorial lens, can only avoid the access question by abandoning its theoretical base.

Perhaps all of these should be taken as strong reasons to reject the combinatorial model in favor of the constitutive one. On the latter, there is no neat separation of behavior into one part purely describable by the language of natural science and another that is an intentional mental state. In terms of meaning, it is the whole of behavior that carries meaning. And this unified behavior is the focus of scholarly investigation, even though that unit is composed of elements, including bodily movements, that are situated in a shared and public environmental, social, and cultural context. On this model, there is simply no question of the need for a scholar to study something that is empirically hidden, no need to access private mental states, no need to span the Cartesian divide. On the constitutive view, interpreting a bit of behavior is part and parcel of an act of identifying something *as* behavioral. That identification is parasitic on describing it in a language that does not neatly separate into a natural science part and a human/social science part. It follows that, on the constitutive view, explanation and interpretation cannot be neatly distinguished, being necessarily and inseparably connected. Postulation of mental states is an inescapable part of the interpretative process of trying to make maximal sense of the behavior. On this view, Schilbrack's second question—"does interpretation require access to someone's mental states?"—appears odd. The constitutive model does not conceive of mental states as something independent of the process of interpretation, and so access to them cannot be seen as a precondition for the possibility of interpretation. By analogy, where Schilbrack's second question asks "do we have to open a fridge to know what it is?" under the constitutive model the question is closer to "does knowing what a fridge is require understanding how the inside and outside are part of a single commercially manufactured appliance, serving to keep food cold and factory workers employed, and so furthering our collective interests?"

What, then, of Schilbrack's third question: *does interpretation preclude causal explanation?* Under the combinatorial model, this is a perfectly sensible question, as behavior splits into a part explainable in causal terms (namely the bodily movements) and a part that is interpretable (namely the meaning-bearing intentional states). Because the model sees these parts as only contingently related, Schilbrack's question is live and open. However, under a constitutive model, the question appears odd, just as the second question did.

The addition of the qualifier "causal" is suggestive, as it opens the door to different *types* of explanations.[4] This is reinforced when Schilbrack says that his third question is equivalent to the following: *does the difference between purposeless [events] and allegedly purposeful [behaviors] imply that human actions are not amenable to the kinds of explanations one finds in the natural sciences?* In the Cartesian version of the combinatorial view, the mental states are taken as possible *efficient causes* of the bodily movements, but making coherent philosophical sense of this has proven so elusive that most nowadays just reject the mind-body dualism that underlies it. Under the constitutive model, the question is whether the sort of explanation appropriate for the bodily movement part needs to be the same as that appropriate for the intentional mental state part. When put like this, it is hard to understand the question. Under the constitutive model, behaviors do not have parts that can be separated out for analysis: i.e., purposeless events (bodily movements) combined with goals (intentional teleological aims). Hence, the question of the relationship between interpretation and explanation can't be expressed in this form. For an analogy, a given ecological phenomenon needs the explanatory resources of (at least) both natural selection and geology. There is no need to see these fields as standing in competition to decide which one truly deserves the epithet "explanation," no need to dissect the phenomenon into one discrete part explained by one and another explained by the other, no need to discredit a richer explanatory meta-model that covers both.

To capture the spirit of Schilbrack's third question under a constitutive model, let's return to the wink-blink example. (Remember that a wink seen as a behavior under the constitutive model does not include the blink's intention as a detachable part.) Can winks be explained:

- with reference *only* to (a set) of mental states?
- *without* reference to neurological processes?
- *without* reference to a shared public environmental social context?

The constitutive model appears to answer "no" to each of these. Behaviors are seen as methodological units that are complexes of non-contingently related "parts"; hence, mentioning only a mental state, or only a neurological process, or only a social context can only provide a *partial* explanation, at best. These would still count *as* explanations, under the constitutive model, just incomplete ones.

For example, if we seek to understand why a person is engaging in a particular ritual, it is possible to highlight different aspects of the issue. Some scholarly approaches frame matters in a way that sets these different partial perspectives as competitors in a metatheoretical zero-sum game. A sharp distinction between interpretation and explanation has this effect, and, as we have tried to show, this particular tension is linked to paradoxical implications of the combinatorial view. On the constitutive view, the very identification of the ritual involves an interpretative process of trying to make sense of what's going on. As a result, a variety of partial explanations needn't be seen as competing:

- because her body is moving in such and such a way;
- because she believes it will achieve such and such an aim;
- because her brain is cognitively processing in such and such a way;
- because that is a social expectation of her group; or
- because of the hierarchical power relations of her culture.

Under the constitutive model, interpreting and explaining are not seen as separable scholarly activities that can be performed on the basic objects that define the subject matter. They are not tools with different points of purchase; they are sides of a coin. To interpret just is to try and explain; the identity of what one is trying to explain is a function of the process of interpretation.

So, which of the two models implicit in Schilbrack's chapter—the combinatorial or the constitutive—betters grounds the very possibility of scholarship in religion? That question should prompt further and useful discussion.

Mark Q. Gardiner is professor of philosophy at Mount Royal University. He works in what he describes as "applied" philosophy of language by exploring and critiquing the linguistic assumptions which underlie talk and thought about a range of human practices. He is especially interested in the semantics of natural languages as embodied in religious contexts, whether text, practices, or institutions, as well as in scholarly reflections on those contexts.

Steven Engler is professor of religious studies at Mount Royal University in Calgary, affiliate professor of religion at Concordia University in Montréal, and professor colaborador at the Pontifícia Universidade Católica de São Paulo. He studies religions in Brazil, as well as theories and methodology in the study of religion.

Notes

1 To be precise, implicit in Schilbrack's chapter is that social scientists are only interested in a subset of behaviors—namely those that are performed purposely and which he labels "actions." While perfectly serviceable, Schilbrack's terminology camouflages the role of the physical body; and it can be potentially confusing to employ the same label both for phenomena the social scientist is interested in (purposive behavior) and those which she is not (non-purposive behavior), as for example when he suggests that a racing heart or the patellar reflex is a behavior which falls outside of the purview of the social scientist. We therefore alter his terminology a bit, but think we've got the same basic framework.
2 The use of "paired" may seem odd, as it suggests that a behavior and its paired bodily movement might be two very different things. Odd as it might sound, we want to keep this option open at this point: to say all behaviors *are* bodily movements (but not vice versa) is to declare the ontological identity right off the bat.
3 On a side note, Schilbrack often talks *as if* a single intentional teleological aim is all that is needed to transform a blink into a wink, but we think this is just a simplifying assumption. We'll come back later to a more complicated account, one still within the spirit of Schilbrack's framework.
4 Egil Asprem and Ann Taves's Chapter 13 in this volume similarly notes different types of explanation, drawing on Aristotle's distinction between efficient and teleological explanations.

Chapter 22

Subjectivity and Meaning

Joshua Lupo

In answering "no" to each of the questions he proposes in Chapter 19 of this volume—"Can one understand human behavior independent of the action's meaning?", "Does interpretation require access to people's mental states?", and "Does interpretation preclude causal explanation?"—Kevin Schilbrack offers a philosophical defense of a hermeneutic approach to religious studies. He re-imagines the study of meaning as the study of collectively articulated norms that govern human cultures. In doing so, Schilbrack opens up a new and more productive approach to meaning that goes beyond traditional accounts of hermeneutic investigation in religious studies.

In my brief response, I want to expand on the second of the two questions around which Schilbrack structures his chapter, namely that of whether interpretation requires access to mental states. Like Schilbrack, I agree that the answer to this question is "no." But I worry that this answer leaves under-investigated the first-person perspective from which knowledge claims are made. In other words, I worry that the role of the individual in shaping meaning is occluded in his socially oriented conceptualization of meaning. I suspect that this occlusion has to do with Schilbrack's desire to not be seen as a defender of an interiorized or ahistorical subject who stands apart from the world, a model of subjectivity that has been criticized by many scholars of religion. To show his distance from this understanding of the relationship between meaning and subjectivity, Schilbrack approvingly quotes Christian Smith, who writes, "The necessary theoretical starting place for understanding religion is what a religious culture or tradition intends its practices to achieve, not the motivations of people practicing them" (Smith 2017: 30–31; emphasis omitted). Schilbrack's endorsement of this claim suggests that scholars do not need to give an account of the role of individual interpretation in understanding the meaning of social practices. And yet without an account of the subject whose motivations matter for conceptualizing meaning, the dynamism of humans' normative worlds is excluded from analysis. Individuals are not only the medium through which norms are expressed, but also the agents who conform to norms, rebel against them, and sometimes change them.[1]

By turning to a phenomenological account of subjectivity, I offer an account of why the first person is important for any analysis of meaning. In the Heideggerean strand of phenomenology followed by thinkers such as John Haugeland and Steven Galt Crowell, the subject does not appear "before" the world comes into existence. Rather the subject comes about as a response to the experience of anxiety (*Angst*) within everyday experience. Anxiety reminds us that the normative world in which we live always matches up imperfectly with our lives as they are actually lived. When I realize that my identity as a scholar is dependent upon adequately adhering to the norms of scholarship, I feel anxious. I feel anxious not because I cannot fulfill such norms, but because there is no certainty that I will be able to do so. For example, I might fail to incorporate an important source into an argument that I am making. What this realization opens up is the possibility of a subject who stands apart from the world. Such a subject still shares a world of meanings with others, but she also plays a role in shaping that world. The norms that determine what it is to be a scholar are not of my own making. But they are norms that *I* take up in the formation of my "practical identity" as a scholar (Crowell 2013: 174). It is this understanding of subjectivity that I want to offer as a supplement to Schilbrack's defense of interpretation.

Giving an account of the first person—of subjectivity—is important for two reasons. I offer a defense of the first here; for reasons of space, I will only gesture towards the second reason in my conclusion. First, it is impossible to account for the dynamism of our normative social worlds without positing an individual for whom such norms matter; second, it is difficult if not impossible to ground scholarly critique as something that has an effect on the world without first providing an account of the kind of subject who can critically engage with that world. I start by taking up the second portion of Schilbrack's argument; then, I show why I think a more robust defense of subjectivity is needed to ground it; and finally, I suggest what such an account can tell us about the nature of scholarly critique.

Schilbrack on Meaning

The first two questions that Schilbrack asks in his chapter are intimately linked, for if one answers "no" to the first question, concerning whether behavior can be understood apart from the meaning of an action, one might immediately fear being critiqued for having implicitly answered "yes" to the second question, that is, of whether interpretation requires access to people's mental states, without justifying that answer. In other words, if one takes some human actions to be meaningful because they are performed by purposeful agents, then understanding those meanings requires accessing the intentions and desires of the agents engaged in such performances. Schilbrack does not believe that this is the case. He argues that we can talk about the meaning of practices without talking about the inner dispositions (or mental states) of individual subjects. This is because the meaning of practices can be read by looking at the norms which govern them, what he calls the practice's authoritative, official, or prescribed meaning (see Chapter 19, this volume). So, to extend one of Schilbrack's examples, an individual might internally see her baptism as an annoying requirement, done merely for the sake of appeasing her parents, while the meaning of the practice itself might be still be understood as a rite which initiates a person into the Christian community. We can access the meaning of the practice without having to delve into the inner mental states of the person who engages in the practice. She might understand her engagement as an expression of filial piety or religious devotion. But when we, as scholars, look for the meaning of a practice we should look at the agreed upon norms that make such a practice intelligible. In doing so, we avoid getting ourselves bogged down in the impossible task of interpreting people's "true intentions."

While I agree with Schilbrack that accessing inner mental states is a difficult task, I do not agree that this means that when scholars investigate the meaning of human actions, they should ignore the motivations of the subjects who undertake those actions. To put it bluntly, norms and practices are always embodied and expressed through the interpretations that individuals proffer. Norms do not stand still; they are not static. Each time a person takes up a practice, or even uses a word, that practice is brought into being in a unique manner (see Brandom 1979: 193).[2] Norms, like a language, are malleable. They respond to the contexts in which individuals employ them. Schilbrack suggests that settling on the meaning of a practice for an individual is an empirical matter, and thus should be distinguished from the practice of hermeneutics. He writes,

> The question whether a gap exists between the prescribed and the personal meaning in any instance is an open question, and it is one that is often worth investigating. But the question of what goes on in the minds of individuals is not the same as the question of the collective meaning of a practice. As [Christian] Smith puts it, to fail to make this distinction is to confuse religion (an analytic concept) with religiousness (an empirical variable). (Schilbrack, Chapter 19, this volume)

But here I worry that Schilbrack has glossed over an important gap, one that reveals how the performance of a ritual, or any sort of practice for that matter, can both draw on a cultural script, but also change that script through its performance. If we stay at the higher level of cultural meanings it is impossible to see this dynamism in social practices.

Let me offer an example to clarify what is at stake in this point. In *Radical Hope: Ethics After Cultural Devastation* (2006), Jonathan Lear argues that the practices of the Crow came into danger when the U.S. government began to take their land and re-organize the political structure under which they lived. This event, along with the disappearance of the Buffalo, led to radical changes in Crow culture. One traditional practice that began to disappear revolved around the meaning of planting what was called a "coup stick." This stick was planted by a Crow warrior at the beginning of a battle with an opposing tribe. For the Crow, it was seen as a mark of bravery when that stick was defended as a line that the enemy could not cross. Over time, general acts of bravery among Crow warriors came to be associated with "counting a coup," such as a Crow warrior taking a horse from a rival tribe or being the first to kill an enemy fighter in battle. When fighters recounted their acts of bravery to each other after the battle, they engaged in a practice that was also identified as "counting coups."[3] The practice of counting coups was one that had been engaged in by the Crow for quite some time. But with the invasion of white persons into the area and the restructuring of political authority, fighting bravely in battle was no longer possible. Indeed, warfare among tribes was not allowed by the U.S. government (Lear 2006: 27). In this situation, "counting coups" was no longer a cultural practice that could be intelligibly enacted. But Lear describes an illustrative moment of the creative interpretation of this cultural practice by Plenty Coups, a leader of the Crow nation during the waning of their tribe's way of life. This occurred at a ceremony for the internment of the Unknown Soldier in Washington, DC. I will reproduce both the account of Plenty Coups's action and Lear's interpretation to illustrate this creative reinterpretation:

> "After the chaplain had completed his prayers, Plenty Coups stepped forward. Dressed in brilliantly beaded buckskin, carrying a coup stick, and wearing an eagle-feather headdress, the seventy-two-year-old warrior's presence was a stunning match for the European generals and the officers from the Mikado's navy who stood in the front ranks of the audience in their polished boots and gold braid. The huge crowd watched in absolute silence as the ... leader—who had first come to Washington with Pretty Eagle and Medicine Crow more than forty years before—removed his war bonnet and laid it on the sarcophagus along side his coup stick."
>
> What was he doing with his warbonnet and coup-stick? Many meanings might attach to such a gesture; but in the context of the current discussion one meaning suggests itself: *he is burying them*. On this interpretation, Plenty Coups is serving as a remarkable kind of witness: he is marking the end of a way of life in which the coup-stick and warbonnet had integral roles. They have reached the end of their traditional lives, and it is time to locate them in a *new ritual*, that of remembering and mourning the valiant deeds of Indians past. (Lear 2006: 33; italics added)

In this passage, Lear shows the dynamism of interpretation among the Crow. Here, a norm (planting a coup stick) is reinterpreted by Plenty Coups in an attempt to make sense of the world in which the Crow now find themselves. Such a meaning could not have been predicted if we were to focus on the meaning of "counting coups" codified through past practices. And yet, Plenty Coups's action here could also not be understood if we were to ignore such a past. Without seeing Plenty Coups as an individual who is able to take up the norms in the past to deal with novel problems in the present, the meaning of such a practice could not be properly understood. In other words, without positing a subject for whom such practices are meaningful, it would be difficult to apprehend the way norms are applied and amended when circumstances require it. This is where I thus differ from Schilbrack and Smith, for whom the meaning of a practice can be discerned independently of its performance. In their account of human behavior, there is no plausible way to explain the differences between our culture in the present and the culture of those who came before us.

What I want to defend throughout the rest of this chapter is a philosophical account of subjectivity that can make sense of the interaction between norms and practices and the people who embody them. What I hope to show is that we do not have to have access to mental states in order to defend subjectivity. What we do need, however, is a more clearly articulated account of how it is individuals are both created by the world in which they live, while also still remaining creators of that world.

Crowell, Heidegger, and Subjectivity

Crowell's recent interpretation of Heideggerean phenomenology offers a resource to help us better understand the necessity for positing the subject as the ground of knowledge. For Heidegger, who I am is linked intimately to what I do. To be a carpenter is to fashion wood for specific purposes—to build furniture, homes, and so forth. To be a father is to care for my children by taking them to school, feeding them, and much more. In other words, my identity is linked up with my performance of specific practices. To put it in Heideggerean terms, my being, as an individual, is intimately tied to my being-in-the-world. But, for Heidegger, as Crowell argues, such an account of identity is insufficient for firmly grounding subjectivity. The very sentence "I am a carpenter" presupposes a subject who stands outside such an identity formation, an I who is not exhausted by carpenter-being (Crowell 2013: 176–179). To see myself as a carpenter is to see myself solely through a social identity that only partially captures what it is like to be a person (ibid.: 173). Further, if being an "I" were co-extensive with my being a carpenter, it would be impossible to differentiate myself from other carpenters. My identity would be anonymous. It is therefore necessary to provide an account of subjectivity grounded in something beyond my practical identity.

Heidegger names the mood that indicates our unique subjectivity *Angst* (or anxiety).[4] In this anxiety "the world is given in such a way that it *no longer* matters at all. Entities in the world no longer speak to me (the pure 'that it is' is all that remains); the world is uncanny (*unheimlich*); my involvements with others 'recede' until I grasp myself as the *solus ipse*" (Crowell 2013: 180). The experience of anxiety is characterized by its objectlessness (Heidegger 1962: 231). There is nothing in the world that drives my anxiety; if there were, the appropriate descriptor of my mood would be fear (ibid.: 234). But because there is no object on which my anxiety can rest, it points to something *about me*—my egoity—that is not determined by my relationship to the world.

One of the ways anxiety shows up in our experience is when our practical identity no longer shows up as meaningful for us (Crowell 2013: 180–181). Let us imagine a person whose identity is bound up in part with being a Protestant: this person goes to church on Sundays, helps out with the food pantry, and reads his Bible every day. Engaging in such practices forms his identity as a Christian. Further, these practices are governed by norms: the requirement to attend the Sabbath, the command by God to give to those in need, and the importance of a personal relationship with God. But let us say at some point that this person's adherence to this set of practices no longer shows up as meaningful. (Perhaps he reads a critique of Christian belief from Christopher Hitchens, or Hume's *The Natural History of Religion*.) At that moment his practical identity as a Christian is unsettled, and he begins to feel anxiety about his self-understanding as a Christian.[5] Here he begins to reflect on what it means *for him* to be a Christian. When Plenty Coups is forced to reinterpret the meaning of "planting a coup" he is engaged in a similar act of existential reflection. He is forced to confront what it means to be a Crow when all the practices that make up such an identity are no longer available. For a person to be able to reflect on the social identity through which he understands himself means that there is something outside that practical identity that defines his being. Such a realization reveals the self that underlies a person's practical identities. This does not mean that one is able to shed all practical identities. It does mean, however, that I am able to see practical identities as identities that are available for me to decide whether to take up or not. As Lear puts it elsewhere, "It is a mark of the human that we do not quite fit into our own skins. That is, we do not fit without remainder into socially available practical identities" (Lear 2011: 50). I would modify this only by noting that it is a mark of *being a subject* that we do not fit into these identities, and it is only as subjects that we can take up different practical identities over the course of our lives.

There are two reasons why I think that Schilbrack's account of meaning needs to be supplemented by this phenomenological account of selfhood. The first concerns how we understand the meaning of social practices. For Schilbrack, as I noted above, to analyze meaning is to stay at the level of the rulebook. My worry is that this account of meaning lacks *dynamism*, a dynamism that only becomes clear once we are able to give an account of the kind of person for whom these norms matter.[6] Social norms might change due to a variety of factors, including some of the non-intentional ones that Schilbrack discusses in his response to the third question. But people also react to those changes. If scientific claims about the unfeasibility of a belief in God come to predominate, it is certainly possible that new ways of imagining the nature of religious faith might come into being. Perhaps instead of praying to a personal God, one might begin to emphasize acting within a community to bring into being the kind of world imagined in the Christian Bible. This shift in meaning might be influenced by external forces, but the re-interpretation of the tradition in light of changing norms must be taken up by self-conscious individuals. If normative traditions were simply a set of rules that people followed, there would be no way to account for the dynamic ways in which individual persons actively interpret their norms as their worlds shift and change. Such a vision of the self need not rest on access to inner mental states. We can still read the meaning of practices off of people's behavior and the ways that they actively engage with normative social structures. Indeed, we do not need to know what was actually going on in Plenty Coups's head at the ceremony to offer a plausible (albeit fallible) interpretation of his actions and motivations for this novel re-interpretation of a "coup." As this example reminds us, what we have no grounds to assume is that meaning is static.

Second, I believe this account offers a ground from which to justify the practice of scholarly critique. When Heidegger points to the everyday experience of anxiety as a grounding condition for the possibility of selfhood, he is employing a method called formal indication, the goal of which is to ground philosophical knowledge in the socially situated, historical circumstances in which everyday life is lived (even by philosophers!) (Heidegger 2004: 38–45). Such a method looks within everyday experience for evidence that "turning around" and reflecting on the conditions that make experience intelligible is possible (ibid.: 8). When Heidegger points to anxiety as the condition for selfhood he is pointing to an aspect of experience in order to ground the possibility of a self that can stand apart from the world and critique it. For Heidegger, such a self is not only necessary to establish an accurate account of norm governed human activity, but also the possibility of philosophical reflection.[7] For if there is no self that stands apart from the world, no self can do anything other than reproduce the social identity into which it has been "thrown" (to use Heidegger's term; Heidegger 1962: 223). If this were the case, when scholars made claims about the world they would simply be solipsistically reproducing their own scholarly discourse rather than making critical claims about the world in which they live. All such attempts would simply be re-iterations of scholars' practical identities, albeit masked in the form of higher-level abstraction. Note that one cannot even explain how the scholar becomes a scholar on a subjectless account of meaning. Doing scholarship requires a person to intervene into, and make critical claims about, the arguments circulating within a discursive community. If a person were to simply repeat the claims of other scholars, then she would not be doing scholarship at all. She would rather be conforming to the established normative meanings that were already circulating within the community. Archiving collectively articulated meanings is the start of a scholarly project; but if it is to be a truly critical enterprise (and therefore, truly scholarly), such archival work can never be the only goal of scholarship.[8]

There is much to be gained from the account of meaning that Schilbrack presents in his chapter. What gives me pause is not his focus on meaning, but the focus on a subjectless interpretation of meaning. Scholars need not be wary of defending subjectivity. We do not have to valorize individual experience as mystical (as phenomenologists of religion such as Rudolf Otto have done in the past), to acknowledge its importance for understanding. We only need to acknowledge that it is individuals who interpret such claims. Without doing so, the intelligibility of scholarship is at risk.

Joshua Lupo received his Ph.D. in religion from Florida State University in 2018. His dissertation, "After Essentialism: Possibilities in Phenomenology of Religion," traces the relationship between the phenomenology of Edmund Husserl and Martin Heidegger and the work of phenomenologists of religion such as Mircea Eliade and Rudolf Otto. He is also the author of articles and reviews appearing in *Soundings*, *Sophia*, *Religious Studies Review*, and *Reading Religion*.

Notes

1 Note that this statement is the inverse of Judith Butler's claim that "when the subject is said to be constituted, that means simply that the subject is a consequence of certain rule-governed discourses that govern the intelligible invocation of identity" (Butler 1990: 198).
2 Brandom references Chomsky's *Aspects of a Theory of Syntax* (1965) as one source of his thinking on this matter.
3 For a summary of the meaning of this practice, see Lear (2006: 13–15).
4 I will say more on Heidegger's methodological principle of "formal indication" later in this chapter.

5   See Burch (2011) for an account of the connections between the failure of one's practical identity, anxiety, and selfhood.
6   Schilbrack does make room for some of this dynamism in his chapter on belief in *Philosophy and the Study of Religion: A Manifesto* (2014: 53–82). But there he limits claims about individual belief to "counterfactuals." In the chapter, Schilbrack treats individual motivation as something that might be accounted for by scholars through inductive practices such as changing the circumstances under which a person engages in a practice. Such an exercise allows the scholar to see if such a change leads the person to behave differently. Nevertheless, this still does not develop an account of the subject who finds himself motivated to act in the world. In other words, it still takes a third-person perspective on motivation, rather than a first-person perspective.
7   See Burch (2011) for an argument on the importance of giving an account of the self for grounding philosophical reflection in Heidegger.
8   Here my position resembles that of Bruce Lincoln's as he articulates it in his final thesis in "Theses on Method" (1999). Schilbrack discusses Lincoln's work in "Bruce Lincoln's Philosophy" (2005). I agree with Schilbrack that Lincoln has philosophical commitments that often go unarticulated and need to be made clear. What I would nonetheless want to further emphasize and argue in favor of is Lincoln's emphasis on criticism as a requirement of scholarship.

References

Brandom, Robert. 1979. "Freedom and Constraint by Norms," *American Philosophical Quarterly* 16(3): 187–196.
Burch, Matthew I. 2011. "The Existential Source of Phenomenology: Heidegger on Formal Indication," *European Journal of Philosophy* 21(2): 258–278. https://doi.org/10.1111/j.1468-0378.2010.00446.x
Butler, Judith. 1990. *Gender Trouble: Feminism and the Subversion of Identity*. New York: Routledge.
Chomsky, Noam. 1965. *Aspects of a Theory of Syntax*. Cambridge, MA: MIT Press.
Crowell, Steven. 2013. *Normativity and Phenomenology in Husserl and Heidegger*. Cambridge: Cambridge University Press. https://doi.org/10.1017/CBO9781139548908
Heidegger, Martin. 1962. *Being and Time*, trans. John Macquarrie and Edward Robinson. New York: Harper & Row.
Heidegger, Martin. 2004. *The Phenomenology of Religious Life*, trans. Matthias Fritsch and Jennifer Anna Gosetti-Ferencei. Bloomington, IN: Indiana University Press.
Lear, Jonathan. 2006. *Radical Hope: Ethics in the Face of Cultural Devastation*. Cambridge, MA: Harvard University Press.
Lear, Jonathan. 2011. *The Case for Irony*. Cambridge, MA: Harvard University Press. https://doi.org/10.4159/harvard.9780674063143
Lincoln, Bruce. 1999. "Theses on Method," in Russell McCutcheon (ed.), *The Insider/Outsider Problem in the Study of Religion: A Reader*, 395–98. London: Continuum.
Schilbrack, Kevin. 2005. "Bruce Lincoln's Philosophy," *Method and Theory in the Study of Religion* 17(1): 44–58. https://doi.org/10.1163/1570068053429848
Schilbrack, Kevin. 2014. *Philosophy and the Study of Religion: A Manifesto*. Malden, MA: Wiley-Blackwell.
Smith, Christian. 2017. *Religion: What it is, How it Works, Why it is Still Important*. Princeton, NJ: Princeton University Press.

Chapter 23

Interpretation

Matt Sheedy

Anyone familiar with Kevin Schilbrack's work would surely agree that he has a knack for bringing together complex ideas in philosophy and the social sciences to bear on the study of religions, that his polemics are both thorough and generous, and that he presents his ideas with an inviting tone that encourages a reciprocal type of response. Such reciprocation can be seen, for example, in the preface to *The Sacred Is the Profane*, where authors Arnal and McCutcheon note that Schilbrack is "among the few" taking seriously the discourse on the category "religion," despite their evident differences (Arnal and McCutcheon 2013: xiii). Lest I come across as too irenic here, I draw attention to Schilbrack's self-proclaimed goal of building bridges between philosophy and the study of religions as not only a necessary task that helps to raise important questions about *what* methods and theories we prioritize and *why*, but also as an inherently fraught terrain that involves trying to convince scholars with different training and different sets of interests what they are missing and how they should rearrange their priorities differently. While I find Schilbrack's arguments to be thought-provoking and highly valuable, I will argue that the priority that he grants to particular methods and theories does not pay enough attention to these situated differences and should shift *emphasis* depending on who he is engaging with—call it *methodological fluidity*—including how we make use of interpretation.

There have been three roundtables published on Schilbrack's book *Philosophy and the Study of Religions: A Manifesto* (2014), along with three critical essays (Dawson 2016; Martin 2017; Sauchelli 2016). One thing that is notable in all of these responses, which include four essays in *Method and Theory in the Study of Religion* (*MTSR*), is that they involve scholars who either describe themselves as philosophers of religion, or, at the very least, have significant training in philosophy and/or theology. The first panel comes from the journal *Sofia*, based on a symposium of the South Carolina Society for Philosophy, and includes a continental philosopher of religion, an analytic philosopher of religion, and a scholar of Mormon Studies and theology. The second comes from the March 2015 volume of the *Journal of the American Academy of Religion*, with contributions from two philosophers of religion (Mikel Burley and Luke Fox) who are more or less on board with Schilbrack's project, and whose work engages intersections between analytic and continental philosophy, comparative (non-Christian) philosophies, and post-modern methods and theories. The other respondent in this roundtable, William Wood, who is an analytic philosopher of religion and theologian at Oxford, offers the strongest objection to Schilbrack's manifesto. At first blush, I found Wood's response almost laughable, as when he agreed with Schilbrack's claim that the traditional philosophy of religion is "narrow, intellectualist, and insular," while adding, "what, if anything, is wrong with this state of affairs?" (Wood in Burley et al. 2015: 249) While Wood's rear-guard, protectionist attitude against cross-cultural and comparative analysis (ibid.: 250) strikes me in some ways as the flailing death-knell of a white Christian male clinging desperately to his power, there is a facet to his argument that I find instructive, if only as a cautionary example—and as recent events have proven, the seeming death knell of white, male, Christian supremacy should not be taken lightly.[1] Wood defends the analytic philosophy of religion's primary focus on "Western theism" and "the rationality of theistic belief" (ibid.: 249), though he does concede Schilbrack's point that "it would be good if more philosophers of religion studied religious practices and rituals" (ibid.: 251). This tiny concession, however, is quickly turned on its head as Wood doubles-down by asserting, incorrectly, that Schilbrack ignores "the role of metaphysics in contemporary analytic philosophy" (ibid.: 252) and concludes with the claim that the philosophy of religion "is at the very heart of the field, and indeed is its summit" (ibid.: 253). Part of what bothers Wood, on my reading, is that his primary concerns are not being taken seriously, leaving him little room to concede to methods and theories that are both foreign to his work, and potentially destructive of its aims. As he puts it in a rather telling passage, "Philosophers of religion who work in religion departments are sometimes struck by the fact that philosophers who work in philosophy departments ignore them and pay no attention to their work ... The state-of-play" he continues, "in religion departments with respect to disputes about the meaningfulness and truth-bearing status of metaphysical assertions lags considerably behind that in most philosophy departments" (ibid.: 252).

Schilbrack's generous reply to Wood's criticism offers a useful parallel when thinking about the question of "interpretation" in the study of religion, how it might be received in critical theoretical circles, particularly when thinking about the priority given to certain methods over others (say, Ricoeurian hermeneutics vs. interpellation), and how we might convince differently situated scholars to take our most prized ideas seriously. Schilbrack's appeal to Wood is simultaneously pragmatic, convincing, and reciprocal. It is pragmatically appealing inasmuch as it clarifies why religious studies often eschews the philosophy of religion on account of its narrow, insular, doctrinal and Christian-centered focus (Schilbrack in Burley et al. 2015: 259–260); it is convincing inasmuch as he demonstrates that philosophy of religion "gets the data on which it works from the interpretative efforts of translators, anthropologists, classicists, historians, and others"; and it is reciprocal inasmuch as he concedes that "[religious studies] scholars who eschew philosophy at the explicit level presuppose answers to philosophical questions about what is rational, what is real, and what is valuable" (ibid.: 259). On this last point concerning the importance of philosophy in general I am in full agreement, and would point to the essays on Schilbrack's book by Jeppe Sinding Jensen, Mark Gardiner, Bryan Rennie, and Kenneth MacKendrick in *MTSR*, along with J. Aaron

Simmons's response in *Sophia*, and Stephen Dawson's essay in *Religious Studies Review* as good examples of current critical scholarship taking these philosophical ideas seriously. In concluding his reply to Wood, Schilbrack clarifies that he is not suggesting that there shouldn't be philosophers of religion working on topics such as the "rationality of theism," but rather that the discipline as a whole should enlarge its vision as a "global project of philosophical reflection on religious beliefs, practices, experiences, and institutions" (ibid.: 260).

My purpose in drawing attention to this particular exchange is not to suggest that we need some "big tent" approach to the study of religion, as was discussed at the 2015 NAASR program in Atlanta, GA, nor to endorse Schilbrack's precise prescriptions *per se*, but rather to provide an example of how even the most obvious and seemingly self-evident arguments for interdisciplinary exchange can founder, thus highlighting the need to appeal to the strengths and preferences of those we are trying to convince to our side—that is, if we deem that there is something useful to be gained in such alliance in the first place. The analytic philosopher of religion, for example, may find certain approaches that Schilbrack highlights to be useful, such as his emphasis on the importance of ritual practices, so long as she (well, he) can be persuaded that they have something important to add to his primary interest in analyzing theological doctrines and propositional beliefs. In my judgment, Schilbrack's recent book provides several juicy carrots to analytic philosophers of religion that are hard to ignore, especially when we consider the continued domination in this domain of male scholars operating within a Christian-centric framework. When it comes to those interested in methods and theories associated with groups like NAASR, including genealogical, deconstructive, and cognitive science approaches, the appeal to philosophies of interpretation and hermeneutics do not, in my estimation, hold the same kind of allure, and it is here that I'd like to focus my attention. Specifically, I will argue that if Schilbrack wants to appeal more persuasively to scholars who are interested in prioritizing genealogical and discourse theoretical methods, he'll need to deep-fry the carrot he's offering in chocolate sauce—in other words, by presenting it in a base much richer in things like ideology critique and interpellation, thereby showing how a focus on "interpretation" might aid *these* academic pursuits.

Schilbrack is clear from the start of his chapter that he wants to address "what is at stake in speaking of 'interpretation' *in the social sciences*" (Chapter 19, this volume; emphasis mine), thus signaling a rather different audience than his previous philosophical interlocutors. Those who answer no to the first questions that he poses—*can one understand human behavior independent of the action's meaning*—aim to connect the explanation of any human activity with the meaning that it holds for participants. Scholars who have taken this "interpretive turn" thereby endorse an "interpretive social science," and are in agreement with the proposition that human actions can be said (1) to be done purposefully (e.g., a wink is purposeful, while a blink is [usually] involuntary) and (2) hold that there is some kind of *meaning* for the person performing an action, which Schilback describes as an ontological claim. Here the difference between the natural and the social sciences hinges on whether or not one is willing to go down this interpretative path and concede that "understanding, explanation, and prediction of meaningful actions and social practices," such as someone going to college to earn a degree, are of a different order from non-purposive actions, such as a rock rolling down a hill. In short, Schilbrack stresses that human actions are certainly influenced by "non-intentional forces" (e.g., biological) but that human activity is not "completely determined" by them (Chapter 19, this volume). On these points, I am in general agreement.

It follows from the first question in Schilbrack's schema that those who reject the idea that we can understand human behavior independent of an action's meaning for participants must also concede that interpretation does not require access to a person's mental state. If one follows this path of the interpretivist, as Schilbrack does, then they must also submit that it is both possible and necessary to grasp a person's "intentions, beliefs, or feelings," which, according to some theorists, requires some sort of "non-empirical method" to gain access, such as empathy or intuition (Chapter 19, this volume). Here he provides an example from Ninian Smart who claims that in order to understand "what it is like to be a Winnebago, one must really make believe that one is a Winnebago." As Schilbrack puts it (via Smart), the scholar must "put himself imaginatively into the position of those he seeks to understand" (ibid.). Crucially, those who reject the claim that interpretation requires access to mental states, also agree that meaning is not a private affair, but is tied to practices, social relations, institutional structures, etc. This means that mental states are not simply subjective ideas or propositions in one's head, but are "intersubjectively constructed" and therefore "publicly available" for scholarly analysis (ibid.). In this regard, Schilbrack follows Paul Ricoeur, who claims that even when a single person authors a text or performs an action, the meaning is not merely individual, but also "a function of collective commitments" (ibid.). Slicing this pie further, Schilbrack makes a distinction between the "cultural meaning" and the "personal meaning" of an action, where the former refers to "a reading of the practice's authoritative, official, or prescribed meaning" (e.g., Vatican encyclicals, to use my own example), which may or may not align well with what an individual does, says, feels, or believes. Taking this idea further, Schilbrack affirms with Christian Smith that the appropriate starting place for analysis is therefore "the culturally prescribed purposes and meanings of the practices" and "what a religious culture or tradition intends its practices to achieve, not the motivations of the people practicing them" (quoted in Chapter 19, this volume). Whether a gap exists between the prescribed or cultural meaning and the personal meaning is, as Schilbrack, writes, "often worth investigating" (ibid.). I'd like to push Schilbrack on this last point (signaling a first question of sorts) that the disjuncture between cultural and personal meaning is "often worth investigating" by suggesting that it is always worth investigating and should, following discourse analysis and ideology critique, be situated in relation to the dominant ideological apparatuses in which a person or community is embedded. The Gadamerian ideal of a "fusion of horizons" that I see embedded in Schilbrack's nod to Ninian Smart strikes me as insufficient at best, and perhaps libel to the charge of idealization—that is to say, by imagining what it's like to be a Winnebago, one necessarily must presuppose some normative core or essence of "Winnebago-ness." It is clear from reading Schilbrack's recent book that this is not what he intends, though what is not clear to me is if he is endorsing the "non-empirical" methodological use of empathy and intuition to analyze the self-descriptions of so-called religious adherents, and if so, to what ends? Allow me to elaborate.

Mark Gardiner summarizes one facet of Schilbrack's position in his recent essay in *MTSR*, noting that he is an *interpretationist* who "hold[s] that the content of a belief is to be identified with the conditions under which it can be interpreted" (Gardiner 2016: 57). This contextualizing move is complimented by Schilbrack's debt to *dispositionalists*, who look to pay attention to a person's dispositions or habits when interpreting their actions (Schilbrack 2014: 66). This is not enough, however, and requires the interpretationist's emphasis on the collective construction of meaning—e.g., "this is a bear, do not pet the bear or it might eat you." In this sense, people's basic beliefs are constructed via "shared reactions to common stimuli" (ibid.: 67) and are thus constituted inter-subjectively, requiring mutual agreement "in their generation and in their intelligibility" (ibid.: 66). If I understand Schilbrack correctly here, and if his nod to Ninian Smart's Winnebago example is meant to suggest that any good interpretation requires depth knowledge of how a particular cultural system is understood inter-subjectivity, including the subject-position of the researcher, then I am in general agreement with this requirement. Much like Bryan Rennie's reply to Schilbrack in *MTSR*, however, I don't think that Schilbrack goes far enough, especially if he wants to appeal to those like myself who are primarily interested in the role of ideology and discourse in shaping people's professed or alleged beliefs.

A recent and unpublished essay by Craig Martin entitled "'Yes, ... But ...': The Neo-Perennialists" touches on part of this concern when he notes that Schilbrack breaks with the philosophical tradition that treats beliefs as internal states and focuses instead on "things third parties *attribute to* agents on the basis of what they say and what they do" (Martin 2017: 7). In this sense, Martin wonders whether Schilbrack's idea of belief is similar to Pierre Bourdieu's concept of habitus, where the focus of scholarly analysis is on discourse and function rather than on the purported meaning of doctrines, creeds, etc. (ibid.: 9–10). As Martin writes, pushing this idea further, "it's quite possible that people might believe they believe their discourses, but may not in fact believe them—much as a person may not believe she is racist but may nevertheless behave in ways that permit outsiders to attribute racist beliefs to her" (ibid.: 10).

In his response, Schilbrack describes Martin's position as "non-realist" and contrasts it with his own "realist" (or critical realist) standpoint, which he is quick to point out includes the poststructuralist idea that, "subjects are the effects of social power and discursive control," before taking a materialist turn, following Constance Furey, with her emphasis on how things like power and discourse impact the body and society and thus condition subjectivity accordingly (Schilbrack 2017: 6). There is, of course, more to Martin and Schilbrack's arguments here, which are part of a much richer and on-going debate that exceeds the boundaries and scope of this paper. What I want to signal from this exchange, however, is what appears to me to be a problem of priority in Schilbrack's account, for nowhere in his chapter of the present volume, nor in his 206-page book, does he appeal substantially or concretely to the value of ideology critique or provide an analysis that foregrounds the role of interpellation in shaping a subject's beliefs. To put it differently, I see a general map for a bridge in his work to these domains of critical theory, though the foundations that he uses to connect to this particular territory remains fuzzy at best. Allow me to provide a concrete example to drive this point home.

In her 2014 book, *The Republic Unsettled: Muslim French and the Contradictions of Secularism*, Mayanthi Fernando brings together ten years of anthropological fieldwork among second and third generation Muslim youth, which includes interviews that explore the intersections between professed religious beliefs and theological influences, secular Republican values, xenophobic racism, and neo-liberal ideology, in order to show how the negotiation of religious identities are conditioned by these dominant structures of power. One of the conclusions that Fernando draws from her rich and wide-ranging analysis, is that Muslim French youth, particularly hijab-wearing women, are caught up in "a series of oppositions between choice and constraint, personal autonomy and religious authority, and self-realization and external norms" (Fernando 2014: 146–147). Here she challenges dominant scholarly interpretations of veiling in France that frame such practices as a matter of personal choice, arguing instead that "such a reading misses crucial aspects of a kind of Muslim French subjectivity"—namely, while presenting Muslim women as "modern religious subjects" they simultaneously restrict "their ability to articulate what it means to wear the veil as a religious duty" (ibid.: 149). Fernando notes, for example, that the women she interviewed stress their adherence and submission to certain religious obligations and religious authorities when speaking in private, which they are often forced to frame in a public context as a result of their own desire and free choice (and that alone, which is an effect of interpellation), thereby excluding personal reasons that are central to their identity formation. Fernando's ideas here align with an observation from Joan Wallach Scott when she writes that scholars should "take as their project not the reproduction and transmission of knowledge said to be arrived at through experience but the analysis of the production of that knowledge itself" (quoted in McCutcheon 2012: 201). To be clear, and in conclusion, while Schilbrack is certainly aware of the importance of analyzing the production of knowledge within his larger framework of analysis, I wonder if he agrees with my suggestion on shifting how we prioritize what methods and theories come first when addressing differently situated scholars, and how his particular approach to interpretation might fit within this grid?

Matt Sheedy (Ph.D) is currently visiting professor of North American studies at the University of Bonn, Germany, and is associate editor of the *Bulletin for the Study of Religion*. His research interests include critical social theory, theories of secularism and atheism, as well as representations of Christianity, Islam, and Native American traditions in popular and political culture. He is currently working on a manuscript that provides a critical examination of Jürgen Habermas's theory of religion in the public sphere.

Note

1   This paper was presented on a panel in San Antonio, TX on November 18, shortly after the election of Donald Trump as president of the United States and Mike Pence as vice president.

References

Arnal, William and Russell T. McCutcheon. 2013. *The Sacred Is the Profane: The Political Nature of "Religion."* Oxford: Oxford University Press.

Burley, Mikel, Luke Fox, William Wood, and Kevin Schilbrack. 2015. "Review Essay Roundtable: *Philosophy and the Study of Religions: A Manifesto* by Kevin Schilbrack," *Journal of the American Academy of Religion* 83(1): 236–260. https://doi.org/10.1093/jaarel/lfu116

Dawson, Stephen. 2016. "Multidisciplinary, Comparative, and Interactive: Toward a Global Philospohy of Religion," *Religious Studies Review* 42(3): 143–174. https://doi.org/10.1111/rsr.12512

Fernando, Mayanthi. 2014. *The Republic Unsettled: Muslim French and the Contradictions of Secularism.* Durham, NC: Duke University Press. https://doi.org/10.1215/9780822376286

Gardiner, Mark Q. 2016. "Reforming Philosophy of Religion: Some Methodological Cautions," *Method & Theory in the Study of Religion* 28(1): 54–67. https://doi.org/10.1163/15700682-12341354

Jensen, Jeppe Sinding. 2016. "Religion, Philosophy, Scholarship and the Muddles Thereof: A Review of Kevin Schilbrack's Philosophy and the Study of Religions: A Manifesto," *Method and Theory in the Study of Religion* 28(1): 39–53. https://doi.org/10.1163/15700682-12341355

MacKendrick, Kenneth G. 2016. "Postmetaphysical Thinking and the Philosophy of Religion," *Method and Theory in the Study of Religion* 28(1): 84–97. https://doi.org/10.1163/15700682-12341353

Martin, Craig. 2017. "'Yes, ... but ...': The Neo-Perennialists," *Method and Theory in the Study of Religion* 29(4–5): 313–326. https://doi.org/10.1163/15700682-12341396

Rennie, Bryan. 2016. "Can Philosophy Save the Study of Religion?" *Method and Theory in the Study of Religion* 28(1): 68–83. https://doi.org/10.1163/15700682-12341358

Sauchelli, Andrea. 2016. "The Definition of Religion, Super-empirical Realities and Mathematics," *NZHTh* 85(1): 1–9. https://doi.org/10.1515/nzsth-2016-0005

Schilbrack, Kevin. 2014. *Philosophy and the Study of Religions: A Manifesto.* Chichester: Wiley Blackwell.

Schilbrack, Kevin. 2017. "The Place of Subjectivity in the Academic Study of Religion: A Response to Craig Martin," *Method and Theory in the Study of Religion* 29(4–5): 327–333. https://doi.org/10.1163/15700682-12341397

Simmons, J. Aaron. 2014. "Toward an Expansive Phenomenology of Religious Existence," *Sophia: International Journal of Philosophy and Religion* 53(3): 373–377. https://doi.org/10.1007/s11841-014-0444-y

Chapter 24

A Reply to My Critics

Kevin Schilbrack

How ought one to theorize the relation of social structure and personal agency? I think that it is illuminating to see the history of theorizing about religions (or, for that matter, theorizing about society in general) as having swung like a pendulum back and forth between a focus on human subjectivity that ignores social conditions (think: William James, rational choice theorists, and other methodological individualists) to a focus on impersonal causes that ignores human subjectivity (think: evolution, disciplinary regimes, or reductive neuroscience). In my work, I seek to develop a methodological approach to the study of religions that avoids both extremes and takes into proper account the contributions to explaining religion from both human subjectivity and its material context. This chapter on interpretation gives me an opportunity to defend the contribution of human subjectivity to religion, though for a complete or balanced account, non-intentional causes would also need to be given their due. Given the contemporary popularity of social theorists who focus on "assemblages" and "networks" and "social power" and who bracket or even deny a role for human intentions, however, I am glad that an essay on the role of interpretation gave me an opportunity to argue for the place of values, purposes, and reasons in the study of religions.

In his response to my own Chapter 19 of this volume, Matt Sheedy (Chapter 23) asks a good question: when interpretivists focus on the meaning of social practices to the participants, how does this relate to ideology critique, critical theory, and discourse theoretical projects in the academic study of religion? That is, if one interprets what people do and say in terms of what they understand themselves to be doing and saying, how does this relate to the influence of forces they don't know? Sheedy illustrates the problem he sees when he refers to the work of Mayanthi Fernando, who contrasts (a) the allegedly "personal," "autonomous," and "free" religious choices (for example, of the Muslim French who do or do not wear a headscarf) with (b) the ways that religious identities "are conditioned by the dominant structures of power." Sheedy worries that to take an interpretivist approach is to focus on (a) rather than (b). For this reason, he says:

> When it comes to those interested in methods and theories associated with groups like NAASR, including genealogical, deconstructive, and cognitive science approaches, the appeal to philosophies of interpretation and hermeneutics do not, in my estimation, hold the same kind of allure. (Chapter 23, this volume)

This is a legitimate worry about interpretive approaches. It is parallel, I think, to Talal Asad's genealogical critique that Geertz's focus on the symbols that give rise to religious moods and motivations ignores the material conditions that actually produce religious dispositions (Asad 1993: e.g., 33). My hope is that chastened, "post-genealogical" interpretivists can avoid this problem. If one treats what people's words and actions mean as always an intersubjective matter (as I do in §2 of my chapter) and if one holds that interpretations of those words and actions does not remove them from the realm of explanations (as I do in §3 of my chapter), then human agency is not treated as "personal" or "autonomous" in any free-floating sense. On this account, human agency is always conditioned by social factors. Such an account of subjectivity does not remove meaningful choices from the influence of impersonal forces. On the contrary, such an account can only help to illuminate how ideology or interpellation works, because on this account, evolution, language, and ideology are what make humans intentions possible.

A complete account of methods in the academic study of religion includes both intentional and non-intentional explanations. I therefore sought to provide an account of human intentions that was intersubjective and explanation-friendly, an account that complements but does not supplant the descriptivist, explanatory, and comparativist methods in this volume. Still, I am glad that I was tasked with giving an account of the place of human meanings in religion because I worry that, without such an account, the genealogical, deconstructive, and cognitive science approaches that Sheedy mentions threaten to slide back into the non-hermeneutic position in which human subjectivity and agency are illusory. Sheedy says that he is in "general agreement" with the both/and position I defend. Nevertheless, Sheedy flirts with the non-hermeneutic position himself when he writes that an individual's choice (not just the conditions for choice) is the effect of interpellation and that knowledge (and not just the conditions of knowledge) is something produced by impersonal forces.[1]

My view is that when a person's intentions are the causes of her actions, an accurate interpretation of those intentions *is* the explanation of that action. In such cases, interpreting and explaining behavior seek the same causes of the behavior. When the person's intentions are not the real causes of her action, then understanding what she is doing or saying requires an explanation in terms the agent may not know. Even this latter case, however, one has to interpret what she thinks she is doing or saying in order to have data to explain. So, for those scholars interested in critical theory, interpretation is what I called the first stage of religious studies. It clarifies what it is one seeks to explain. But if such scholars think that they can identify human behavior without interpretation—that is, with no reference to the participants' meanings—then they offer a descriptive reductionism that I would argue is, in the end, incoherent.

Like Matt Sheedy, who worries that interpretation as a method may fit poorly with critical theory, Jennifer Eyl (Chapter 20, this volume) points out that interpretation may not appeal to those influenced by post-colonial studies. Interpretation is suspect as a method in the first place, Eyl suggests, because the interpretivist claim that people's intentions are not exhaustively explained by their genes or their environment implies that human minds are somehow "outside the natural world." It is suspect in the second place because the interpretivist claim that it is possible to interpret others accurately implies that one can somehow interpret another independently of the lenses created and conditioned by our own cultures, practices, interests, experiences, mores, and intersectional identities.

I think that these two worries can be answered. First, although some have claimed that human subjectivity "transcends" the natural world in some sense, we no longer have to choose between (i) a reductive physicalism in which there is no subjectivity and (ii) a Cartesian or Kantian dualism in which minds are immaterial substances or noumenal realities. Rather, those who adopt the stratified ontology I sketched can see human agency as grounded in and emerging from the physical, chemical, biological, psychological, and social levels of human being so that all human cognition and agency is embodied, embedded, extended, and enactive.[2] Second, although any interpretive approach does have to hold that it is possible to interpret others accurately, accuracy does not require interpreting them independently of one's historical or cultural lenses. In fact, the insistence that this is not possible—that the interpreter always has to read the other from one's own perspective, with one's own prejudices—is pretty central to the hermeneutic tradition (certainly since Gadamer's *Truth and Method*, published in 1960) and not a criticism of it.

Eyl provides an excellent example with which to see the place of interpretation in the social sciences, namely, the actions that entangle people in the criminal justice system. People commonly interpret criminal activity as chosen by those involved, but, as Eyl points out, the social and economic factors that predispose certain people toward entanglement with the criminal justice system—"poverty, racial bias in law enforcement, drug dependence and the so-called war on drugs, stability of home life, access to education, success-affirming role models, etc."— are not intentions. These factors nevertheless have their say: "social forces determine the very field of possible choices and actions before the individual chooses." No adequate account of human action can ignore them.

Eyl compares the impersonal forces that make rain predictable to the social forces that make political strife predictable. And this is exactly right: human beings are material beings and neither their bodies nor their minds escape the causal patterns of the world that make behavior predictable. Despite the effects of the impersonal forces, however, my view is that human actions are to some extent self-caused. Eyl does not reject this idea. On the contrary, she proposes that the difference between an action's meaning and its environment is a matter of what she calls "proximity" or "magnitude": the scholar can either zoom in to focus on the individual's choice or pan out to see the social forces at work. This sounds like the both/and view for which I am arguing. However, though one might speak of the difference between intentional and non-intentional causes *metaphorically* as a difference between the proximity of the observer from the phenomenon or the magnitude of one's picture, I would want to insist that this difference is not a product of one's distance from those one studies, let alone a difference merely "in the eye of the beholder" or "manufactured" or "invented" by the scholar's perspective as some post-structuralists claim. The difference between social structure and subjectivity is, on my account, an ontological difference, since agents have one kind of causal power and social structures have another (Elder-Vass 2010), and both of these kinds of causes can operate even when scholars are not looking.

My view is that human agency always emerges from a particular context that enables some possible choices while it constrains or eliminates others. No choices are made or can be understood free of those non-intentional factors. Scholars should therefore take a complementary approach in the study of religions that includes both intentional and non-intentional explanations. Eyl's statement that "we are nothing if not *homo interpretans*" and her talk of reconciling deterministic Epicurean science with non-deterministic Epicurean ethics suggest that she imagines a methodological pluralism like the one I advocate. However, she writes that the intentional and non-intentional approaches are "ever at odds," and I hope that this is not right. My hope is still that we can find an account of human practices that does not simply provide two rival explanations but rather one that weaves together intentions and non-intentional factors—both what agents know of themselves and what they do not know—into a coherent explanatory whole.

Joshua Lupo (Chapter 22, this volume) argues that the third-person account of the meaning of religious practices in my chapter needs to be supplemented by a first-person account of subjectivity. His argument, we might say, is that hermeneutics needs to be supplemented by phenomenology. I judge that Lupo is exactly right, both about the incompleteness of the account I give in this chapter and for the need for a first-person account to complement it.

I was concerned to argue, first, that the study of religions should not leave subjectivity out—those who study social practices have to interpret what the practices mean to the participants—and, second, that to interpret the meaning of a social practice could be accomplished without mind-reading. For that reason, I distinguished between the ways that a community might understand a ritual offering to a God and why an individual participant might engage in that ritual, and I argued that identifying the former does not require scholars to know the latter. Lupo considers this distinction between collective subjects and individual subjects coherent, but he worries that it encourages scholars of religion to focus on collective meanings and to overlook the question of how individuals take their cultural scripts, put them into practice, and change them over time. As Lupo puts it, unless scholars also ask what the practice means to individuals, the analysis of meaning stays "at the level of the rulebook."[3]

Lupo's intervention helps me to address the question of what it means to be a realist about groups. Some scholars hold that, strictly speaking, a group is not a thing in the world. These ontological individualists hold instead that our labels for groups are simply heuristic devices for speaking about an aggregate of individuals, about what Gardiner and Engler (Chapter 21, this volume) call a "concatenation" of individual behaviors. Other scholars are ontological holists who explain the behavior of individuals in terms of the needs or functions or pressures of the whole, and they see individuals simply as parts of a larger organism or machine that is ultimately responsible for what its parts do (cf. Sheehy 2003). By contrast, my distinction between collective and individual meanings reflects a stratified, two-level account that sees both individuals and groups as emergent realities with properties and powers not possessed by their parts. Given this emergentist account, what a practice means to a single participant is distinct from what it means to the collective, but both are real in the sense that both have causal powers.

Lupo argues that a first-person, phenomenological account of subjectivity shows that the norms in which we live match up imperfectly with our lives as they are actually lived. Scholars cannot understand how group norms are resisted and how they change unless they include that first-person perspective. I completely agree.[4] Moreover, I would say that unless one includes how collective meanings are taken up by individuals, one cannot understand *any* action the group does. On the emergentist account I recommend, though a group is a real thing in the world, a group does not act except through its members. Collective meanings do not do anything by themselves, and collective subjects have no hands other than those of their members. Thus, one might correctly say that some person was baptized or excommunicated "by the church," but the actions of the group will always be carried out by some particular members. In this way, the first-person perspective is needed not only to explain how novelty is introduced or how norms are changed, but also to explain everything the group does.

Mark Gardiner and Steven Engler (Chapter 21, this volume) see an ambiguity in my chapter between what they call the combinatorial and constitutive views of meaning. Both views take human actions as meaningful and so, on either view, actions require interpretation. But the important distinction Gardiner and Engler are making reflects the critique of empiricism that began more or less with Quine (1951) and it has implications for the study of religious practices. On the combinatorial position, one can conceive of an action as having two combined parts: the behavior, plus the behavior's meaning. On this view, one can separate the publicly observable bodily movements from the private meanings. The connections between the two are merely contingent. On the constitutive position, however, there are not two "parts" that have been combined. There is only a single "part," namely, the meaningful action. It is the whole of the behavior-in-its-context that "carries" the meaning and neither the action nor the meaning can be grasped without simultaneously grasping the other. On this view, any connection between action and meaning would be necessary, not contingent.

Now, I would not agree that my chapter is as ambiguous as they claim. They say that my chapter "often" takes the combinatorial position and the constitutive position is "less prominent" with only "scattered hints" of it to be found. But they give no examples of the combinatorial position in the chapter, claiming only that it is "implicit" there, even while they quote the chapter's statement that "The meaning the behavior has for the participants is part of the very constitution of what they are doing," which could not be a more explicit statement of the constitutive position. The constitutive view is also the one championed by Ryle and by Geertz in their Wittgensteinian opposition to thin (that is, merely empiricist) descriptions of actions, and this is precisely why I cite them. Perhaps the ambiguity that Gardiner and Engler see is a product of the fact that the three questions that structure my chapter are intended to capture real nineteenth and twentieth century debates about interpretation. Those structuring questions were therefore phrased in ways that permit the combinatorial position, even though my own stated view is that actions are constituted by their meanings.[5]

In any event, Gardiner and Engler are right that, given a constitutive view of meanings, it is the behavior-in-its-context that "carries" the meaning, and my chapter did not make this clear. As a consequence, the argument in my chapter can be improved or clarified by saying that interpretivists who say no to the second question—that is, interpretivists who do not think, like Schleiermacher, that grasping someone's meaning requires psychologistic access to his hidden or private mental states—should shift their investigation from the private to the public. But this recommended shift is not from what goes on in the mind of individuals to what is publicly available in groups. Rather, the shift is from the combinational assumption that meaning is hidden in minds (either of an individual or of the members of a group) to the constitutive position that meaning (whether individual or collective) is found in the give and take of what people say and do in their physical and cultural contexts. This means that those who try to interpret another about whom they know nothing (those who are sometimes called "radical interpreters") can make a reasonable first stab at understanding the other's meaning it by triangulating the other's gestures and words with aspects of a shared world. And it means that those who know a great deal of what the other person fairly well may actually perceive the visible parts of the other person's mental states (Krueger 2012). Interpretation is now understood in a post-Cartesian world. This understanding is the work of scholars working across boundaries between the hermeneutic tradition, philosophy of mind, and philosophy of social sciences. Though this work is still unfinished, I judge not only that interpretation is ineliminable from the academic study of religion, but also that its future is promising.

Kevin Schilbrack writes about philosophical questions raised by the academic study of religion. A graduate of the University of Chicago Divinity School, he is now professor and chair of the department of Philosophy and Religion at Appalachian State University. He is the author of *Philosophy and the Study of Religions: A Manifesto* (Blackwell, 2014) and he is presently interested in the relevance of embodied cognition and social ontology for understanding what religion is and how it works.

Notes

1 Similarly, Craig Martin (2017) has critiqued my work for including human subjectivity despite "the wave of poststructuralist critiques of religious studies."
2 For this "4E" account of cognition, see https://4ecognitiongroup.wordpress.com (accessed February 27, 2018).
3 Lupo judges that I over-emphasize collective meaning. But accounting for both agency and structure is a tricky balancing act, and it may be that he errs in the opposite

direction. When Lupo argues that we need a subject-based account of society and not what he calls a subjectless account, he seems to identify individuals with subjects and collectives with dead scripts or rulebooks. I hope that it is clear that I reject subjectless accounts (both in §1 of my chapter as well as in my responses to Sheedy and Eyl here). My view is that a collective subject, a "we," is still a subject.

4 I hasten to point out that this demand that the study of human behavior cannot exclude the first-person perspective is not solely a demand made in phenomenology or Continental philosophy. It can also be found in analytic philosophy (e.g., Baker 2013) and Indian philosophy (e.g., Ganeri 2013). For a defense of first-person authority in the study of religion, see Godlove (1994).

5 Gardiner and Engler also claim that my chapter "implicitly" says (i) that the proper object of scholarly investigation is social behavior, not the behavior of individuals, and (ii) that social scientists are only interested in purposive actions and not non-purposive bodily movements. But to distinguish as I do between the social and the personal meaning of a practice is not to exclude the latter from scholarly investigation (even from sociology, let alone from psychology). And to distinguish as I do between purposive from non-purposive behavior does not deny the importance of the study of hormones, neurons, and all the other embodied aspects of behavior.

References

Asad, Talal. 1993. *Genealogies of Religion: Discipline and Reasons of Power in Christianity and Islam*. Baltimore, MD: Johns Hopkins University Press.

Baker, Lynne Rudder. 2013. *Naturalism and the First-Person Perspective*. Oxford: Oxford University Press. https://doi.org/10.1093/acprof:oso/9780199914722.001.0001

Elder-Vass, Dave. 2010. *The Causal Power of Social Structures: Emergence, Structure, and Agency*. Cambridge: Cambridge University Press. https://doi.org/10.1017/CBO9780511761720

Gadamer, Hans-Georg. 2013 [1960]. *Truth and Method*. London: Bloomsbury.

Ganeri, Jonardon. 2013. *The Self: Naturalism, Consciousness, and the First-Person Stance*. Oxford: Oxford University Press.

Godlove, Terry F., Jr. 1994. "Religious Discourse and First Person Authority," *Method and Theory in the Study of Religion* 6(1): 147–161. https://doi.org/10.1163/157006894X00073

Krueger, Joel. 2012. "Seeing Mind in Action," *Phenomenology and the Cognitive Sciences* 11(2): 149–173. https://doi.org/10.1007/s11097-011-9226-y

Martin, Craig. 2017. "'Yes, ... But ...': The Neo-Perennialists," *Method and Theory in the Study of Religion* 29(4–5): 313–326. https://doi.org/10.1163/15700682-12341396

Quine, W. V. O. 1951. "Two Dogmas of Empiricism," *The Philosophical Review* 60(1): 20–43. https://doi.org/10.2307/2181906

Sheehy, Paul. 2003. "Social Groups, Explanation and Ontological Holism," *Philosophical Papers* 32(2): 193–224. https://doi.org/10.1080/05568640309485123

Afterword

Gregory D. Alles

> The word ... "research" is probably one of the dirtiest words in the indigenous world's vocabulary. (Linda Tuhiwai Smith 2012: 1)

In March 2013 two professors of English at colleges in Chhotaudepur and Pavi Jetpur *talukas*, a predominantly *adivasi* ("tribal," "indigenous") area in the eastern central part of Gujarat state, India, distributed surveys for me to assembled undergraduate students (*n* =100 and 75).[1] The surveys were written by me in Gujarati and thoroughly revised by native multilingual speakers of Gujarati and English (none was simply bilingual) both in the United States and in the local area. The main part of the survey consisted of a couple of story tasks—stories followed by a series of questions—designed to uncover what the students thought about people who had died. I wanted to know this, partly because accounts of such beliefs have figured prominently in the development of the cognitive science of religion, but also partly because for several years in visits to the area I had been setting aside, as instructed, small portions for ancestors before eating and drinking myself. To what did these people think I was setting aside food and drink?[2]

I never did publish the results—apologies to Joseph Bulbulia, who encouraged me to do so—because at the time I did not find them particularly interesting or conclusive. Looking back now, I wonder if that was a mistake. Certainly, one result still strikes me as intriguing and somehow worth pursuing. It came not from the story tasks themselves but from the demographic data that I asked participants to provide at the end of the survey. After asking about such things as age, gender, home village, community, year in college, and observances at home, I naively posed a question that, I thought, would begin to uncover an appropriate local vocabulary with which to talk about the human person: "Do you think that (a) a person (*mānasa*) is just a body (*mātra śarīra*) or (b) a person is not just a body but also something else (*bījuṃ kamīk*).[3] If your answer is (b), please explain." Later that year, I gave a similar survey to undergraduate students at two colleges in Maryland (*n* = 159 and 199). Largely convinced by claims about intuitive folk dualism (Stanovich 1989; Bloom 2004; Cohen et al. 2011; Slingerland 2013), I expected most participants, whether in Gujarat or Maryland, to choose (b) in reply to the question about the human person. I was wrong.

To summarize briefly: roughly 96 percent of Maryland students answered this question,[4] and in line with my expectations, 77 percent of them thought a human being was more than a body. In general, students in Gujarat had more difficulty with the process of taking a survey, and only 72 percent of them answered this question. Of those who did, however, only 45 percent claimed that a human being was more than a body—a statistically significant difference (Pearson chi-square $p < 0.001$, $\varphi = 0.306$) that seems to call the notion of an intuitive folk dualism into question. Most surprising to me was the breakdown by gender.[5] At the Maryland colleges, more men than women tended to think of the human being as just a body, but among the Gujarati students the distribution was the opposite, and by a very wide margin. In Chhotaudepur the men who answered the question split evenly, but a full 75 percent of the women answered that a human being was just a body. In Pavi Jetpur the results were even more striking. There only 19 percent of the men thought that a human being was just a body—several percentage points lower than Maryland men—but once again a large proportion of the women—73 percent—selected the "body only" option. Of course, as a pool gets subdivided, the numbers shrink, and statistically significant results become harder to achieve, but these differences still proved to be statistically significant ($p = 0.015$). To summarize: women college students at these two Gujarati colleges, heavily populated by "tribal" students, favored a body-only monism by a very wide margin (3 to 1). In this they differed not only from college women and men in Maryland but also from their male counterparts, especially in Pavi Jetpur, where a larger percentage of men than either Maryland men or women asserted that a person is more than a body. What is going on here?

I know colleagues whose work focuses on method and theory, and I very much respect what they do. For me, however, methods are valuable because of what they allow us to do, and theories are valuable because of what they allow us to see. As I read through the essays, the responses, and the responses to the responses in this volume, I found very much to admire. Clearly, the discussion of method is thriving in NAASR today, and one hopes that it continues to do so for a long time to come. I also kept asking myself, "To what extent will these discussions help me as I try to make sense of what I encounter among people who have become the focus of my professional interest, the *adivasi* people of eastern central Gujarat?" There are, of course, many questions about these people and their practices with which I could try to engage here, and some no doubt would fit some of the discussions better than others, but it will be enough to focus on the survey described above.

Engaging the Essays

I have no intention of usurping the role of a respondent. In general, the respondents have made whatever points I thought needed to be made, they have made them well, and they have made even more points besides. I simply want to note, in some detail, that while the content of the essays and responses is undeniably rich, the methodological boundaries circumscribing them are somewhat too narrow for my comfort.

Let me start with Part II, on description. In all honesty, I am not overly concerned with how my question above gets classified. Some may consider it a question about religion; others may consider it a question about philosophy or folk beliefs or indigenous knowledge or something else. Certain extraneous factors incline me toward the term "religion." My official training is in the history of religions, and I came to this question because I wanted to know something about the offerings that I had been presenting to the ancestors. If, however, I am meant to think of religions as "vestigial states within more dominant jurisdictions," defining a vestigial state as "sets of institutions and practices that reference former governments as historically based and/or imaginatively elaborated sovereign powers," I will happily say that I am not investigating religion. This is because it makes no sense to refer to the practices I have been engaged with as somehow relating to a vestigial state. Before Indian independence, the people who interest me were subjects of states ruled by Rajput princes; they have no traditions of having their own independent rulers or having their own states and governance. (They do celebrate revolutionary leaders from the nineteenth and twentieth centuries like Birsa Munda and Govind Guru; e.g., see Singh 1983; Hardiman 2003.) So to talk about vestigial states is beside the point. To be clear: I am not saying that Naomi Goldenberg's project does not make sense; it just does not extend to my interests. If adopting this view of religion is the cost of admission to the ranks of scholars of religions, I will just keep my money.

One other point from this section puzzles me. Goldenberg writes:

> instead of citing "religions" as if the word named a distinct genre of phenomena, I identify the traditions and ideologies that pertain to the particular issue I am discussing. I refer to Christianity, Judaism, Islam, Buddhism and Hinduism even though I realize that these are also problematic generalizations. Whenever I can, I attempt to be even more precise: Lutherans, Evangelicals, Catholic, Baptist, Hasidic, Lubavitch, Sunni, Shiite, Theravada, Hindutva, etc. Perfection is impossible. (Chapter 7, this volume)

Fair enough, even if for second-level categories I prefer Bauddha dharma and Hindu dharma. On Goldenberg's statement Ian Cuthbertson comments:

> perhaps Goldenberg does not go far enough in this productive direction. While I agree that scholars ought to replace 'religions' with the most specific terms available and write about Catholics or Lutherans instead of Christians, these more specific categories nevertheless depict Catholicism or Lutheranism as coherent and stable social groupings or objects of study that are worthy of scholarly attention and about which meaningful generalizations might be made. (Chapter 8, this volume)

As a most unusual but still practicing Lutheran, I am very grateful for Cuthbertson's more precise specification. At the same time, I am puzzled that Goldenberg, Cuthbertson, and others seem to recognize only two options for description: essentializing overgeneralization or individual description. While it is tempting but dangerous to take descriptive shortcuts like "*adivasi* women in Chhotaudepur and Pavi Jetpur *talukas* think a person is just a body," I see nothing wrong with saying that when presented with an option, 73 to 75 percent of the women college students who happened to show up to take my survey—or x percent of some kind of representative sample of people who self-identify as Catholics or Lutherans—chose option (a). The descriptions may be thin; indeed, as I have presented them, they are extremely thin. But this is a different matter.

What Kevin Schilbrack says about interpretation in Part IV makes a good deal of sense. When instructed to set aside bits of food or allow drops of a beverage to fall on the ground, one could respond with unquestioning obedience, but given enough opportunities or simply the right occasion, some people, especially those engaged in fieldwork, will ask, "Why?" It is always possible that the response one receives to this question is insincere, and that one is being made the object of a local joke. Nevertheless, this is a risk that most fieldworkers will be willing to take, especially those who are cognizant of "the challenge of including the voices of the colonized Other in all the stages of the research process" (Chilisa 2012: 16). Of course, none of this precludes explanations in which agents' intentions do not figure.

My survey, however, presents other pressing issues of interpretation that Schilbrack does not take up. These are issues related to an etymological sense of *interpretatio* as translation, the transfer of a statement from a source to a target code. What is a *śarīra*, that it can be said that it is all that a person is? There are sophisticated theories about bodies in South Asia. Do any of them apply in this instance? What is that second something that appeared most commonly in the responses of the Gujarati students who chose (b), the *ātman*? The word is so burdened with philosophical baggage that simply leaving it untranslated still leaves an enormous range of questions unanswered. To what extent did the men and women taking the survey understand *śarīra* in the same way? If pressed, would those who said a person is just a *śarīra* acknowledge the *ātman* as well? And how do the answers to these questions mesh with the responses to the stories that formed the main content of the survey? Some participants told me later that they realized their responses were inconsistent, but that they had answered each question honestly.

This is not all. Honesty compels me to admit that, despite my best efforts, my question was poorly formulated—in a manner that reminds me of Gadamer's notion of horizons. The issue is not an implicit mind-body dualism. It is that, as I now know, at least one strong Hindu missionary movement in the area teaches quite forcefully that a person is *not* a *śarīra* but rather *only* the *ātman*, pure and simple. Since this is a movement with which many survey participants identified, several participants might have wanted to select "neither (a) nor (b)" in reply to my question, but they were not given the chance. If they had been, how would their views compare with Jesse Bering's claim that a ghost is just a mind without a body (Bering 2002: 269; cf. Hodge 2011; Pereira 2012)?

Aaron Hughes establishes some very stringent criteria for comparison in Part I. He requires historical sensitivity, linguistic dexterity, and theoretical sophistication. (He can perhaps be forgiven for claiming that historians, philologists, and area studies specialists lack theoretical sophistication; some may, but certainly not all.) But he also states, "For me, comparison cannot be cross-cultural, comparing texts or phenomena from different times and places" (Chapter 1, this volume).

Understandably, Hughes is reacting to the excesses and mistakes of the past, excesses and mistakes that few would dispute. But as Lucas Carmichael points out, historical sensitivity, linguistic dexterity, and theoretical sophistication did not in themselves prevent past excesses. More importantly for me, if I want to work with *adivasi* people, as I do, then cross-cultural comparison—comparison across different places and perhaps different times—is both unavoidable and useful.

Cross-cultural comparison is unavoidable because it is a major feature of indigenous life today. Over the last several decades, perhaps beginning with the adoption of ILO convention 107 in 1957, indigeneity has been constructed as a specific identity through conversations, conventions, and movements involving people as diverse as the Maori of Aotearoa/New Zealand, First Nations peoples of Canada, Native Americans in the United States, aboriginal peoples of Australia, the Sami in the Nordic countries of Europe, native peoples of Latin America, sub-Saharan Africans, and, not to be forgotten, "tribals" in India, a country that is home to the largest grouping of such peoples of any country in the world, over 100 million (Wilmer 1993; Niezen 2003; Smith 2012: 111–119; Clifford 2013). Clearly, these are disparate peoples. They are diverse geographically, historically, culturally, economically, socially, and in a great many other ways. Not surprisingly, it has proven impossible to come up with a single account of what makes them all indigenous (some further comments in Alles, Guzy, Skoda, and Valk 2015: 7–8). Nevertheless, the United Nations has adopted a Declaration on the Rights of Indigenous Peoples, and these peoples have themselves found something that they think they share. To quote the Maori scholar, Linda Tuhiwai Smith (2012: 218), "There are also shared discourses, visions and aspirations that resonate across many indigenous contexts—cultural and linguistic survival, self-determination and the right to remain indigenous are some examples of the shared discourse that has been the platform for indigenous activism." This sharing also extends to what most people consider religions (cf. Johnson and Kraft 2017). Whatever one thinks of these developments, it is impossible to begin talking about them without engaging in cross-cultural comparison—or for that matter by talking only about specific groups but not about "indigenous people," despite an apparently latent commitment that some people have to the notion that the only concepts worth using are essentializing ones (cf. the good comments by Daniel McClellan and Emily Crews in Chapters 9 and 10 of this volume).

The constructed indigenous identity that I have been discussing largely depends upon a sweeping contrast with the "Euro-Western" (Kovach 2009; Smith 2012; Chilisa 2012). Even without engaging in such generalizations, however, a case can be made that the survey results with which I began become more interesting precisely because of cross-cultural comparison: precisely because the women in the survey appear to differ not just from men in their communities but also from at least some of their peers in the U.S. I also find it useful to use comparison to note similarities, however rough they may be, especially when dealing with people whose very designation as "indigenous" or "tribal" may evoke all sorts of misconceptions associated with extreme otherness. Thus, in a recent article critical of traditional notions of sacred space, I compared ritual sites of the *adivasis* with whom I work to portals in science-fiction films (Alles 2017). Some people may find this comparison jarring, but it may serve to remind us that although their access to televisions and cinemas is limited, many of the people with whom I work have in fact watched science-fiction films. Nor is it inconceivable that an indigenous person would draw this analogy. Here is Kathy Absolon, an Anishnabe woman, as recorded by Margaret Kovach:

> If you experience a fast, I know what that is like and so I know what comes for you. It's different for everyone. I know that experience is sacred. What do you call it, like in sci-fi movies, a portal? I know that there are portals and when you go into a sweat lodge there are portals. When you go into different ceremonies, there are portals for knowledge to come through. (Kovach 2009: 154)

The question that I posed about my survey results—"What is going on here?"—intersects directly with the kind of new mechanistic explanation advocated by Egil Asprem and Ann Taves in Part III of this volume. I do not know the theoretical literature particularly well, but I find their view of explanation congenial, perhaps for personal reasons: for years my closest local colleague was a younger philosopher of science with connections to many of the people that Asprem and Taves cite. But what sort of new mechanistic explanation will work in my case?

I have no doubt that structures shaped by evolution lurk in the background, but how relevant are they to my question? Certainly, if there were a consistent gender distinction, such that women consistently identified persons with bodies more frequently than men, or vice versa, I would look to evolution. But otherwise I worry that the insistence upon evolution is a little like insisting that an insurance adjustor provide accounts of the origins and functioning of internal combustion engines, steering mechanisms, suspension systems, drive trains, inflatable tires, drilling for oil and its fractional distillation, and so on in explaining every accident. Paul Kenny (Chapter 16, this volume) has made the same point with a different example.

I do not have a firm explanation for the difference I noted in my survey, but I suspect that the most relevant explanation lies in a different direction. Although *adivasis* in the area where I work make up the vast majority of the population—roughly 95 percent—non-*adivasis*, that is, caste Hindus, are still seen as representing the cultural mainstream. Their identification as such has to do with matters of history, economics, politics, society, and education. One consequence is that there is a divide in the community between those who insist on adopting the habits of the cultural mainstream, and those who preserve, whether consciously or by inertia, traditional *adivasi* ways. Some preservationists are *adivasi* activists with a formal education, but conversion to mainstream lifeways, which are seen as more "civilized," is especially attractive to *adivasis* who have received a formal education. Historically, formal education has attracted more men than women; one sees the difference still in the 2011 Census, according to which slightly over half of *adivasi* men were literate, in comparison to slightly over a third of *adivasi* women. Conversion also seems to be a means by which men receive social and professional status. So there may be good reasons having to do with this community's interaction with other social groups, seen as more advanced, and the way gender differentiation has worked in this interaction that inclines young, college-age men with certain kinds of aspirations to adopt views of the human person peddled by caste Hindu missionary groups. That proportionately more men would do so in Pavi Jetpur than in Chhotaudepur may result from the different interactions of the two constituencies with the so-called mainstream and the different aspirations of those who attend the two colleges; the college in Chhotaudepur is several decades older and physically a little more worse for wear than the college in Pavi Jetpur.

NAASR and Beyond

NAASR has always been something of a sect. It began as a split-off from the larger, more theologically inclined American Academy of Religion, and in this character lies its strength. NAASRites may at times make exaggerated claims, and they may focus narrowly, but doing so has allowed them to explore issues in depth in a way that has influenced the study of religions worldwide. To that extent, I am neither surprised nor particularly bothered that these essays are not completely relevant to the question my survey raised. But I think it is also good to think a little about NAASR in relation to the world beyond.

One of my concerns as the editor of an international journal, and indeed, of the journal of the international association of which NAASR is a regional affiliate, is that the content and perspectives of the journal address an international scholarly constituency, in fact, a global one. There have been exemplary moments when NAASR and those prominent within it have engaged with such a constituency. Recall, for example, Luther Martin's extensive activities in Eastern Europe (e.g., Dolezalova, Martin, and Papoušek 2001). In this volume, however, I see little engagement with academics beyond NAASR. Lucas Carmichael is perhaps most forthright about these limited horizons:

> Since I am writing in English and in connection with the North American Association for the Study of Religion (NAASR) to an audience who most likely belongs to NAASR and the American Academy of Religions (AAR) among other organizations, I will venture to suggest that a significant portion of all our research, publishing, and teaching relates to religion/s in America and is accomplished through English translation. Most of us, in our backgrounds, training, and employment, are deeply enmeshed in contemporary Anglophone conceptions of religion, even in our efforts to document, articulate, and translate alternative ideas from other times, places, and languages. (Chapter 2, this volume)

Carmichael's observations are fair enough, so long as they do not become an excuse for ignoring the rest of the world, including North America outside of NAASR. If they do become such an excuse, that would be a shame, because as I see it one of the challenges facing scholars of religions today—and not just scholars of religions—is competing claims to knowledge arising from different research cultures. It may be relatively easy to ignore these dynamics if one's work focuses on dominant North American cultures or if one is primarily concerned with people from the past, in other words, with people who cannot talk back. If one's research requires interaction with people in other parts of the world or in significantly different North American cultures on a regular basis, or one's responsibilities include evaluating scholarship originating in various research cultures, one may find such claims more difficult to ignore.

Consider my opening example. Along with the development of an indigenous identity over the last several decades have come extended reflections on indigenous research methodologies. Adapting a phrase by Salman Rushdie ("the empire writes back"), itself adapted from George Lucas and picked up as a title by Bill Ashcroft, Gareth Griffiths, and Helen Tiffin (1989), these scholars advocate projects of "researching back" (Smith 2012: 8; Chilisa 2012: 51–57). It is possible to see just how different these projects can be by contrasting the subdivisions of this volume — description, interpretation, comparison, and explanation — with the "indigenous research agenda" formulated by the Maori scholar, Linda Tuhiwai Smith. In her agenda, which self-consciously uses island metaphors, research is active in four cardinal directions: decolonization, healing, transformation, and mobilization. In each direction she identifies four "tides," that is, "conditions and states of being through which indigenous people are moving": survival, recovery, development, and self-determination (Smith 2012: 120–122).

In other words, among some indigenous people there is a deep suspicion of research conducted by "Euro-Western" scholars—scholars like those represented in this volume, myself included. Smith (ibid.: 1) sums up the suspicion succinctly: "The word itself, 'research', is probably one of the dirtiest words in the indigenous world's vocabulary." According to this perspective, academic research has objectified the indigenous person, "assum[ing] that the researcher belonged to the dominant cultural group and was 'doing' research to, for, and sometimes with, a minority group" (ibid.: 228). On this view, academic research has been a form of colonization. It has tended to marginalize or dismiss indigenous knowledge, for example, when dealing with HIV/AIDS in parts of Africa (Chilisa 2012: 73–95). It has also tended toward extraction. When "Euro-Western" researchers have found something of value in indigenous knowledge, they have appropriated it for themselves with little concern for the welfare of the people whose knowledge they have taken. As scholars of religions know well, "Euro-Western" research has also frequently denigrated indigenous religious and spiritual practices as savage and superstitious. For its part, research in education has often sought simply to determine the most effective means of eradicating the indigenous, an aim articulated in Macauley's infamous "Minute."[6] What lies at the root of the problem, in this perspective, are ontologies, epistemologies, and axiologies that are incompatible with and ultimately antithetical to indigenous perspectives and ways of life. To quote Linda Tuhiwai Smith again, "Indigenous peoples have been, in many ways, oppressed by theory" (Smith 2012: 39).

In response to this view of Euro-Western research, indigenous people, including scholars, have demanded that indigenous research be "informed by the resistance to Euro-Western thought and the further appropriation of their knowledge"

(Chilisa 2012). If research is to be done, it should not be done "on" indigenous people for the "betterment of mankind" (cf. Smith 2012: 2, 26, 122, 226). It should be done by and with indigenous people for their own betterment. Important considerations include the following: "Did the research assist the community, and could the community make sense of the research? Dissemination of the research is a central issue, and it is important to ensure that the research is available to the community in a manner that is accessible and useful" (Kovach 2009: 149). Furthermore, research needs to take indigenous knowledge—and indigenous epistemologies, ontologies, and axiologies—seriously. Especially one element of this requirement should interest NAASR members. It concerns one dimension of the concern for respecting the holism of indigenous knowledge. In the words of Bagele Chilisa:

> Social science research needs to involve spirituality in research, respecting communal forms of living that are not Western and creating space for inquiries based on relational realities and forms of knowing that are predominant among the non-Western Other/s still being colonized. I have always been disturbed by the way in which the Euro-Western research process disconnects me from the multiple relations that I have with my community, the living and the nonliving. (Chilisa 2012: 3)

To be sure, the fundamental dualism that frames this vision of indigenous methodologies—Euro-Western vs. indigenous—belies the claim that indigenous methodologies are inherently holistic, even if it also understandably reflects the political experiences of indigenous people at least since the time of Columbus. It could also provide scholars who see themselves as Euro-Western with an opportunity to turn their backs completely on indigenous methodologies and assert that they, too, are thinking within their own context, as they must do.[7] It would benefit all concerned, however, if this opportunity were resisted.

To start with, not all indigenous scholars embrace indigenous methodologies. More pertinent to the present discussion, not all proponents of indigenous methodologies are dismissive of the "Euro-Western." In this regard, it is worth noting comments by the Maori scholar, Graham Smith, as recorded by Margaret Kovach:

> It is not an either/or situation, and I think this is a really important point to emphasize ... I am not going to say Western theory is useless, that it's white man's knowledge and we shouldn't use it and all that stuff. That's a load of bull—we need to use all the very best available theoretical and methodical tools, and where necessary develop new approaches when these tools are inadequate. (Kovach 2009: 89, 91)

Even many of those scholars who seem most adamant about rejecting Euro-Western research do not actually do so completely (e.g., Chilisa 2012).

It can at times be difficult for those of us who are "Euro-Western" to recognize the representations of "Euro-Western" research practices by some proponents of indigenous methodologies as anything more than stereotypes drawn from the worst excesses of people from whom one would like to distance oneself as far as possible. Scholarly research by Europeans and their descendants in North America and elsewhere is hardly monolithic. Many critiques of this research by those who advocate indigenous methodologies also seem to assume—falsely—that a critical analysis of the circumstances in which knowledge claims have been produced is a sufficient critique of the claims themselves, although in this mistake they are certainly not alone. Moreover, proponents of indigenous methodologies may appear at times to be demanding special treatment for their traditions that others, including, I presume, all NAASR members, would never demand for their own, such as equating claims about gods and spirits with knowledge. Is the ability to be comfortable with these critiques just a sign of the privilege of the conqueror?

Nevertheless, those of us whose interests tend in the direction of the religions of indigenous peoples can hardly afford to ignore these methodological agendas. Not only do they both define the parameters within which we work and inform the people with whom we interact, but they also in many respects make extremely important points; they critique claims and behaviors that we should want to avoid and point out directions in which we should want to go. Nor should an interest in these and other methodologies be limited only to those NAASR members who study indigenous peoples. If the study of religions as practiced paradigmatically in NAASR is not to become an isolated enterprise, NAASR, too, will need to participate in other conversations about how to study religions more than the essays in this volume do. From my vantage point as an editor of an IAHR publication, this would be an important contribution that NAASR could make. Presumably all of us can rally around the claim that "An activist must get the story right as well as tell the story well, and so must a researcher" (Smith 2012: 226). Or, to adapt a comment that the scholar of history and Middle Eastern studies, Michael Gomez, made in his keynote address to the conference, "Expanding Earth: Travel, Encounter, and Exchange," at the University of Pennsylvania on March 2, 2017, the issue in revising representations of indigenous peoples is not political correctness; it is accuracy—a venerable scholarly ideal. To this I might add the moral dimension of treating people with courtesy and respect, especially those who are kind enough to allow us to write about them and to assist in our endeavors.

I have been referring exclusively to indigenous research methodologies for the sake of illustration. The issues raised are more general, but in the space that is left here I will simply remain with the illustration. What implications might we draw for method as discussed in this volume?

First, perhaps we should add another category that is logically if not always chronologically prior to description, interpretation, comparison, and explanation: data gathering. Given the manner in which researchers have gathered data in the past, this topic is of inevitable interest to indigenous peoples. If anyone needs a reason why, that person need look no farther than the sad tale of Ishi recounted, among others, by James Clifford (2013: ch. 4). There is a significant amount of literature on both qualitative and quantitative approaches to research within an indigenous studies framework (e.g., Walter and Andersen 2016). I have to admit that my own attempts at quantitative research have been clunky at best, so perhaps I should point instead to the experiences which lay behind them. At least I like to think that they go part of the way in the direction of what Margaret Kovach calls cultural grounding: "Researchers incorporate ceremonial practices to show respect and give protection to the knowledge shared. A Cree protocol is to offer tobacco to teachers" (Kovach 2009: 116). Among the Rathvas with whom I work one offers food and drink to the ancestors and liquor, chickens, and perhaps a goat to ritual specialists.

Second, we should be aware of the implications of the terms we use and the topics we explore for the people whom we study and others like them—people who may in fact be our colleagues and students. For example, I personally have no objections to the terms "naturalistic explanation" and "evolution," but I do understand why indigenous people would see these terms as danger signals (Smith 2012: 50, 65). At the very least those who want to promote naturalistic explanations rooted in evolution should be aware of what their terms are signaling—to quote a proponent of indigenous research methodologies, of "the psychological harm, humiliation, embarrassment, and other losses that these theories ... [have] caused to the researched colonized Other" (Chilisa 2012: 60)—and be prepared to demonstrate why in their case these fears are misplaced. Similarly, if I were to pursue further the survey results I introduced at the beginning of my remarks, I would need to address more than I have done the manner in which some indigenous people see a mind-body dualism as a legacy of Euro-Western colonizing.

Third, to what extent does our research positively benefit the communities that we study, and to what extent should it (Smith 2012: 175–176)? Some of us may have become interested in the topics we study out of a concern for the people involved. I personally became interested in *adivasis* when I encountered the stereotyped views one sometimes hears about them, such as the common slur that they act like monkeys. Studying *adivasi* culture and religion may not promise material benefits the way studies in pedagogy or medicine might, but I like to think, perhaps wrongly, that in some small way I help to counter negative images of *adivasis* and their cultures. Nevertheless, it is worth considering the extent to which demands that research benefit communities and that local political bodies control research are detrimental. Similarly, to what extent might demands to respect local knowledge interfere with the processes of scholarship, which at times are necessarily critical? For that matter, to what extent would we agree to call into "question that most fundamental belief of all, that individual researchers have an inherent right to knowledge and truth" (Smith 2012: 176)? Or to what extent can and should scholars be expected to be advocates for the people they study?

To the extent that proponents of indigenous methodologies demand that scholarship take religious realities seriously, NAASR should have an important role to play. As we know, colleagues in many other disciplines may not take the effects of claims about religious and spiritual realities seriously in their accounts. At the same time, taking these claims seriously does not mean granting that the realities exist. To my mind an article forthcoming in *Numen*, "Spirits in a Material

World: Mediation and Revitalisation of Woodcarvings in a Village in Nagaland, India" by Arkotong Longkumer, a scholar at the University of Edinburgh, strikes the right note. Furthermore, given what have traditionally been NAASR's concerns, the association could make an invaluable contribution to two sets of issues that involve conceptualization. One is the concern with what constitutes an appropriate second-order, analytical vocabulary, a concern that has been exercising scholars of religions for the last several decades, starting with the category of "religion" itself. The other is the more basic translational difficulty of trying to understand just what indigenous people mean by the expressions they use. This goes beyond simply talking about "superhuman beings," to the kinds of difficulties examined by Marisol de la Cadena (2015) in trying to understand precisely what two Quechua speakers with whom she was close meant when, among other things, they referred to mountains as persons.

Finally, a note frequently sounded by indigenous people in a variety of cultures is the need to respect ancestors, a respect that indirectly informed the survey with which I began. Proponents of indigenous research methodologies include this respect within the standards of scholarship. Thus, Bagele Chilisa (2012: 21) quotes Shawn Wilson as writing, "you are answerable to all your relations when you are doing research" (attributed to Wilson 2008: 56). It is probably expecting too much to expect most members of NAASR to adopt such a perspective toward our disciplinary ancestors, but presumably everyone would agree upon the need for accuracy as a shared value. In the interests of this value it may be prudent to extend Aaron Hughes's insistence upon knowledge of the original languages to the works of our ancestors. Hughes himself provides an example. He writes, "The traditional use of comparison, in short, does little to make us uncomfortable precisely because it refuses to destabilize our understanding of 'religion'" (Chapter 1, this volume). This is a common enough sentiment, but is it correct?

Rudolf Otto is widely castigated for having identified the essence of religion in a *sui generis* experience of the numinous. For those who read Otto only in English, this view makes sense, especially given the way Otto is normally presented. For those who read Otto in the original, however, and read him thoroughly, such a critique may appear one-sided. Here is one example among several.

It is unfortunate that the translator of Otto's article on Schleiermacher in *Religious Essays* concluded the translation where he did, because Otto's text actually continues with words that it would have been well for his Anglophone successors to take into account. Otto asks: Did Schleiermacher, in his speeches *Über die Religion*—his speeches, we might say, "on religion with a capital R"—really discover "the essence of religion"? The answer, he says, is no, first of all because, "as a thousand failed attempts have sufficiently demonstrated, it is not possible to give a definition of 'religion'" (Otto 1932: 134). In fact, he says, it is a mistake to think that there is some absolute unity "religion." Religion is not something that is everywhere the same. Instead, there are only historical givens that we call religion. What Schleiermacher depicted was not "religion" but "*his own* religion" (ibid.: 135, italics original). A couple of pages later Otto makes some more general methodological observations:

No one first finds a general "essence" of religion that he [sic] then divides and classifies according to a *principium individuationis* a priori [an a priori principle of individuation]. In truth each person starts from what he [sic] knows and recognizes as religion. He then proceeds through an ever expanding survey to find analogues, to compare and distinguish, to find connecting features, and, to the extent that it is possible, to arrive at types. To one person these will seem to come together into an ultimate, unitary "fundamental essence of religion;" to another they will seem much more to form competing types and oppose one another; to yet a third they may seem to center on fundamentally different spiritual attitudes, despite having significant features in common. (Otto 1932: 138-139)

And so on.

Granted, this passage does not make Otto a late-twentieth-century deconstructionist, nor should we expect it to. I would maintain, however, that it and others like it do raise questions about our notion that traditional comparativists refused to destabilize our understanding of religion. I cannot speak as an indigenous person or for the indigenous—a category that, too, can and should be destabilized—but I wonder whether from an indigenous perspective this oversight might not seem to typify another failing of "Euro-Western" scholarship.

Gregory D. Alles is professor of religious studies at McDaniel College, Westminster, MD, USA. His fieldwork over the last decade has focused on Rathvas and other *adivasis* in eastern central Gujarat. He has published widely in the history of religions, including *The Iliad, the Ramayana, and the Work of Religion* (1994) and the edited volume *Religious Studies: A Global View* (2008). He is currently co-executive editor of *Numen*, the journal of the International Association for the History of Religions.

Notes

1 The survey was approved by the Institutional Review Board of McDaniel College. I sought similar approval at the colleges in India but was told that no similar mechanism was in place and that the permission of the principals was sufficient. Thanks are due to Prof. Subhash Ishai, S. N. College, Chhotaudepur, and Prof. Arjun Rathva, M.C. Rathva Arts College, Pavi Jetpur, for assistance in formulating and administering the survey, as well as to Profs. Shannon Kundey and Elizabeth MacDougall, Hood College, Frederick, Maryland, for administering the survey, and to Akshay and Ila Vidyarthi, Hanover, PA, for linguistic assistance.
2 Perhaps I should add that I was not particularly concerned about the representativeness of the pool because I thought of the survey as something of a dry run. I knew from experience that adults in the area, especially those with little or no education, had difficulty grasping the idea of a survey, as did for that matter some literate people who were willing to help. I wanted to try out some options on a group of people likely to be more familiar with surveys.
3 This is the phraseology I was told by local sources that the students would understand the best.

4   In the English version the question read:

> I think that
>
> a a human being is only a body
>
> b a human being is more than a body
>
> If you select b, please explain what more you think there is to a human being besides a body.

5   This is in part surprising because there are some claims in the literature that women are more innately dualist in their outlook on human persons than men are (cf., e.g., Cohen et al. 2011: 10).

6   Cf. Linda Tuhiwai Smith (2012: 222–223): "Remember, for example, that colonial processes such as religion and education actively set out to destroy the existence of indigenous knowledge or systems for knowing in many ways."

7   I worry that one finds hints of this perspective in, for example, Paden (2016).

References

Alles, Gregory D. 2017. "Ritual Space as Borderland: Building and Breaching Ritual Borders in Eastern Central Gujarat," *International Journal of Dharma Studies* 5: 19. https://doi.org/10.1186/s40613-017-0057-9

Alles, Gregory D., Lidia Guzy, Uwe Skoda, and Ülo Valk. 2015. "Contemporary Indigeneity and Religion in India," *Internationales Asienforum* 46(1–2): 5–15.

Ashcroft, Bill, Gareth Griffiths, and Helen Tiffin. 1989. *The Empire Writes Back: Theory and Practice in Post-Colonial Literatures.* London: Routledge. https://doi.org/10.4324/9780203426081

Bering, Jesse M. 2002. "Intuitive Conceptions of Dead Agents' Minds: The Natural Foundations of Afterlife Beliefs as Phenomenological Boundary," *Journal of Cognition and Culture* 2(4): 263–308. https://doi.org/10.1163/15685370260441008

Bloom, Paul. 2004. *Descartes' Baby: How the Science of Child Development Explains What Makes Us Human.* New York: Basic Books.

Cadena, Marisol de la. 2015. *Earth Beings: Ecologies of Practice across Andean Worlds.* Durham, NC: Duke University Press. https://doi.org/10.1215/9780822375265

Chilisa, Bagele. 2012. *Indigenous Research Methodologies.* Thousand Oaks, CA: Sage.

Clifford, James. 2013. *Returns: Becoming Indigenous in the Twenty-First Century.* Cambridge, MA: Harvard University Press. https://doi.org/10.4159/9780674726222

Cohen, Emma, et al. 2011. "Cross-Cultural Similarities and Differences in Person-Body Reasoning: Experimental Evidence from the United Kingdom and Brazilian Amazon," *Cognitive Science* 35(7):1282–1304. https://doi.org/10.1111/j.1551-6709.2011.01172.x

Dolezalova, Iva, Luther H. Martin, and Dalibor Papoušek (eds.). 2001. *The Academic Study of Religion During the Cold War: East and West.* New York: P. Lang.

Hardiman, David. 2003. "Assertion, Conversion and Indian Nationalism: Govind's Movement amongst the Bhils," in Rowena Robinson and Sathianathan Clarke (eds.), *Religious Conversion in India: Modes, Motivations, and Meanings,* 255–284. New Delhi: Oxford University Press.

Hodge, K. Mitch. 2011. "On Imagining the Afterlife," *Journal of Cognition and Culture* 11(3–4): 367–389. https://doi.org/10.1163/156853711X591305

Johnson, Greg, and Siv Ellen Kraft (eds.). 2017. *Handbook of Indigenous Religion(s).* Leiden: Brill. https://doi.org/10.1163/9789004346710

Kovach, Margaret. 2009. *Indigenous Methodologies: Characteristics, Conversations, and Contexts.* Toronto: University of Toronto Press.
Niezen, Ronald. 2003. *The Origins of Indigenism: Human Rights and the Politics of Identity.* Berkeley, CA: University of California Press.
Otto, Rudolf. 1932. *Sünde und Urschuld.* Munich: C. H. Beck.
Paden, William E. 2016. *New Patterns for Comparative Religion: Passages to an Evolutionary Perspective.* London: Bloomsbury Academic.
Pereira, Vera, Luis Faísca, and Rodrigo de Sá-Saraiva. 2012. "Immortality of the Soul as an Intuitive Idea: Towards a Psychological Explanation of the Origins of Afterlife Beliefs," *Journal of Cognition and Culture* 12(1–2): 101–127. https://doi.org/10.1163/156853712X633956
Singh, K. S. 1983. *Birsa Munda and His Movement, 1874-1901: A Study of a Millenarian Movement in Chotanagpur.* Calcutta: Oxford University Press.
Slingerland, Edward. 2013. "Body and Mind in Early China: An Integrated Humanities-Science Approach," *Journal of the American Academy of Religion* 81(1): 6–55. https://doi.org/10.1093/jaarel/lfs094
Smith, Linda Tuhiwai. 2012. *Decolonizing Methodologies: Research and Indigenous Peoples,* 2nd edition. London: Zed Books.
Stanovich, Keith E. 1989. "Implicit Philosophies of Mind: The Dualism Scale and Its Relation to Religiosity and Belief in Extrasensory Perception," *Journal of Psychology: Interdisciplinary and Applied* 123(1): 5–23. https://doi.org/10.1080/00223980.1989.10542958
Walter, Maggie, and Chris Andersen. 2016. *Indigenous Statistics: A Quantitative Research Methodology.* Abingdon: Routledge.
Wilmer, Franke. 1993. *The Indigenous Voice in World Politics: Since Time Immemorial.* Newbury Park, CA: Sage. https://doi.org/10.4135/9781483326610
Wilson, Shawn. 2008. *Research is Ceremony: Indigenous Research Methods.* Black Point, Nova Scotia: Fernwood.

Index

Abington School District v. Schempp 2
Abrahamic religions 16
Absolon, Kathy 264
Abu-Odeh, L. 90
academic study of religion (ASR) 186, 187, 190
accidental relationships 189
adapted cognitive features 186
Adivasi 259, 263
aim
    purpose 229, 230, 231, 233, 234, 235, 236
    teleology 229–230, 231, 233, 235, 236n
Althusser, Louis, 67
American Academy of Religion 1
analytic philosophy 246, 247
anxiety (*Angst*) 238, 241–243
Aporia 185
Arab Jewishness 19
Arabia (Hijaz) 18–20
Aristotle 139–141, 145, 187–189, 192, 187, 188, 189, 191 n6
    causation 187, 188, 191n6
    explanation 191 n6
    physics 2, 188
    posterior analytics 191 n6
    rhetoric 2 191 n9
    teleology 188, 189
Arnal, William 245
Arora, K. S. and Jacobs, A. J. J. 89
artificiality of 15
Asad, Talal 212, 219, 253
Atran, Scott 182
authority 50–53
axiology 173–175, 193–195, 197, 199

Baldas, T. 89
Barnavi, Elie (scientific advisor, Museum of Europe) 38, 83
Barton, Carlin 91
Batnitzky, Leora 87

Before Religion: A History of a Modern Concept (Nongbri) 90
belief 169, 170–173, 174–175
behavior 228–236
    combinatorial model of 229, 230–232, 233, 234, 235, 236
    constitutive model of 230–231, 234–236
Bible 87
biology 181, 182
Book of Mormon 159
boundary 108, 109
Bourdieu, Pierre 50–51, 212, 249
Boyarin, Daniel 72–73, 87, 91
Brauer, Jerald 1
Braun, Willi 190 n2, 191
British North American Act 88
Buchanan, F. 85
Buddhism 87, 92

Cadena, Marisol de la 270
Cady, L. 90
Canadian Constitution 88
Canadian Museum of Civilization 82
Canadian Museum of History 82
Cardinal, Douglas (architect) 81
Carmichael, Lucas 263, 265
category 106–111, 114
causality/causation 187, 188, 190
    causal explanations 186
    causal factors 189
    causal mechanisms 189, 190
    causal power 188
    causal relationships 189
Cavanaugh, William 85–86
Chilisa, Bagele 267, 270
Christianity 87
Christianity, rise of, 60–61
Churchill, Winston 183
circumcision, as religious 89
Citizens for Constitutional Freedom 158

Classics and Religious Studies, Department of (University of Ottawa) 79
cognition 225-226
  human 179, 180
cognitive science of religion 23, 71, 110-111, 133, 198
Cohen, Roger 92, 93
common vocabulary, 55-56
comparison 262-263
  artificial activity 65-66, 68
  context of, 66
  idiom of, 67
  metaphors and models 54-55
  natural activity, 65-66
  responsible 64
  triadic model of, 65
comparative religions 37
comparative religious ethics 48, 49-50, 52
complex cultural concepts (CCC) 137-138, 154, 163-164, 168-169, 176, 179, 182, 193
concepts—complex cultural 168-169, 173, 175
conceptualization 106, 110
constructionism 136-137, 233
contexts of 25-30
correlative relationships 189
Couillard, Francois (Baha'i Community) 85
counterfactual experiments 190
craft analogy 188
craft, techne 188
Craver, Carl 134-135, 141, 145, 147-148
Crawford, James 86
creation 189
Crews, Emily 263
critical religion 80, 97, 98, 103, 104, 129,
critical religious studies 114
Crow Nation 239-240
Crowell, Steven Galt 237-238, 241
cults, plurality and diversity of 57-59
Cuthbertson, Ian 261

Daode jing (Tao Te Ching) 41, 43
Darwin, Charles 138, 161, 164, 181, 182, 188
data
  as a category, 66
  primary and secondary sources as, 66
Decolonizing Methodologies 66
deconstruction 114

definition 97, 106, 107, 109-111
Dempsey, Corinne G. 22, 24
Dennett, Daniel 181, 182, 183, 184
Descartes, Rene 5, 141, 146
description 106, 109, 110
descriptive explanations 186
descriptive method 117, 118
Deutsche, David 178,179, 183, 184
Dilthey, Wilhelm 149, 171-172, 194, 211, 222-223, 226
discourse 66, 68, 109-111
dispositionalists 249
distance, critical 66, 68
divine will 189
Droysen, Johann Gustav 149
Druids 87
dualism, duality 180
dualism, folk 259
Durkheim, Émile 117

effective history (history of effects, *Wirkungsgeschichte*) 39-40, 43, 44
efficient (moving) cause 188, 189
Einstein, Albert 182
Eisenhower, Dwight 88
Eliade, Mircea 1, 171
Ellen, Roy 138
emergence 207, 208, 216, 218
emergent phenomena 182, 183, 184
Emergentism 183-184, 197, 207-208, 216, 256
emotion 189
Empire, effects of, 56-58
Empire, Rome, 56-57
Engler, Steven 255-256, 256-257
Epicureanism 224, 226
essence 114, 116, 188, 189
essentialism 17, 64, 68, 135-137
Euro-centrism 223
European Union 81
Eusocial 184, 185
evolution 134, 136, 144-145, 150, 151, 178, 181, 195
explanation 169-175, 209, 214-217, 219-220, 222, 226, 228, 229, 234-236
explanatory priority 188
explanatory reduction 189
Eyl, Jennifer 253-235

faith-based courts 87
feature 106–109
feminism 88
Fernando, Mayanthi 250, 252
Fessenden, Tracy 90
final cause 188, 206
Fitzgerald, Timothy 122
formal indication 242–243
Frankfurter, David 209
future of 30–31

Gadamer, Hans-Georg 39, 43, 74, 211, 219, 223, 248, 254, 262
Gaon, Saadya 25
Gardiner, Mark Q. 255–257
Gatineau, Quebec 81
Geertz, Clifford 212, 214, 215, 216, 219, 219–20, 253, 256–257
gender 88, 115, 117
generalization 99
Geonim 25–26
ghulat 26–27, 30–31
goal oriented activity/behavior 189
god
    in Canadian Constitution 88
    in U.S. Pledge of Allegiance 88
"God(s): A User's Guide" (museum exhibit) 81–85
Godhra railway station 93
Goitein, Shlomo Dov 18–20
Goldenberg, Naomi 86, 261
Gomez, Michael 268
governance 115
Greek mythology 87
Gujarat riots 93

Habermas, Jürgen 222, 223
Haugeland, John 237–238
Heidegger, Martin 135, 211, 214, 223, 237, 237–238, 241–243, 244
Hempel, Carl 142
heresiology, 59–61
hermeneutics 39, 40, 42, 222, 223
historical 173
historicity 37, 39, 44
history 17–20
history of religions 1
Hobbes, Thomas 141, 146
homa (Asian fire rituals) 24–25

Hughes, Aaron 64–68, 262–263
Hume, David 141–143
hypothetical experiments 190

Ideology critique 247
Illari, Phyllis 149
Imagine No Religion: How Modern Abstractions Hide Ancient Realities (Barton and Boyarin) 91
Imagining Religion: From Babylon to Jonestown (J. Z. Smith) 85
The Impossibility of Religious Freedom (Sullivan) 91
incarceration 224
India 87
Indigeneity 263–264
Indigenous methodologies 266–270
Indigenous peoples
    and Christianity 66
    spirituality 66
"The Inspiration of Ample India" (Cohen) 92
intelligent design 189
intelligibility 65, 67
intention, intentional, intentionality 229–236
interacting components 187
interpellation 246, 247, 250
    interpretationist 249
    interpretivist 248
interpretation 205–17, 222–226, 229, 230, 232, 234–236
Isawiyya 25, 27–28, 47, 52
Ishi 268
Islam 17–20, 72

Jackson, Michael 6
James, William 181, 183, 184, 185, 252
Jews of 21–22
Joint Attentional Scenes 180
Journal of the American Academy of Religion 3
Judaism 17–20, 87

Karaites 25, 29, 73
Kitagawa, Joseph 1, 2
Kovach, Margaret 264, 267

La Mettrie, Julien Offray 141
Labor 48–49, 51

language
  academic 67
  analogy 65
  dexterity 67
  idiom 67
Latter Day Saints 158, 159
Lear, Jonathan 239-240, 242
learning outcomes (Department of Religious Studies, University of Ottawa) 79, 93
legal status 97
Lincoln, Bruce 3, 50-53
linguistic dexterity 40-43
logical positivism 142-143
Longkumer, Arkotong 270
Lucretius 224
Lupo, Joshua 255-256

Macaulay, Thomas Babington 266
Mahmood, Saba 89, 90, 212
manipulability 189
marketplace model of religion, 58, 60, 62
Martin, Craig 81, 122, 249,
Martin, Luther 265
Marx, Karl 48-49
Masuzawa, Tomoko 85
McClellan, Daniel 263
McCutcheon, Russell 6-8, 120, 245, 250,
Mead, George Herbert 180
meaning 228, 229, 231-2, 233, 234
  "meaning" 224-225
  social 232-233
mental states 229, 231-2, 233, 234, 235
  access problem of 229, 230, 232, 233, 234
Menzies, Peter 220
method 1-10
Method and Theory in the Study of Religion 4, 245, 246, 249
Mexican Day of the Dead 82
micro 70-71
mind-body dualism 207-8, 211, 218, 254, 262
Modi, Narenda 93
moral psychology 189
Mormonism (see Latter Day Saints)
Moroni 159, 163
Mufti, Aamir 89
Muhammad 21, 25
Müller, Max 1, 15, 36-38, 41

Museum of Europe 82
Muslim Spain (al-Andalus) 21

natural causes 189
natural purposive structures 188, 189, 191 n7
natural selection 150, 188, 191 n8
naturalism 135-136, 153, 160, 178, 187, 189, 199, 208, 218
naturalistic 187
neo-liberalism 87
neo-perennialists 240
new mechanism 139, 144-150, 153, 168-169, 175, 178-183, 187-189, 195, 197-199
new mechanistic causal approach 187
new mechanists 187
Newton, Isaac 182
Nongbri, Brent 90, 91, 117, 121
non-realist 249
non-religion 101-103
normative 118
North American Association for the Study of Religion 4, 64, 68, 80, 245
Notre-Dame Cathedral Basilica (Ottawa) 82

objectivity 66, 68
ontogeny 179, 185
Orsi, Robert 6-7
Orwell, George 92
Ottawa 81, 82, 83
Ottawa Citizen 85
Ottawa City Hall 85
Otterman, S. 89
Otto, Rudolf 210-211, 219, 270-271

Paden, William E. 22-23, 24
Pals, Daniel 135
Parliament of Canada 81
pedagogy 104
"the personal is political" 88
phenomenology 17, 207, 237-238, 241-243, 255
Philosophy and the Study of Religions: A Manifesto 245
philosophy of science 139-146, 190
Plato 189
Plenty Coups 240-242
poetry 65

politics 88
"Politics and the English Language" (Orwell) 92
Politics as a Vocation (Weber) 86
Politics of Piety: The Islamic Revival and the Feminist Subject (Mahmood) 89, 90
possibilities of 21–25
Postmodernism, 54, 61
postsecular, as emergent orthodoxy 89
prescriptive method 117, 118
Presentism 31, 36, 38–40, 44
private, spheres of life considered as 89
problems of 17
Prothero, Stephen 21–22, 24
prototype 108, 109
Proudfoot, Wayne 134, 138–139, 149, 162
psychologism 210–11, 213, 257
Putnam, Hilary 212

Rabbinic Judaism 21, 25, 28–29, 59, 72, 73
Rabinow, Paul 211–2
Rappaport, Roy 182
Realist 249
recidivism 224
redescription (of religion) 80, 90, 91–92
reduction 169–171, 174–175
reduction, reductionism, reductive method 178, 179
reductionism 6, 47, 133–134, 136–138, 160, 171, 178–179, 192, 194, 217, 253
religion 106, 109–111
   and an apparatus of recognition 67–68
   and government, jurisdiction, sovereignty 86
   and peacefulness 87
   and secular 88, 92
   and science 120, 124–125
   as abstraction 80, 84
   as anachronism 80, 91
   as apolitical 90
   as event 100
   as object of study, 64–65, 68
   as once and future state 86
   as redescriptive concept 91
   as vestigial state 86
   as a given 88
   category of 119, 122–124
   comparative religion 64, 68
   deconstruction of 91
   defined as limited government 89
   definition of 261, 270–271
   destabilizing religion, 64
   effort to define 83, 91
   in relation to group identity 66–67
   "it" as pronoun for 80
   linked to violence 86, 87
   popular discourse about 83
   popular representation of 84
   religion-secular binary 119, 124
   rethinking of 89
   uncritical use of term 92
   women, sex, and gender (subject areas) 89
"Religion, Religions, Religious" (J. Z. Smith) 83
Religion, the Secular and the Politics of Sexual Difference (Cady and Fessenden) 90
religioning 100
religionization 100–101
Religionsgeschichteschule 1
Religious Difference in a Secular Age: A Minority Report (Mahmood) 90
religious studies 79, 80, 83–84
   vocabulary of 92
religious violence 81, 93
rhetoric 67
Rice, Waubgehig (First Nations group) 85
Risjord, Mark 220
Rosenberg, Alexander 220
Rushdie, Salman 266
Russo, Federica 144
Ryle, Gilbert 207, 256–257

Salmon, Wesley 135, 143
Schilbrack, Kevin 262
Schleiermacher, Friedrich 210, 211, 212, 219, 222, 223, 226
scholar
   demands on 66
   disciplinary apparatus 67–68
   position of 65, 68
   scholar-subjects 67–68
scholarship
   context of 66
Science of Religions (*Religionswissenschaft*) 1, 36, 37
scientific theories of explanation 190
secular 88, 90, 92

Sedley, David 191, 191n7
Segal, Robert 171
Sheedy, Matt 252–253
Shiʿism (Twelver) 27, 29, 30
Skousen, W. Cleon: 158
Slingerland, Edward 206, 207, 210, 211, 218
Smart, Ninian 135, 210–211, 212, 219, 248, 249
Smith, Christian 213–214, 218, 219, 248
Smith, Graham 267
Smith, J. Z. 17–18, 54, 55, 65, 83, 85, 114, 115, 116, 119–120
Smith, Joseph 150–152, 161, 162, 164, 190
Smith, Linda Tuhiwai 66, 259, 263, 266
Smith, Wilfred Cantwell 209
Snow, C. P. 143
social theory 65, 67
sovereignty, 115
Stanton, Elizabeth C. 89
state, in international law 86
Stausberg, Michael 133, 137, 182
Stereotyping Religion: Critiquing Clichés (Stoddard and Martin) 81
Stoddard, Brad 81
stratified ontology 208, 216, 254
subjectivity 237–243
sui generis 187
Sullivan, William 91, 211–212
Sullivan, Winifred 117
supernatural causes 190, 191 n5
symbiosis 18–19

Taira, Teemu 122
Taves, Ann 264
Taylor, Charles 211, 219, 220
teleology 188, 222, 226
telos 188, 189
theological 173–174
theoretical sophistication 43–45
theorizing causation 190

theory 133
theory laden 184
Tinbergen, Nikolaas 154
Tomasello, Michael 179, 180
translation 40–43, 44, 45

United Kingdom 87
United States Pledge of Allegiance 88
universal/global versus local, 61
unwillingness to engage history 17

Venuti, Lawrence 42
Verteshen 210
vestigial states, 86, 87, 115, 119, 121–123
violence
  legalized 89
  linked to religion 87
  management of 86
  "religious" 93
Vygotsky, Lev 180

Wallach Scott, Joan 250
Wasserstrom, Steven M. 27
Watson, Jim (Mayor of Ottawa) 85
Weber, Max 86, 89, 123, 173–176, 194–196, 198
Weinberg, Robert 191
Wicca 87
Williamson, Jon 144, 149
Wilson, E. O. 185
Wilson, Shawn 270
Winch, Peter 214–5, 216, 219, 220
Wittgenstein, Ludwig 91, 180, 211, 212, 214, 219, 256–257
women and religion (as subject area) 89
Wood, William 245, 246
Woodward, James 189, 191
World Religion Day (Ottawa) 85
world religions discourse 84–85
worldviews 194–195, 199–200